Gustav Klimt
MASTERWORKS

Art Nouveau & the Vienna Secessionists

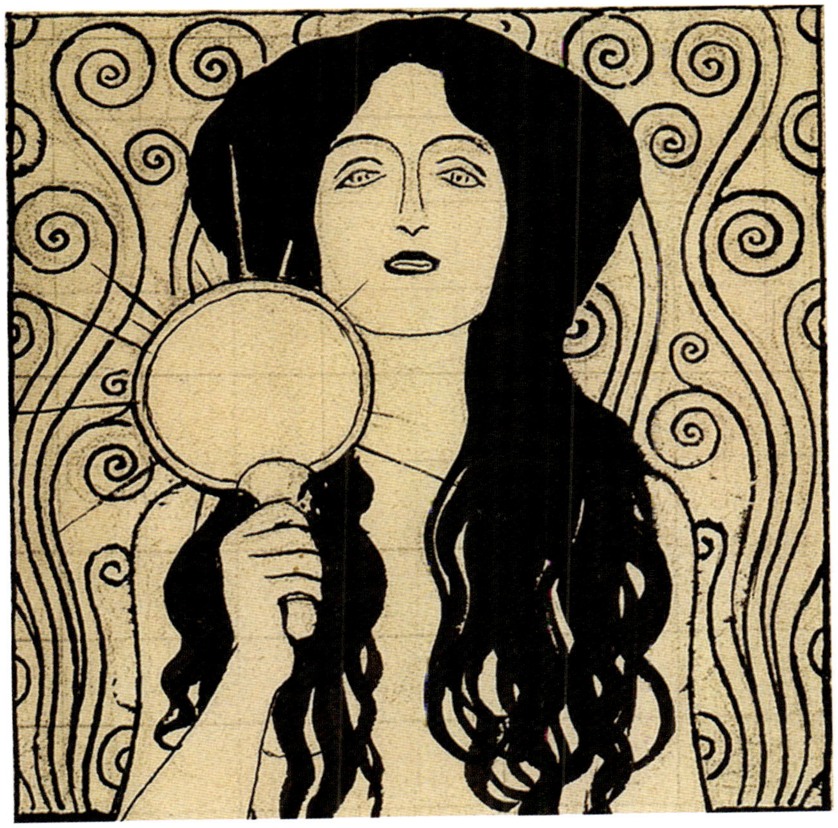

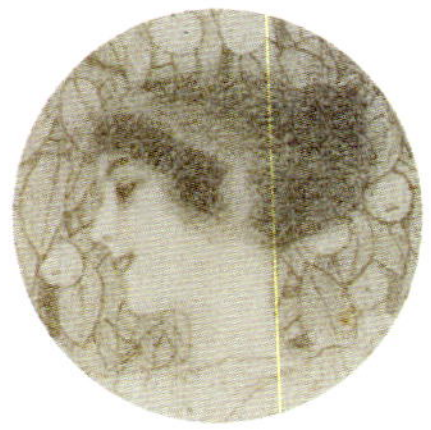

Publisher and Creative Director: Nick Wells,
Senior Project Editor: Laura Bulbeck,
Art Director: Mike Spender
Special thanks to Karen Fitzpatrick, Dawn Laker,
Eileen Cox, Gillian Whitaker, Ramona Lamport

FLAME TREE PUBLISHING
6 Melbray Mews
Fulham, London SW6 3NS
United Kingdom

www.flametreepublishing.com

First published 2015

26 28 30 32 31 29 27
7 9 10 8 6

ISBN 978-1-83562-801-0
Special ISBN: 978-1-80694-281-7

Front cover: an adapted version of The Kiss, 1907–08, © Belvedere, Vienna
Back cover: Fulfilment (The Stoclet Frieze), c. 1905–09, courtesy of Artothek/Blauel/Gnamm.

A CIP record for this book is available from the British Library upon request.

Printed in China

Represented in the EU for product safety and compliance by
Authorised Rep Compliance Ltd, Ground Floor, 71 Lower Baggot Street,
Dublin, D02 P593, Ireland. Contact at www.arccompliance.com

FSC www.fsc.org MIX Paper | Supporting responsible forestry FSC® A000532

Gustav Klimt
MASTERWORKS

Art Nouveau & the Vienna Secessionists

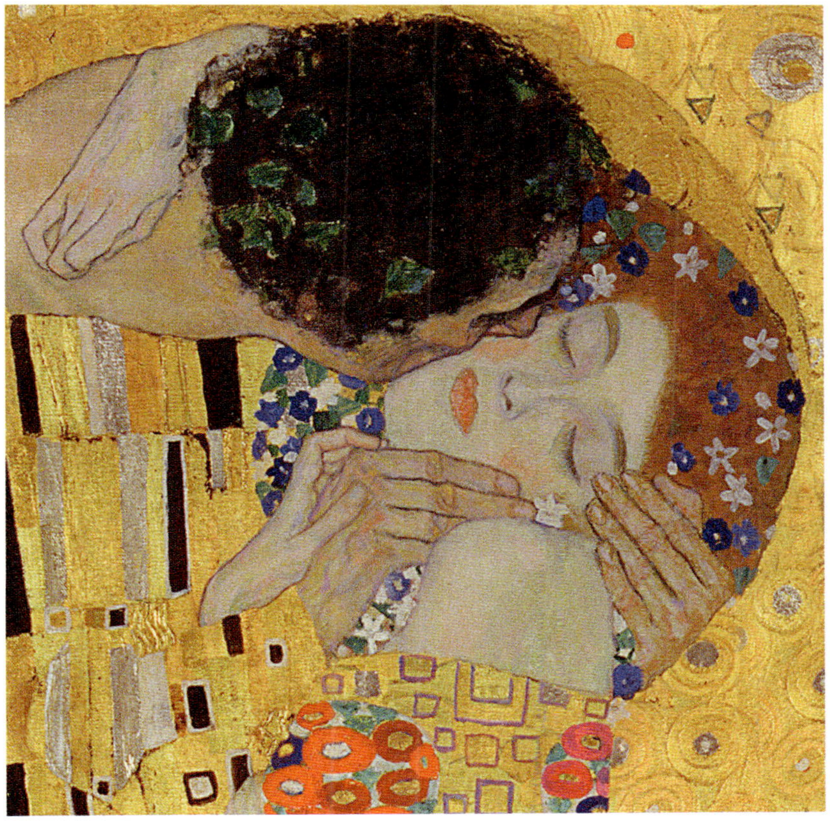

Michael Kerrigan

FLAME TREE
PUBLISHING

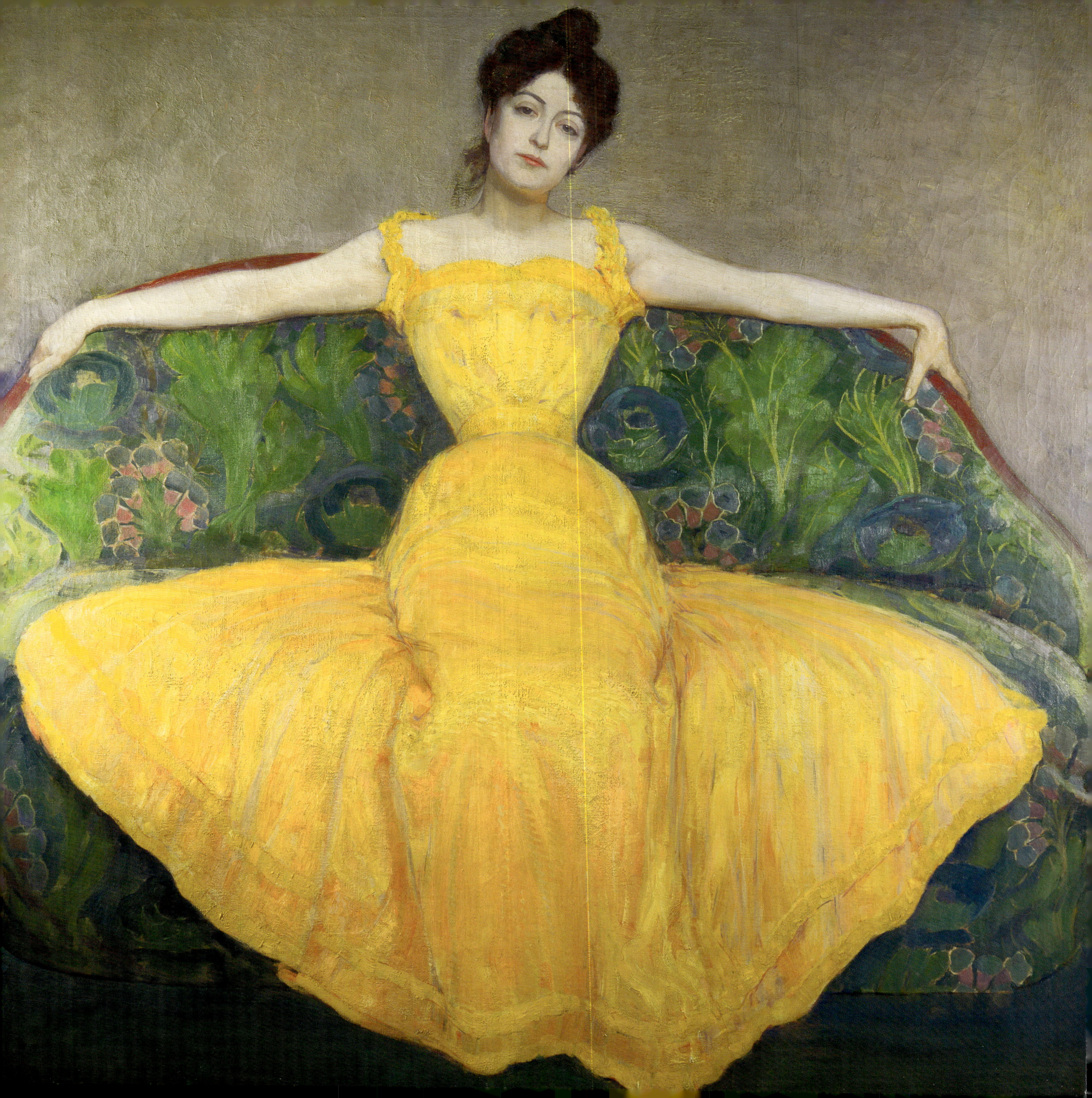

Contents

WOMAN IN A YELLOW DRESS, 1899, MAX KURZWEIL (1867–1916)

INTRODUCTION

THE 1890s were a time of sweeping change across the world of art. Post-Impressionism was on the march in France. If the Impressionism of Claude Monet (1840–1926) and Pierre-Auguste Renoir (1841–1919) had carried classical realism to its logical conclusion in (as Hamlet had it) holding a 'mirror up to nature', recording what the artist saw with an unprecedented immediacy, painters like Paul Cézanne (1839–1906), Vincent van Gogh (1853–90) and Paul Gauguin (1848–1903), and sculptors like Auguste Rodin (1840–1917), were unabashedly bringing their own ideas and emotions into their work.

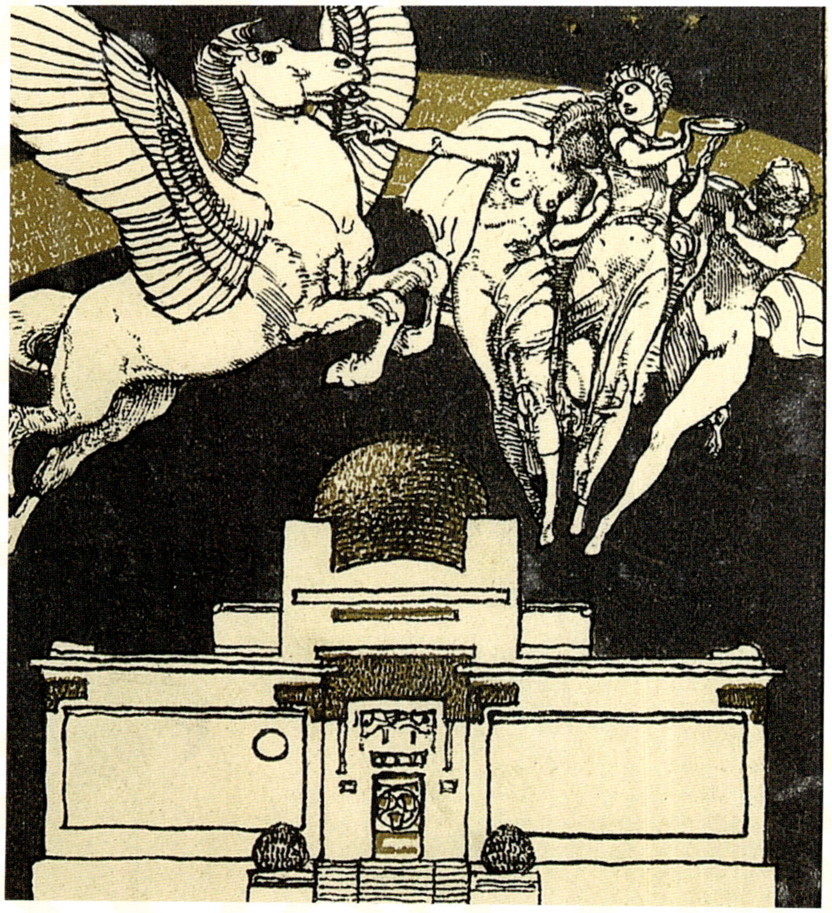

Paris had long been at the cultural heart of things, of course. But extraordinary things were happening elsewhere too. Oscar Wilde (1854–1900) was mesmerizing London with his wit and daring. The adulation with which this outrageous personification of *fin de siècle* decadence was received when he toured the United States in the 1880s showed that even America, 'provincial' as it may still have appeared to be from a European perspective, was ready and indeed eager for artistic innovation. A self-consciously progressive Society of American Artists had been founded as long ago as 1874. Even creaky old Russia had its *avant-garde*.

In Vienna, though, art and sculpture slumbered on as though the last generation hadn't happened; as though the nineteenth century would never end. What should have been a modern metropolis, the glittering capital of the rich and powerful Austro-Hungarian Empire, the city seemed no more than a backwater. Central Europe had never felt less central. But in 1897 all that changed, and Austria had a rude awakening when the Vienna Secession sent a shockwave not just through the region but through European art itself.

The Black Duchess

The Black Duchess, her fine features etched stark in black and white, as austere as she is beautiful, dominates the scene, stage-left in Koloman Moser's (1868–1918) *Duchess and Footboy* (1901, *see* page 7). At the same time, however, she appears to be receding before our eyes, sinking into a black-and-white lozenged background that possesses an animation all its own. Facing her, on the right-hand side of the picture, we see the bright new form of an orange-red patterned Page Boy emerging. Or rather not quite facing her, in fact, for his eyes are downcast – in bashful reticence or simple sadness? – as though to avoid a gaze

LEFT ■ : POSTCARD OF THE VIENNA SECESSION, 1906. RUDOLF JETTMAR (1869–1939)

that is in fact averted in its turn. For the Duchess too has her head tilted slightly downward and away – not just from the Page Boy but also from the viewer. Even if there's dialogue here, there's no real communication.

Behind and below the Duchess, elongated white diamonds and orange-centred squares pick out a broad black border on which she leans back, as though gaining support. The black-and-white geometric pattern picks up that of the checkerboard squares which seem to shimmer and heave before her at the centre of the picture, its living heart – more vibrant, perhaps, than the two personified figures on either side. Behind and above the boy, meanwhile, the black border, more solid in itself, is also more strongly studded with orange lozenges – as though bright colour were warring with monochrome.

The Arrival of Spring

There are no prizes for guessing what these two figures are supposed to represent, for the image accompanies the richly decorated pages of a printed poem. The same lozenged patterns, the same solid borders in black, white and orange adorn the text of 'Vorfrühling' ('Early Spring') by Rainer Maria Rilke (1875–1926). We don't need to be told that the Duchess stands for winter and its rigours – for age and sterility, for darkness and for death. Nor that the Page is spring, the embodiment of life, youth, fertility and possibility – though the optimism he should show is tempered here by a certain melancholy air. When asked why, by the Black Duchess, in Rilke's words the Page explains his plight more clearly. His life, in all its hopefulness, cannot but be clouded by the loss of his late mother – in her beauty and her gentleness she had to be seen to be believed.

RIGHT • DUCHESS AND FOOTBOY' FOR THE POEM 'VORFRUEHLING', VER SACRUM, 1901.
KOLOMAN MOSER (1868–1918)

Frames of Reference

'Illustration' seems too weak a word for a work in which pictorial and decorative imagery flow into one another – just as the darkness of death and loss overshadow the new sun of spring. The border that at first appears to frame the picture, demarcating it from the text it accompanies, is ultimately a bridge between the two. This is a work that counterpoints visual art and literary lyricism, which sets poetry and picture on equal terms in an aesthetic that disregards the traditional generic boundaries.

Koloman Moser created this elaborate presentation for a poem Rilke had written specifically to appear in the Viennese magazine, *Ver Sacrum* (*Sacred Spring*, 1901, Issue IV). This publication was explicitly dedicated to the idea of the *Gesamtkunstwerk* or 'total work of art'.

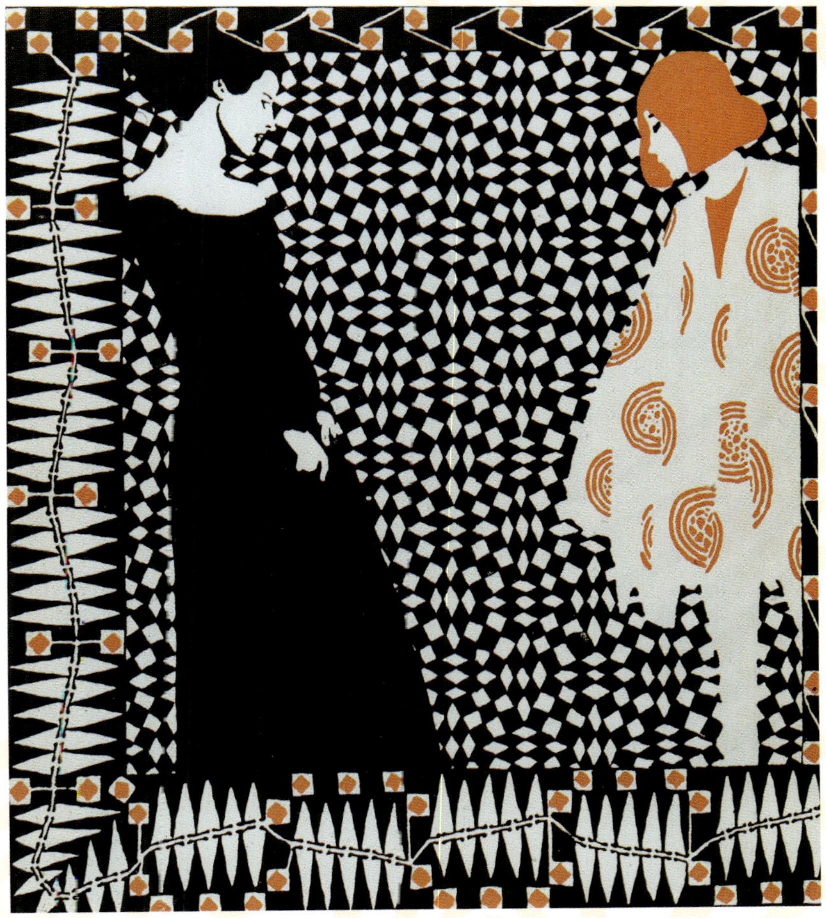

Founded just a few years before, *Ver Sacrum* provided a platform for an exciting new generation of Austrian and Central European artists who hoped to usher in a new approach to creativity in the arts: the Vienna Secession.

Out of This World

Not that there was anything absolutely wrong with the work of painters like Hans Canon (1829–85) or of sculptors such as Viktor Oskar Tilgner (1844–96). To modern eyes, perhaps, their work seems a little too obviously conservative; too content to strive for canons of correctness established originally by the classical Greeks and Romans, and then revived in the Renaissance by the masters of European art. Like their forebears, they were allegorical in intent: their figures embodied identifiable virtues, vices or philosophical principles; they told little stories in which moral messages were enacted. Line, symmetry, balance and proportion: these were the artistic ideals of classicism, just as moderation – the 'golden mean' – was its most important moral value. As timely a message for the end of the nineteenth century as for ancient Greece or Rome, or fifteenth-century Florence, perhaps, but no longer one that occasioned too much excitement. These tasteful scenes of nymphs and shepherds; these superbly proportioned nudes; these colonnaded temples; these beautiful historic events, only underlined this art's allegiance to ancient cultural ways the rest of the world had left behind.

The World Confined

And the art in its turn left the world behind: whether landscapes, portraits, still lifes or representations of historical or mythical events, the sort of conventional paintings by members of the Austrian Artists' Society, displayed in the galleries of Vienna's Künstlerhaus as the end of the nineteenth century approached, invariably began and ended with their frames. Plain or ornate, varnished or gilt, the frame contained the artist's vision, made the picture a sort of window on to the world. But in doing so, it also held that world at bay – defined it as something separate, 'other' from the reality in which it had been created. And in defining it, it made it finite, pinned it down.

Art itself, in fact, existed in a space apart, sectioned off from the world in which it was created, confined to the museum; if in the home, it was raised above the realm of the everyday, up on a wall. Where it intersected with daily life – as wallpaper, furnishing or fashion – it tended to be implicitly relegated to an ancillary role, dismissed as 'decoration' – something subordinate, the merest afterthought.

Transgressive Talents

The most talented artists (as the most talented artists always do) push up against the limits of the conventions within which they work. Take the Austrian historical painter Hans Makart (1840–84), for example. The customary characterization of his style as 'realistic academicism' barely begins to do justice to the warmth and vividness with which his exotically-imagined works make use of colour, or the arresting emotion and unmistakeable glamour of his greatest works. It hardly matters whether this extravagant painterliness originated – as his critics carped – in Makart's comparatively late development as a draughtsman. The character is there, and it resonates powerfully in his work.

This resonance was powerful enough to catch the eye – and the imagination – of a younger Viennese painter. Gustav Klimt (1862–1918) was an ardent admirer of Makart's work. No natural-born revolutionary,

Klimt unquestioningly accepted the traditional aesthetic values of academic art and strove to attain them in his own early paintings. And he didn't do too badly: the classically-influenced allegorical works he produced as a young man in the 1880s do display a tremendous talent – even if it is one that has comfortably accommodated itself to the conventions of its time. In the intensity of the colours though, we see not only a reflection of Makart's painterly technique, but also an anticipatory hint of the bejewelled blaze that was to shine out of Klimt's later and more celebrated paintings. Klimt's great late works are remarkable for the way in which colour and decorative detail displace conventional outline and contour from their traditional primacy; for the way they let passion and emotion usurp the purely visual.

Boundary Breaking

But there's a message too in the artistic contexts for Klimt's later paintings: several are to be seen as the centrepieces for ornate ceilings or on elaborately marbled walls – not hung there as finished artworks, but actually executed there as frescoes. One commission Klimt inherited from his idol Makart in the 1890s was the continued decoration of the walls of Vienna's Kunsthistorisches (Art History) Museum. In the Greek and Egyptian rooms, Klimt painted female figures, standing nude or dressed in stylized antique costumes, their arms upraised to frame the curvature of the arched doorways.

As far as their execution goes, these figures are utterly conventional. Nor does the amount of gilding – although no doubt raising the odd eyebrow in the Imperial works department when the bills came in – seem especially out of place in these sumptuous surroundings. But with the benefit of hindsight, it doesn't seem too fanciful to see signs of the Klimt to come, the Klimt who loved to douse his female forms with gold and enamelling; and who showed us woodlands shimmering with mother-of-pearl or gleaming with autumnal bronze.

More important in this case though, is the relation these figures bear to their architectural context, and to the archaeological treasures displayed in the museum space itself. Although it made sense to have antique-looking ladies in galleries of Greek and Egyptian art, Klimt's decision clearly went well beyond appropriateness in the everyday sense. Having created an artistic continuity between architecture and decorative artwork, he was also creating a continuity between the ornamental motifs he used and the array of antique items on display in the rooms below.

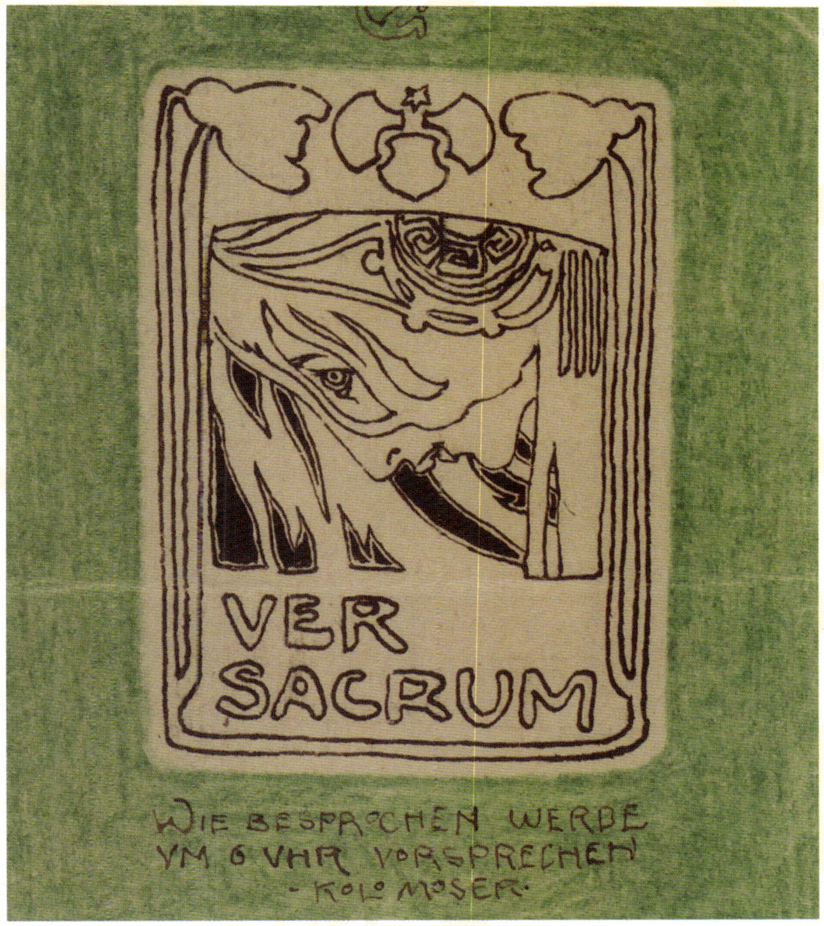

ABOVE • POSTCARD TO CARL MOLL WITH A DESIGN FOR VER SACRUM. 1897. KOLOMAN MOSER (1868–1918)

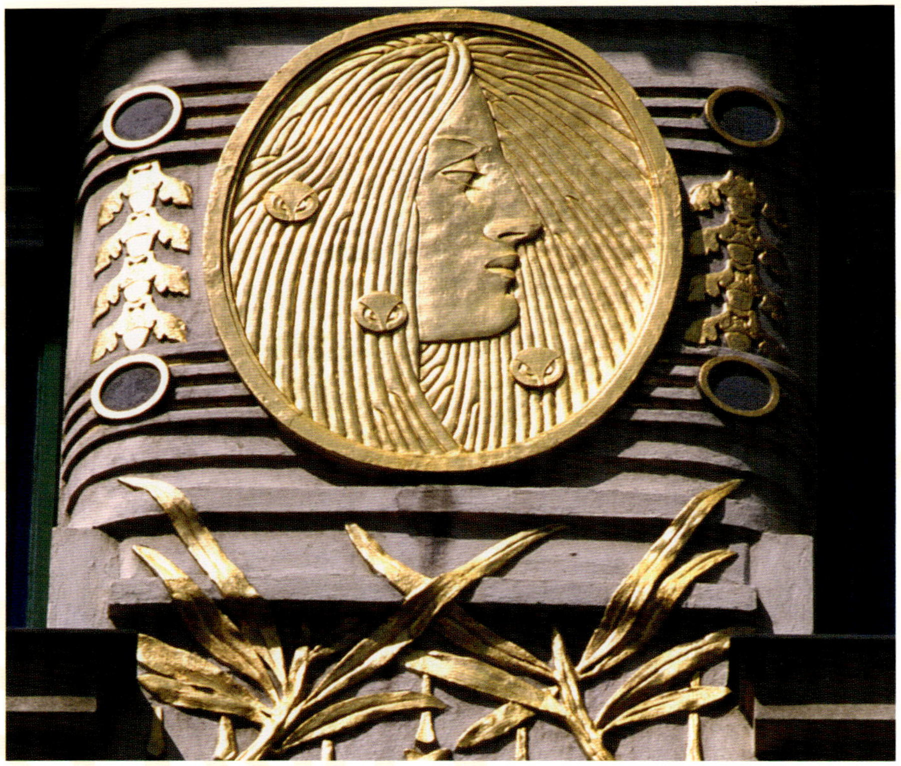

This was, of course, a chronological as well as a spatial continuity. Klimt's ladies were created to engage in an active dialogue between modern and ancient art. Time moves on, and with it, taste: aesthetic beauty is at once eternal and of its moment; universal and yet at the same time, utterly of its place. More boundary-breaking, in other words. As Moser would with Rilke's verses, Klimt was seeking art's transcendent essence by worrying away at the relations between creation and context, work and genre; between universal, timeless beauty, and the here and now.

Unbounded Beauty

In Klimt's later and now more famous works, these preoccupations are immediately apparent. Take *Portrait of Adele Bloch-Bauer I* (*see* page 189), which Klimt created in 1907. As much a radiance as a woman, the wealthy industrialist's wife emerges, face and form, out of a radiance of patterned gold too complex and kinetic in its own right to be called a background. The swirls of the patterns of the wallpaper behind her are amplified in the spiralling whorls of the upholstery amid which she sits enthroned – as they are in her jewelled choker; in the tumbling (yet somehow still rigid) billows of her dress. There's a clear continuity of patterning, here; a character of fine metalwork, marquetry or stained glass only underlined by the flatness of a painting in which perspective is not much more than a memory. Where does this sumptuously decorated room end, exactly, and the sumptuously decorated Mrs Bloch-Bauer begin?

The largest open areas of uninterrupted colour here are the black stab of hair at the very top and the pallid white of the bosom just below. Between, black and white interpenetrate in the features of a face that the work as a whole has had the effect of disembodying almost completely. Below, another decorative motif among the multicoloured circles, squares and triangles of her dress, stylized eyes look back at us – as boldly as its wearer's do above.

Breaking Free

The word 'secession' is generally used when the section of a state breaks away and achieves its own autonomy, as the American South sought to do in 1861 at the outbreak of the Civil War – or as activists of various national groups (such as Magyars and Serbs) tried to do in the Austro-Hungarian Empire in the 1890s. The goals these movements aimed for were never really attained, though the pressure they exerted did, by 1914, help plunge Europe into a devastating conflict, and the First World War left behind it a continent in ruins, its political map redrawn, its frontiers and its territories transformed.

ABOVE • DETAIL OF MEDALLION HOUSE, 1898–99. DES. BY OTTO WAGNER (1841–1918). DECORATION POSSIBLY BY KOLOMAN MOSER (1868–1918)

By comparison with such upheavals, the decision of a group of young Viennese painters, sculptors and architects in the final years of the nineteenth century to strike out in a new direction might not seem so significant, but they too in their way brought about far-reaching changes. Their secession was not from a state, however, but from the establishment represented by the Austrian Artists' Society, from whose authority – on 3 April 1897 – they formally broke free to form the *Vereinigung Bildender Künstler Österreichs* (Union of Austrian Artists).

In doing so, these artists were articulating a wide and varied range of grievances, from the hanging policy of the Society (which placed canvases so high up on the walls of the Künstlerhaus that they could barely be seen from the floor below) to the absence of foreign artists from its exhibitions. Broadly though, they felt that an old and complacent hierarchy in Viennese art was keeping down everything that was fresh and new. More specifically, they were copying the group of young German artists who, led by sculptor Bruno Piglhein (1848–94) and painter Paul Hoecker (1854–1910), had in similar circumstances five years before staged what was becoming known as the 'Munich Secession'.

Gestures and Realities

What's in a name? The artists of the *Vereinigung Bildender Künstler* were referring to their movement as a 'secession' before they'd actually seceded from anything. There was an air of boyish bravado about their stance. Their desire for change was real, though, as were their agitations for reform within the Austrian Artists' Society – and the irritation their campaign caused to many older, more hidebound members of the leadership. Ultimately, secession was thrust upon them: in May 1897, at a meeting in the Künstlerhaus, a vote of censure put the youngsters in their place. Gustav Klimt led a walk-out there and then.

This abrupt – and ever so slightly farcical – action did, however, only confirm the break Vienna's young artists had already made in their hearts and minds. This was certainly a secession waiting to happen. As soon as it did, moreover, the painters and sculptors who had left the Künstlerhaus with Klimt were joined by architect friends who felt they were engaged in the same fight. The rulebound classicism of nineteenth-century Viennese painting and sculpture had its parallel in an inability to imagine a prestigious building without its share of Graeco-Roman columns, pediments and domes. Talented architects were tired of endlessly reworking the same designs.

Artistic Visions

This book sets out to tell the story of the Vienna Secessionists, not from a biographical point of view, but from the artistic perspective they surely would have wanted.

Even so, telling their story presents something of a challenge, for the artists of the Vienna Secession did not form a single 'school'. They were individuals, many of whom worked in very different fields, and they certainly approached their work in very different ways. In acknowledging their uniqueness, however, we also have to recognize the extent to which they shared similar goals and priorities – not just with one another, but also with other young artists active internationally at the time. The French creators of Art Nouveau; the German devisers of the *Jugendstil*; all may be seen as having wrestled with comparable problems with comparable aims in mind. Antoni Gaudí (1852–1926) in Barcelona; Charles Rennie Mackintosh (1868–1928) in Glasgow; Louis Comfort Tiffany (1848–1933) in New York … all enormously different in their approaches, yet all producing art that spilled over longstanding generic boundaries and disregarded time-honoured demarcations of

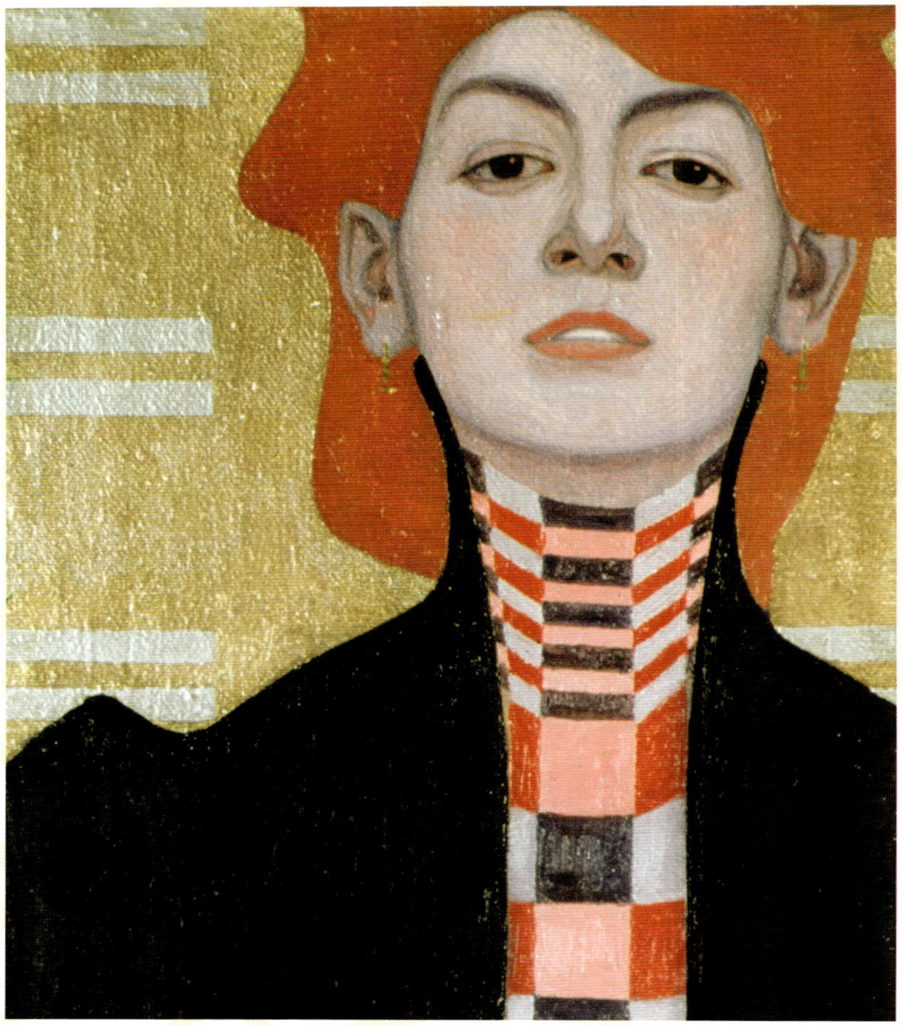

medium and material, just as the Vienna Secessionists were to do in their bid to build the *Gesamtkunstwerk*.

Modernism, Music and Mortality

Already, in Rilke's collaboration with Koloman Moser in the pages of *Ver Sacrum*, is a reminder that literary 'Modernism' was to share this impatience with the old boundaries. The great Bohemian-Austrian poet Rilke had started out as a student of art history and philosophy before he made literature his life in the mid-1890s. He remained open to other artistic media even then, making music a central metaphor in his verse. This symbolism was made explicit in the sonnets Rilke addressed to Orpheus, the ancient bard, who in Greek legend descended to the underworld to fetch back his dead wife Eurydice. Hearing his pleas and taking pity, the King of Hades allowed Orpheus to lead his love back up to her home in the world above – just so long as he did not at any point look back. Just as he reached the end of his journey, Orpheus unthinkingly glanced back at his wife, and Eurydice was snatched back down into the realm of death.

For Modernist writers, music became emblematic of the inadequacy of artistic expression at the conscious level: sound, symbol and colour communicated better than words could. Orpheus, the original musician-poet, represented the writer's descent into the deep unconscious to bring back insights that – though inexpressible – held secret meanings for the human soul. The idea that the most important truths might be 'subconscious' had been in the back of the modern mind for quite some time, at least as a vague inkling, but by the middle of the 1890s, this notion was being explicitly formulated for the first time.

Profound Patterns

Also in Vienna, the controversial psychologist Sigmund Freud (1856–1939) had, by 1896, devised his own method of tapping into the unconscious mind by asking his patients to put together their thoughts and impressions randomly as they occurred, in a process he was calling 'free association'. By reaching into the inarticulate reaches of their minds this way, his patients were accessing deeper – and ultimately more fundamental – feelings than they could by explaining how they felt and what they thought at the conscious level. In the years that followed, Freud was to explore the ways in

ABOVE ◆ PORTRAIT OF A WOMAN, 1909, EGON SCHIELE (1890–1918)

which subconscious longings might force their way into the open through dreams or jokes – or those accidental 'Freudian slips' in which we reveal our secret feelings despite ourselves.

Later, during the First World War, the Dadaists would make random 'word salads' the basis of a (mostly) serious intellectual movement, while André Breton (1896–1966) would make Surrealism into an important artistic creed. For now though, these developments – like the fame of Freud, even in his own city – still lay several years in the future: it is highly unlikely that any of the Secession artists would even have known his name. For Freud's part, cultivated as he was, the Vienna Secession would only have been something he read about in the papers; there's no reason to think that the artists influenced his thinking or that he made any impression on theirs. But Freud's work, like theirs, was boundary-breaking – not just because it was new and radical, but because it was all about the crossing of the border between the conscious and the subconscious mind.

Beyond the Bounds

It might also be argued that the way in which 'free association' elevated inarticulate babble and unformulated impressions above the level of coherently marshalled thoughts had implications for the art the Vienna Secessionists were producing. When Mrs Bloch-Bauer can be upstaged by the dress she's wearing and its folds can in their turn be subsumed into the room around her, it's clear that all sorts of conventional hierarchies are being up-ended; that we are coming at the world in a very different way. In Klimt's vision, we see the person as being of a piece with the armchair and the skirting board, her individuating outline breaking down. Repetitive patterning serves something of the same function as the nonsensical narratives of dream, depriving what we see of all its normal bounds and meanings. Conscious reality is fragmented and opened up, and we start to sense a surreality beyond.

Born or Made?

So who were they, the men and women who, in turn-of-the-century Vienna, had the desire and the self-confidence to rebel against so many generations of conformism in creative art? In a sense, it shouldn't matter: they are their work. Klimt certainly thought so: 'Whoever wishes to know something about me,' he once said, 'should look at my pictures attentively and try from them to recognize what I am and what I intend.' Is this a purist position that art is all, or the defensiveness of a successful painter of obscure origins; a rich and successful but essentially self-made man?

That this son of Baumgarten, one of Vienna's less inspiring lower-middle-class neighbourhoods at the end of the nineteenth century, should have seen things this way is unsurprising – understandable, even. But we don't have to take him entirely at his word. Who he was – his social and familial background – comes across in his creative work in several ways. Klimt's father Ernst, a gold and silver engraver, was an immigrant from the little town of Drabschitz in what is now the Czech Republic. Although he worked in rich metals, Ernst Klimt never made much money himself: he and his family, including seven children, lived in poverty. Gustav's mother Anna (née Finster), a native of Vienna, had ambition to be a singer, but she had been unable to fulfil her talent professionally.

Naturally enough, Klimt felt that he had started out on his artistic career at a disadvantage, but if he really thought his vocation had come out of nowhere, he must have been deluded. Central, surely, to his developing vocation were not only the deep and thoroughgoing background he had in craft, but also the insistent sense of unfinished artistic business, of yearning aspiration, his family circumstances instilled in him.

Precious Metals

Although the connection between Ernst Klimt's skills in metalwork and those his son later showed in his art is obvious, it would be perverse just to ignore it: how many academically trained artists would have had the basic technical competence to create the effects Gustav did in his most famous works? It's perhaps more interesting to wonder whether a painter from a more middle-class background would have had Klimt's mental and emotional ability to break the aesthetic taboos of his time and incorporate the blue-collar skills of the craftsman into 'high' artistic work. While in his earlier career, Klimt strained in aspiration to produce academic art, he quickly opened up his paintings to imagery and techniques derived from 'merely' decorative fields, of which the establishment had always taken a condescending view.

The Bourgeois Bricklayer

Klimt's friend and fellow secessionist Joseph Maria Olbrich (1867–1908) was the son of a wealthy brickworks owner who also had business interests in wax manufacture and confectionery. So although much more privileged than Klimt, Olbrich's background was again marked by (a broadly defined) creativity; one in which artisanal skills commanded respect. Olbrich's decision to turn his back on formal education to embark on an apprenticeship as a bricklayer can hardly have delighted his rich and respectable parents, but they appear to have accepted it with good grace. In any case, Olbrich's work quickly took him into more prestigious areas of creativity or art through a back door: he went to a vocational school to train in architecture.

Such was Olbrich's promise that he soon attracted the attention of Otto Wagner (1841–1918), at that time the head of one of Vienna's leading firms. Wagner's radical credentials were already as well established as his reputation as an architect and urban planner. In 1890, he had been commissioned to conceive a whole new vision of Vienna. With the exception of a new *Stadtbahn*, or light railway system, Wagner's conception had not been carried through, but he was still held in the highest regard in his home city.

Industrial Relations

Max Kurzweil (1867–1916) was also the son of a factory owner, who moved with his family to Vienna from Bzenec, Moravia, in 1879. Compared with his Secessionist contemporaries, Kurzweil's artistic interests retained a relatively narrow focus, though his works are often more radical than they first appear. Josef Hoffmann (1870–1956) was another industrialist's son. His father had made a fortune in cotton, and became the mayor of the family's home town of Brtnice in Moravia. The folk traditions of this province continued to influence Josef Hoffmann's work as an architect and designer long after he had shaken off the old conventions of formal art.

Koloman Moser broke this trend: he was brought up in a cottage in the grounds of the Vienna school in which his father worked as an administrator. Once classes were over, however, the young Moser had the run of the main building with its workshops and art rooms, and he seems to have enjoyed this freedom to the full. Did the opportunity he had at this time to poke his nose here and there, to play with this or that piece of equipment, this or that material, help explain the breadth of Moser's skills and interests in later life? Even by the standards of a movement that made a point of defining art in the widest possible terms, Moser is astonishing in the breadth of his accomplishments. With achievements in everything from architecture and graphic arts to tapestry, glassware and jewellery design, he was a one-man Renaissance in his own right.

A Late Arrival

Some young painters stuck to brush and canvas and to figurative work, while at the same time taking on important Secessionist values. Helene Funke (1869–1957) was one of these artists. A late arrival to the Secessionist party, she was born in Chemnitz, in Germany, and studied art in Munich before spending several years in Paris. Not until 1911 did Funke arrive in Vienna; hence, understandably enough, the tendency of art historians to see her work through the prism of French Fauvism – the audaciously antirealistic style employed by Henri Matisse (1869–1954), André Dérain (1880–1954) and friends in the 1900s. Yet Funke's work may, as art historian Julie M. Johnson suggests, make as much artistic sense in association with the work of those more famous male Viennese Secessionists in whose circles she moved once she was living in Austria. In her still lifes and scenes from nature, we see an emphasis on the same sort of repeated patterning as we do in work by Klimt and Moser; a comparable questioning of the conventional 'realist' view.

Foreign Bodies

Two more immigrants who became naturalized Secessionists were the Russian artists Elena Luksch-Makowsky (1878–1967) and Teresa Feodorovna Ries (1874–1956). The very presence in Vienna of these

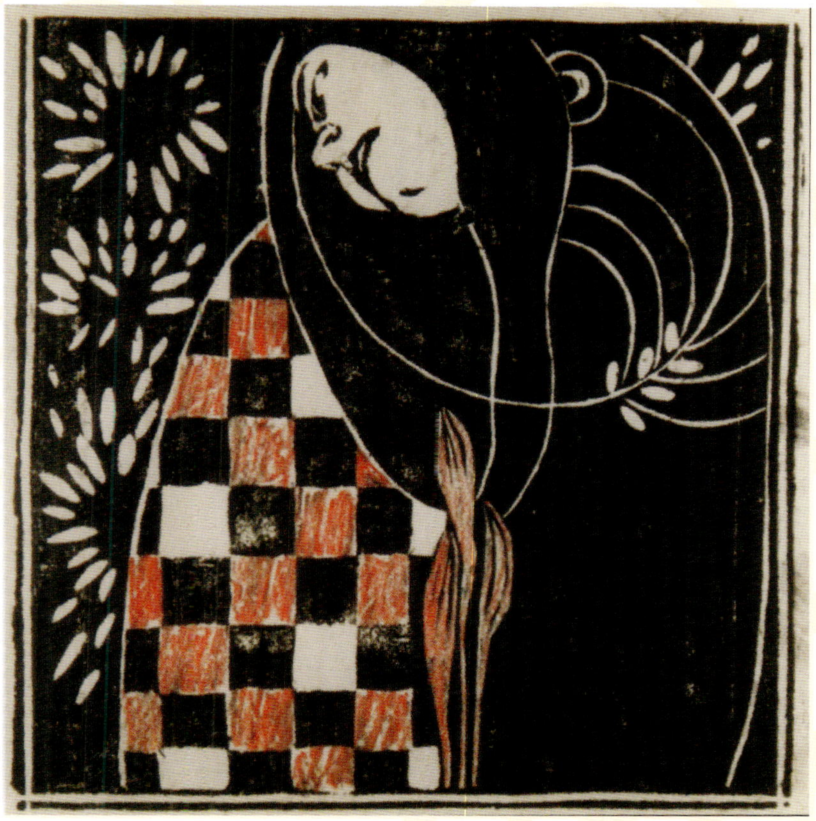

emigrées represented a crossing of frontiers, of course, as did the influences from Russian historical tradition and folk art they brought with them. They were also concerned, however, with breaking the old boundaries of medium and genre, and both threw themselves enthusiastically into the Secessionist experiment; both became as skilled in graphic arts as in figurative painting.

St Petersburg-born Luksch-Makowsky, the daughter of the celebrated radical-realist artist Vladimir Makowsky (1846–1920), had moved to Munich before arriving in Vienna in 1900 after marrying the Austrian sculptor Richard Luksch (1872–1936). Ries, a larger-than-life personality who created larger-than-life sculptures (of everyone from Lucifer to Mark Twain), was to some extent overshadowed by her own celebrity. So successful were her statues – Rodinesque meditations in

ABOVE ◆ DANCER, 1903. KOLOMAN MOSER (1868–1918)

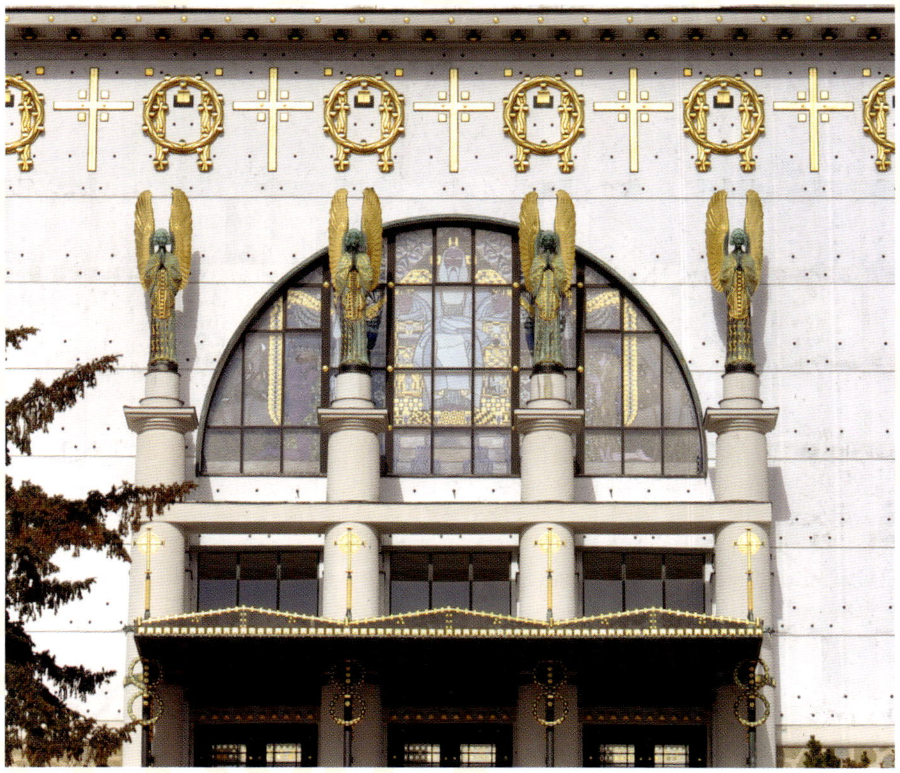

stone – that envious male contemporaries were sick of hearing about them, though between her gender and her Jewishness, her fame was subsequently to be suppressed. Even while her renown endured, however, the breadth of her vision tended to be disregarded, her work in painting and graphic arts ignored: like the male Secessionists, she believed in an art that transcended the normal bounds.

Subconscious Revealed

The Jewish daughter of a military architect from Sanok, Galicia, Broncia Koller-Pinell (1863–1934) and her family moved to Vienna, where her father ran a textile factory, at the age of seven. Although technically as 'foreign' as Luksch-Makowsky and Ries, then, she had much in common with men like Josef Hoffmann and Max Kurzweil, with whom she also shared a great many artistic values. Like Helene Funke, she conformed notionally to well-established genres, such as still life and landscape, but sought out semi-abstract patternings in her scenes. Koller-Pinell's paintings didn't so much tell stories as reveal subconscious feelings: 'I often want to express something and narrative pictures are impossible for me. I found a new language,' she confided to her daughter in 1924.

ABOVE ◆ KIRCHE AM STEINHOF (CHURCH OF ST LEOPOLD), VIENNA, 1903–07.
OTTO WAGNER (1841–1918)

A Man Apart

Egon Schiele (1890–1918) was an outlier in just about every imaginable sense. For a start, he was by far the youngest of the group. Just a child when the Secession took place, this son of a stationmaster in the little town of Tulln, Lower Austria, spent much of his solitary boyhood obsessively drawing trains. Slow at school, he was further isolated by being kept behind with younger children. As an adolescent, he alarmed his parents by his clear – and quasi-incestuous – attachment to his younger sister. Despite his obvious abilities, Schiele did not fit in at Vienna's conservative Academy of Fine Arts, where he studied – or attempted to – from 1906. Although he stayed at the Academy for three years, from 1907, he was at best a semi-detached student, being mentored increasingly closely by Gustav Klimt.

Mutual Talent

Why Klimt felt a kinship for Schiele is less immediately clear – though his generosity to younger artists was widely remarked on at the time. Both men, of course, were insistently erotic in their interests. As he grew older, Schiele's obsessions shifted from railway rolling stock to sex and women's bodies – or girls' bodies: in 1912, he was prosecuted for the abduction and seduction of a minor. In fairness, those charges were dropped and replaced with the much lesser ones of exhibiting indecent images where they could be seen by children.

Was this bourgeois morality gone mad? Or a justified response to what many even now believe was essentially a pornographic talent? Klimt's exotic sirens may be unmistakeably sexual in their allure, but they're also achingly dreamy, soft-focus figures of wistful yearning and desire. Schiele's nudes are shockingly direct in the way they face us, stripped not just of clothing but also of 'femininity' as romantically constructed: frank, unabashed and defiant in their gaze.

Klimt's and Schiele's approaches to art were very different too: impure as Schiele's thoughts may have been, his work was fastidiously figurative; nor did he show much interest in other media, unlike Klimt and the other Secessionists. It might seem merely facetious to say that the boundaries Schiele was most interested in breaking were those of sexual morality and conventional decorum, but at the same time, it's at least partly true. That said, to be as resolutely transgressive as Schiele is an artistic achievement in itself. Klimt surely recognized a talent as unusual as his own.

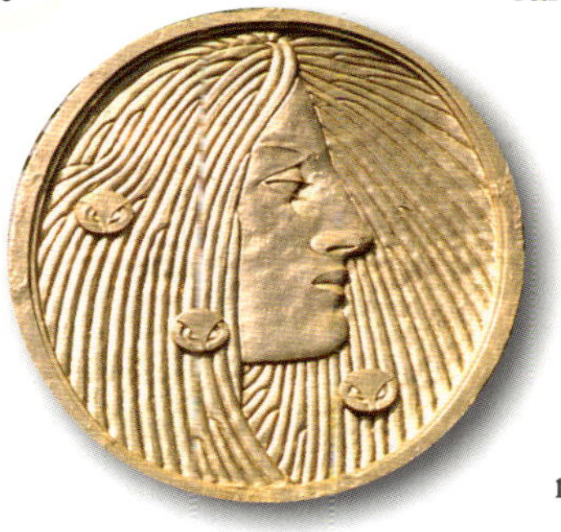

Friends in High Places

But if Egon Schiele cut an odd figure in the company of the Secession artists, he can hardly have seemed more out of place than their choice of first honorary president, Rudolf von Alt (1812–1905). Wondrous as they are in their luminosity and skill, Alt's watercolours appear to be nothing if not conservative in style. A founder member of the Künstlerhaus (and indeed its president since 1874), Alt was pretty much the epitome of the establishment artist. But it isn't difficult to see why the Secessionists sought the patronage of such a figure; Alt's former colleagues were certainly in no doubt of the significance of his defection.

Alt's involvement was emphatic confirmation that the Secession was, first, serious and, second, much more than a fit of pique on the part of a few young hotheads. It was vital to Klimt and his friends that these points were made. But Alt was also important as an emblem of continuity, and even of conservatism, a mark of the movement's loyalty to timeless principles. In embracing the modern, they weren't turning their backs on beauty. Alt's presidency underlined this fidelity to the aims of art.

Forward!

Why Alt himself wanted to throw in his lot with the Secessionists is a little less clear – though there's no real reason to question his good faith. A dedicated servant to Viennese art, Alt wanted it to be all that it could possibly be. He'd seen the future in the works of Klimt and the others and found it exciting. There's a danger that, in appreciating the radicalism of the great Modernists in art, we dismiss the real achievements of those against whom they rebelled. 'Academic' art doesn't necessarily have to be devoid of either integrity or talent – even if the rigidity of its conventions did, on the one hand, deter innovation and on the other, let lesser artists succeed by simply going through the motions. The original aims of the Künstlerhaus had been to produce the best work possible: the paintings of Makart were still revered by the younger generation. There may have been a fair few time-servers on the Künstlerhaus committee, but Austria's older artists needn't be dismissed as mediocrities en masse.

The time for change had clearly come, however, and in the Vienna Secession, it had a self-appointed vanguard. Great things were to be expected, that seemed sure.

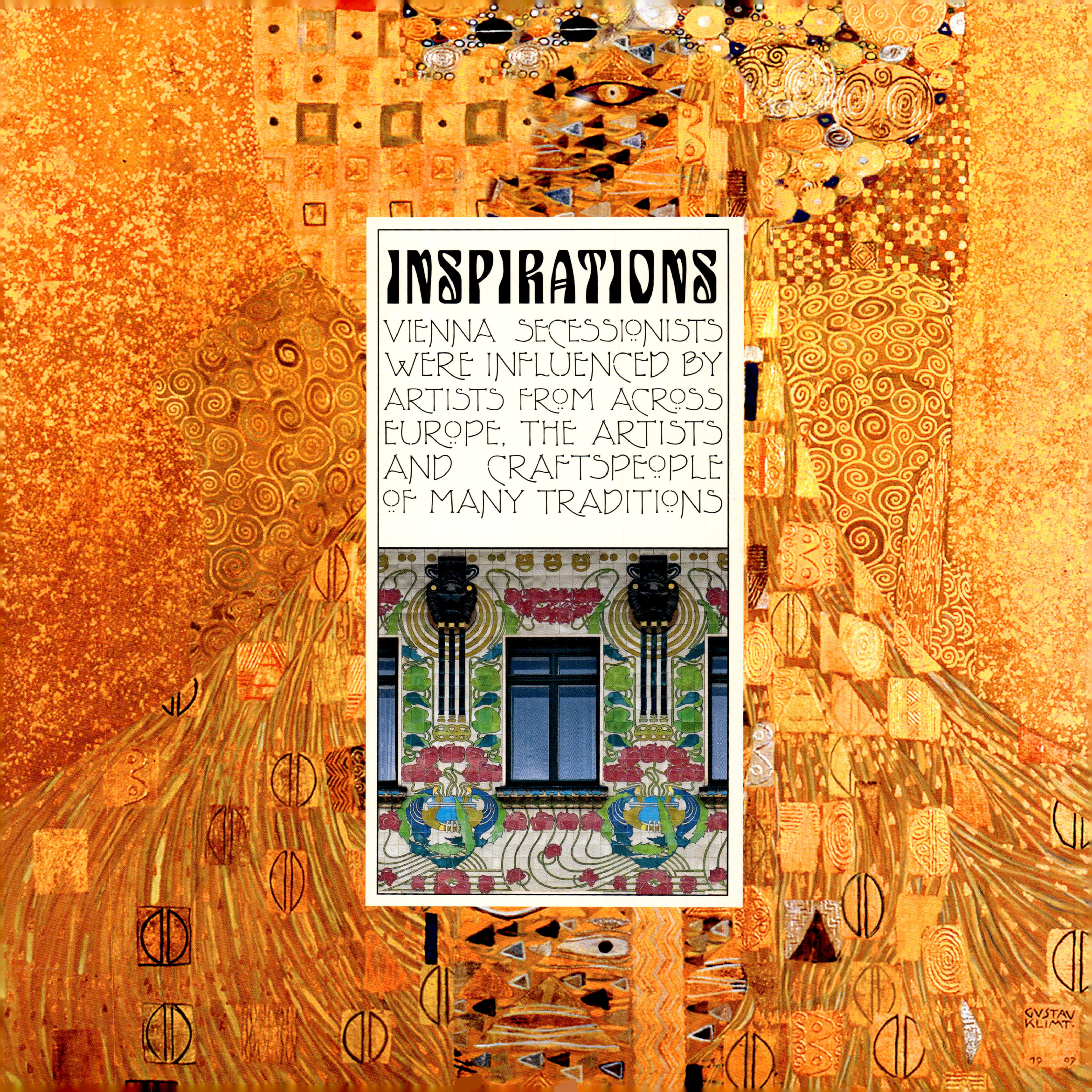

INSPIRATIONS

VIENNA SECESSIONISTS WERE INFLUENCED BY ARTISTS FROM ACROSS EUROPE, THE ARTISTS AND CRAFTSPEOPLE OF MANY TRADITIONS

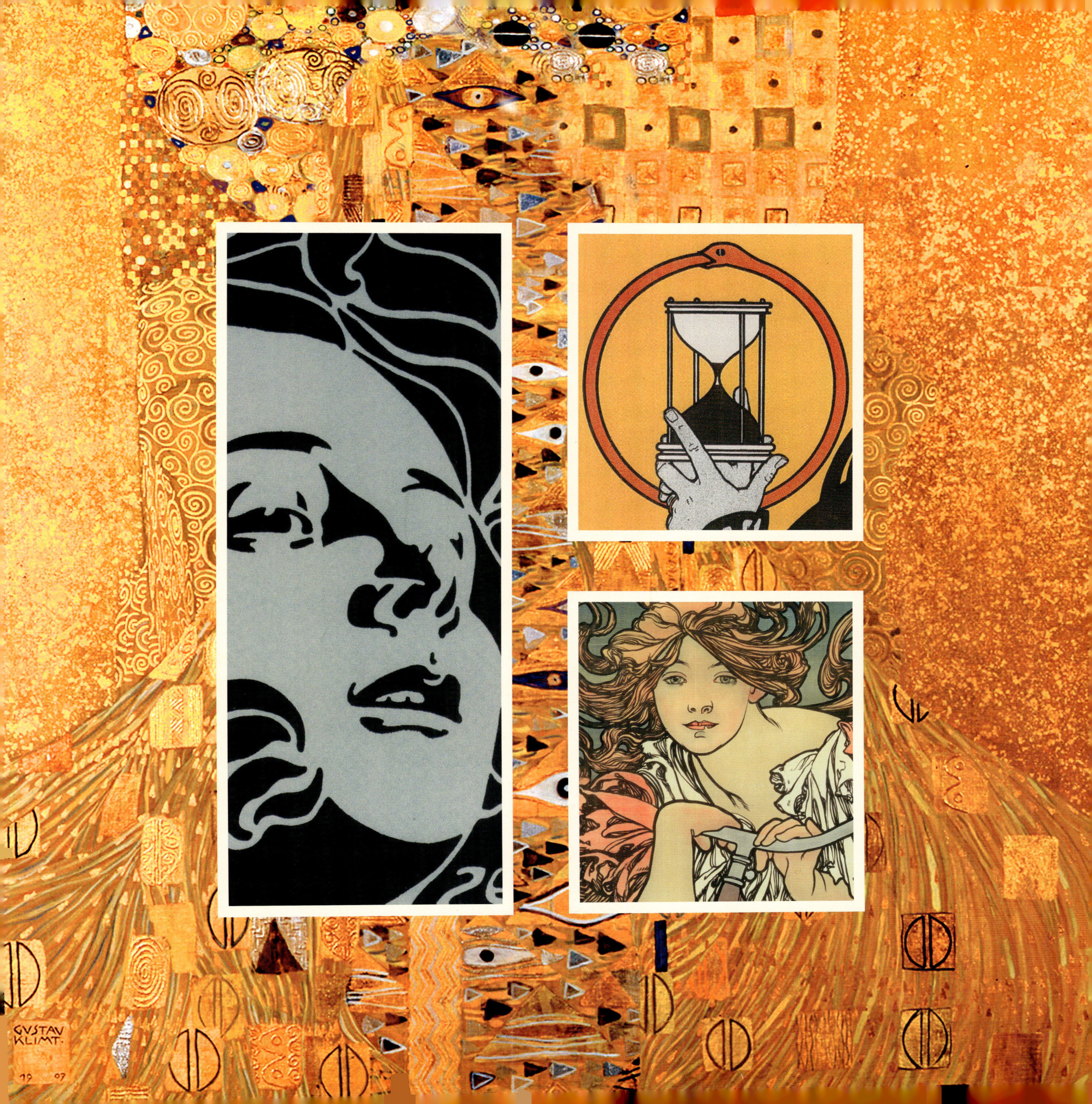
GVSTAV
KLIMT

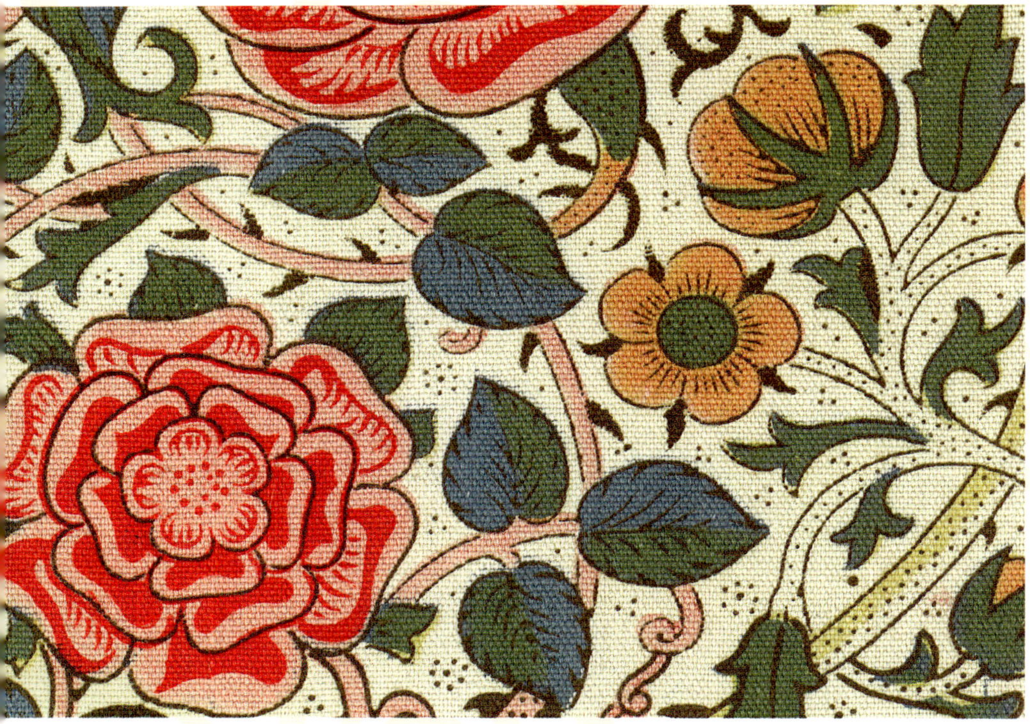

THE Vienna Secession may not have been a unified movement in terms of style, but they could all look to the powerful new artworks coming out of the Munich and Berlin Secessions, keen to break away from what had been before, to Art Nouveau developing in other countries, to the Glasgow Four and the Arts & Crafts movement, and even non-Western influences like Japanese art.

Digging Up the Past

Those who joked that Joseph Maria Olbrich's Secession Building (*see* page 132) looked like an 'Assyrian public lavatory' were on to something – the sneering note apart. Olbrich had rushed to design this imposing (but undoubtedly odd-looking) hall just off the Ringstrasse as a headquarters for the Secession, in whose galleries his colleagues' works could be displayed; and in whose own exterior form the values of the movement could be advertised. It was indeed constructed (very loosely) in Mesopotamian style, as far as this was apprehended at the time. Literally the 'land between the rivers' (the Tigris and Euphrates), a wide alluvial plain at the centre of what is now Iraq, Mesopotamia had seen the emergence of some of the world's first civilizations some 4,000 years ago.

More to the point, perhaps, Mesopotamia offered a paradigm for human cultural endeavour that owed nothing to Greek or Latin antiquity. Hence the style of the Secession Building: no classical colonnades – just blank walls, with recessed panels (or ornamental patterning); no triangular pediments – just rectangular blocks or squared-off towers. Nor were there any domes – just a peculiar 'golden cabbage', which might or might not have been the sort of thing the Mesopotamians liked, but assuredly had no precedent in Athens or in Rome. And this, of course, was the point. The Secessionists had seceded not only from the Künstlerhaus but also from the classically-inspired traditions they'd been schooled in – and, they felt, in artistic subjection to for much too long. But whether Olbrich understood it clearly or not, there was more to his choice than this: Mesopotamia had other associations for the modern mind.

Twenty years before, another young man had studied art and architecture in Vienna. He too had found the experience unsatisfactory; so much so that Brunswick-born Robert Koldewey (1855–1925) had dropped out of his chosen courses altogether and embraced the pursuit of archaeology. There was nothing particularly surprising about this choice: the idea that human history lay buried beneath our feet had caught the imagination of nineteenth-century Europe, especially perhaps in the German-speaking countries. The ruins of Rome and Italy had of course been above ground in open view since medieval times. They had given the Renaissance a template of civilization, characterized by symmetry and order.

ABOVE LEFT • ROSE, 1883, WILLIAM MORRIS (1834–96)
OPPOSITE • FELSENHUHN, 1910–12, WIENER WERKSTÄTTE

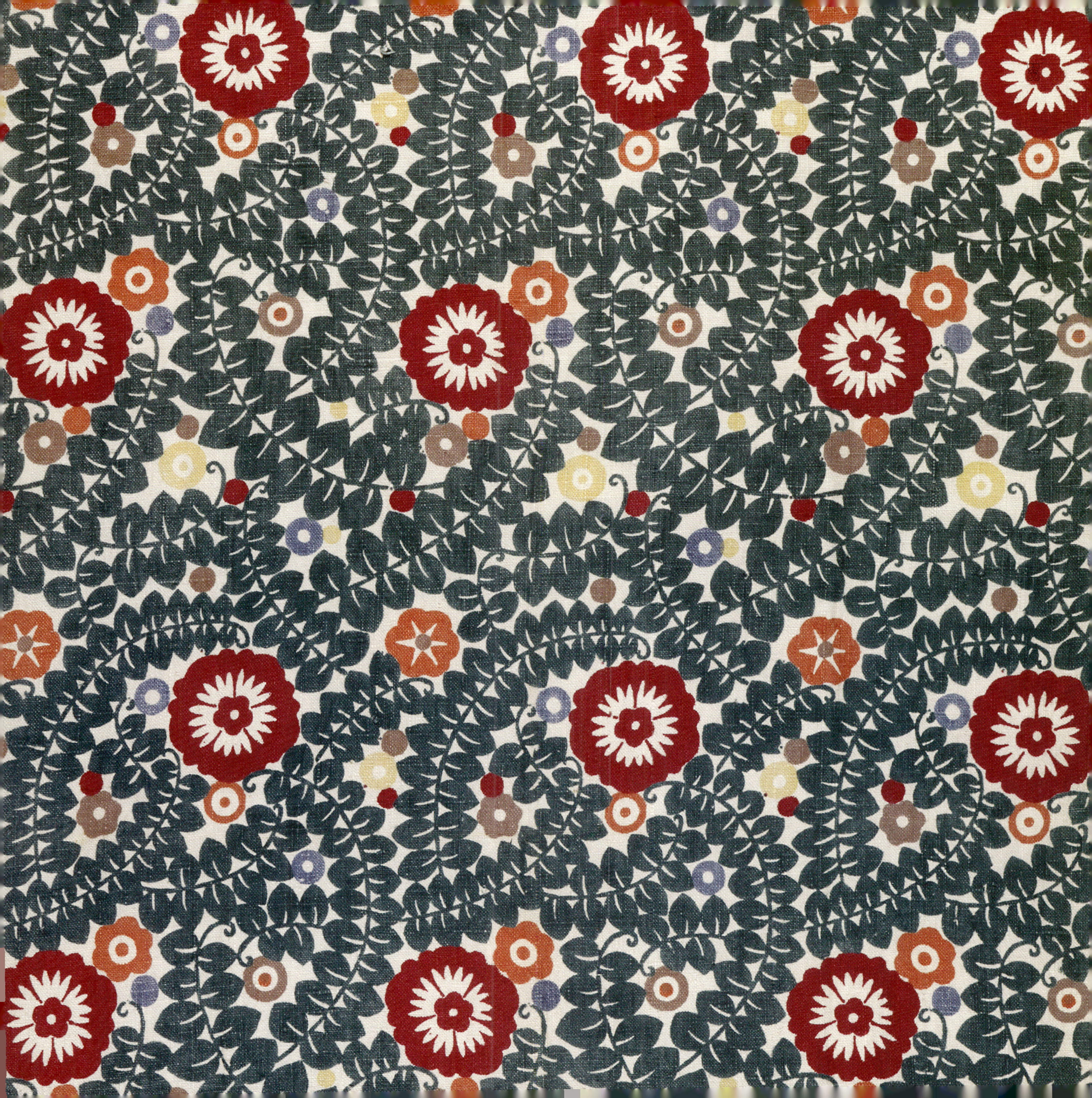

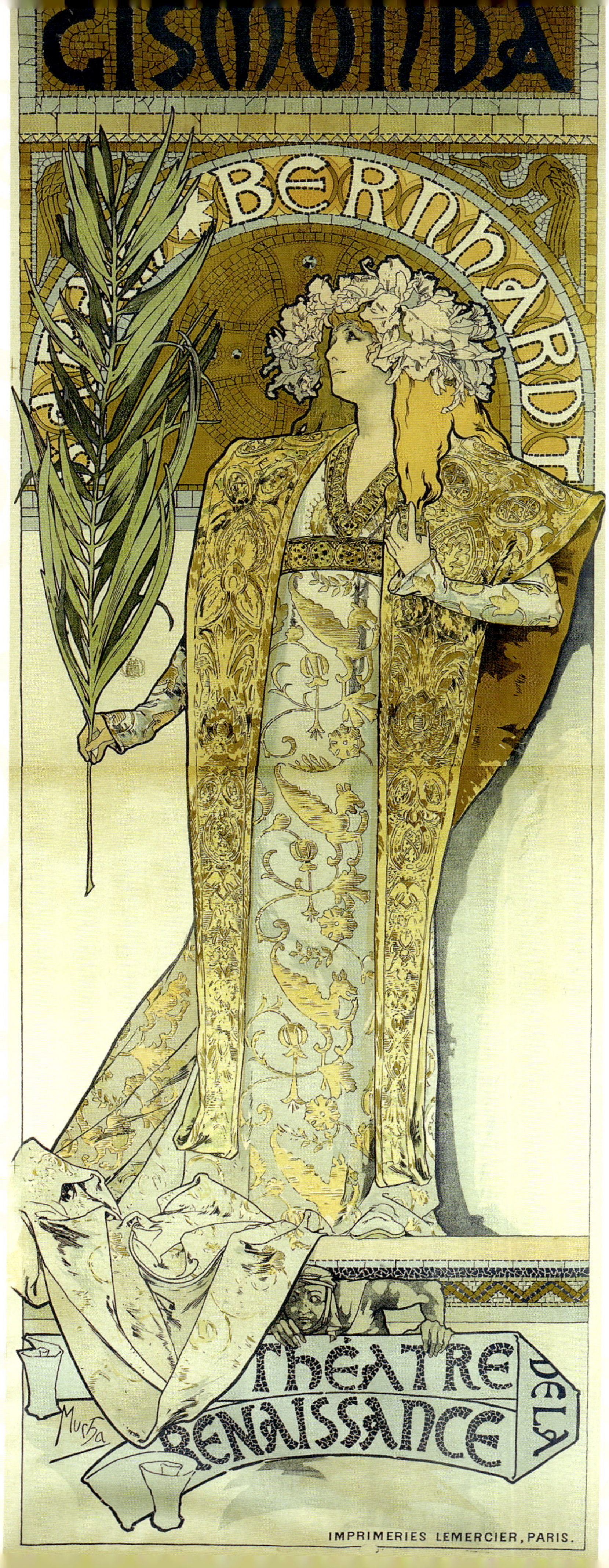

The unearthing of the lost city of Pompeii in the eighteenth century gave the Romantic age that followed an era-appropriate paradigm – of the inner life, the secret history that goes unseen. By the 1870s, Heinrich Schliemann (1822–90) was delving deep into the annals of ancient legend, excavating what he insisted were the ruins of Troy, in Turkey – ancient Asia Minor. It's a strange sort of scholarship that feels the need to establish the historic authenticity of classic stories, but Schliemann's theories resonate to this day, in part perhaps because – in their literalistic way – they recognize the importance of the imaginary and the mythical to human life.

Like many archaeologists of his time, Koldewey began by examining Western Europe's antecedents in the Graeco-Roman world, exploring sites at Assos on Turkey's Aegean coast and on the isle of Lesbos. Valuable as his work may have been, in excavating here, he was really only uncovering more of what was already known. By 1887, however, Koldewey had moved on to the Middle East. Inspired at first by biblical references, archaeologists had been busy in Palestine since the 1830s. Further east, in Mesopotamia, work had been underway at the ancient Assyrian cities of Nineveh and Nimrud since 1842. But Koldewey's digs further to the south at the old Sumerian sites of Surghul and al-Hiba, near Telloh, were to revolutionize archaeological research.

Secret Cities

Raised up on Mesopotamia's open, flat and fertile floodplain, the great cities of Sumer had been built with bricks of mud. With sticky clay available in such abundance and the heat of the sun to bake it dry, there had really been no need to work in stone. Mud bricks were used in the construction of whole cities, with massive defensive walls and prestigious buildings: extensive palaces; gigantic step-pyramids; and imposing temples.

LEFT ◆ GISMONDA, c. 1894. ALPHONSE MUCHA (1860–1939)
OPPOSITE ◆ STAINED-GLASS WINDOW, c. 1901. JOSEPH MARIA OLBRICH (1867–1908)

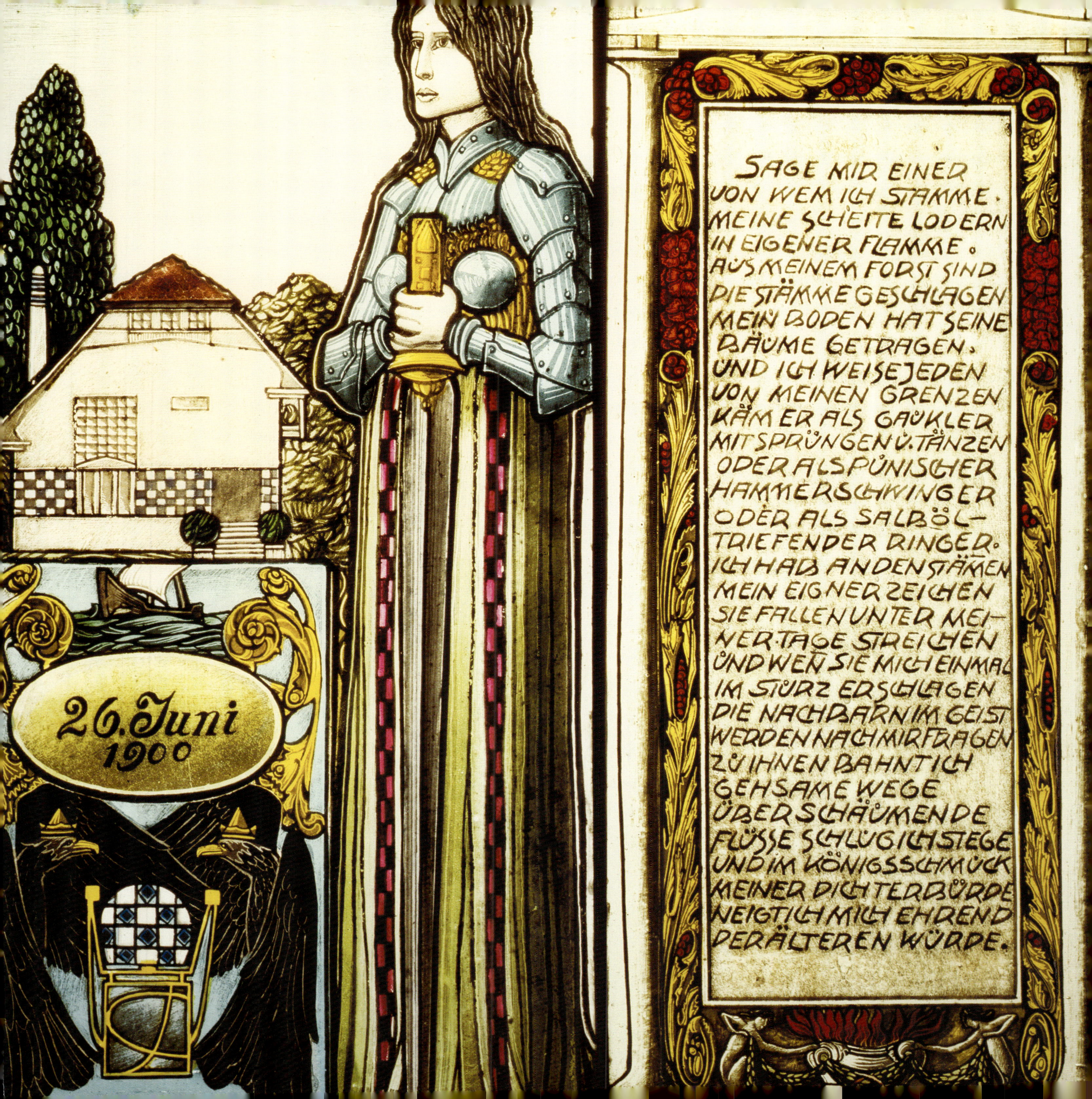
26. Juni
1900
SAGE MIR EINER
VON WEM ICH STAMME.
MEINE SCHEITE LODERN
IN EIGENER FLAMME.
AUS MEINEM FORST SIND
DIE STÄMME GESCHLAGEN
MEIN BODEN HAT SEINE
BÄUME GETRAGEN.
UND ICH WEISE JEDEN
VON MEINEN GRENZEN
KÄM ER ALS GAUKLER
MIT SPRÜNGEN U. TÄNZEN
ODER ALS PUNISCHER
HAMMERSCHWINGER
ODER ALS SALBÖL-
TRIEFENDER RINGER.
ICH HAB AN DEN STÄMEN
MEIN EIGNER ZEICHEN
SIE FALLEN UNTER MEI-
NER TAGE STREICHEN
UND WEN̄ SIE MICH EINMAL
IM STURZ ERSCHLAGEN
DIE NACHBARN IM GEIST
WERDEN NACH MIR FRAGEN
ZU IHNEN BAHNT ICH
GEHSAME WEGE
ÜBER SCHÄUMENDE
FLÜSSE SCHLUG ICH STEGE
UND IM KÖNIGSSCHMUCK
MEINER DICHTERBÜRDE
NEIGT ICH MICH EHREND
DER ÄLTEREN WÜRDE.

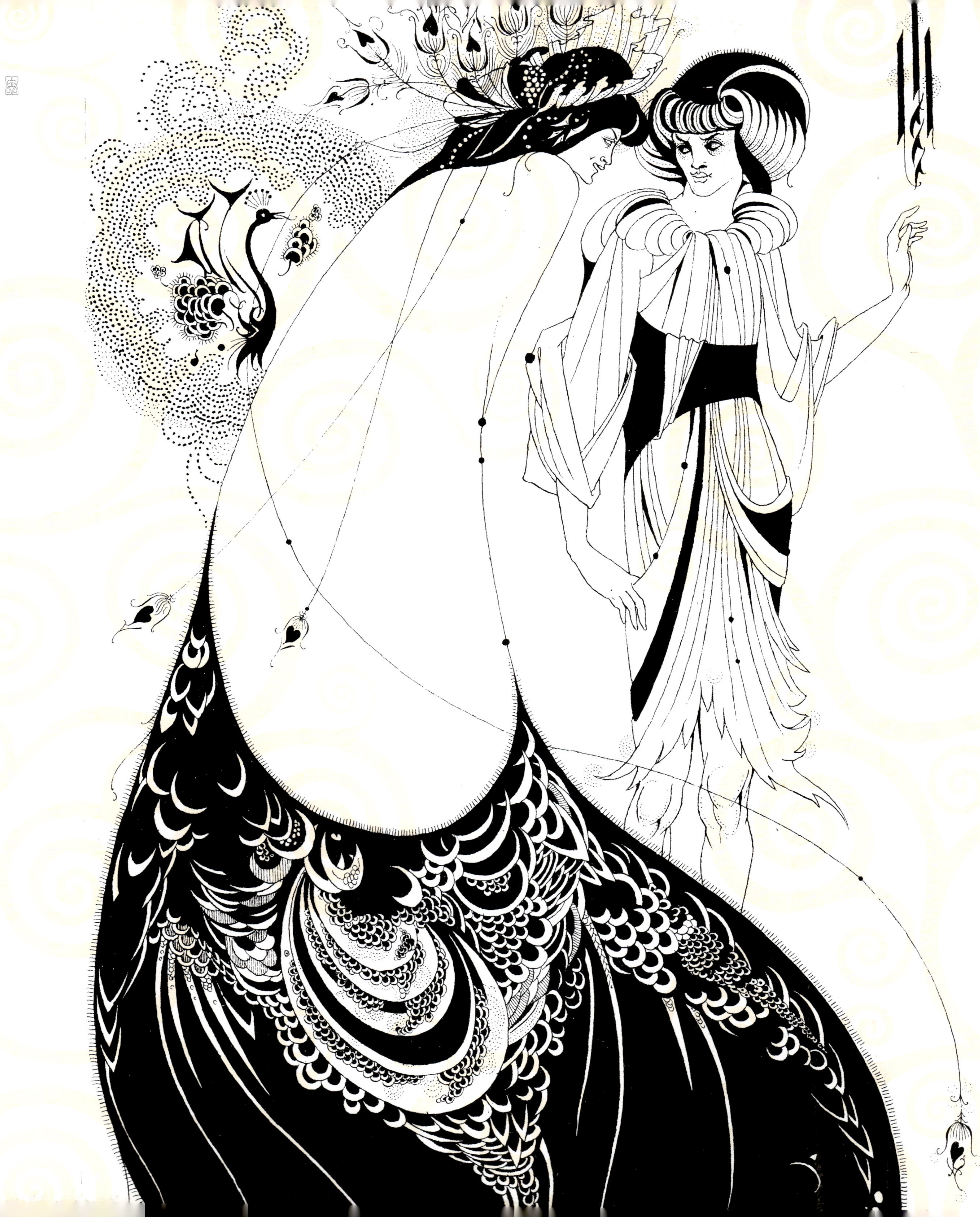

The trouble was, to modern archaeologists seeking after treasures from the ancient world, these mud-brick structures were well-nigh indistinguishable from the sun-baked clay they were concealed in. We can now hardly guess how many precious ruins were dug straight through – by investigators who ended up disregarding entire cities to triumphantly turn up tiny stone or ceramic fragments or metal artefacts. In developing techniques for identifying and then safely excavating courses of unbaked mud-brick, Koldewey revolutionized Mesopotamian archaeology.

Story of the Soil

If Schliemann had given the stories of 'Troy' a site, placing legendary settings in the real world, Koldewey did something much more interesting. With his skill in reading messages of which the earth itself appeared unconscious, he became a sort of psychoanalyst of the sites he worked. Just as Sigmund Freud was to do a few years later, stepping back and listening quietly while his patient reeled off words in screeds of 'free association', Koldewey adopted a comparatively passive posture before the sites he studied. Rather than hacking away after disparate 'finds', he learned to let the soil tell its own story, revealing the larger structures that lurked beneath the surface, only now revealed. Over the next few decades, the German archaeologist and the new generation of researchers he trained were to excavate one of the very greatest cities of antiquity: Babylon.

Remembering Babylon

The historical home of Hammurabi and Nebuchadnezzar, the biblical site of the Tower of Babel and the Jewish captivity, Babylon had a strange and semi-mythical status. The Book of Revelation's world

OPPOSITE ◆ THE PEACOCK SKIRT, FROM 'SALOME' BY OSCAR WILDE, 1893. AUBREY BEARDSLEY (1872–98)
RIGHT ◆ NUDA VERITAS, 1898. GUSTAV KLIMT (1862–1918)

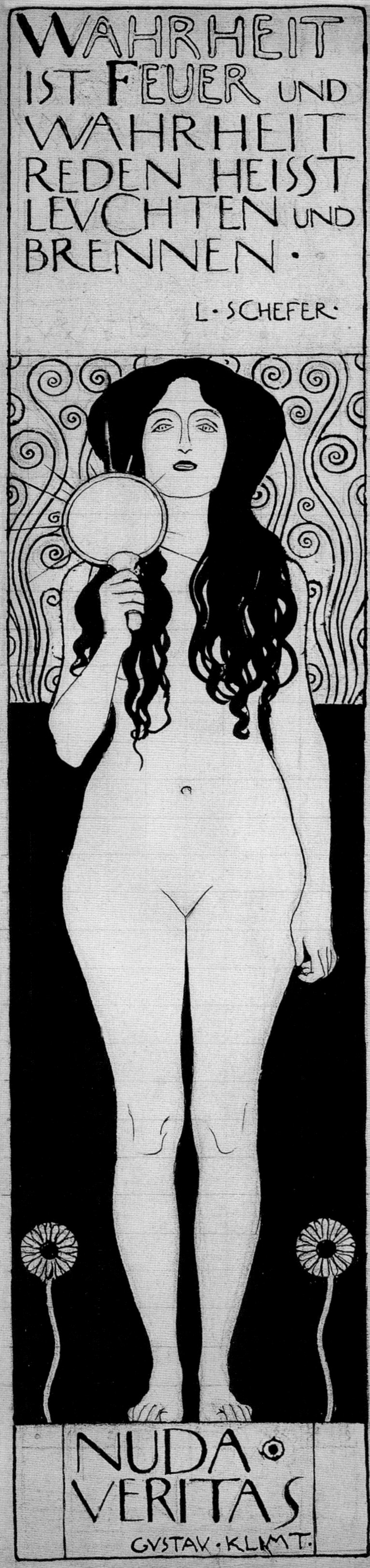

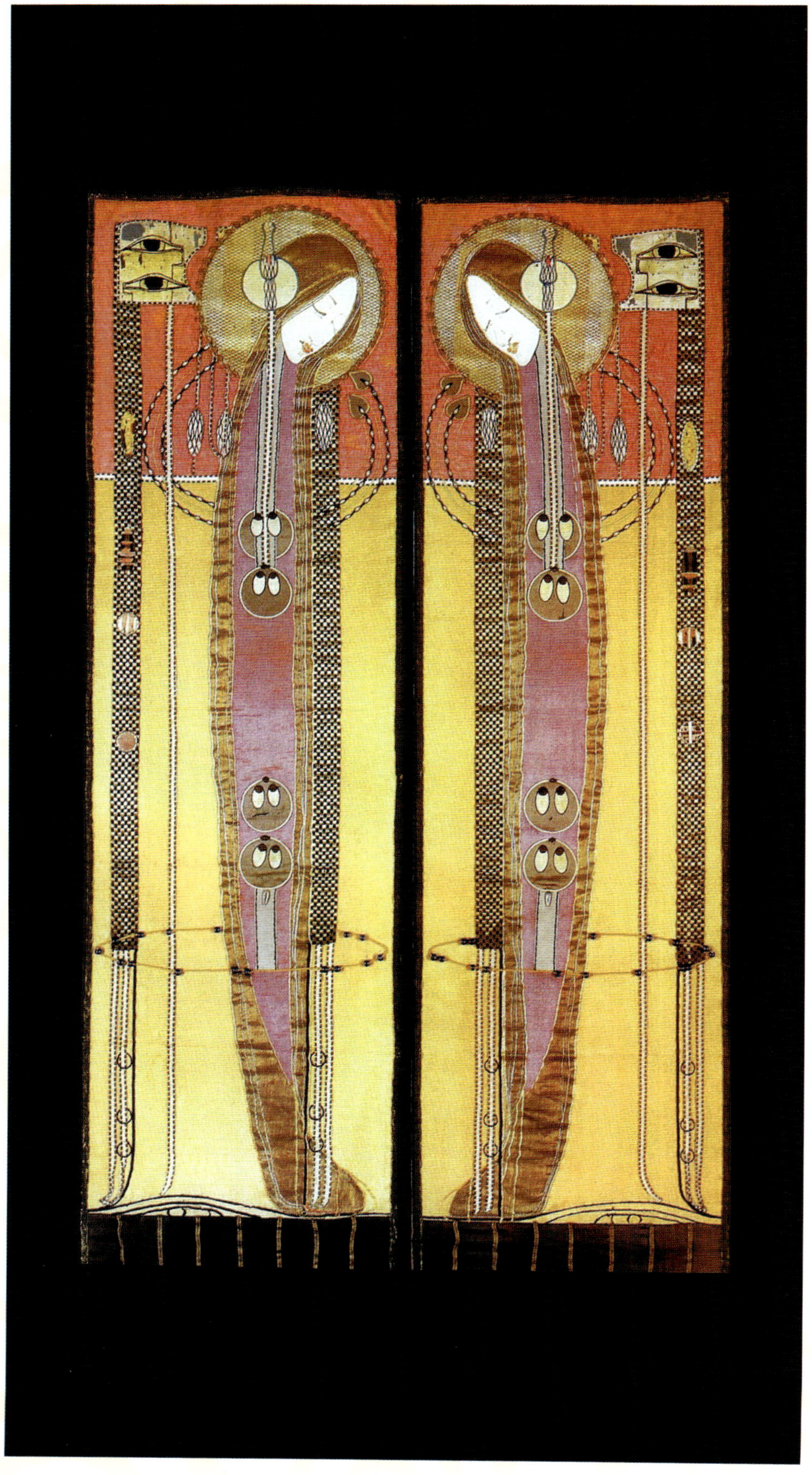

capital of sin, it lurked like some secret fantasy in civilization's subconscious, its excavation a sort of psychoanalytic exposure of the Western mind. The shift of archaeological focus to Mesopotamia may have been an accident of imperial history – the new researches accompanied an expansion of Western colonialism into the region. But mere chance can't account for the excitement their findings caused.

If classicism had come to represent all those values to which Western civilization consciously aspired, how were its unconscious yearnings to be symbolized? The original builders of Babylon would surely have been utterly astonished if they could have seen the lurid colours in which posterity was to paint their home, but if Babylon had not existed, it would have had to be invented about now. After all – as Freud was to claim – there was no such thing as coincidence.

Dressed to Kill

The 'purity' of classical art and architecture had always been held up as their justification, but what did they offer an age which sensed that the excitements of art – as of life – were likely to be impure? Such excitements were most obviously – although by no means solely – to be found in the area of sexuality. Even where it was ostensibly erotic, classical art was not completely convincing any more. It's pretty much a cliché that clothing can be more erotically suggestive than bare flesh. The classical female nude, beautiful as she may be, is austere even in her nakedness. She certainly seemed strait-laced beside the surging sexual allure of the women Klimt was painting, studies in exoticism, in their sinuous postures, their spangled forms and their gaudy gowns.

Again, it's about the opposition between what is explicitly set out and what's only implicitly suggested, between appeals to the conscious and

LEFT ◆ EMBROIDERED PANELS, 1902. MARGARET MACDONALD (1864–1933)
OPPOSITE ◆ INSET PANEL (DETAIL), c. 1904. KOLOMAN MOSER (1868–1918)

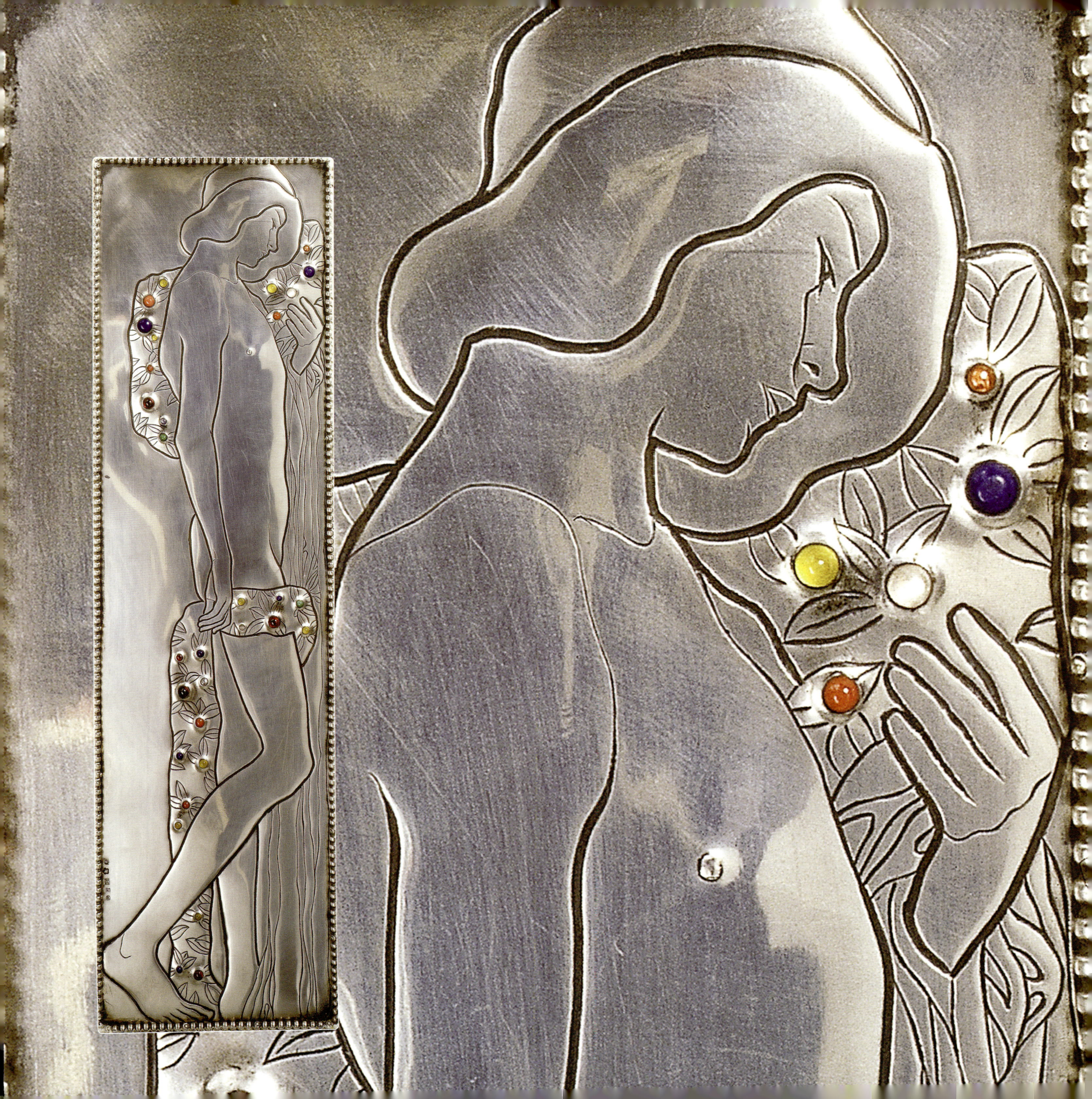

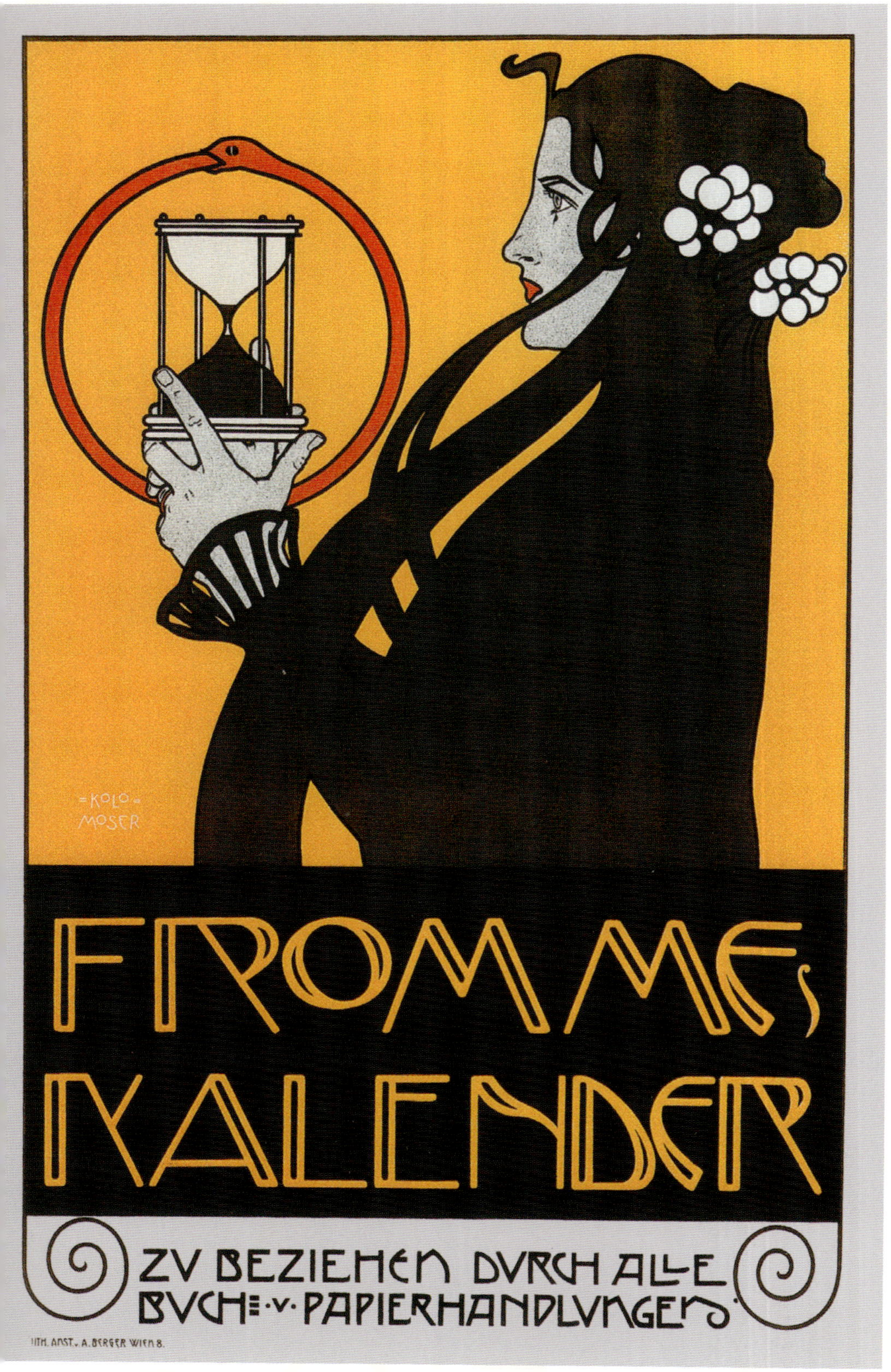

to the subconscious mind. For better or for worse, Klimt's women are seldom subjects in their own right. What we see is inseparable from the way we see it. The 'backgrounds' in these pictures don't know their place; instead, they bundle up their subjects in a wider, more extravagant vision so that they seem to evoke the imagery of a dream.

Or, of course, a nightmare; for paradoxically, the more sumptuously and sensually Klimt represented the women in his paintings, the more we feel we're gazing into sexuality's deep, dark heart. Freud had yet to formulate his famous association between *eros* and *agape* – desire and the 'death wish' – but Klimt was clearly on to it already. As well indeed he might be: as long ago as 1857, in his landmark collection *Les Fleurs du Mal*, the French poet Charles Baudelaire (1821–67) had made this association a major theme in European literature and art, but it had never been conveyed as clearly and powerfully as it was in Klimt's great works.

Dangerous Liaisons

There were, art historian Frank Whitford reminds us, more prosaic reasons for the association of death and sex than the deep-lying dream imagery described by Baudelaire, by Klimt and then by Freud. Bourgeois morality being what it was, young ladies were expected to be virgins until they wed. Young men had to wait until they were well established in their careers before they married – though they didn't necessarily wait so chastely. With such an industry of prostitution – so many young maidservants, seamstresses and shopgirls looking for love, or fun, not to mention the occasional bored matron – there were any number of opportunities for gentlemen prepared to show a little generosity and lack of scruple. That there might well be a price to be paid, and not only on the female side – even if an inconvenient

LEFT • ADVERTISING POSTER FOR FROMMES CALENDAR, 1899. KOLOMAN MOSER (1868–1918)
OPPOSITE • POSTER ADVERTISING THE SUN. LOUIS JOHN RHEAD (1857–1926)

pregnancy could be shrugged off when the man was of a higher social class than the expectant mother – was the risk of many sexual encounters.

It was in 1897 that the Austrian playwright Arthur Schnitzler (1862–1931) wrote *Reigen* or *La Ronde*, his notorious drama about the social and sexual merry-go-round of modern life. In a series of scenes – such as 'The Prostitute and the Soldier', 'The Soldier and the Parlourmaid', 'The Parlourmaid and the Young Gentleman', 'The Young Gentleman and the Young Wife', 'The Young Wife and the Husband' – he traced contacts and connections that otherwise went unseen. And of course in doing this, he hinted at the possible transmission of syphilis, which could corrode the body and ultimately destroy the mind. So the sexual impulse, hard as it might be to resist, could – quite literally – drive people to sickness through to insanity, and at the last to death.

A Dread Disease

Nor did the disease stop there: congenital syphilis was passed on to the children of any such contaminated relationship. Worse still, such children were born with the sickness at its secondary stage, working away at their central nervous system. Stunted, sickly, mentally defective or even mad, syphilitic children bore living testimony to the sins of the fathers, visited upon the next generation. This then was a disease that didn't just attack the individual, but went to the heart of the nineteenth century's most venerated institution: the family.

Again, of course, there's that mismatch between what was consciously acknowledged and what was actually the case: the bourgeois family was often founded in hypocrisy. What made syphilis the most powerful

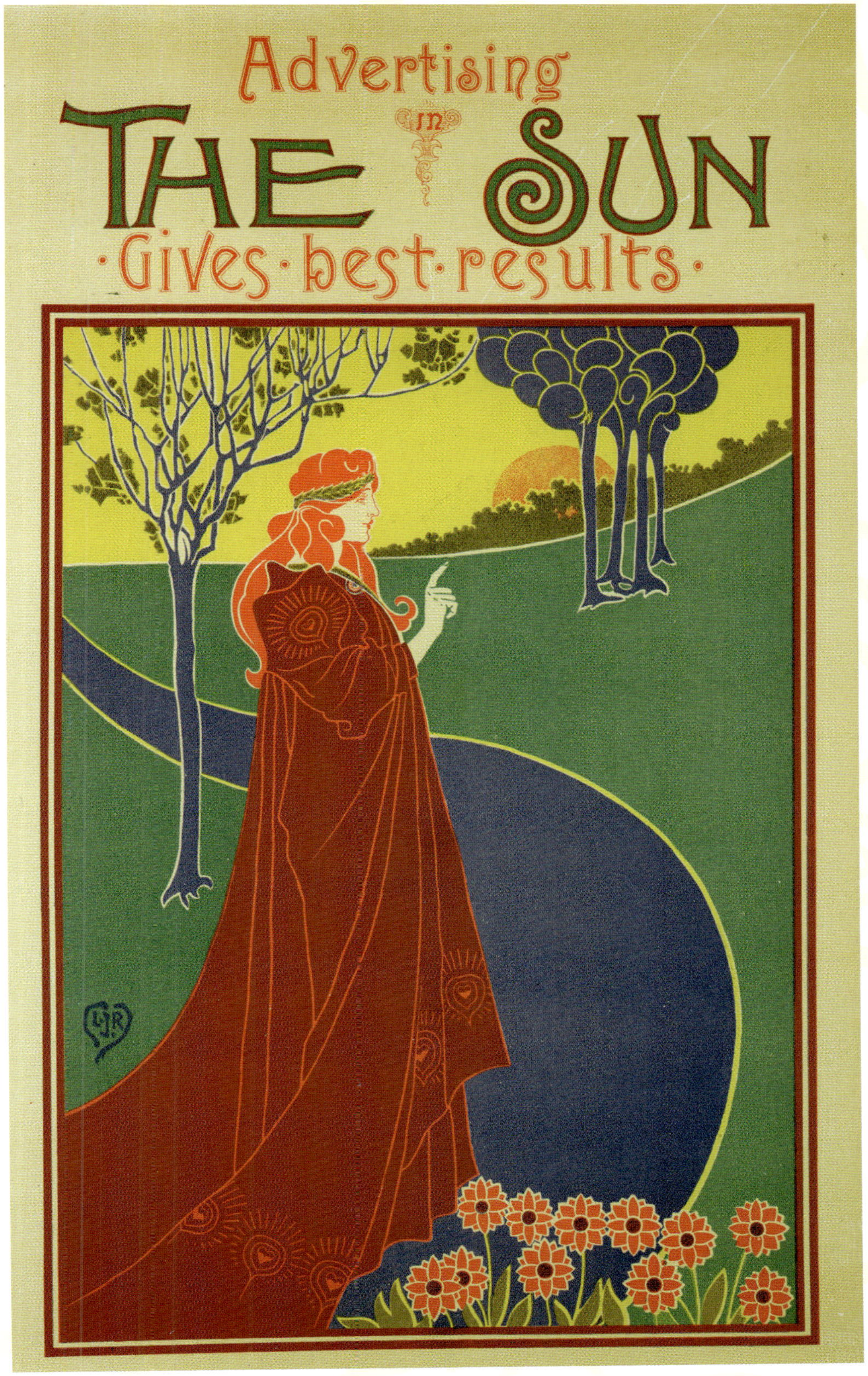

metaphor for moral evil and for social disintegration was the way in which its prevalence undermined the most comforting myths of middle-class respectability.

No wonder then that the male sexual passion should have been viewed – by men themselves – as a source of horror, or that the feminine beauty which sparked it should have inspired as much fear as it did love. The thought of the *vagina dentata* – the fanged vagina, which bit off the male member even as it gratified its desires – seems to have haunted the male imagination of the nineteenth century.

Art and the Everyday

We're a long way, admittedly, from the decorative pendants of Koloman Moser, Josef Hoffmann's high-backed chairs or an Otto Wagner church. But if so much emphasis has so far been placed on what might be described as the 'artistic unconscious' of the *fin de siècle*, that's because – by definition – it's both vitally important and very easy to overlook. But there were of course conscious echoes too, not least a very obvious debt to *Jugendstil* and the Art Nouveau on which the German form was founded.

There was also an obvious debt to the Arts and Crafts movement to which, in its turn, the modern French style owed so much. This was established by William Morris (1834–96) in the 1880s. The Englishman's insistence that a well-designed wallpaper or tablecloth could be as important to the quality of life as a beautiful painting stemmed in part from his socialist concern for a labour force he saw as having been left de-skilled and alienated by the mechanistic methods of industrial production; and, at the same time, his belief that consumers were being fobbed off with shoddy factory goods. But

RIGHT • MAJOLICA HOUSE. 1898–99. DES. BY OTTO WAGNER (1848–1918)

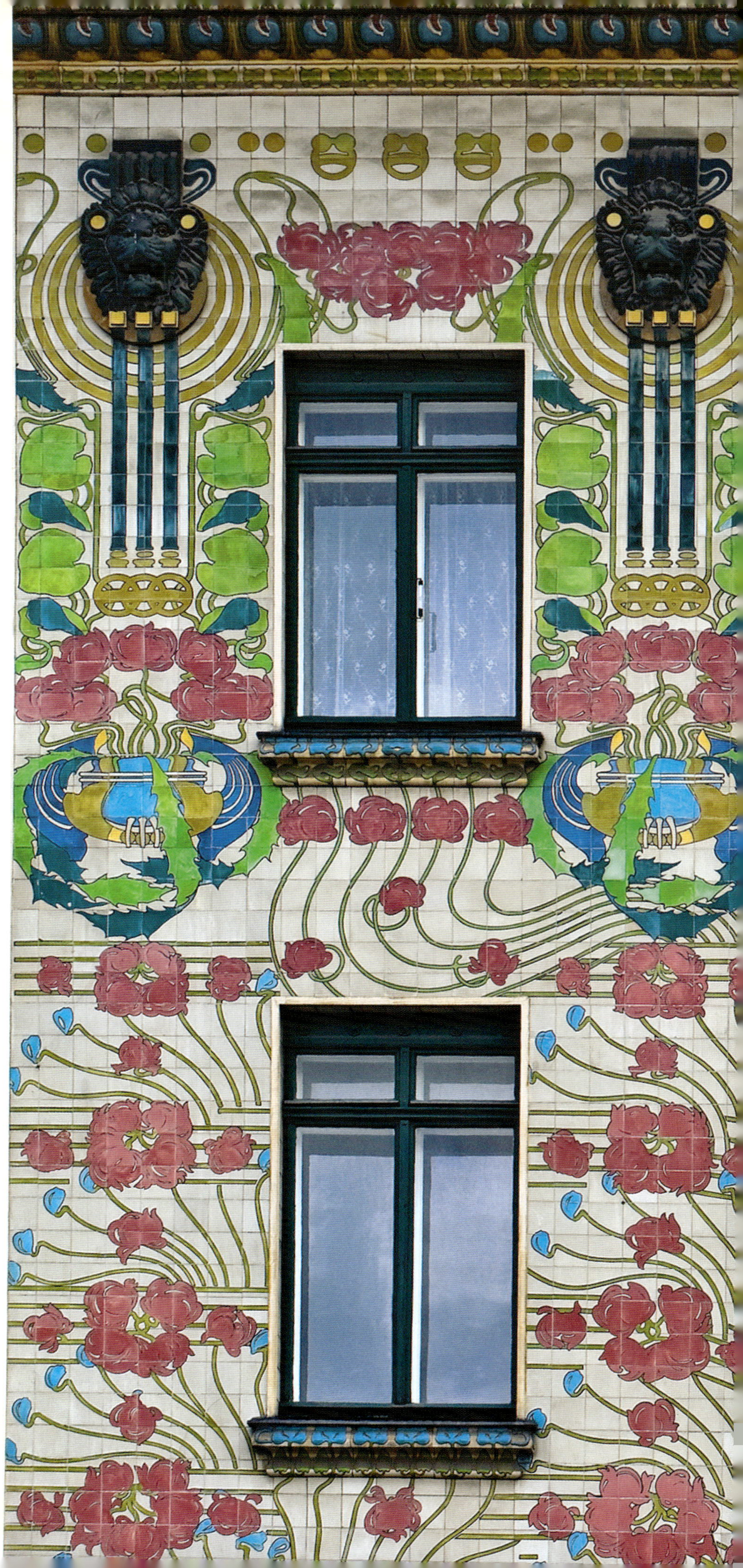

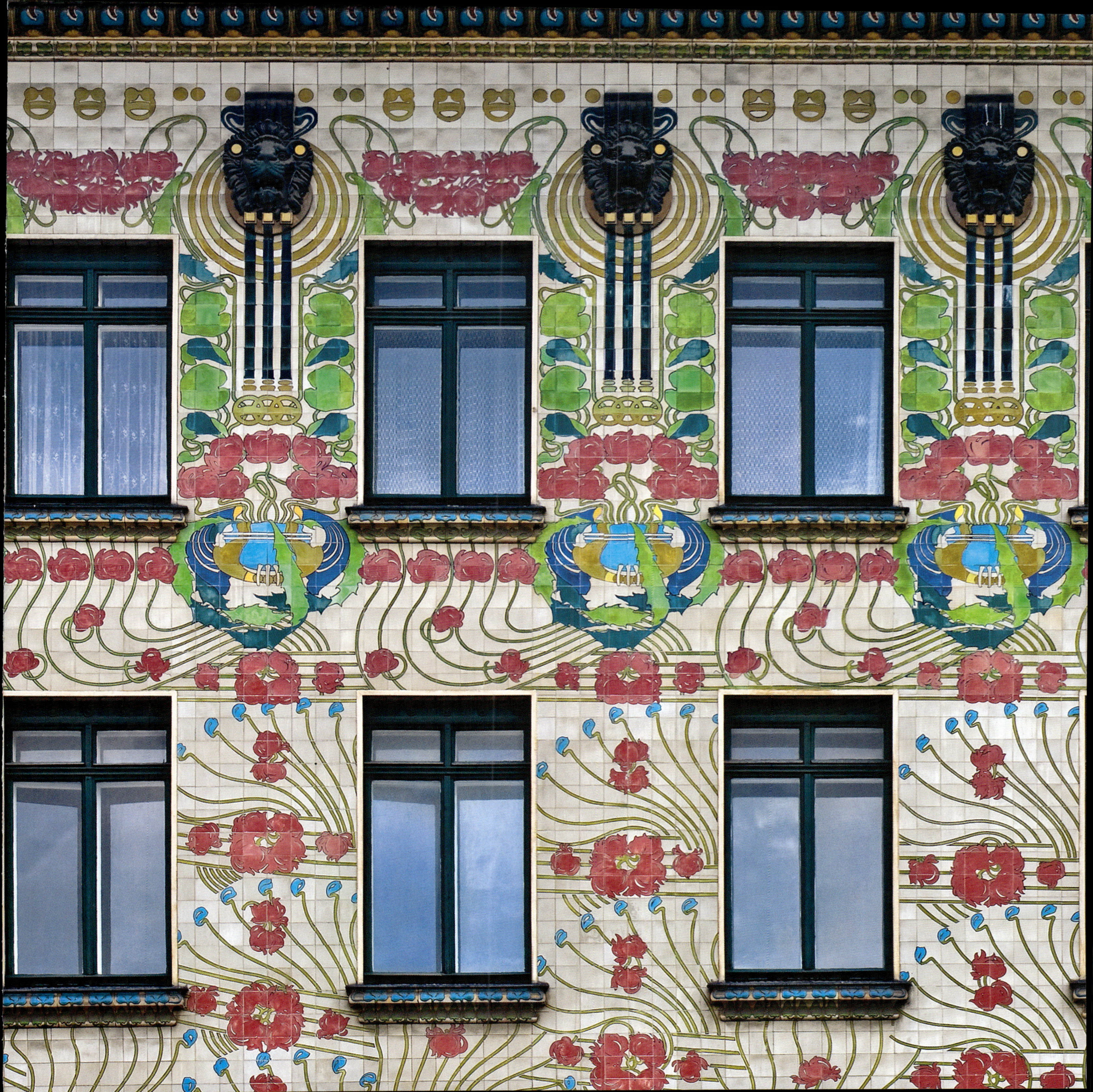

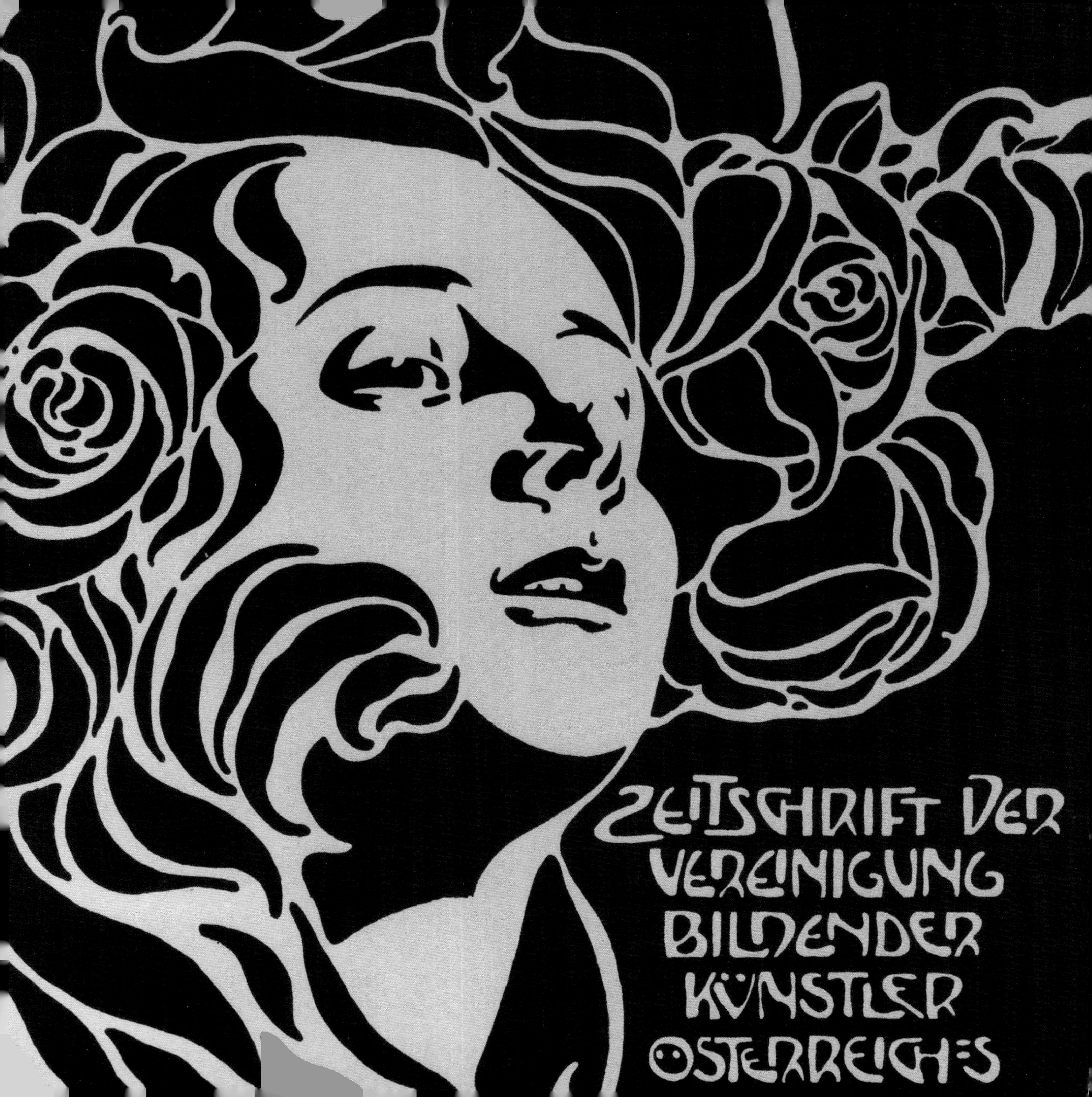
ZEITSCHRIFT DER
VEREINIGUNG
BILDENDER
KÜNSTLER
ÖSTERREICHES

Morris's belief that art had a place in every area of daily life had an appeal that extended far beyond the revolutionary left.

The work of Moser, Hoffmann and their fellows from the Secessionist craftsman's group, the *Wiener Werkstätte*, from 1903 onwards, was very much in the William Morris spirit (*see* pages 20–21). Working hard to bring 'high' artistic standards to workaday items in a way that would beautify life, they produced everything from business cards to glassware.

Foreign Forms

Long before this, however, the Arts and Crafts project had stirred a response across the English Channel in France, in the luxuriantly ornamental Art Nouveau. Ethnically as well as artistically hybrid, this style was launched in Paris by the Czech-born painter and designer Alphonse Mucha (1860–1939). Raising advertising to the standards of high art, the posters he created in 1885 for the actress Sarah Bernhardt (1844–1923) brought decorative design features into a sensuous and exciting form of figurative painting (*see* page 22). (At the same time, arguably, they lowered art to the level of advertising, given that the stunning jewellery he showed the stage star wearing was available for purchase – and indeed sold in impressive volumes.) It is easy enough to see in Mucha's works a foreshadowing of the way in which (for example) Gustav Klimt or Helene Funke would work ornamental patterning into pictorial forms.

The rich colour of Mucha's work contrasted sharply with the stark black-and-white of the ink drawings made by the Englishman Aubrey Beardsley (1872–98). Audacious in their counterpointing of spindly black line and extensive empty space, these drawings too are adventurous in the way they make complex ornamentation in

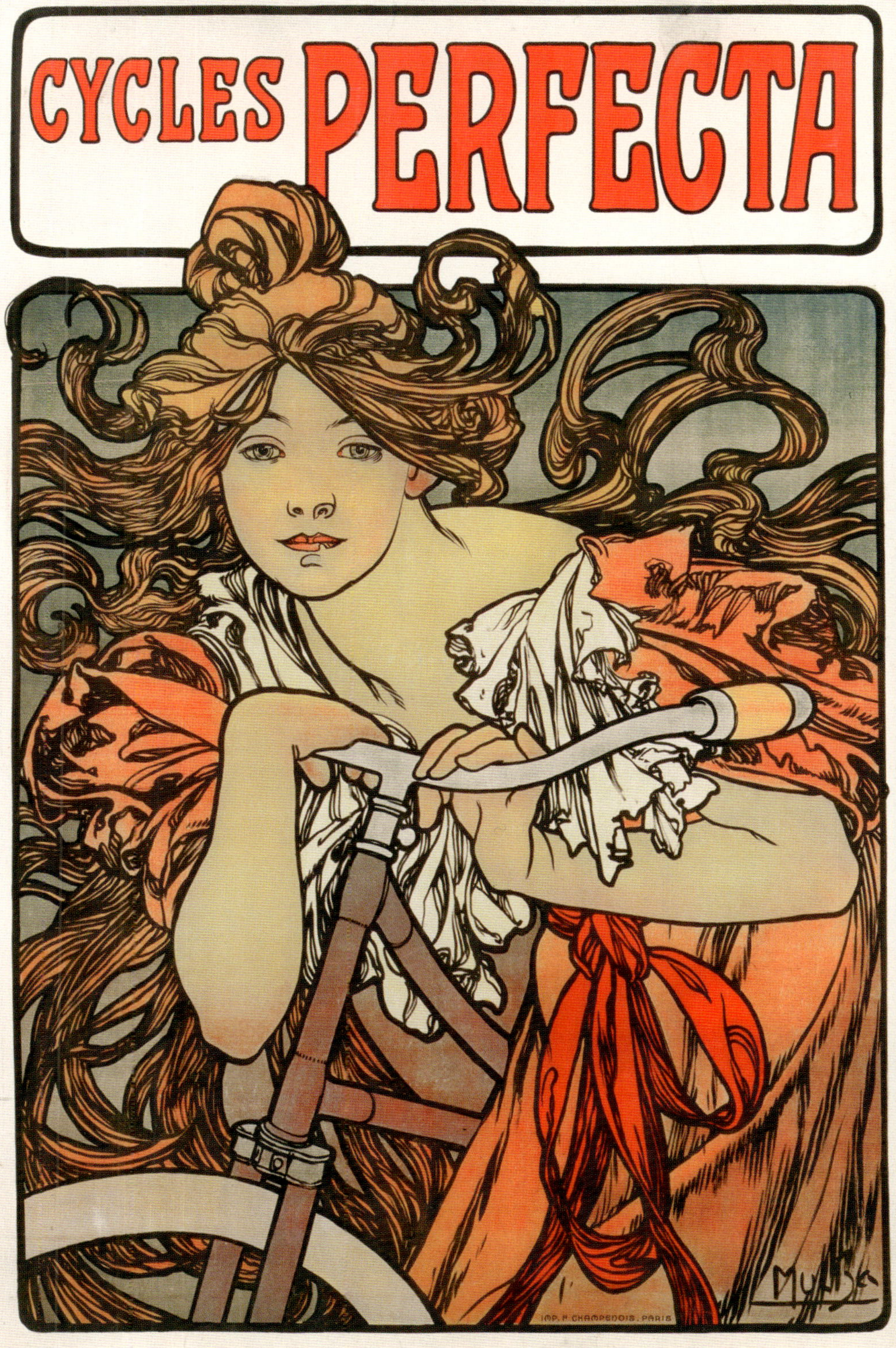

OPPOSITE ◆ HEAD OF A WOMAN, VER SACRUM, COVER DESIGN, 1899, KOLOMAN MOSER (1868–1918)
ABOVE ◆ POSTER ADVERTISING 'CYCLES PERFECTA', 1902, ALPHONSE MUCHA (1860–1939)

black do the work of suggesting warmth and colour (*see* page 24). Beardsley clearly revels in his power to make his pallid forms evoke glamour and eroticism.

Art from the Orient

Beardsley's work is only one of the most obvious examples of the influence of Japanese woodblock art that was very much in vogue in Europe at this time. The great oriental artists, like Katsushika Hokusai (1760–1849) had never really bothered with Western theories of perspective and had always been happy to present reality in highly stylized forms. Hokusai's land- and seascapes in particular reveal his readiness to subordinate representative realism to the decorative figures he can find in anything from a treetop to a waterfall.

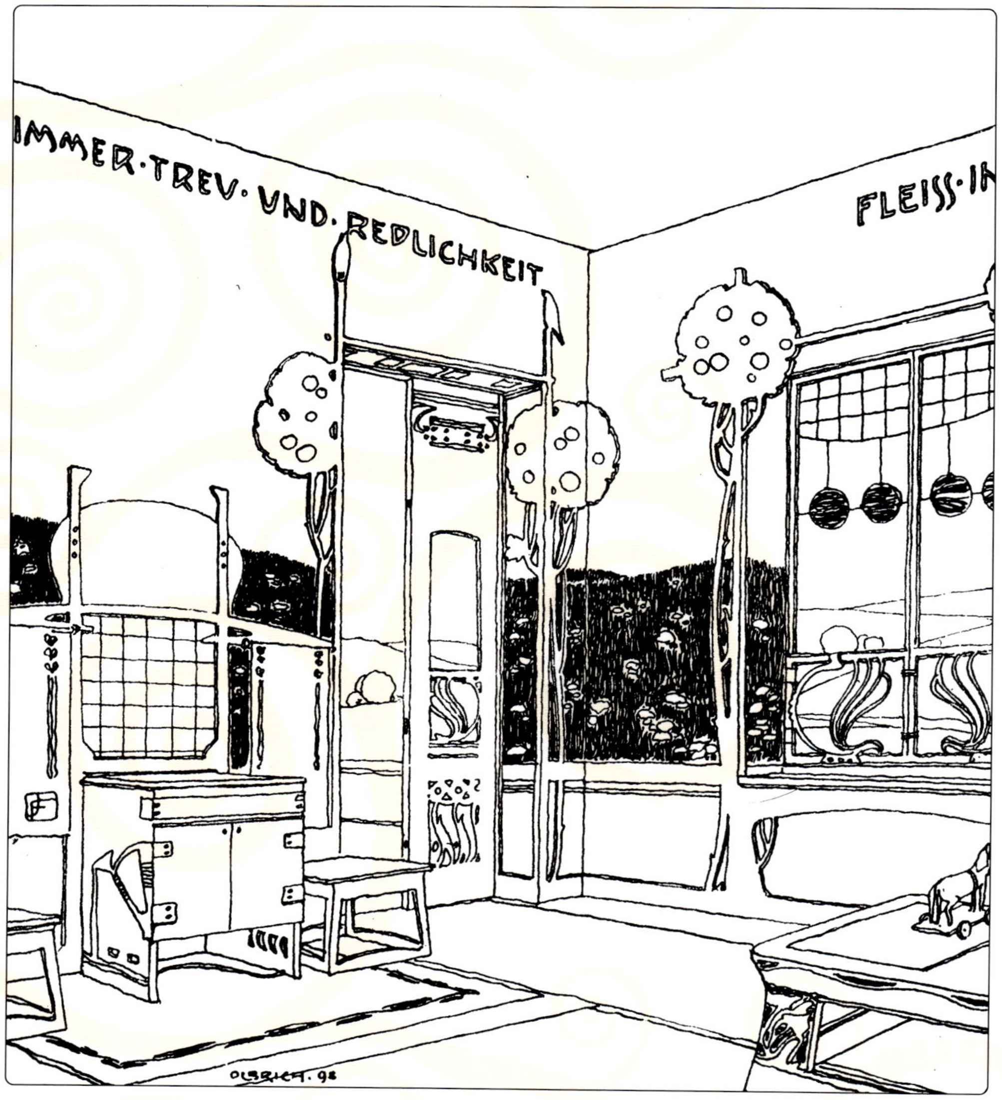

ABOVE ◆ INTERIOR DESIGN FOR VILLA FRIEDMANN, 1898. JOSEPH MARIA OLBRICH (1867–1908)

From Glasgow to Vienna

Japanese influences also arrived in Austria via Scotland when members of the Glasgow School exhibited in Vienna in 1900. Charles Rennie Mackintosh (1868–1928) was an innovator in everything from typography to architecture and furniture design. His influence, like that of his wife Margaret Macdonald (1864–1933), her sister Frances Macdonald (1873–1921) and their friend Herbert McNair (1868–1955), can also be traced in the works of the Secessionist artists and designers.

Margaret Macdonald's frequent use of gold, her employment of craft techniques – and her embedding of figurative women in decorative backgrounds in a work like 'Embroidered Panels' (1902, *see* page 26) – may well have had an impact on Gustav Klimt (though as we've seen, Klimt already possessed metalworking skills).

In reality, the list of significant influences on the Vienna Secessionists might be endless. Morris's demystification of the skills of art had to some extent worn away at the Romantic cult of the individual 'genius' and made it easier for egotistical artists to trade influences, to lend and borrow. Morris had also, as we've seen, eroded the boundary between art-for-exhibition and art-for-use, raising the possibility of a life that might be attended by beauty every day. The influence of this

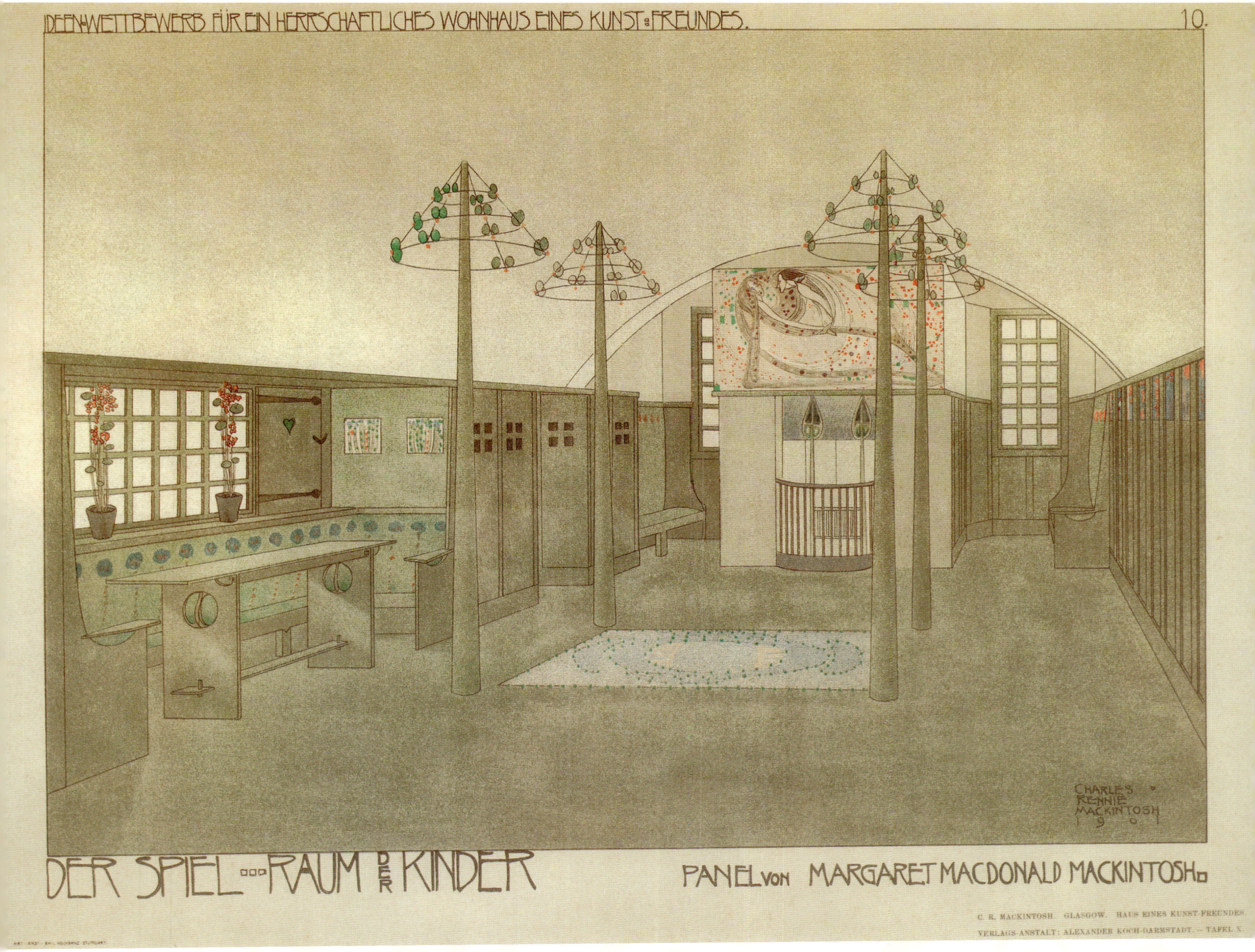

ABOVE ♦ HOUSE OF AN ART LOVER: THE CHILDREN'S NURSERY ROOM, DES. 1901.
CHARLES RENNIE MACKINTOSH (1868–1928)

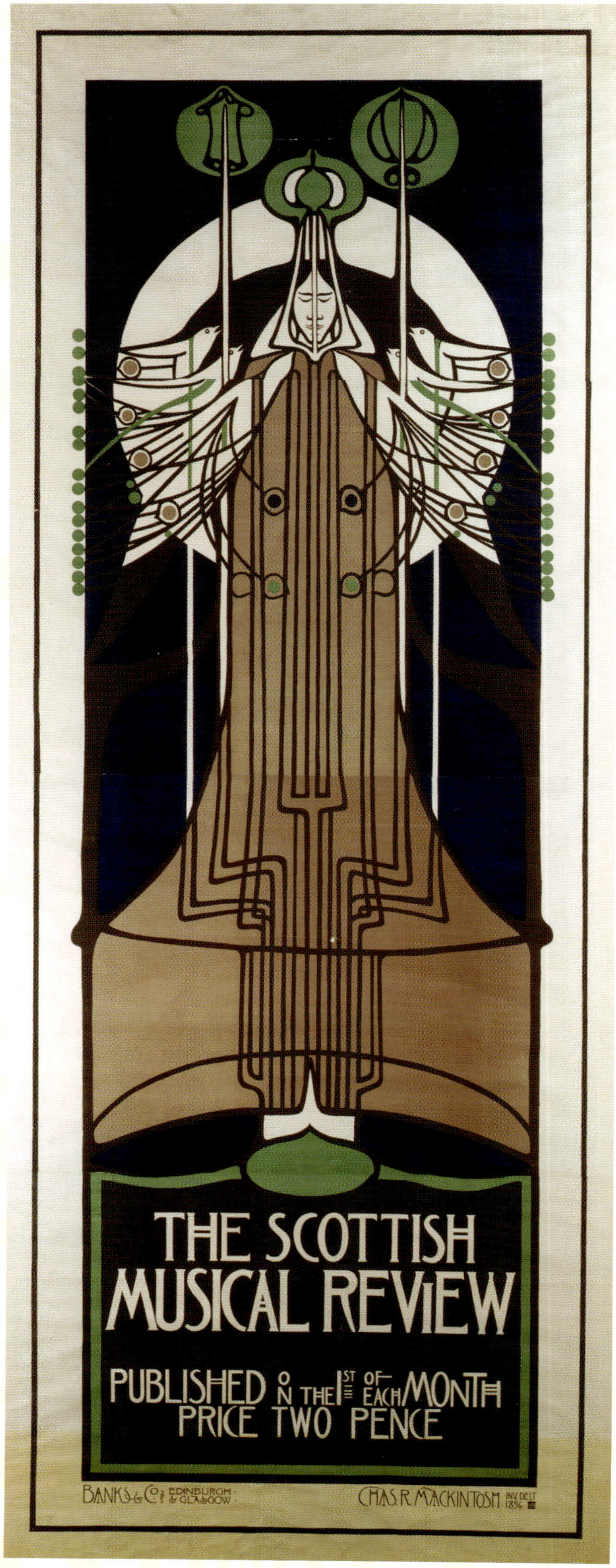

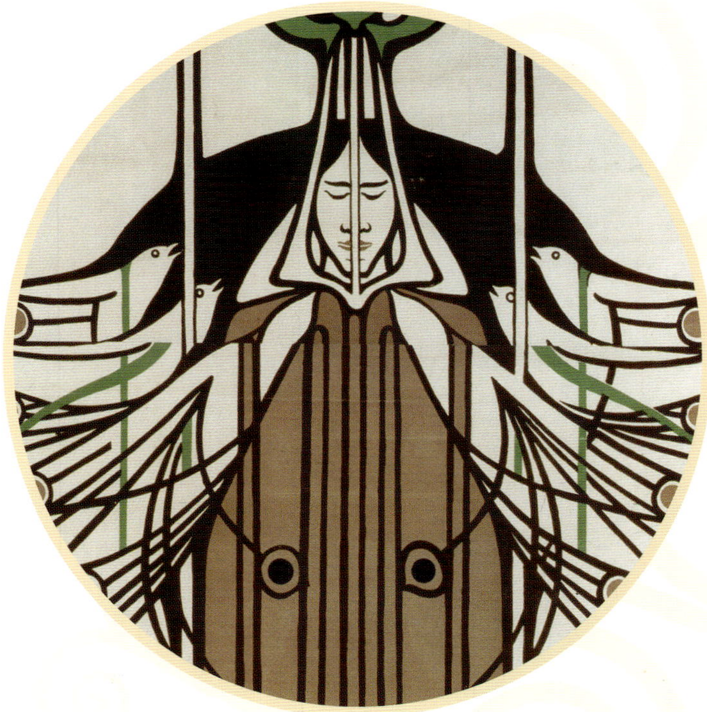

belief was soon to be as evident in the sophisticated salons of Vienna as it already was in the drawing rooms of London and the halls of the Paris Métro. It was as much a sensibility as a school, as much an attitude as an aesthetic.

A Metropolitan Muse

This belief was also – like so much of modern life – essentially urban. It made a point of celebrating the man-made. Although Secessionists did create some stunning landscapes – those of Klimt and Funke stand out, along with some of Kurzweil's works like *Pine Grove at the Seaside* (*c.* 1908), they primarily made play with the decorative possibilities they found in the features of the countryside, and were never more than secondarily supposed to be a window on to nature.

This was in keeping with the spirit of the age. Even for a religious writer like G.K. Chesterton (1874–1936), God's creation was less

LEFT • POSTER ADVERTISING THE SCOTTISH MUSICAL REVIEW, 1896.
CHARLES RENNIE MACKINTOSH (1868–1928)

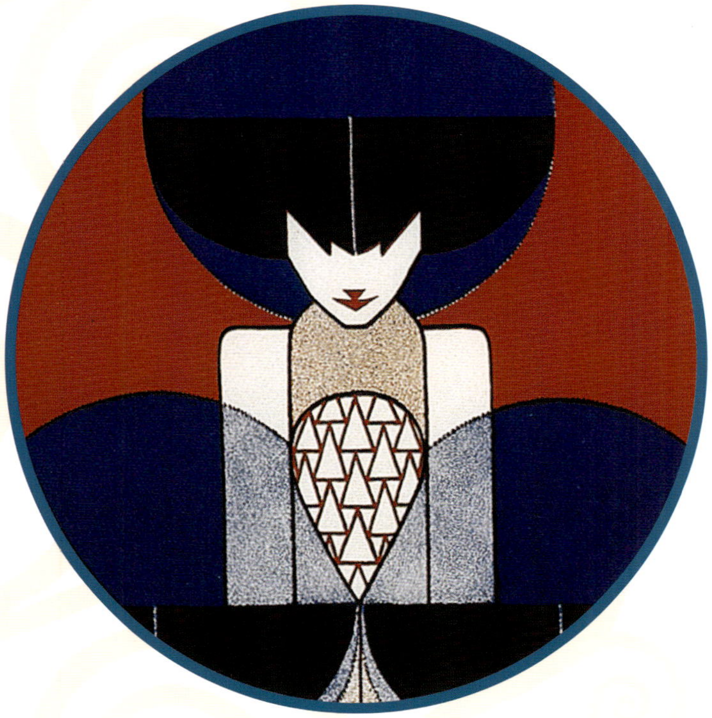

inherently suited to artistic celebration than humankind's. 'A city,' he wrote in 1901:

> *...is more poetic even than a countryside, for while Nature is a chaos of unconscious forces, a city is a chaos of conscious ones ... there is no stone in the street and no brick in the wall that is not actually a deliberate symbol ... The narrowest street possesses, in every crook and twist of its intention, the soul of the man who built it, perhaps long in his grave. Every brick has as human a hieroglyph as if it were a graven brick of Babylon.*

What St Petersburg became for the novelist Andrei Bely (1880–1934), Dublin for James Joyce (1882–1941) and Berlin for Alfred Döblin (1878–1957), Vienna was for the Secessionist movement as a whole. But it wasn't just their subject: it was their setting, the city they inhabited; the place they built their buildings, made their artworks, lived their lives.

RIGHT ◆ VIENNA SECESSION 13TH EXHIBITION POSTER, 1902. KOLOMAN MOSER (1868–1918)

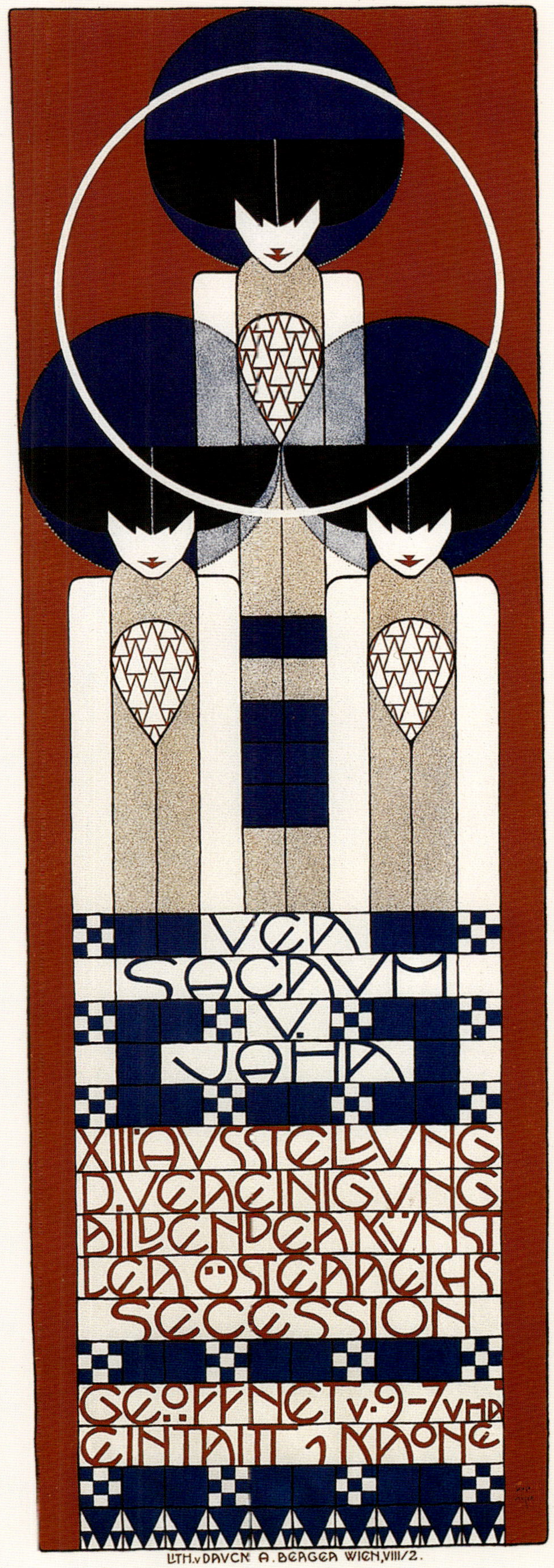

ART & LITERATURE

FOR THE SECESSIONISTS ART AND LITERATURE WERE INTERTWINED AS TWIN FORCES OF CREATIVITY IN THEIR CHANGING WORLD

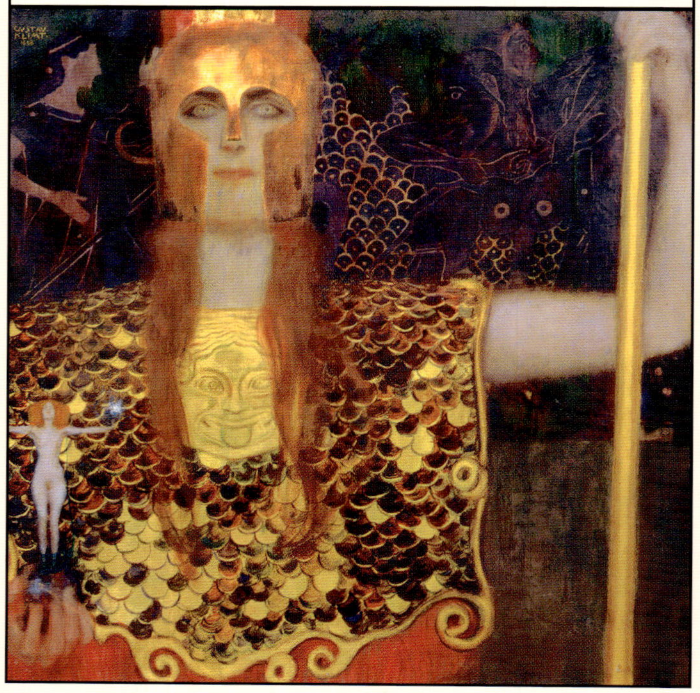

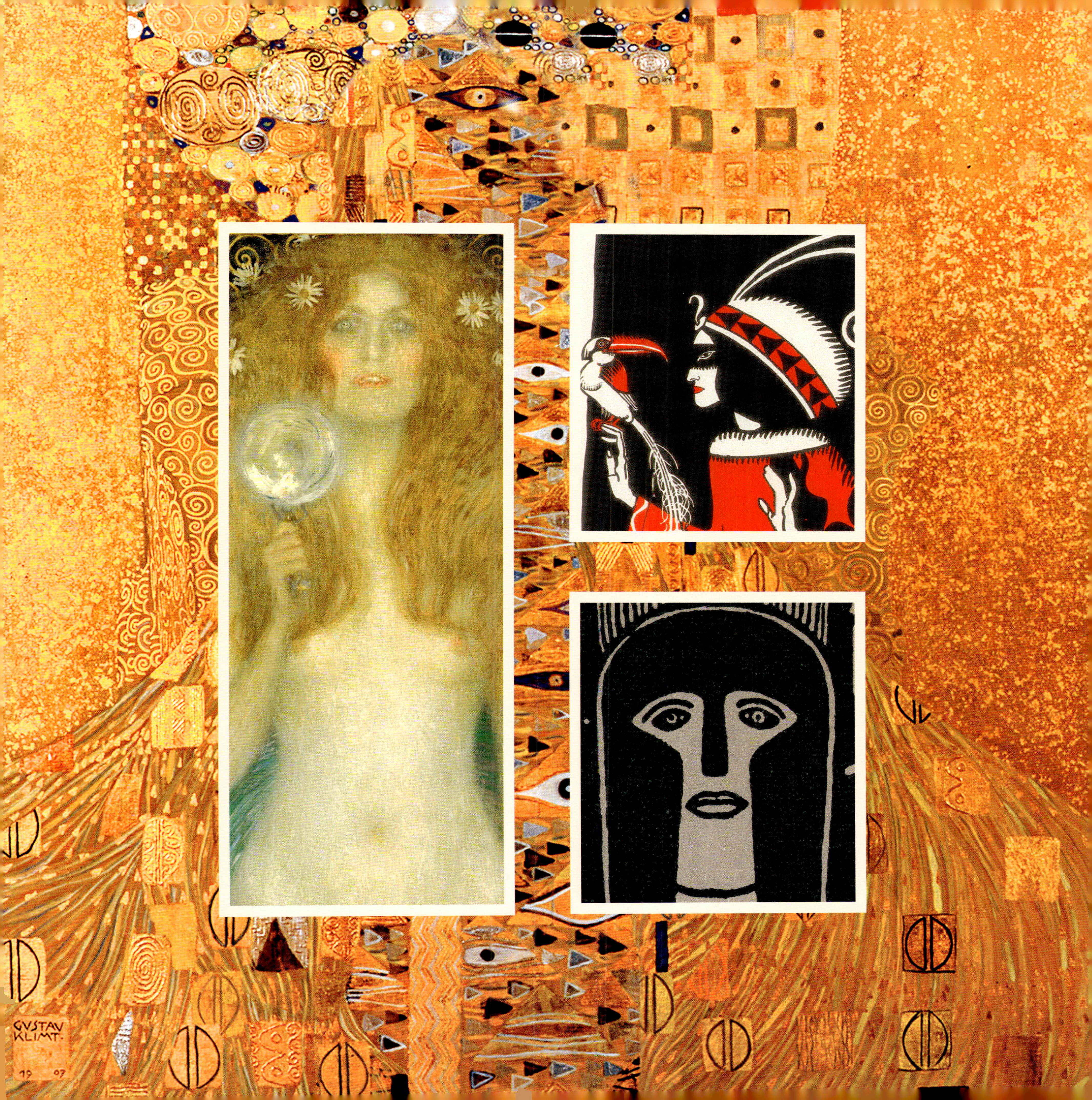
GVSTAV KLIMT.
19 07

WE'VE already seen that the Secessionists were no great believers in boundaries in the arts, but they seem to have attributed an especial importance to literature. Klimt, his most ardent admirers insisted, kept copies of classic books in his pockets at all times: Petrarch's *Sonnets*; Dante's *Divine Comedy*; Goethe's *Faust*. Although we may wonder how far this was literally true, the claim is as consistent with Klimt's inclination (and those of the Secession in general) to extend his interests across established boundaries of genre and of medium as it is with his autodidact's reverence for the monuments of the past.

She is older than the rocks among which she sits;Like the Vampire,She has been dead many times,And learned the secrets of the grave;And has been a diver in deep seas,And keeps their fallen day about her;And trafficked for strange webs with Eastern merchants;And, as Leda,Was the mother of Helen of Troy,And, as St Anne,Was the mother of Mary;And all this has been to her but as the sound of lyres and flutes,And livesOnly in the delicacyWith which it has moulded the changing lineaments,And tinged the eyelids and the hands.

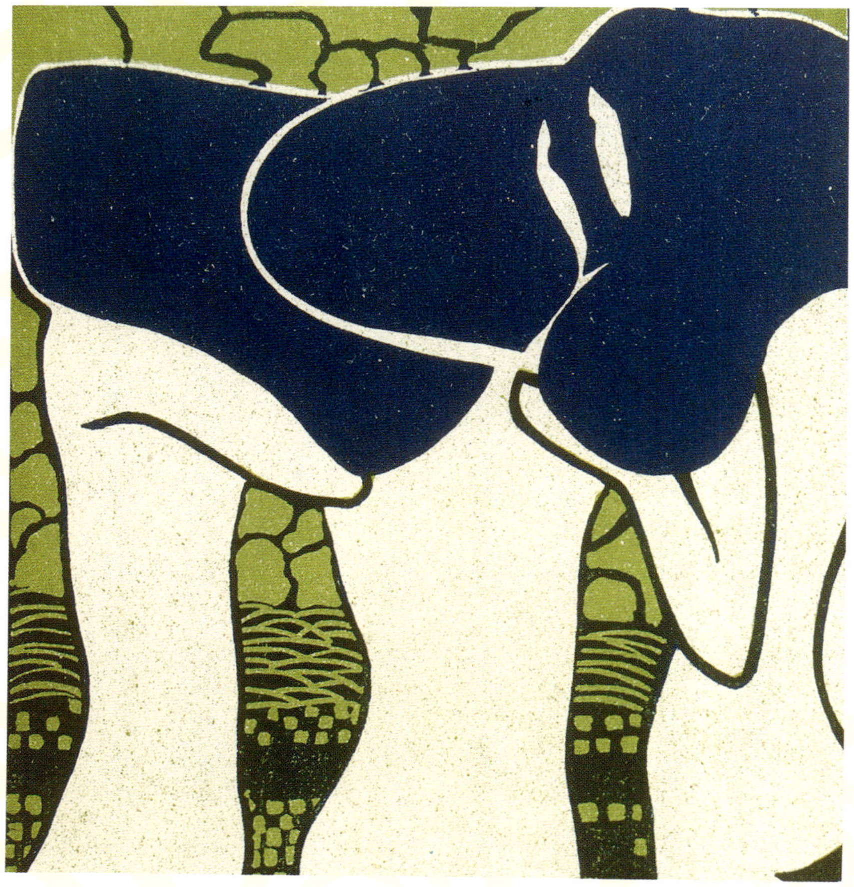

The passage above, originally written in prose by the English critic Walter Pater (1839–94), was set out as a poem by W.B. Yeats (1865–1939) for inclusion in his Oxford Book of Modern Verse (1936). Taken from 'The Renaissance' (1873), the lines represented Pater's response to the Mona Lisa (c. 1505), the famously enigmatic painting by Leonardo da Vinci (1452–1519). If the most immediately striking thing about this meditation is the far-flung extravagance of its references (ranging over everything from Gothic horror and history to mythology and religion), our more enduring impression is of the essential unity of art. So a painting becomes a piece of prose, which in its turn becomes a poem, which having mentioned music ('the sound of lyres and flutes') makes a momentary suggestion of sculpture ('moulded the changing lineaments') before finally coming full circle, back to painting ('tinged the eyelids and the hands').

Literary Leanings

The swiftness with which the writing passes from one area of reference to another is positively mesmerizing – as though Pater really wanted to leave his reader in a spin. So difficult is it to keep track that – as Yeats was to appreciate – the words seem almost to part company with meaning. Instead they transport us to another realm – of strange and exotic imagery, assuredly, but first and foremost of sonority and rhythm. Sound here starts to push aside meaning as the motive force of Pater's writing – though of course this sound may have a meaning all its own.

LEFT ◆ IN FELICIAN MYRBACH, 1902 (DETAIL), NELLY MARMOREK (1877–1942)
OPPOSITE ◆ JANUARY CALENDAR SHEET, VER SACRUM, 1901, GUSTAV KLIMT (1862–1918)

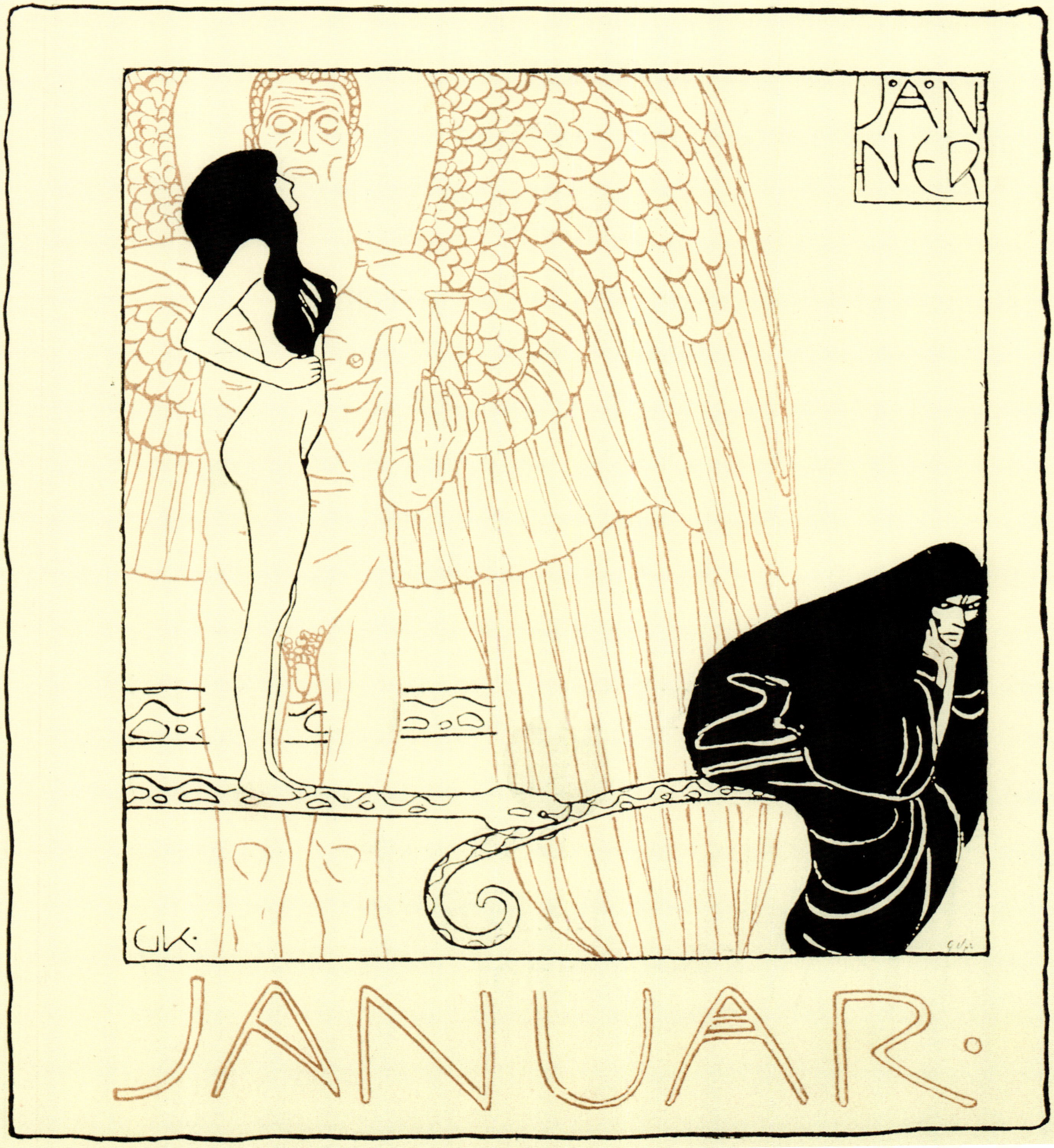
JÄN
NER
GK
JANUAR·

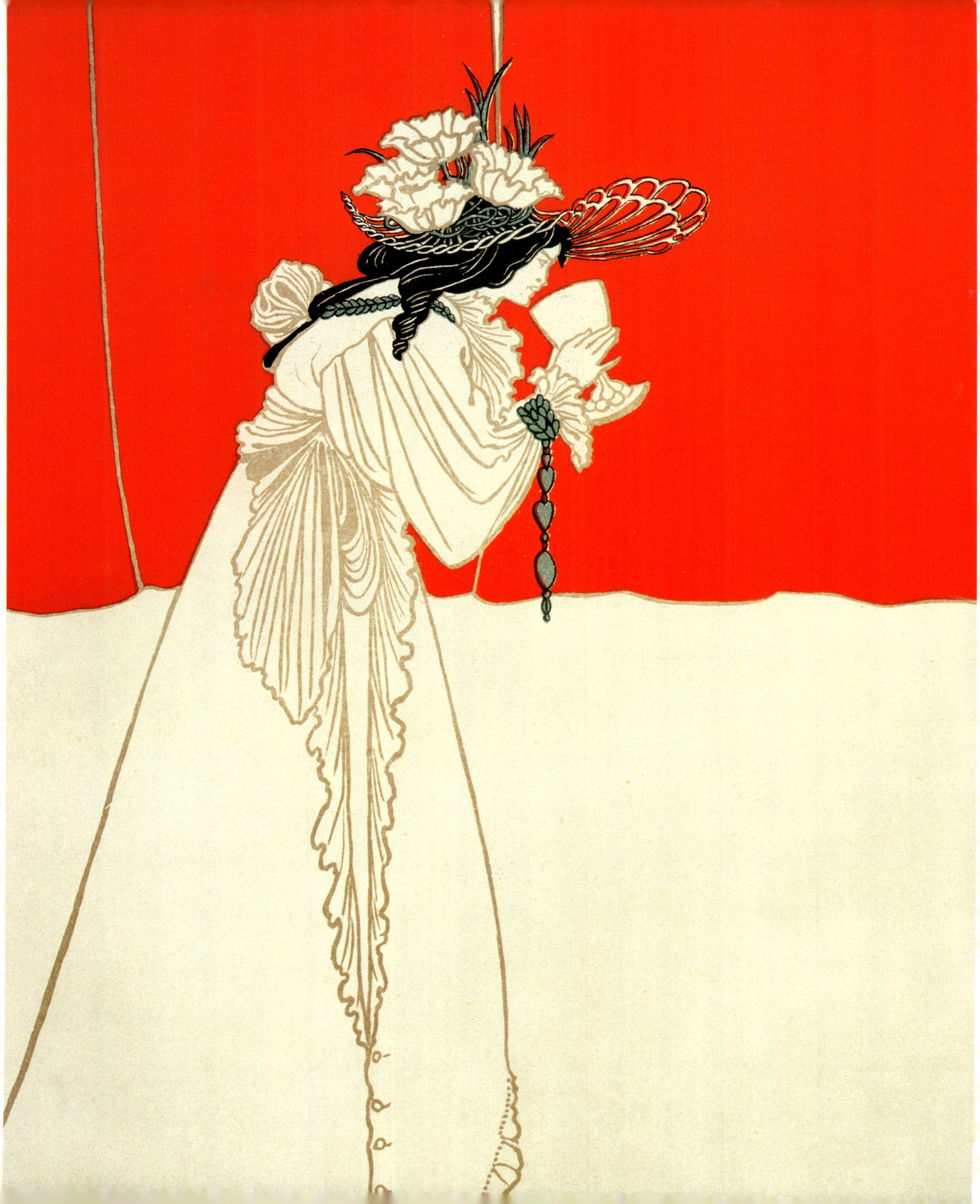

German Pride

These specific choices make sense too: Johann Wolfgang von Goethe (1749–1832) was seen as representing the very height of cultural achievement in the German-speaking countries. The Secessionist sculptor Edmund von Hellmer (1850–1935) had in 1900 created a bronze statue of the poet to be placed in the Opera Ring in the centre of Vienna.

Nowhere had Goethe's work reached a higher summit than it had in *Faust* (1808, with a second part appearing posthumously in 1832), which also carried an important lesson for the world of art in general. Based on the medieval legend of the learned doctor who sells his soul to the Devil in return for scholarly knowledge and divinatory power, it encompasses both the majesty of human endeavour and its limitations.

German Romance

Like many of his Secessionist friends, Klimt also celebrated the defiance of convention represented by Goethe's friend, the Romantic poet Friedrich Schiller (1759–1805). His notorious avowal 'To please many is bad' was inscribed by Gustav Klimt at the top of his outrageously audacious painting *Nuda Veritas* ('Naked Truth', 1899, *see* page 49). Schiller also turns up in the *Beethoven Frieze*, understandably enough, given that Beethoven's Ninth Symphony was inspired by (and contains a choral setting of) Schiller's 'Ode to Joy' (1785). A quotation from the poem is incorporated in the frieze – 'Joy, beautiful sparks of the gods, this kiss for all the world' – and is illustrated (perhaps over-literally) by a pair of naked lovers in a close embrace.

The centenary of Schiller's death was well-timed for commemoration by the Secessionists. Indeed, it afforded the

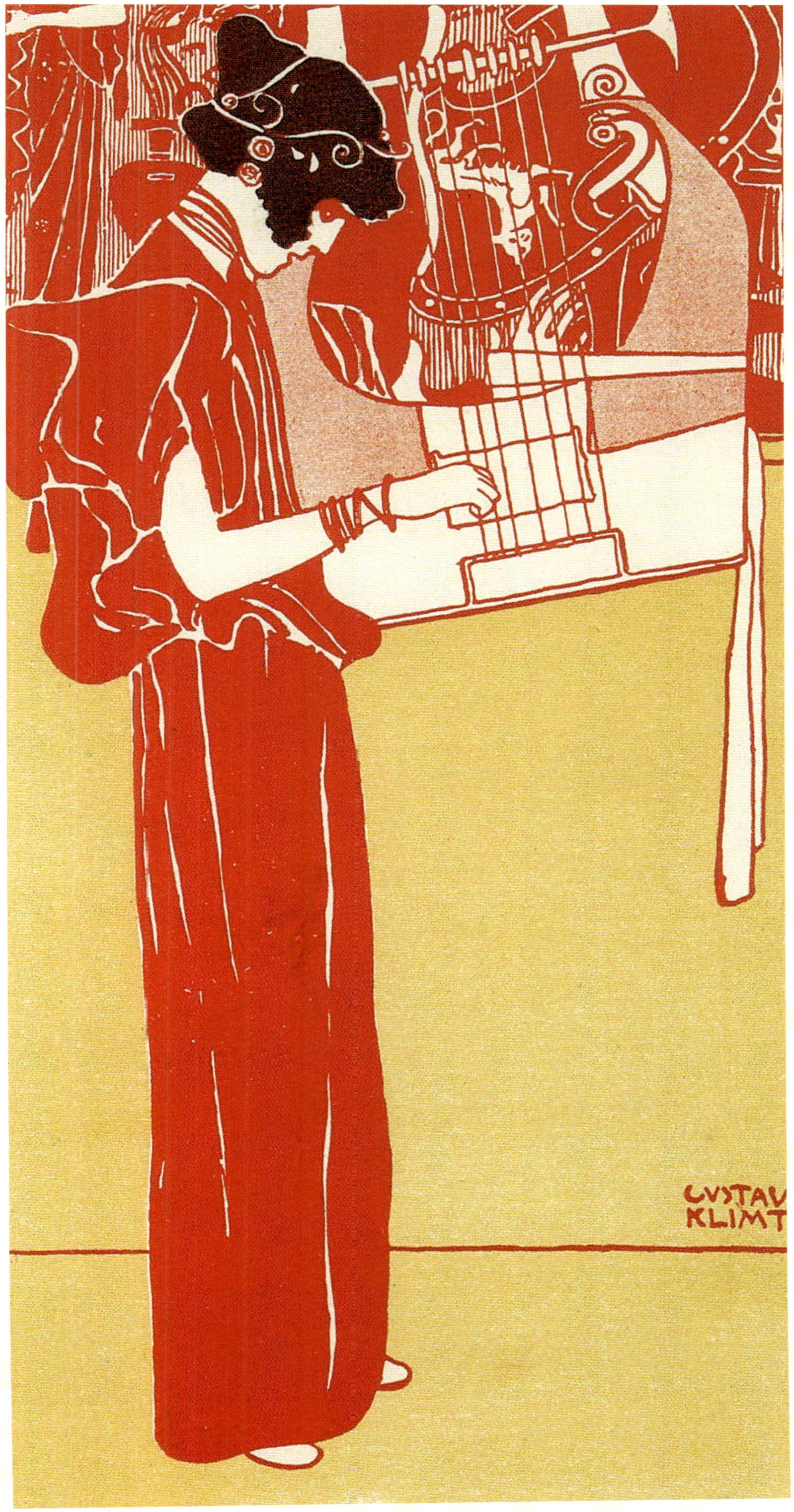

OPPOSITE ◆ ISOLDE, 1895, AUBREY BEARDSLEY (1872–98)
RIGHT ◆ MUSIC (STANDING LYRIST), VER SACRUM, 1901 GUSTAV KLIMT (1862–1918)

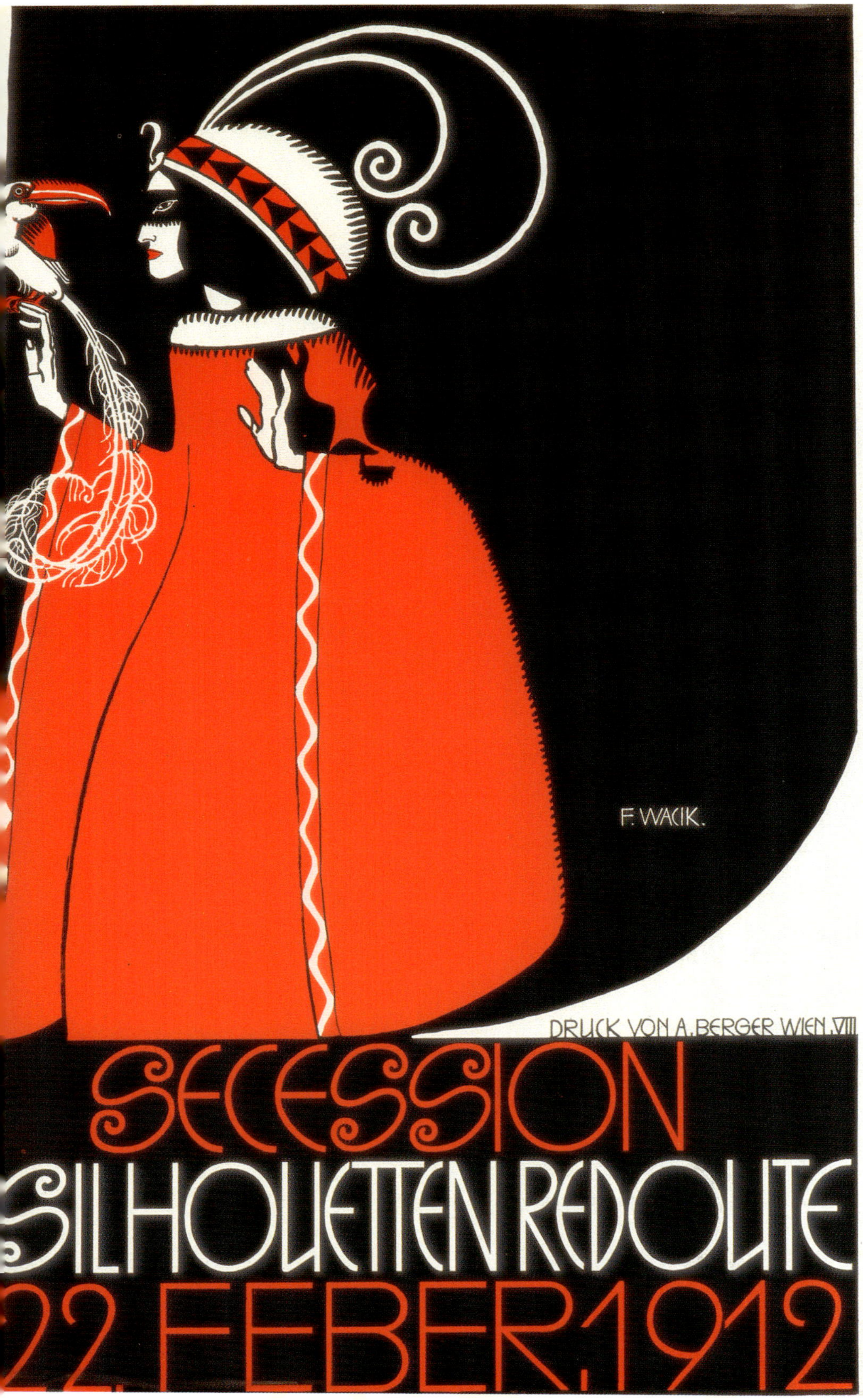

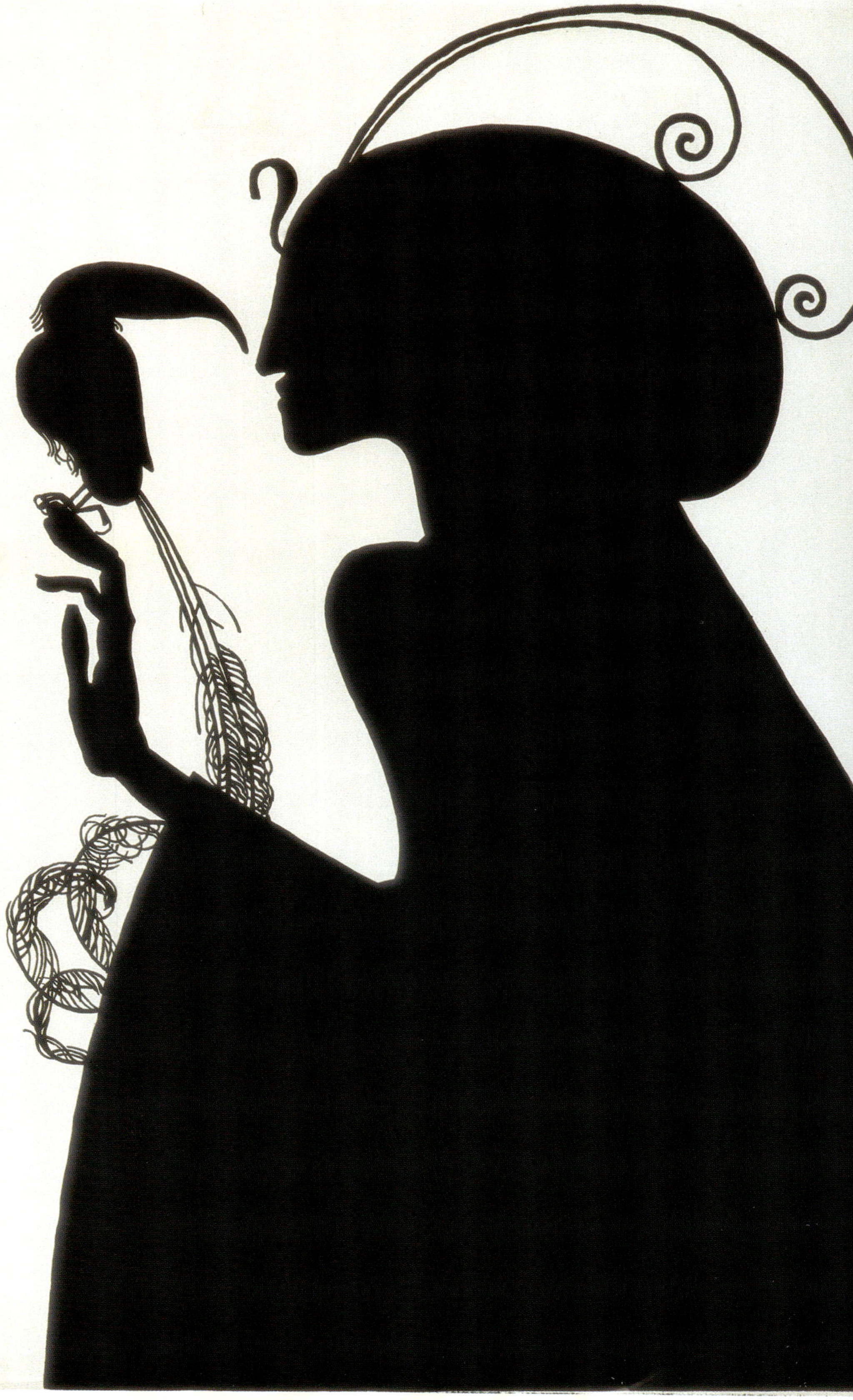

ABOVE • POSTER OF THE SILHOUETTEN REDOUTE IN THE VIENNA SECESSION, 1912
FRANZ WACIK (1838-1938)

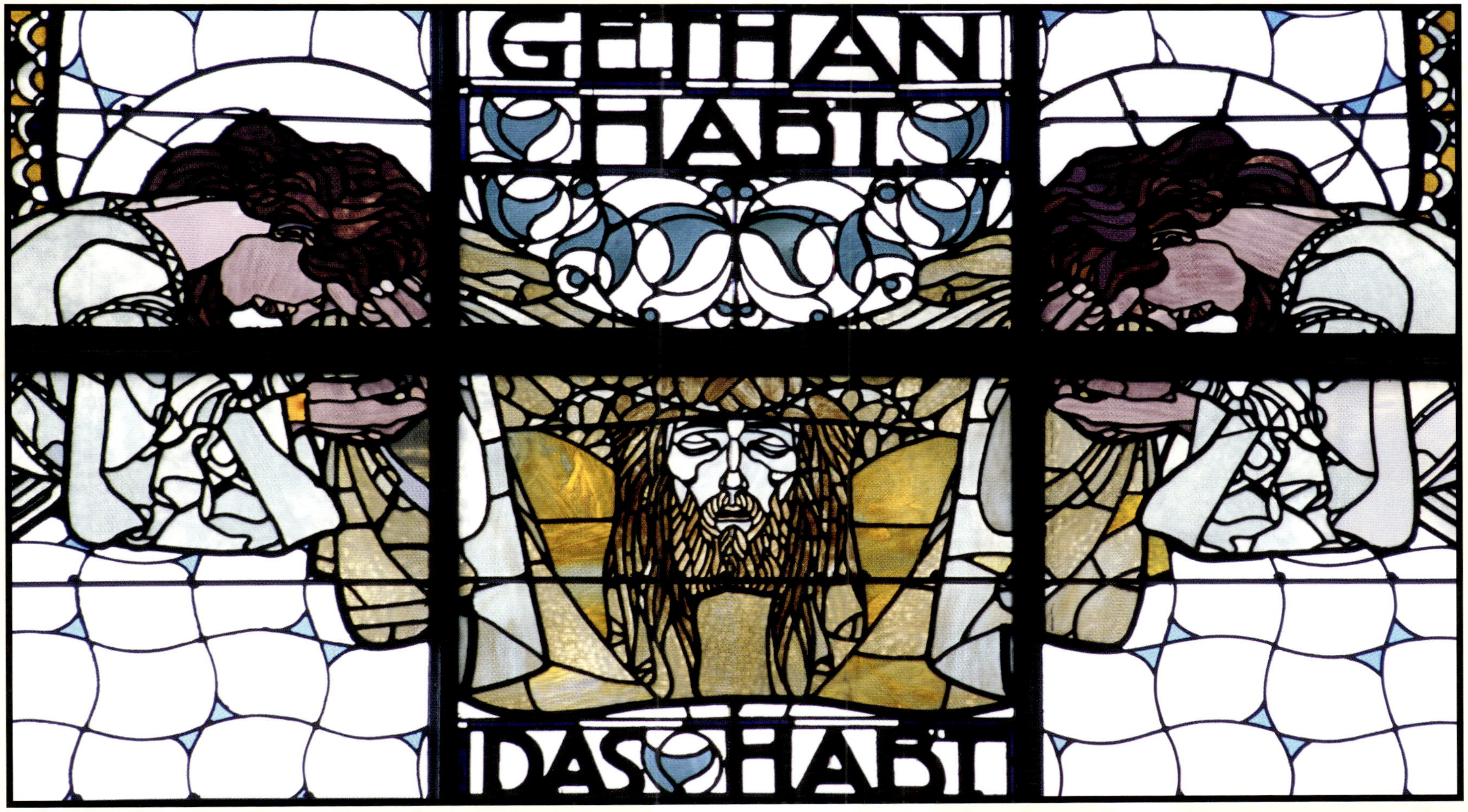

movement a unique opportunity to get its message 'out there' to Vienna as a whole. When it was decided that a short collection of the great poet's work should be issued to all schoolchildren, the job of designing it fell to Heinrich Lefler (1863–1919). The stunning volume that resulted found its way into virtually every household in the city, carrying with it a radical message of what might be achievable in art. Introducing a poet renowned as a classic, its cover referenced that eternal status with its central image of a lyre, like that of Orpheus, rhymed visually with curving swan-shapes and vegetal cascades. Wit and erudition, elegance and symmetry – and all cheaply available in two-colour printing: this was mass production of real art for a whole city.

ABOVE ✱ STAINED GLASS WINDOWS IN THE KIRCHE AM STEINHOF (CHURCH OF ST LEOPOLD), VIENNA, 1903–07. KOLOMAN MOSER (1868–1918)

Infernal Vision

As for the Florentine poet Dante Alighieri (*c.* 1265–1321), his *Divine Comedy*, completed in 1320, inspired awe in its ambition even as it moved the emotions through its beautiful verse. Imaginatively too, it was extraordinary. Never had the black-and-white characters of a written or printed text evoked more colourfully the sights and sounds not just of the world but of the universe. Although Dante's overall schema allowed for a *Purgatorio* (Purgatory) and of course a *Paradiso*, or Heaven, for the blessed, in the nineteenth century, the focus tended to be on the hideous punishments visited on the sinners in his Hell

(*Inferno* in Italian). Even here, however, humanity shines through: hard as it is for the modern mind to imagine such sufferings being inflicted by a system underpinned – as Dante insists it is – by Love, the poet's sympathy is always powerfully evident.

Tragically, the work of Klimt that showed the influence of Dante most directly was destroyed at the end of the Second World War. *Philosophy* (1899), one of a trio of ceiling paintings commissioned by the University of Vienna for its faculties of Philosophy, Medicine and Jurisprudence, was not the upbeat allegory the University had had in mind. Instead, a luridly fantastical scene showed a column of naked human forms suspended in misty space – sometimes clinging together in couples, as though for security; sometimes single, seized with seeming horror or distress. Out of the emptiness behind these living, suffering beings looms the face of a sphinx, impassive and indifferent, symbolizing Philosophy, the 'Question of the World'.

This was an *Inferno* re-envisioned for an atheistic age, a fact that the paintings Klimt did for *Medicine* (1897, *see* page 161) and *Jurisprudence* (1903) only underlined. Again men and women writhed helplessly, let down by an unheeding and essentially unjust universe. In the face of determined opposition from outraged academic faculties, none of these paintings was ever placed in its intended position. Though kept concealed, they seem to have been burned by retreating German soldiers in 1945.

Divine Effulgence

Dante created much more than a vision of hell – even for the *fin de siècle* world that found his infernal imagery so arresting. Taken as a whole, the poet's *Divine Comedy* represented the ability of art to encompass absolutely everything in human existence – both to soar the radiant heights of heaven and to plumb the dark depths of desolation. Klimt was only one of many artists and intellectuals who made the pilgrimage to the tomb in which Dante's bones were laid to rest after he died – a political exile from his home city – in Ravenna. This little town on Italy's northeastern, Adriatic coast was in early-medieval times an outpost of the Byzantine Empire, which had its capital at Byzantium or Constantinople – later (after its conquest by the Ottoman Turks in 1451) known as Istanbul. An exclave of Orthodox Christian culture in Catholic Europe, Ravenna was remarkable for its old churches, their walls resplendent with religious mosaics – vast, jewelled images worked in tiny shards of glass and semi-precious stones.

Art and craft crossed over in the workmanship of these great pictures in which painstaking, close-up labour was miraculously transformed into a shimmering radiance that seemingly partook of the divine. The use of gold, silver and semi-precious stones literally embedded value into these extraordinary images, which then blazed forth their beauty to the world. Their originators presumably saw this effulgence as representing the influence of the numinous, the godly in the affairs of earth. For the *fin de siècle* artists, though, they displayed the wondrous sanctity of human creativity.

Golden Influence

W.B. Yeats's poem 'Byzantium' (1927), believed to have been prompted by the sight of similar mosaics in the ancient Church of Hagia Sophia in Istanbul, spelled out the relation the poet saw between these holy pictures and the holiness of a human creativity, which left behind the body to inhabit a heaven of beauty and of art:

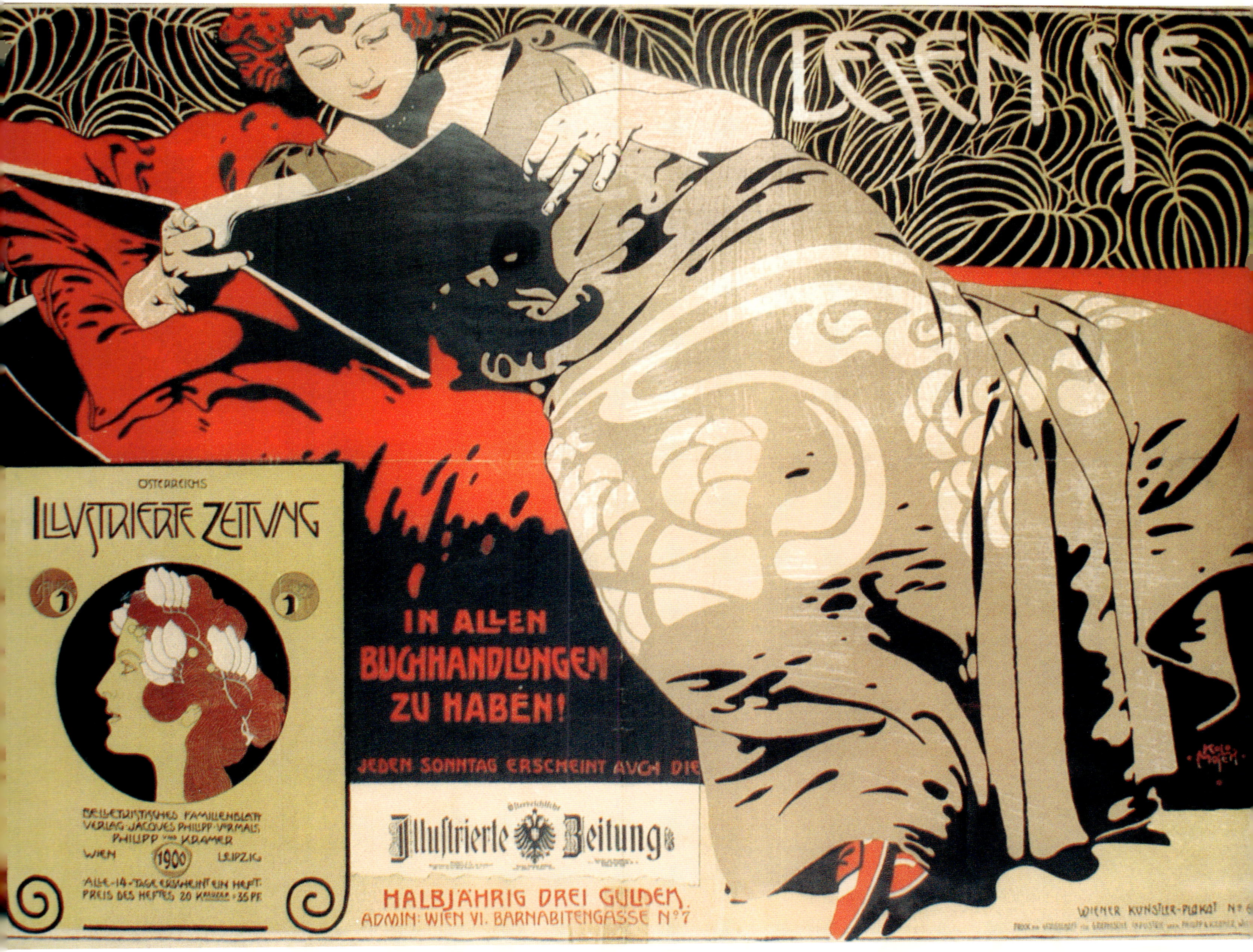

ABOVE ◈ ADVERTISING POSTER FOR 'ÖSTERREICHS ILLUSTRIERTE ZEITUNG', 1900.
KOLOMAN MOSER (1868–1918)

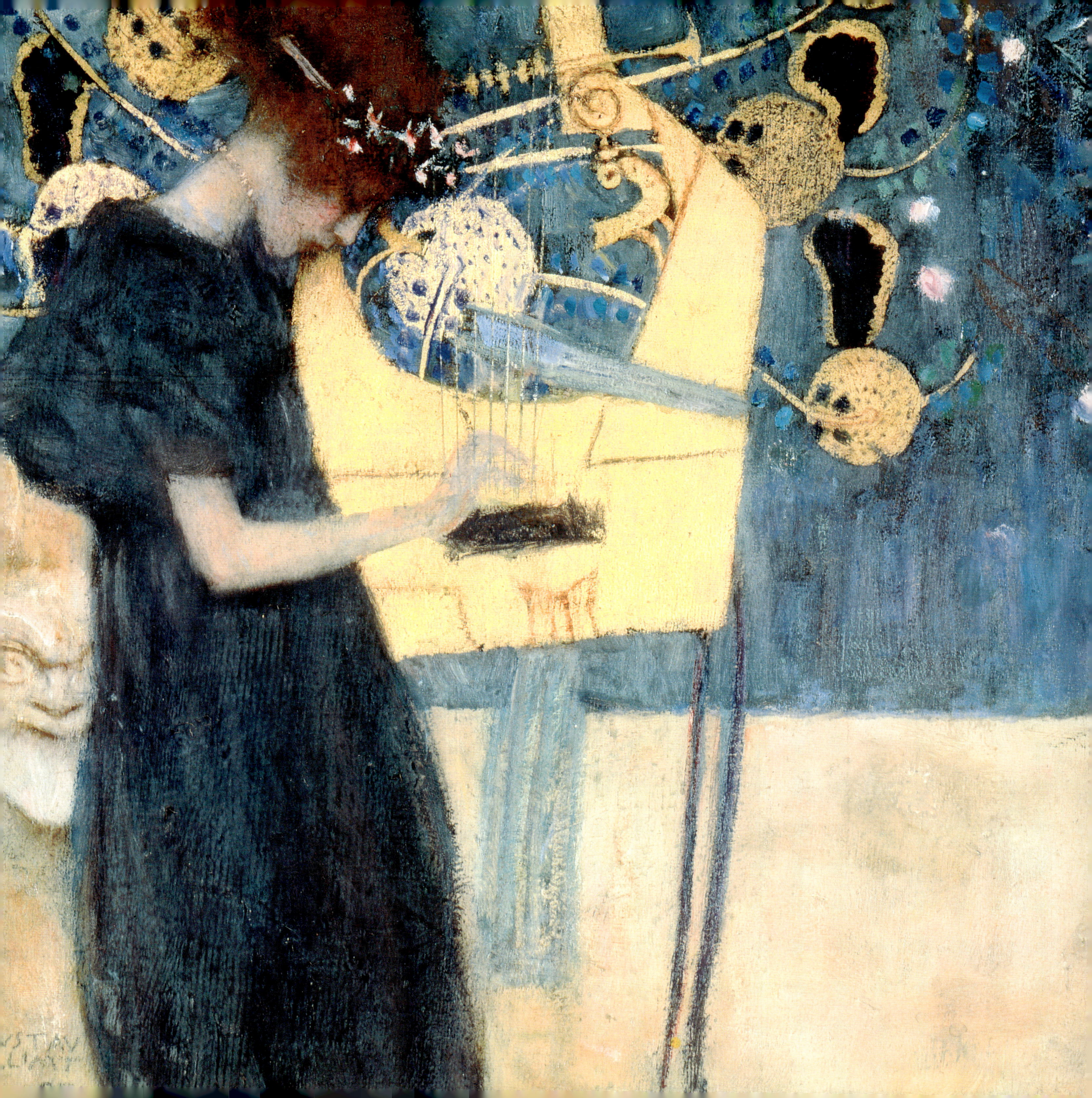

O sages standing in God's holy fire
As in the gold mosaic of a wall,
Come from the holy fire, perne in a gyre,
And be the singing masters of my soul.
Consume my heart away; sick with desire
And fastened to a dying animal
It knows not what it is; and gather me
Into the artifice of eternity.

Once out of nature I shall never take
My bodily form from any natural thing,
But such a form as Grecian goldsmiths make
Of hammered gold and gold enamelling …

Gustav Klimt was long dead by the time the Irish poet wrote these lines, but they may still help us understand the impact his first experience of this kind of mosaic art made on the Austrian goldsmith's son when he visited Ravenna in April 1903. So strong an impression did the images he saw in San Vitale Church make on Klimt that he came back again at the end of the year. The transporting influence of what he saw here is attested over and over again in the radiant splendour of the paintings of the artist's 'golden phase'.

Ice, Fire, Inspiration

The great lyric poems of Francesco Petrarca ('Petrarch', 1304–74) had taken the medieval convention of 'courtly love' – a characteristically unrequited yearning for a feminine ideal of beautiful unattainability – and elevated it into something like a pathology; a paralysing contest between icy chastity and fiery passion. For all their seeming frankness, Klimt's paintings frequently hint, as we have seen, at more sexuality than they

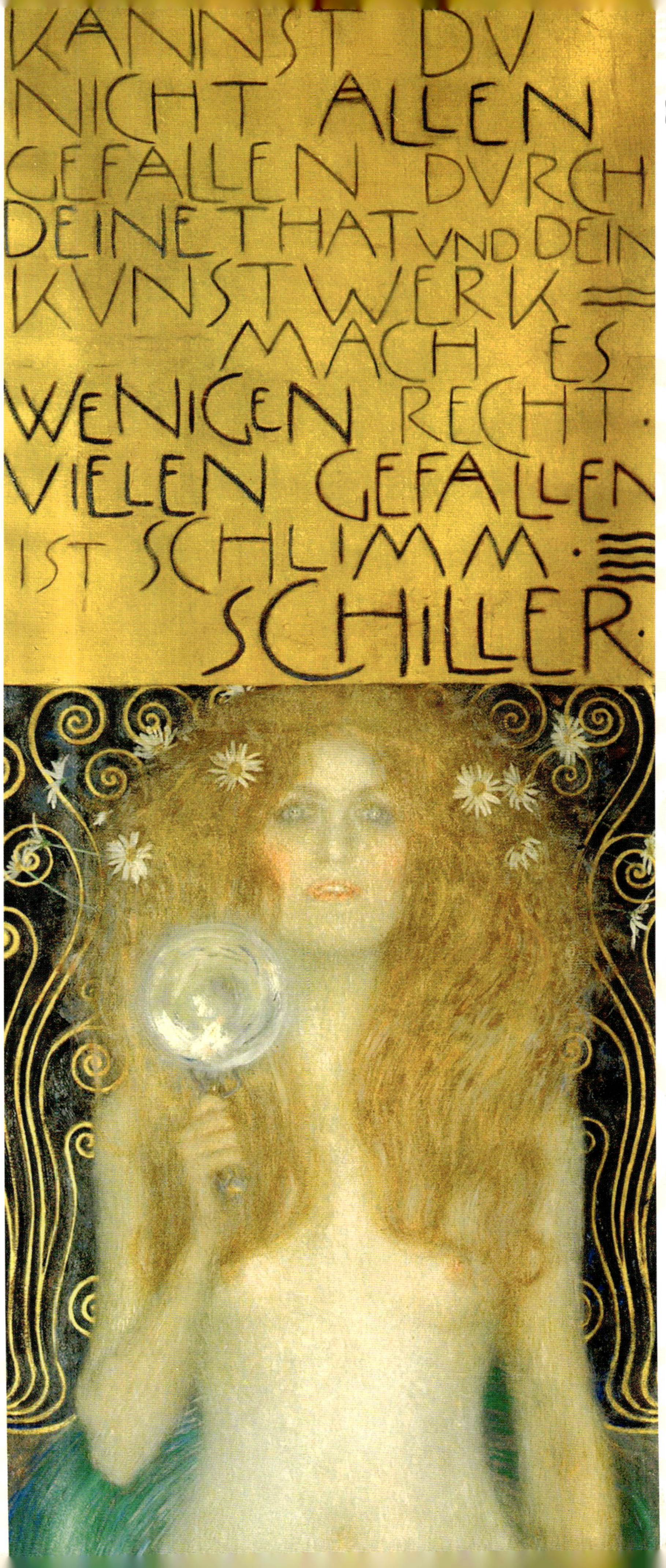

OPPOSITE ◆ MUSIC, 1895 (DETAIL). GUSTAV KLIMT (1862–1918)
RIGHT ◆ NUDA VERITAS, 1899 (DETAIL). GUSTAV KLIMT (1862–1918)

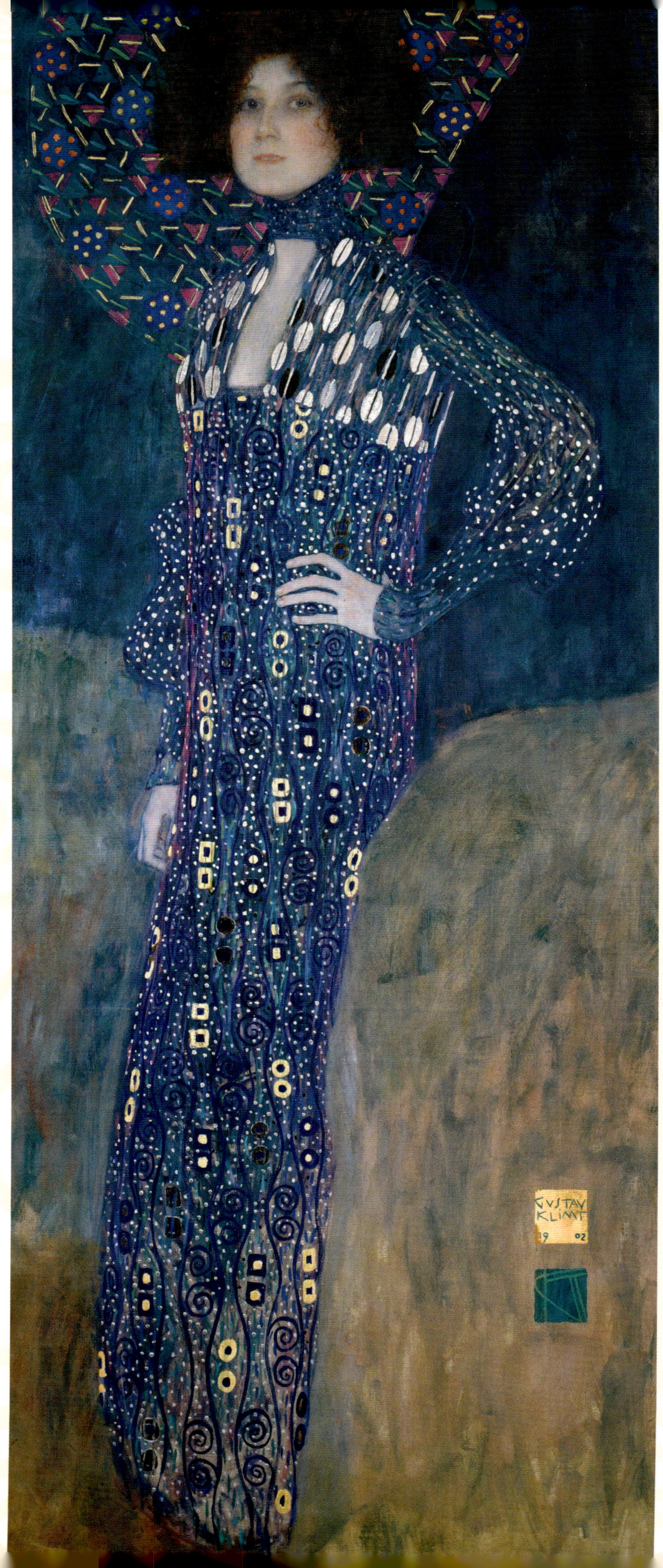

display. Klimt's (carefully cultivated?) reputation as a cynical philanderer didn't necessarily preclude a fascination with feminine chastity. He quoted extensively from Petrarch in a letter he wrote in 1896 to Emilie Flöge (1874–1952). This dress designer, feminist and famous beauty became the subject of one of Klimt's most famous portraits in 1902. She also became the long-term companion of his life, though there remains real doubt as to whether the two were lovers in the sexual sense.

A One-sided Embrace

It's been suggested that Emilie Flöge is the woman in *The Kiss* (1907–08, *see* page 51), which for many art lovers would make her the ultimate Klimtian woman. And it's been further suggested – far from conclusively, but by no means unconvincingly – that this picture also has a literary theme. Whether it does indeed show Emilie or not, the situation in the picture bears obvious similarities to that of Daphne in the ancient myth.

The Latin poet Ovid (43 BC–AD 18) relates the story of Daphne in his *Metamorphoses* (AD 8), an epic celebrating shape-shifting, boundary-breaking and transformation of every kind. Seeing the beautiful naiad, or water nymph, the sun god Apollo fell in love with and pursued her; Daphne fled through fields and woods, but was finally caught. Although she called on her father, the god of the nearby river, to save her, he was only able to turn her into a laurel tree where she stood.

The laurel tree was thenceforth sacred to Apollo: its leaves were fashioned into garlands to crown his champions in poetry and sports. In his remorse, the sun god made the laurel tree an evergreen, an eternal symbol of beauty and of youth. Daphne herself, having given up if not her life then her essential nature in the name of chastity, became an emblem of heroic maidenhood. It was only natural, then,

LEFT ◆ PORTRAIT OF EMILIE FLOEGE, 1902. GUSTAV KLIMT (1862–1918)
OPPOSITE ◆ THE KISS, 1907–08. GUSTAV KLIMT (1862–1918)

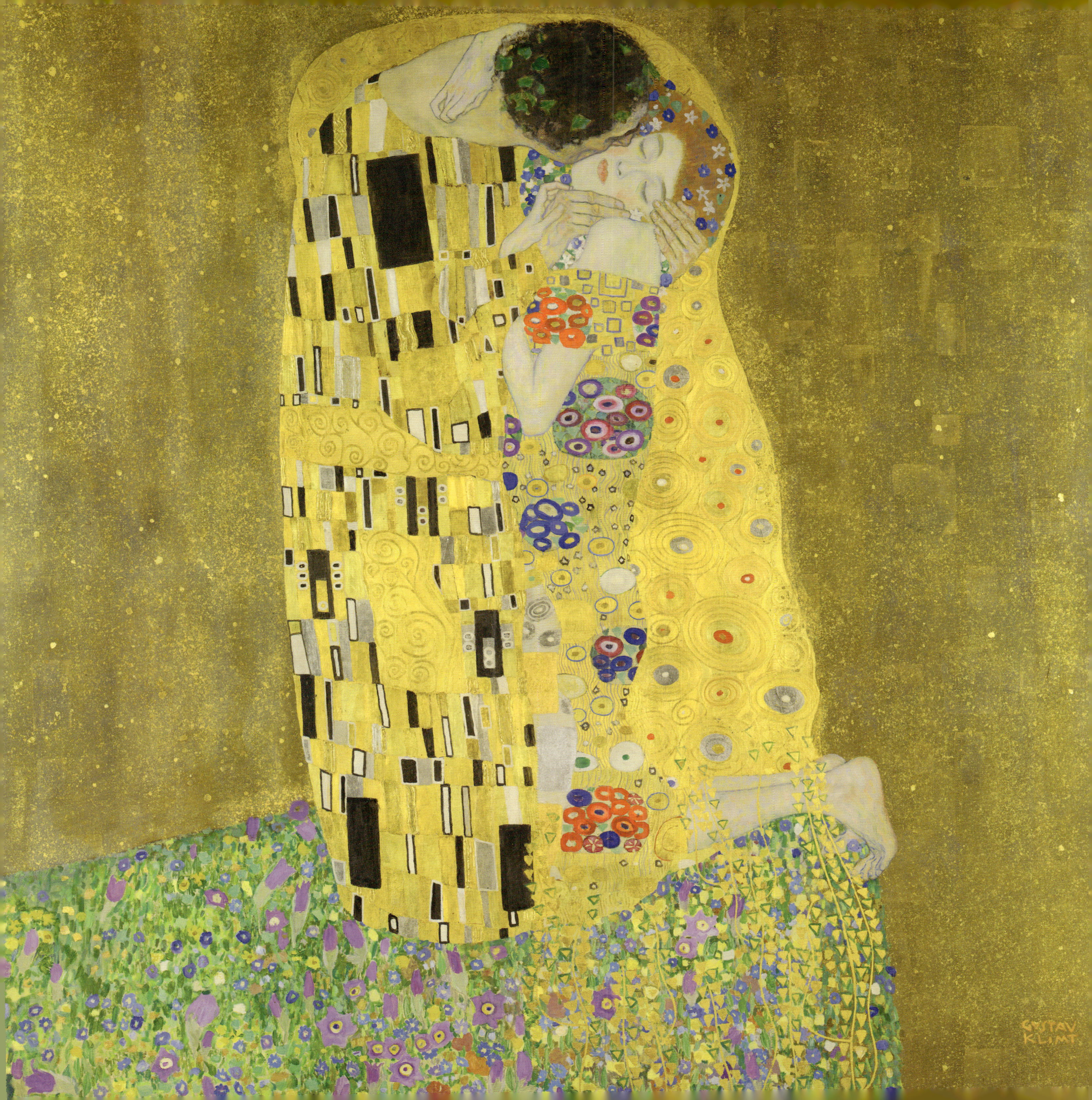
GUSTAV
KLIMT

that Petrarch should have made repeated use of the story in his poetry; that the laurel shared a name with that of his beloved, Laura, only added to the appeal.

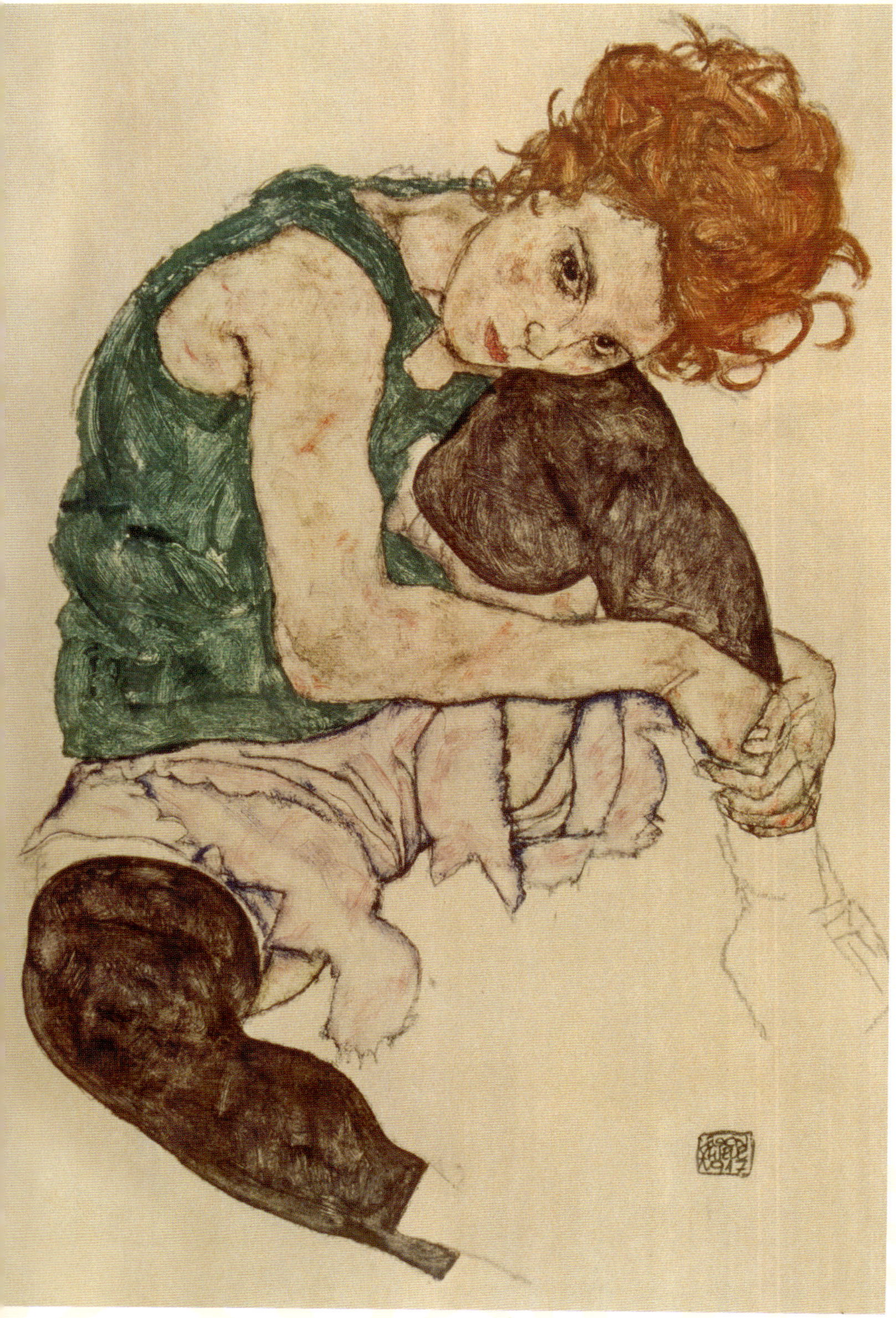

Viewed from this perspective, the profound ambiguity in Klimt's most celebrated painting becomes apparent. The poetic references aren't especially prominent, but they are there. While the masterful male figure wears a circlet of leaves on his head, more leaves may be seen before her feet, while her tight-fitting dress seems to take on the wavy pattern and texture of tree bark. Her swooning, kneeling posture thus becomes more questionable than it might at first appear: is she melting in desire, fading into lifelessness – or both? To show us her lovely face, moreover, she has to have it turned away from her lover's. She isn't actually a participant in this famous kiss.

Men and Mountains

Egon Schiele's women can hardly seem further removed from Petrarch's idealizing vision of femininity – if anything, in their defiantly confrontational air and their bold contortions, they seem much more like demons out of Dante's *Inferno*. But Schiele revered Petrarch – not for his reverence for womanhood, but for his appreciation of humanity's relationship with the world we live in. Unimaginable as it may seem (and utterly unverifiable as it may actually be), there's reason to take seriously Petrarch's claim to have been among the first men ever to have climbed a mountain just for the experience.

A victory for civilized man over wild nature, a triumph of the assertive individual will, Petrarch's ascent of Mont Ventoux in 1336 has often been regarded as the start of the Renaissance. Only since the nineteenth century, though, since just as that century's Romanticism rediscovered and reinterpreted Dante's essentially medieval vision, it also reimagined Petrarch's epiphany on the peak. The poet, while waxing spiritual and sententious in his account of what he saw, and claiming to be the first man up the mountain since antiquity, hadn't

LEFT • SEATED WOMAN WITH BENT KNEE, 1917, EGON SCHIELE (1890–1918)
OPPOSITE • HEAD OF A WOMAN (UNFINISHED), GUSTAV KLIMT (1862–1918)

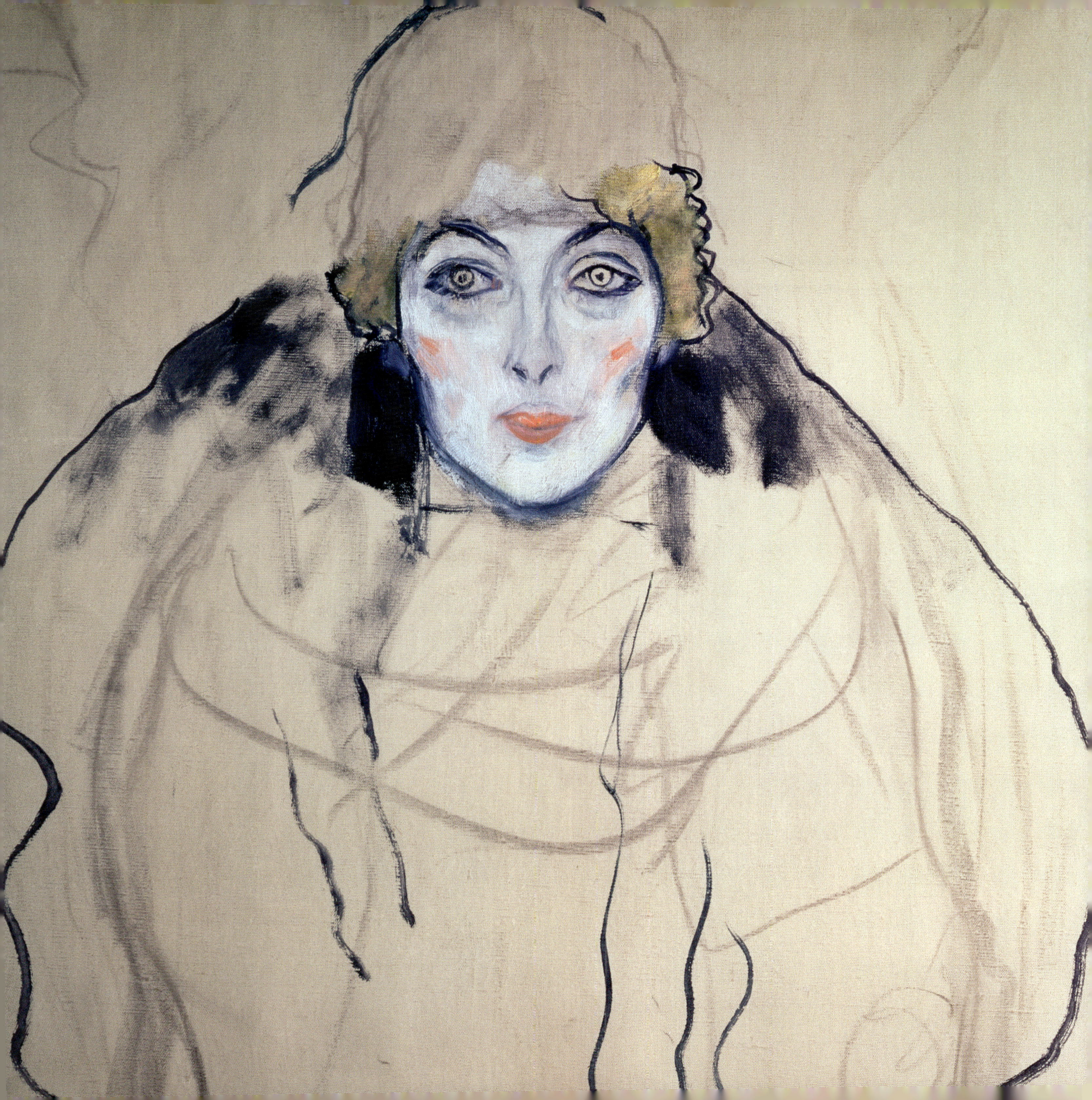

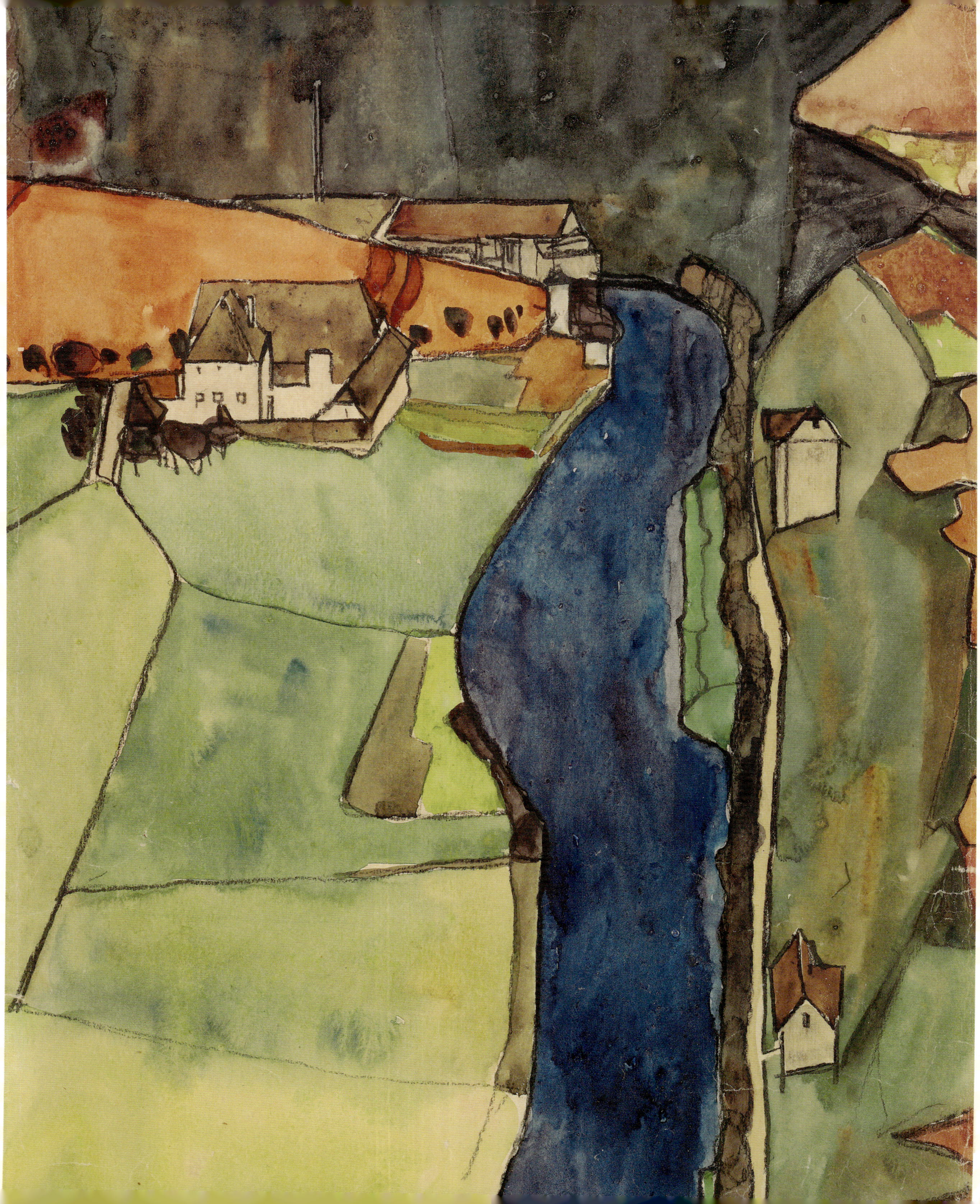

sacralized the climb itself in any way. In hindsight, however, it seemed to anticipate the sort of communion with nature envisaged by the English poet William Wordsworth (1770–1850) – or the sort of psycho-melodrama imagined by the German painter Caspar David Friedrich (1774–1840) in works like *Wanderer Above the Sea of Fog* (1818).

Landscape and Summit

Lent a book about the art of the great Gothic cathedrals, Schiele was thrilled by everything he found inside, but most of all by the way in which the medieval craftsmen had incorporated little landscape scenes. 'The men in the Middle Ages, now they had culture!' he enthused to his friend, the scholar Arthur Roessler (1877–1955):

> *The Gothics discovered the landscape for humankind. Gothic painters were certainly the first artists who gave a landscape background to the portrayal of man. Petrarch, who was in his essence a Gothic poet, was also really the first man who climbed up a high mountain in Europe and let himself be inwardly shaken in the strongest way by what he experienced on the peak.*

A painting like *Town on the Blue River, Krumau* (1910, *see* page 54) or *Summer Landscape, Krumau* (1917, *see* page 55) finds Schiele showing us a scene from a vantage point above, as though he himself were looking down from a mountain summit.

Falling Apart

So much for the poets of the past. What of the up-and-coming writers of the *fin de siècle*? As far as they themselves were concerned, they were going nowhere fast. Literature had been plunging into a major

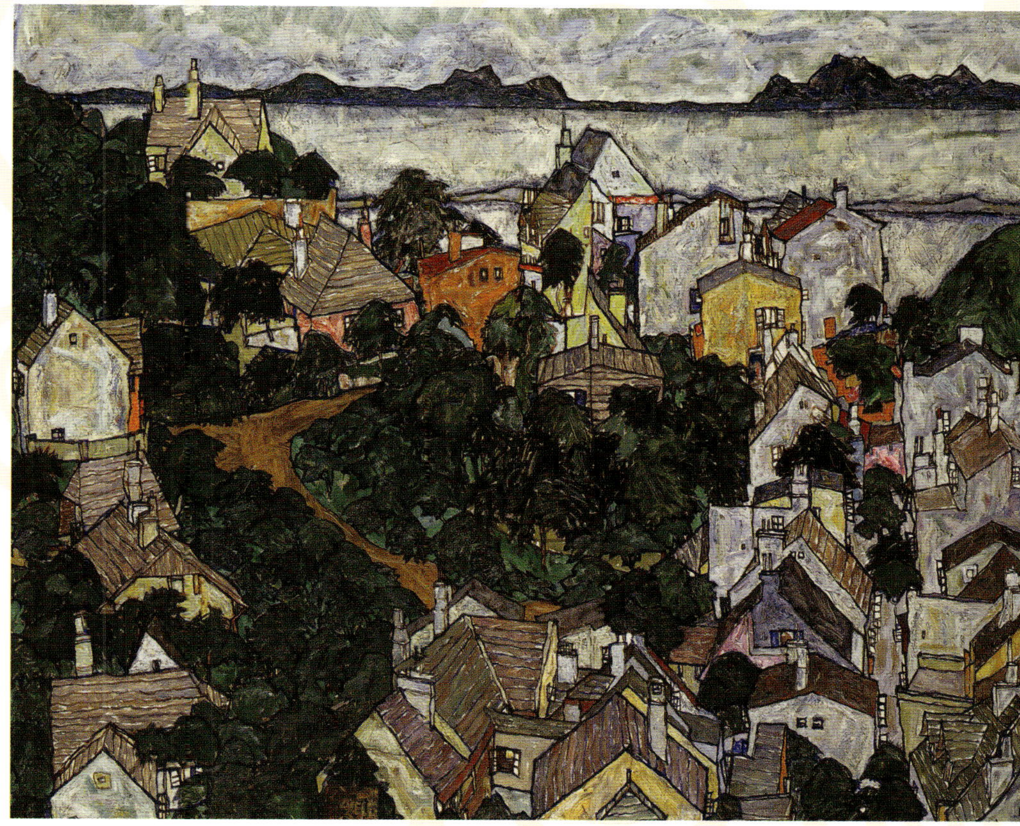

collective crisis of confidence, stemming from a frustration with language which, though ostensibly a means of communication, had a tendency to obscure those truths that it was charged with transmitting. As the Belgian writer Maurice Maeterlinck (1862–1949) lamented in an essay of 1896:

> *As soon as we put something into words, we devalue it in a strange way. We think we have plunged into the depths of the abyss, and when we return to the surface the drop of water on our pale fingertips no longer resembles the sea from which it comes. We delude ourselves that we have discovered a wonderful treasure trove, and when we return to the light of day we find that we have brought back only false stones and shards of glass; and yet the treasure goes on glimmering in the dark, unaltered.*

OPPOSITE ◆ TOWN ON THE BLUE RIVER, KRUMAU, 1910, EGON SCHIELE (1890–1918)
ABOVE RIGHT ◆ SUMMER LANDSCAPE, KRUMAU, 1917, EGON SCHIELE (1890–1918)

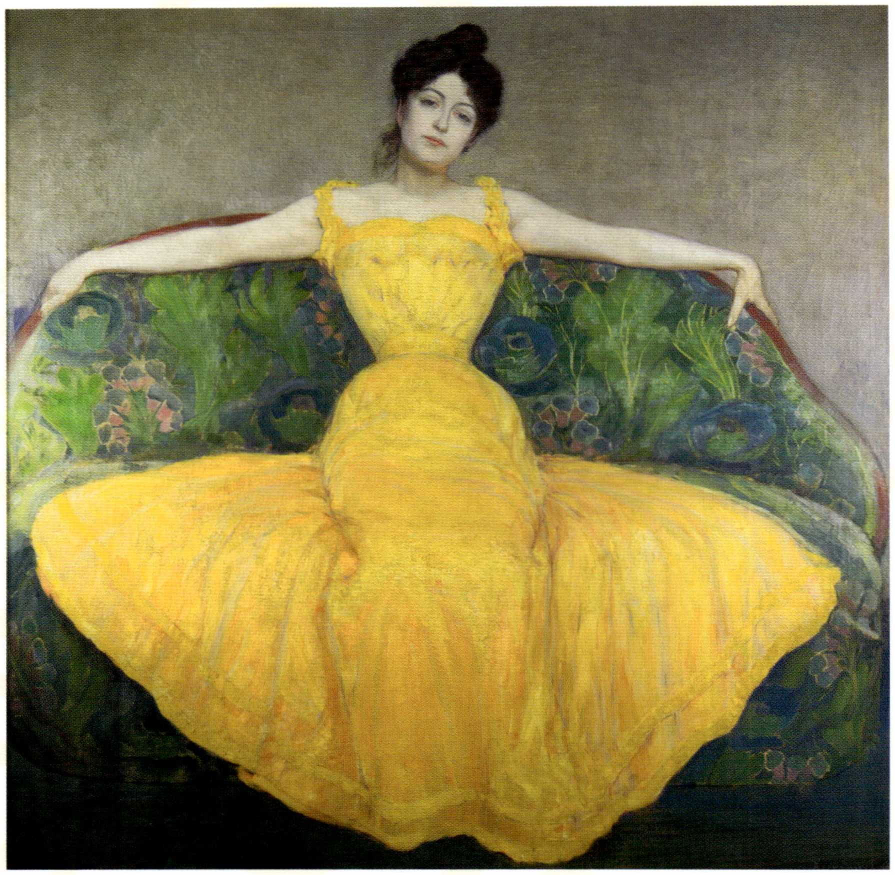

The Irretrievable 'I'

This crisis was of course philosophical in its origins – though it hardly helped that science itself appeared to be against the thinking, feeling individual who wished to have some real sense of what he or she actually *was*. Taking a lead from the German thinker Arthur Schopenhauer (1788–1860), the physicist Ernst Mach (1838–1913) was arguing by the 1880s that 'we' were daily being modified and reconstituted by a jumble of impressions, and that it followed from this that there was really no such thing as 'us'.

In 1907, Hermann Bahr (1863–1934), the writer, dramatist and director who had become an important articulator of the Secessionists' aims, took this idea and ran with it in his essay 'The Irretrievable I'. Where Goethe had famously observed that *individuum est ineffabile* ('the individual is ineffable – too great and complex to be summed up in words'), Bahr had substituted a far less flattering view. Inherently unstable, utterly inconstant, we were in our very essence existential flibbertigibbets – so much so that our subjectivity, our 'I', was 'irretrievable'. We were, in other words, existentially adrift, without either an established place in the universe or any means of securing psychological integrity. For the writer, it was going to be a real challenge to find forms for self-expression when it was far from clear that there was a self to be expressed.

Fragmented Spirit

The same went for what William Hazlitt (1778–1830) in England had referred to as 'the Spirit of the Age' and which German-speaking intellectuals had, since Georg Hegel (1770–1831), come to call the *Zeitgeist* (literally 'time spirit'). The idea worked well enough when there was apparent consensus of thought and feeling and when there were obviously shared artistic aims, but proved problematic in a time whose 'spirit' was a sense of personal, intellectual (and ultimately political) fragmentation. Across Europe – and indeed beyond – writers and artists were united only in their common concern to reconcile what seemed irreconcilable aesthetic aims.

Culture Shock

The irritated feeling conservatives had that young writers and artists were simply out to shock, being new and different for the sake of it, was by no means altogether without foundation. The old forms had indeed come to seem exhausted to them; there did indeed seem to be

ABOVE LEFT ◆ WOMAN IN A YELLOW DRESS, 1899, MAX KURZWEIL (1867–1916)
OPPOSITE ◆ THE CUSHION, 1903, MAX KURZWEIL (1867–1916)

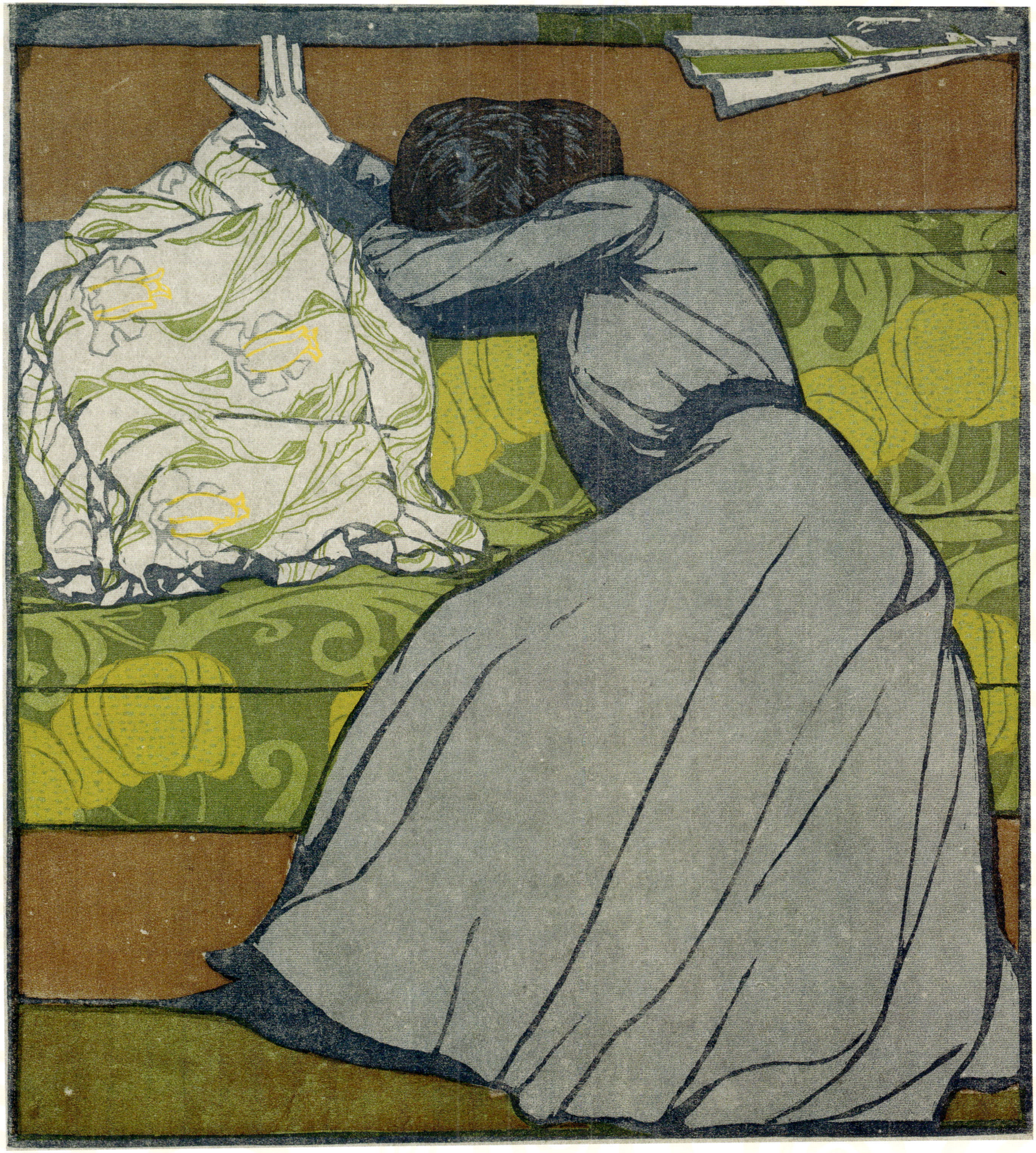

a need for art to jolt the public out of the complacency that too longstanding a familiarity with the same conventions is bound to bring.

Describing the excitement accompanying the first appearance on the literary stage of Hugo von Hofmannsthal (1874–1929) as star of the 'Young Vienna' circle, the writer Stefan Zweig (1881–1942) later recalled that the hero's youth had in itself seemed to underline the newness – and the importance – of his work.

Above all there was one figure that fascinated, enticed, roused and captivated us, that wonderful and unique phenomenon, Hugo von Hofmannsthal, in whom our youth saw not only its higher ambitions but also absolute poetic perfection come into being, in the person of one of its own age.

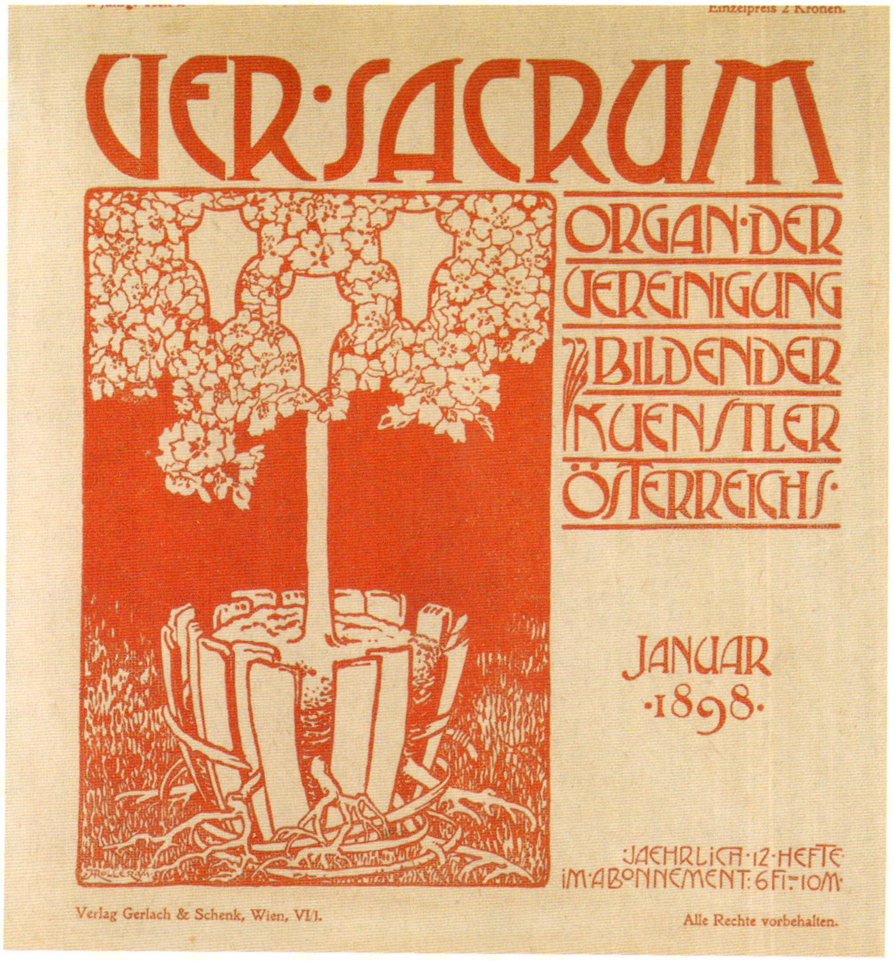

All the exciting young talents were young, Zweig said: the age's enthusiastic investment in youth contrasted dramatically with the attitudes of that 'age of circumspection' which had gone before. Until now, the artistic establishment had been most reluctant 'to distribute its favours prematurely to anyone, before he had proved himself by years of "solid" achievement'. Now solidity was seen as dullness: a single spectacular work or dramatic performance was enough to rocket a young genius to artistic stardom.

Modern Energy

This made perfect sense, given the insights from Mach and Bahr, the people of the age; its sense that the 'I' was being constantly reinvented, was ever new. As Hofmannsthal himself was to have it, the past was – almost literally – dead; a feeling only underscored by the commencement of a new century in 1900. 'With us,' he said:

nothing is left but a kind of frozen life, a blank, dull reality, lame farewells. We have a sentimental memory, a lamed will, and the strange gift of disengaging from our own lives. We watch ourselves. We look for the cup and yet remain thirsty … we experience loss at the moment of possession, failure in the moment of experience. We have no roots in life; we drift, clear-sighted yet light-blinded, like shadows.

The energy that animated Modernism, Hofmannsthal suggested, stemmed not from 'life' but from neurosis: it was a sort of nervous twitch, a convulsive spasming of creativity. The age was frank in its contradictions, he argued:

Two things do seem modern, the analysis of life, and the flight

LEFT ◆ COVER OF THE FIRST ISSUE OF THE MAGAZINE VER SACRUM. 1898. ALFRED ROLLER (1864–1935)
OPPOSITE ◆ OPERA OF THE SEA. c. 1902. MARGARET MACDONALD (1864–1933)

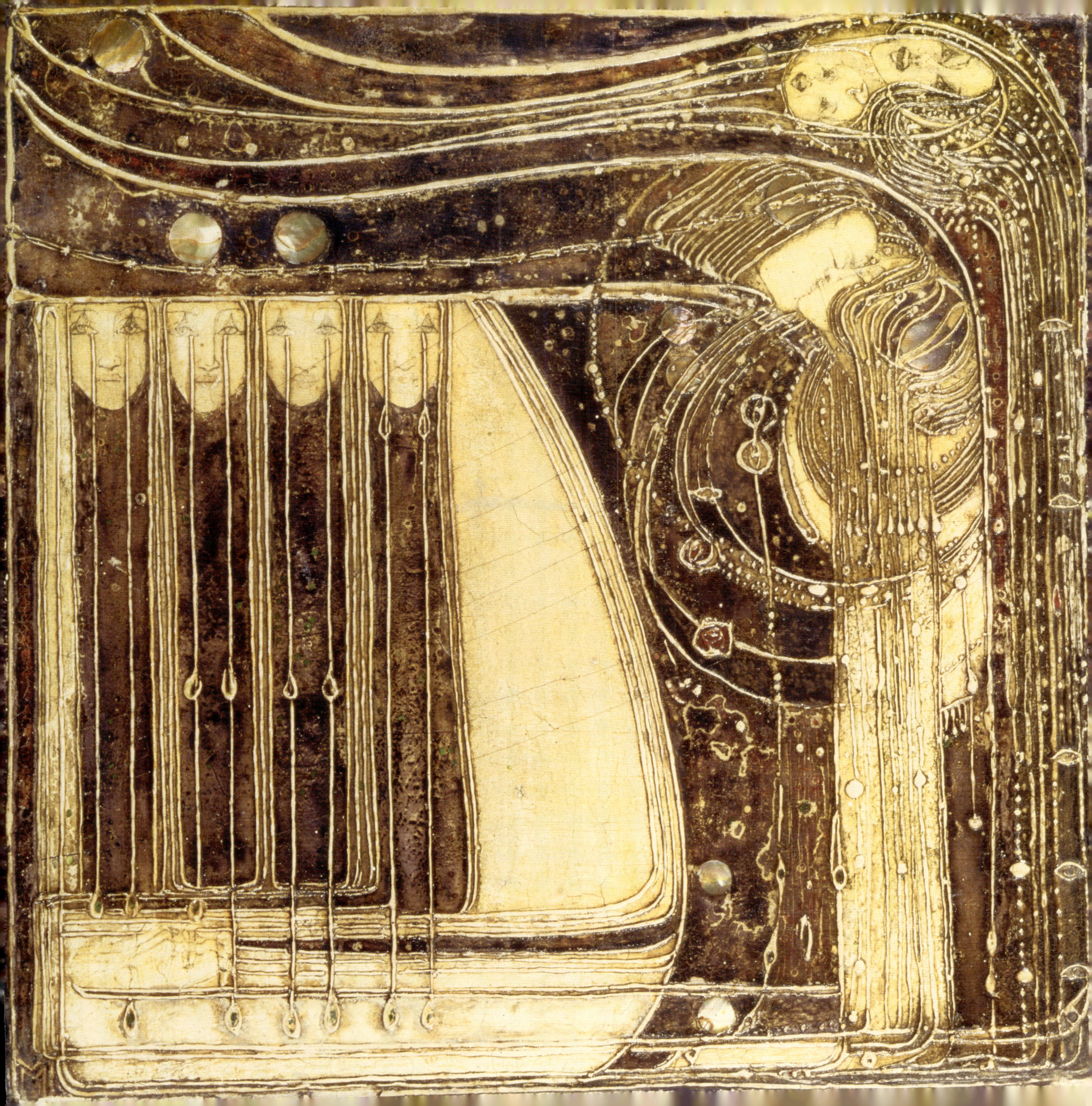

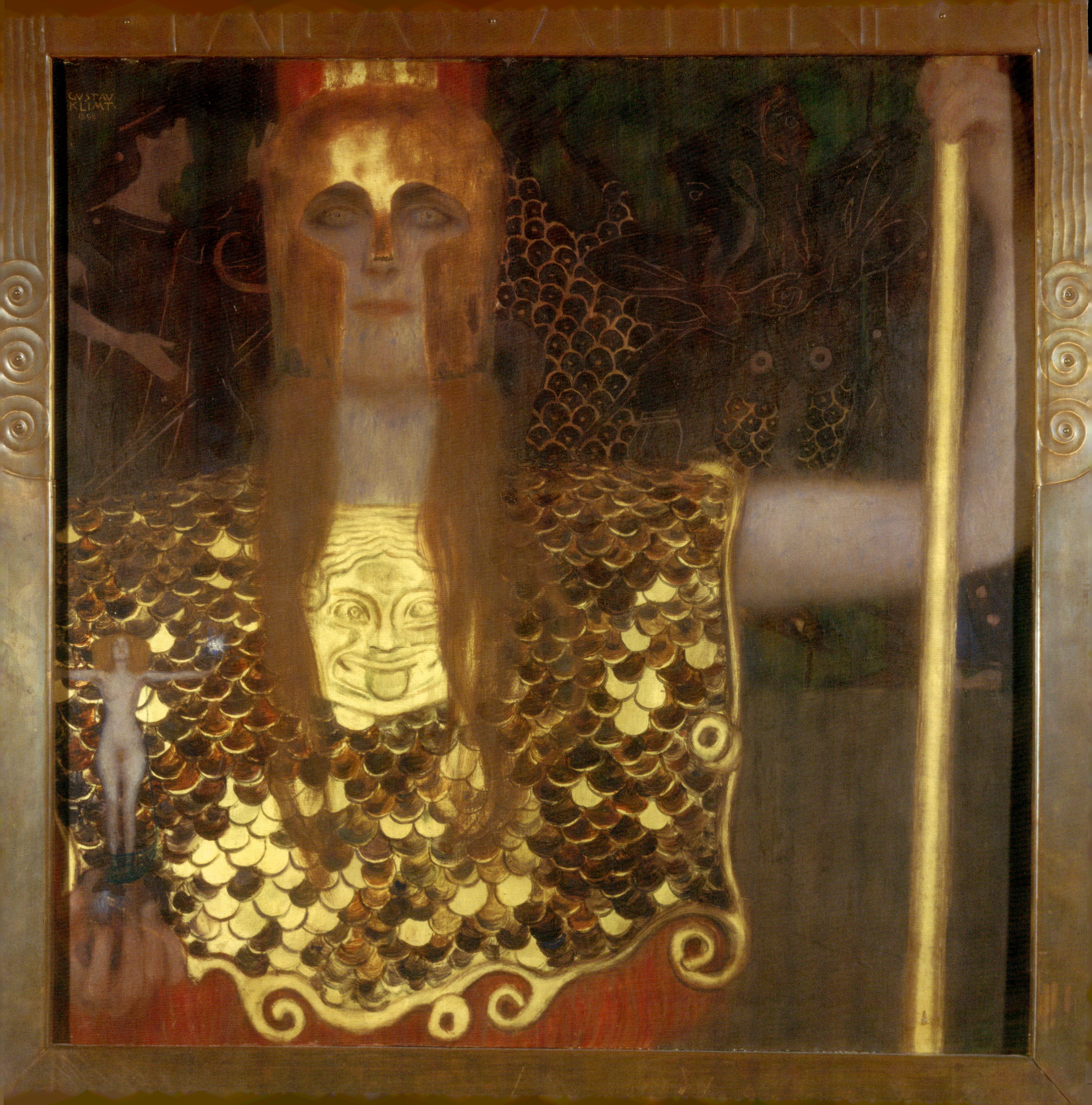
GVSTAV
KLIMT

from life ... One examines the anatomy of one's own life, or one dreams. Reflection or fantasy, mirror images or dream images. 'Modern' means old furnishings and young nervousness.

Hofmannsthal's aesthetic ideal of *zusammenschauen* ('seeing together') involved much on the sensory spectrum – from sight and smell to taste and touch – being evoked together in the same sort of simultaneity with which they were apprehended by the individual consciousness in real life.

Structures of the Self

Hofmannsthal's theories bring us back to the idea of the 'total work of art' whose complexity re-echoed that to be encountered in real life. Nowhere was this experience captured with more literal reality and immediacy than in architecture and interior design. That the one was the continuation of the other seemed self-evident to Otto Wagner and his disciple designers of the younger generation. Wagner's vision of a whole new city – the ultimate *Gesamtkunstwerk* – was never actually realized, but the stations he designed for the *Wiener Stadtbahn* (*see* pages 88–89), his *Kirche am Steinhof* and his Majolica House (*see* page 31) all embodied these principles in their different ways; and they embodied them both inside as well as out, in everything from their lamp-fittings to their flooring.

To walk into a building like this was to enter a work of art, to be bombarded with impressions on every side, like the 'I' making its way through the wider world. Josef Hoffmann's designs for the new sanatorium at Purkersdorf, outside Vienna (1903), encompassed everything from the shape of the roof to the form of the table lamps in the breakfast room. Built-in *zusammenschauen*, in other words.

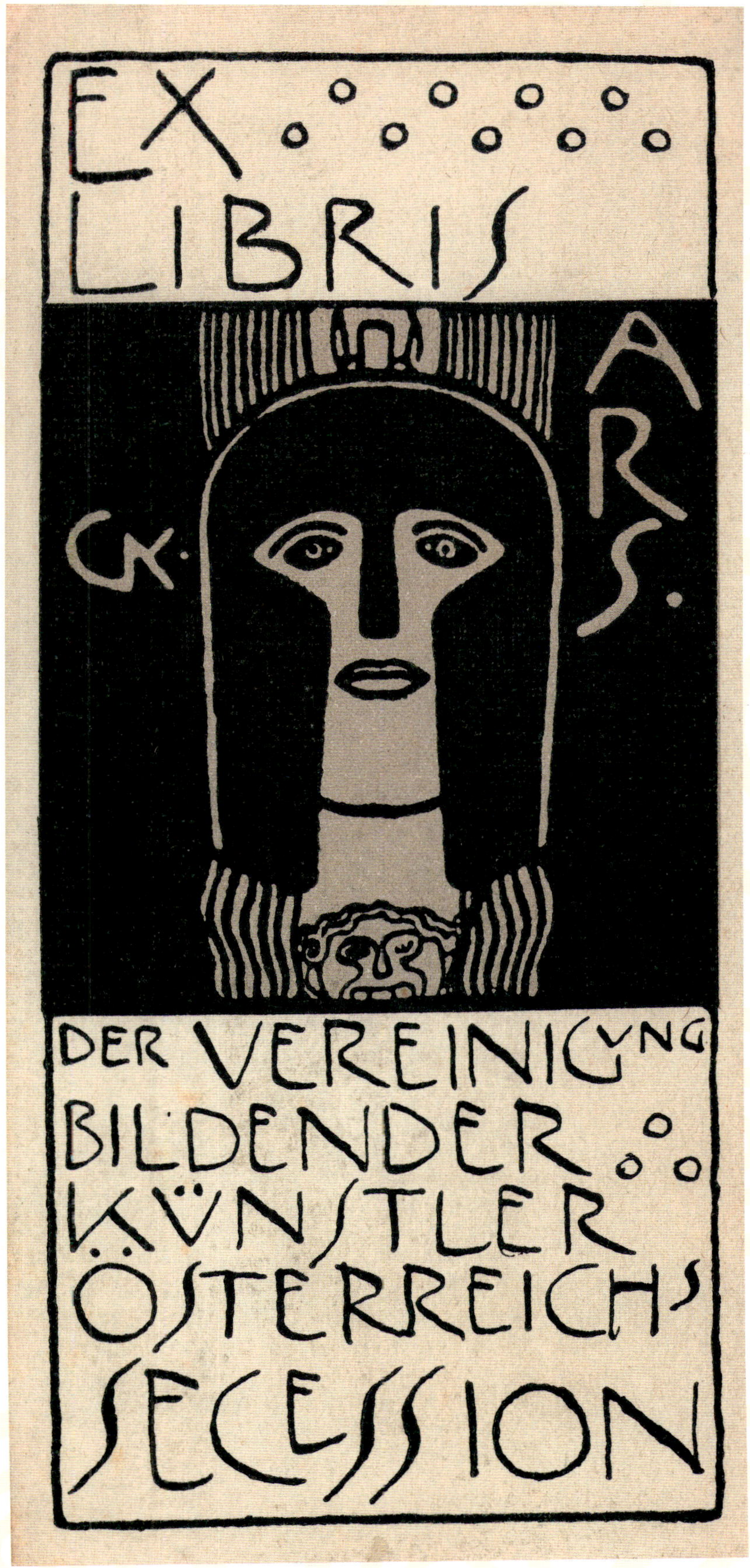

OPPOSITE ◆ PALLAS ATHENA. 1898. GUSTAV KLIMT (1862–1918)
RIGHT ◆ EX LIBRIS. 1899/1900. POSSIBLY GUSTAV KLIMT (1862–1918)

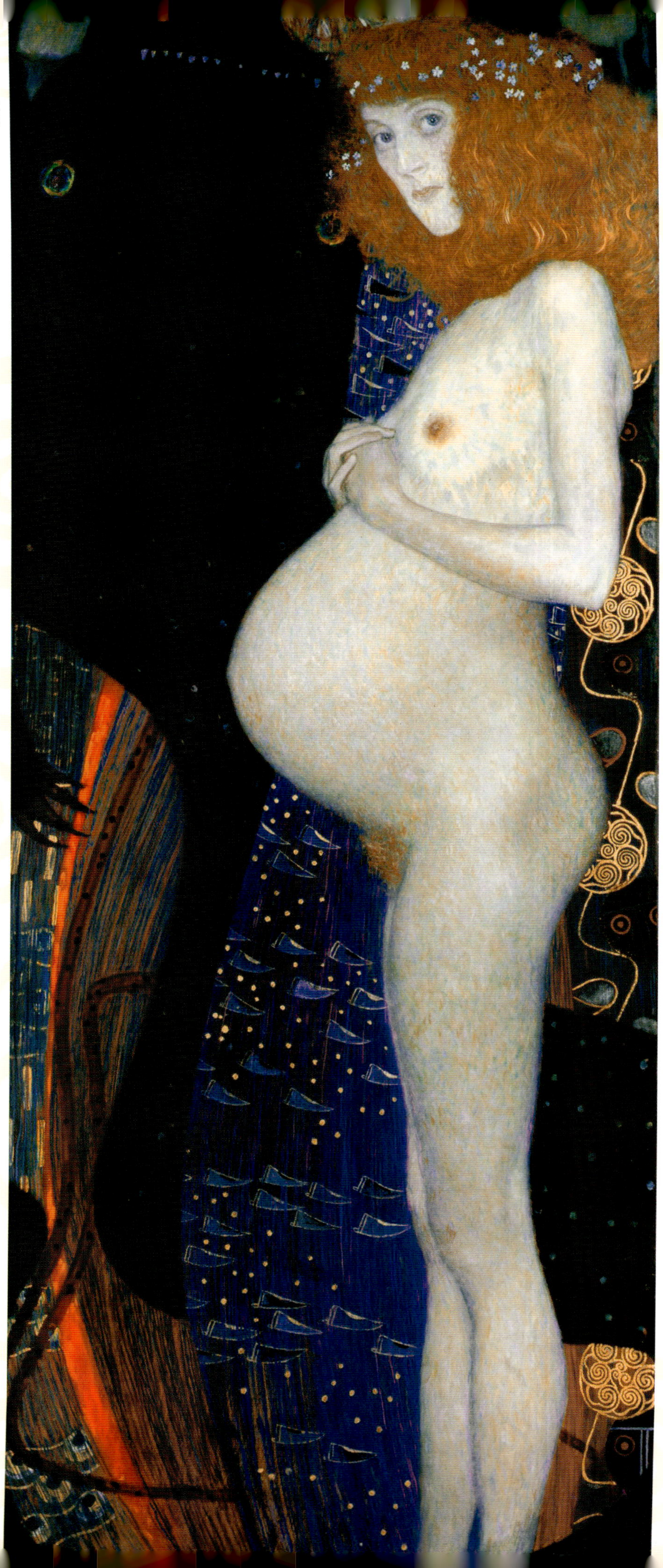

It was, then, in theory – and in certain places, in practice – possible to live the larger part of one's life within an environment, every inch of which had been designed. Previously the bourgeois Austrian had typically experienced the arts as an interruption to what was basically a prosaic and philistine routine. The occasional visit to a gallery; a night at the opera; a piano recital; a poetry reading … these existed outside the normal rhythms of the everyday. Now though, it seemed that the intersection of architecture and interior design was somehow elevating the routines of daily life to create a more artistic environment.

Working Model

As eloquently as he had expressed the most problematic preoccupations of his times, Hugo von Hofmannsthal erred in suggesting that '"Modern" means old furnishings and young nervousness'. A nicely turned phrase, no doubt – and he was definitely right about the 'young nervousness' – but Secessionist designers were coming up with innovations in furniture and fittings of every sort. Nothing was beneath the attention of a talent like Josef Hoffmann's, which concerned itself not just with spires and staircases but also with cutlery, flower-holders, bathroom mosaics and kitchen chairs. Colleagues in the *Wiener Werkstätte* ('Vienna Workshop') – a craft-centred subdivision of the Secession that Hoffmann and Koloman Moser formed in 1903 – created mustard pots and pendants, rings and bracelets, belt buckles and brooches.

They created clothing too, so a fashionable hostess might pose for a photograph (as did Moser's wife Editha in 1905) wearing a *Werkstätte*-designed dress seated on a *Werkstätte*-designed chair or sofa. As we saw with Klimt's *Portrait of Adele Bloch-Bauer I* (*see* page 189), there was an aesthetic excitement in the overspilling of one artistic medium into another. (We see something of the same in Max Kurzweil's earlier

LEFT ❖ HOPE I, 1903. GUSTAV KLIMT (1862–1918)
OPPOSITE ❖ MISS RIA MUNK ON HER DEATHBED, 1912. GUSTAV KLIMT (1862–1918)

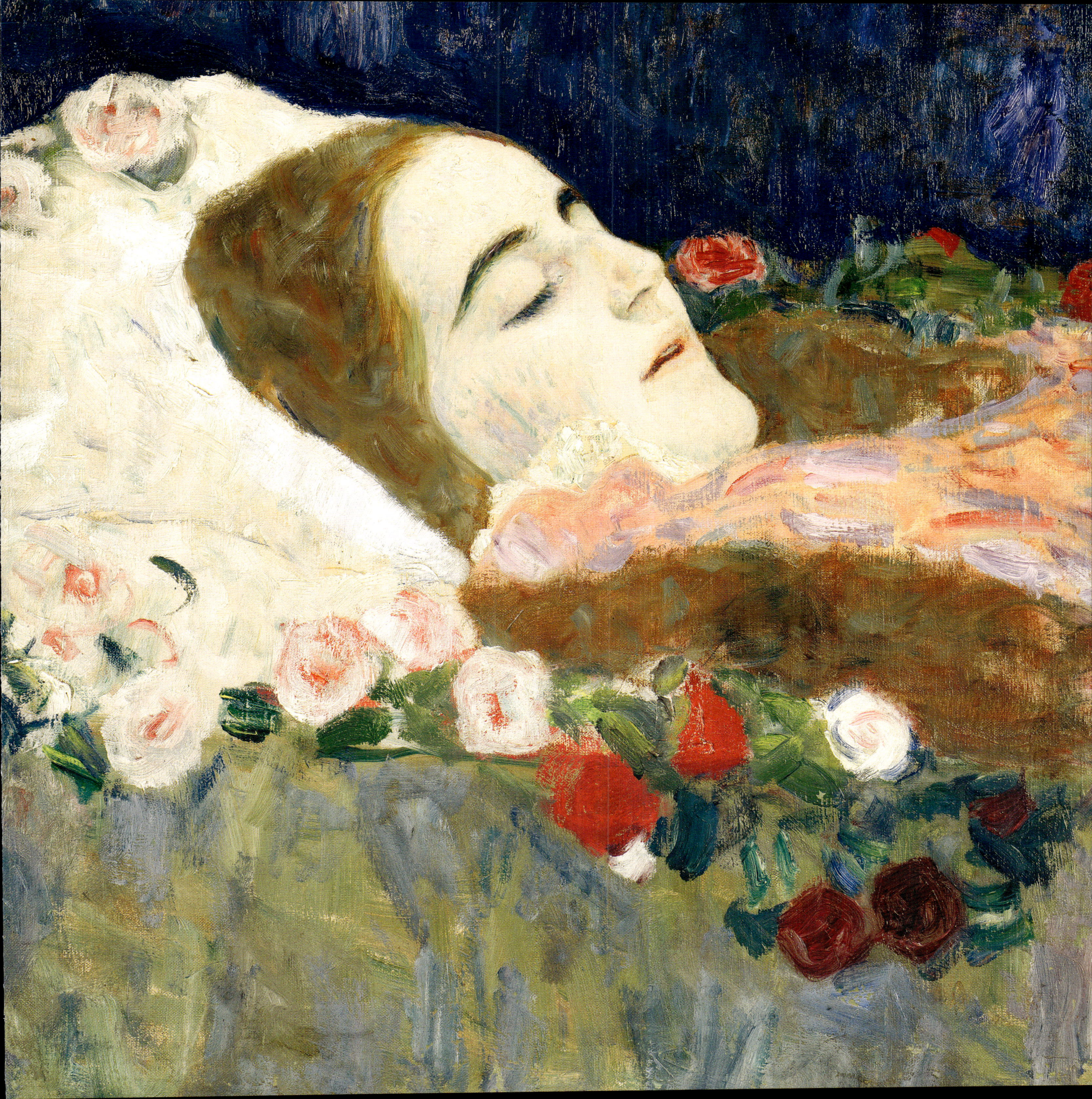

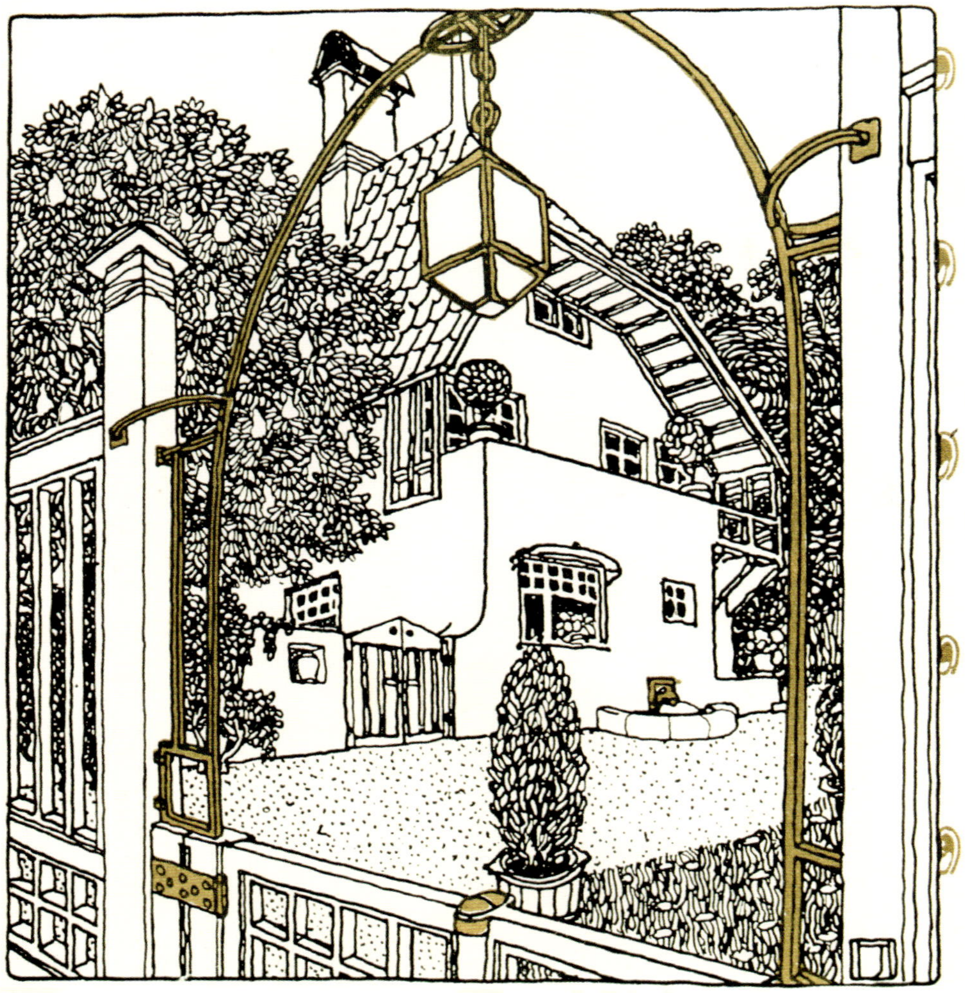

Woman in a Yellow Dress (1899, *see* page 56). Here, the way the subject's dress is draped 'rhymes' visually with the sofa on which she sits – though it could hardly contrast more strongly when it comes to colour.) It's not surprising, perhaps, given the trouble he took to make the dresses of his female subjects in his famous portraits part of the pictorial composition as a whole, that Klimt did design actual dresses and gowns for women from time to time.

Quality Control

The *Wiener Werkstätte* ethos clearly had a lot in common with that of the Arts and Crafts movement. Josef Hoffmann might have been echoing William Morris when he called for 'close contact between the public, designer and craftsman' to make a 'good and simple household object':

> *The limitless harm done in the arts and crafts field by low-quality mass production on the one hand and by the unthinking imitation of old styles on the other is affecting the whole world like a giant flood.*

And equally important to Hoffmann and his fellow craftsmen was their parity with practitioners of the 'fine' arts:

> *The value of artistic work and its design needs to be acknowledged and appreciated once more. The work of the craftsman is to be held to the same standard as that of the painter and sculptor.*

He should also, Hoffmann insisted, be able to derive the same rewards – artistic and financial – from his labours as the painter and the sculptor did from theirs:

> *We cannot and will not compete with cheapness; it is mainly achieved at the expense of the worker, and we feel that recapturing for him the joy of creation and a humane existence is our foremost obligation.*

Community Art

The plans that Joseph Maria Olbrich drew up for the Mathildehöhe district of Darmstadt may have been less ambitious than those of Otto Wagner for Vienna, but unlike Wagner's plans, Olbrich's were actually achieved. The commission came from Ernest Louis, the Grand Duke of Hesse (1868–1937), an enthusiastic amateur writer and musician, who

ABOVE LEFT ◆ CALENDAR SHEET. VER SACRUM. 1901. JOSEF HOFFMANN (1870–1956)
OPPOSITE ◆ MARCH CALENDAR SHEET. VER SACRUM. 1901. FRIEDRICH KÖNIG (1774–1833)

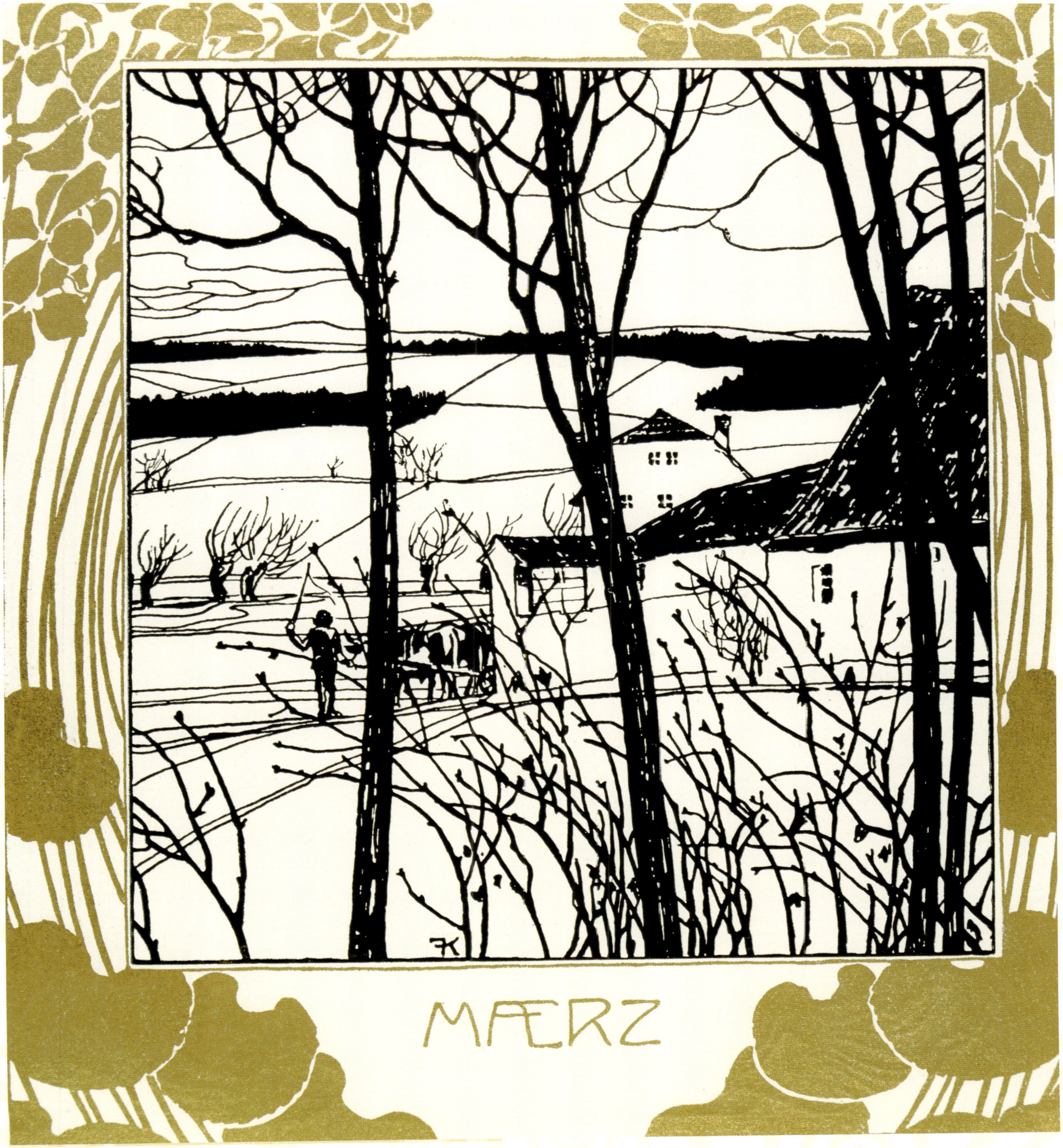
MÆRZ

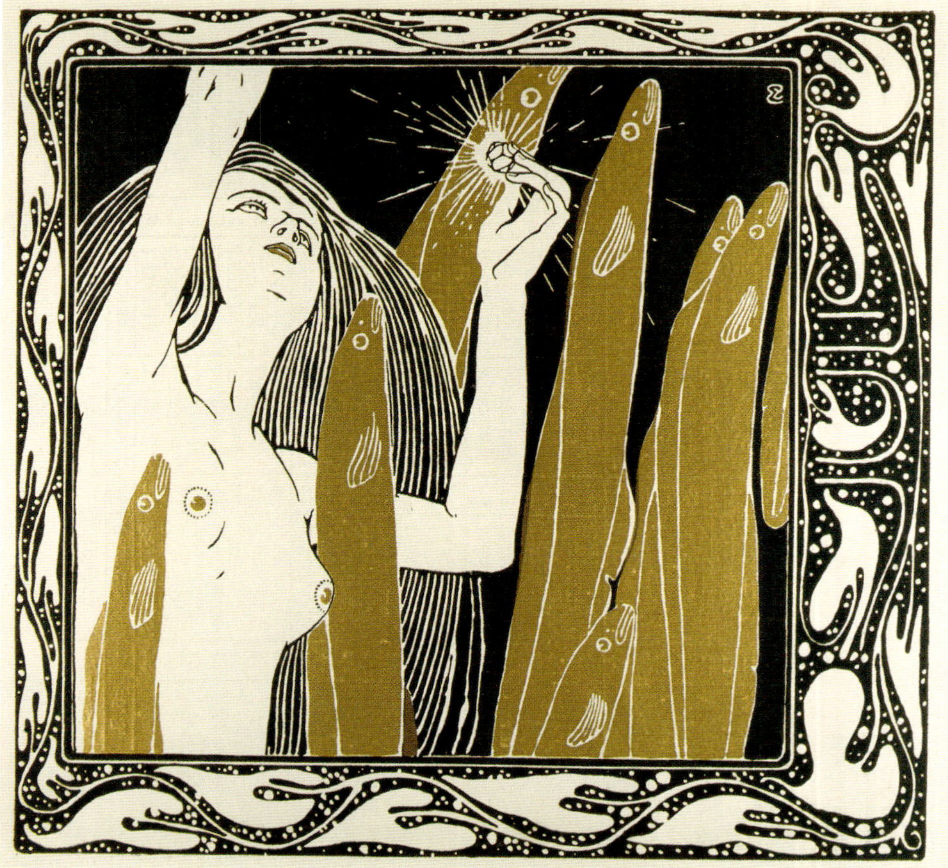

was eager to make his Duchy an important centre for the arts. Arranged around a shared atelier, Ernst Ludwig House (*see* page 84) doubled as a meeting place and exhibition hall. Twin male and female statues ('Strength' and 'Beauty') stood on either side of its ornate front door. Around this centre were spread the houses of the individual artists and architects – some self-designed, others built by Olbrich. Again, there was a clear emphasis on the importance of a total artistic environment, a sense of art and beauty being brought into the very heart of daily life.

Music and Meaning

Given all the ways in which the other arts were starting to impinge on everyday existence, ideas of the different media and genres as 'pure' and self-contained were fast retreating. Art and literature were both affected. Poetry (as the word 'lyric' reminds us) had in its origins been associated with music in the form of song. But so too now, in the understanding of the *fin de siècle* intellectual and aesthete, was artistic creativity in general. 'All art', Pater had summed up, in his essay 'The School of Giorgione' in *The Renaissance*, 'constantly aspires towards the condition of music.'

Why should this be? Why should the visual arts, with their ability to show, and writing and poetry, with their ability to use words to tell and make communications with real meanings, find themselves envying the inarticulacy of music? Could it be because that very lack of a communicable message or meaning enables music to bypass our conscious, thinking mind, and speak directly to our emotions, to our psyche, to our soul?

The great Modernist writers were clearly fascinated by musical composition. Though deceptively straightforward beside his notoriously complex and difficult later works like *Ulysses* (1922) and *Finnegans Wake* (1939), the short story collection *Dubliners* (1914) by James Joyce (1882–1941) is more multilayered than it seems. Read closely, its text just about constantly throws out references to music, from light opera to the drawing-room ballad, from amateur concerts to musical soirées in private homes. Joyce recognized that song – however sentimental it might seem – communicated in a way that even the greatest writing could not.

T.S. Eliot (1888–1965) called his breakthrough work 'The Love Song of J. Alfred Prufrock' (1915). His great long poem *The Waste Land* (1922) referenced a range of music from Wagnerian opera to ragtime; he called a later collection *Four Quartets* (1945).

ABOVE LEFT ✱ JULY CALENDAR SHEET, VER SACRUM, 1901. KOLOMAN MOSER (1868–1918)
OPPOSITE ✱ THE BLOOD OF FISH, 1898. GUSTAV KLIMT (1862–1918)

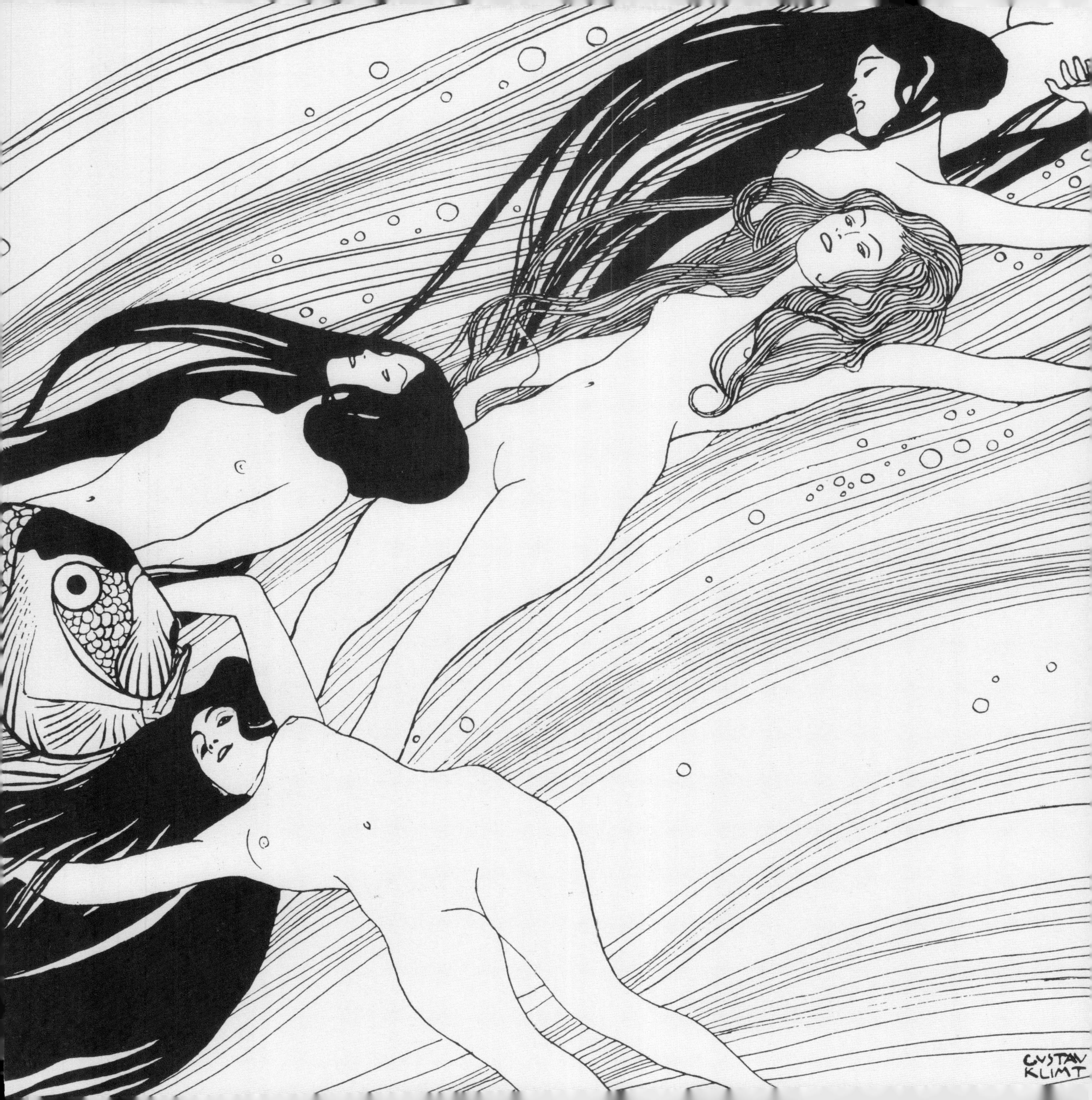
GUSTAV
KLIMT

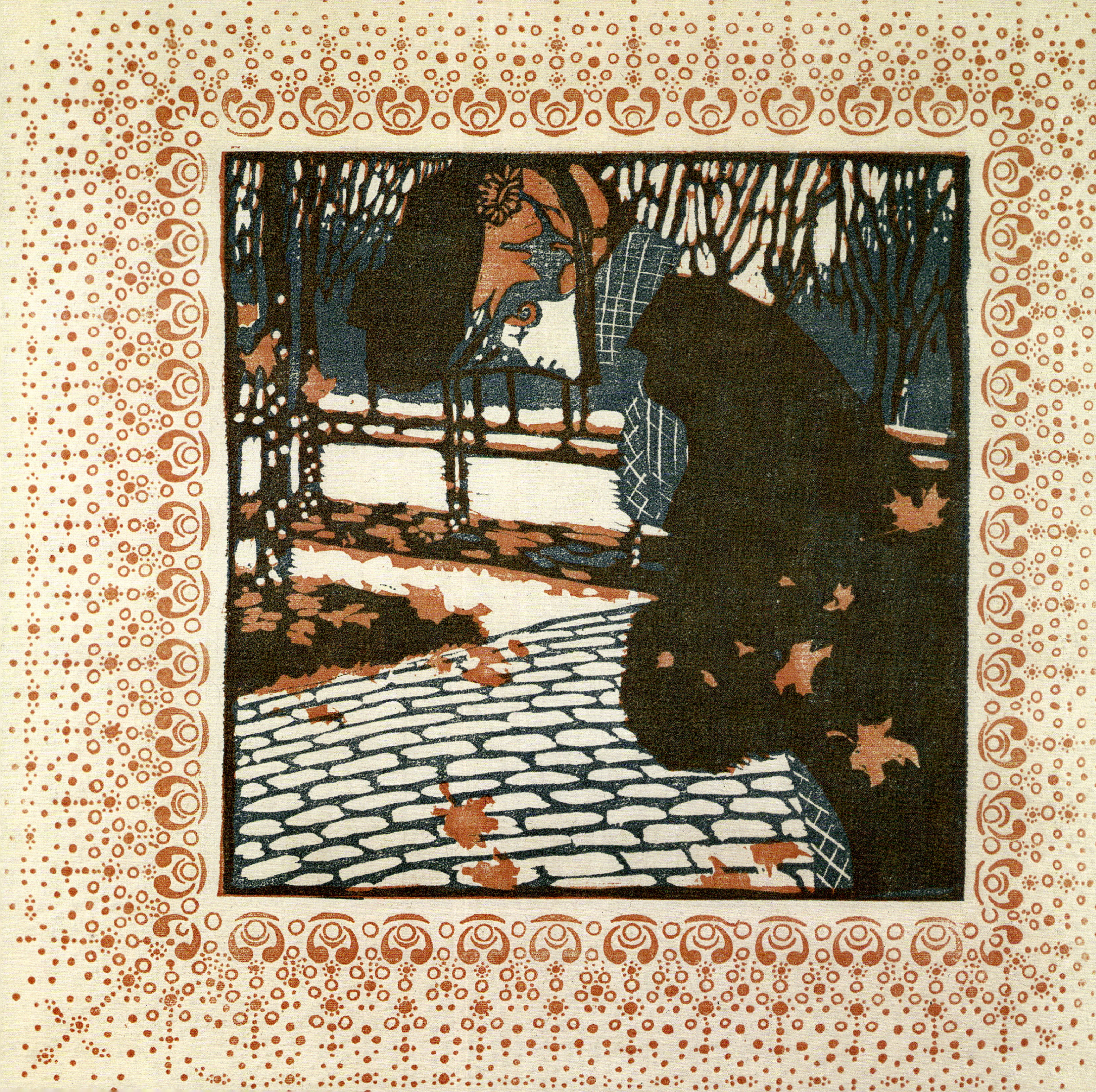

Deeper Exploration

What readers experienced as the difficulty – even the obscurity – of the Modernist writers may be seen as stemming from a desire to break the hold of conventional narrative and a 'commonsense' perspective, which only recycled the same old insights and dressed them up as new. As Friedrich Nietzsche (1844–1900) wrote, arguments from philosophical reason were essentially circular: 'When somebody hides something in a bush and then looks for it in the same place and finds it there, they haven't done anything especially praiseworthy.'

But much the same might be said of literature as a means of exploring truth. An old-fashioned story was all very well, but if it carried the reader along, simply skating along the surface of existence, how was writing supposed to get deeper into the heart of things? A rhyming poem expressing love, loss or nostalgia might be charming, but what did it do for insight, for the exploration of real feeling? In reality, it couldn't do much more than set out thoughts and insights embedded in it consciously by its author – like Nietzsche's seeker, finding what they themselves have hidden in the bush.

Easiness a Difficulty

If writing were to achieve the same effect, it was going to have to find its way past the distractions of meaning. W.B. Yeats put this well in a letter to a younger friend in 1930. Margot Ruddock had let her technique grow sloppy, he said, allowed herself to use the obvious rhyme, the self-evident image. As a result, she had let her verses seem 'second-hand'; too easy. 'There is no difficulty,' he complained, 'to force you down under the surface. Difficulty is our plough,' the great poet concluded.

Music didn't face these problems. Mozart's *Requiem* or Beethoven's *Pathétique* sonata didn't express any ideas or betray the slightest sign of thought, but somehow seemed to fathom the deepest regions of the human heart. All those intractabilities that made the great Modernist texts seem like so much outrageous mumbo jumbo to ordinary readers of the time were attempts to transcend the realm of story and idea to access the less articulable truths to be found beyond.

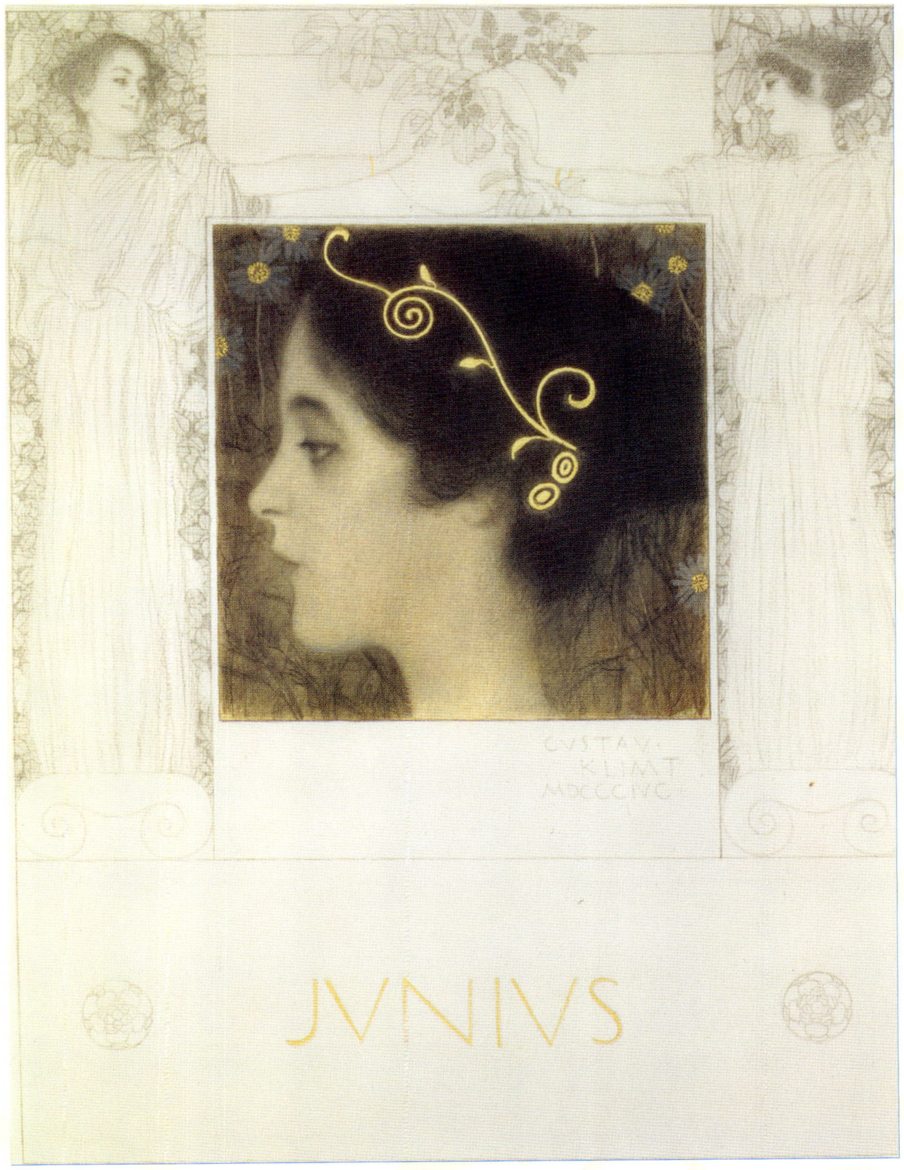

OPPOSITE ◆ NOVEMBER, 1903. KOLOMAN MOSER (1868–1918)
RIGHT ◆ SKETCH FOR THE ALLEGORY JUNIUS, 1896. GUSTAV KLIMT (1862–1918)

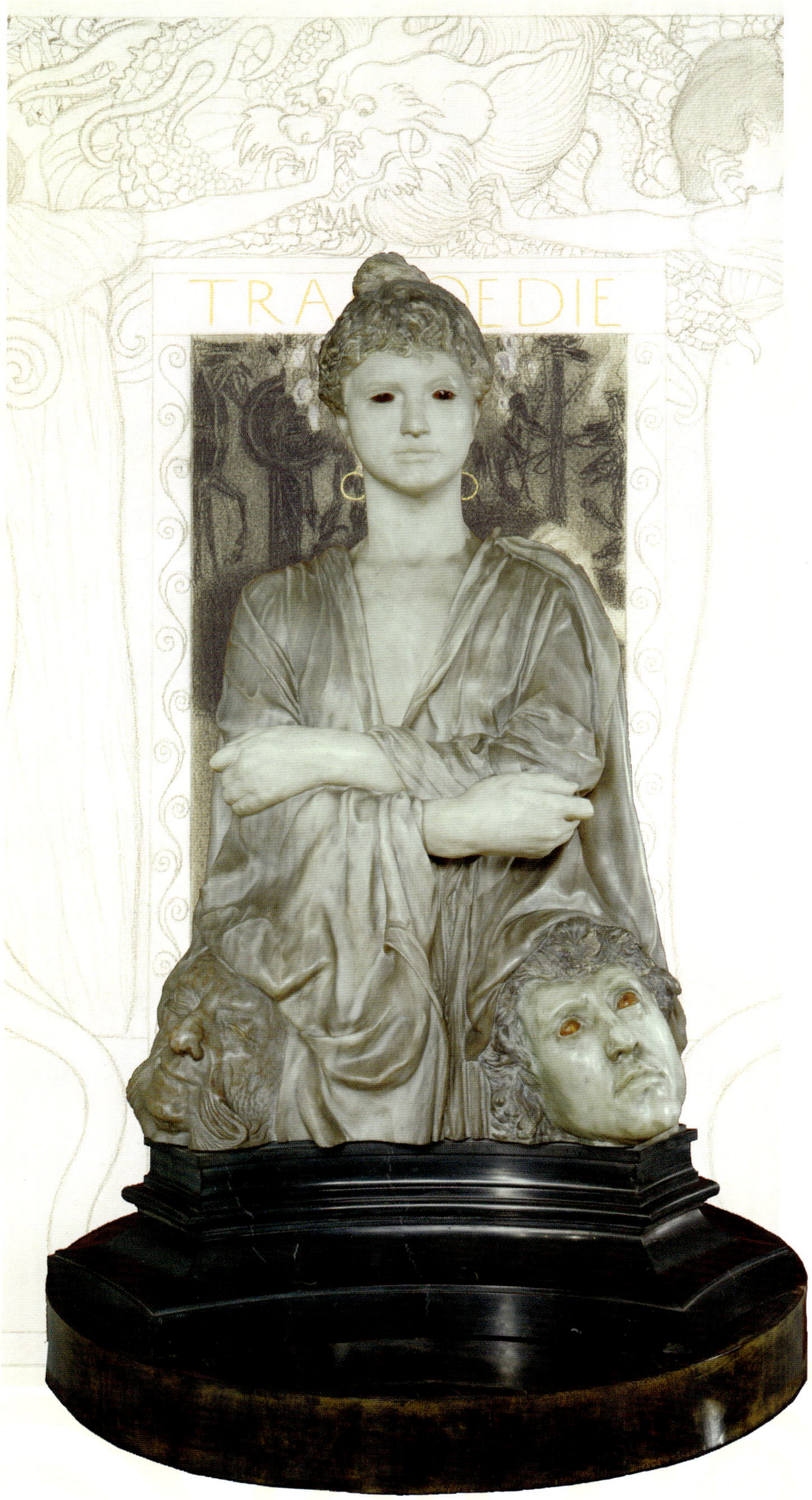

When we look into the visual arts for the closest approximation we can find of what makes music music, it is not to be found in figurative painting. By 1911, Wassily Kandinsky (1866–1944) was creating what have come to be seen as the first works of 'abstract' Modern art, finding a visual version of the deliberately difficult writings of the Modernist novelists and poets. In hindsight, however, it isn't difficult to see the shift in sensibility that paved the way for this taking place much sooner, in the elaborately decorative products of Art Nouveau, the *Jugendstil* – and, of course, the Vienna Secession.

Use, Ornament and Art

The fact that this shift wasn't immediately apparent at the time is down to the strictly ancillary function attributed to ornamentation in established art. The decorative might have its incidental place wallpapering a home or making a woman's jewellery box a little more appealing – or even setting off a 'proper' picture in a frame. Yet William Morris's recognition that a decanter or upholstered chair could be as artistic as a picture was at least as revolutionary as those idealistic yearnings that drew him to become a member of the Marxist Socialist League, campaigning for the world's workers to rise up and overthrow the existing order. Morris's views on knick-knacks – trivial though they may have seemed – put him entirely at odds with an artistic establishment that still drew a clear and rigid distinction between mere decoration and serious, actual art.

Aesthetically too, Morris's wallpapers, fabrics and stained-glass door-surrounds can in hindsight be seen as being ahead of their time. The very qualities that made decorative art appear trivial – the absence of obvious significance, the repetitive use of set motifs – were what made these designs most like music. Like the metronomic beat of a

LEFT ◆ SALOME. MAX KLINGER (1857–1920)
OPPOSITE ◆ TRAGEDY, 1897. GUSTAV KLIMT (1862–1918)

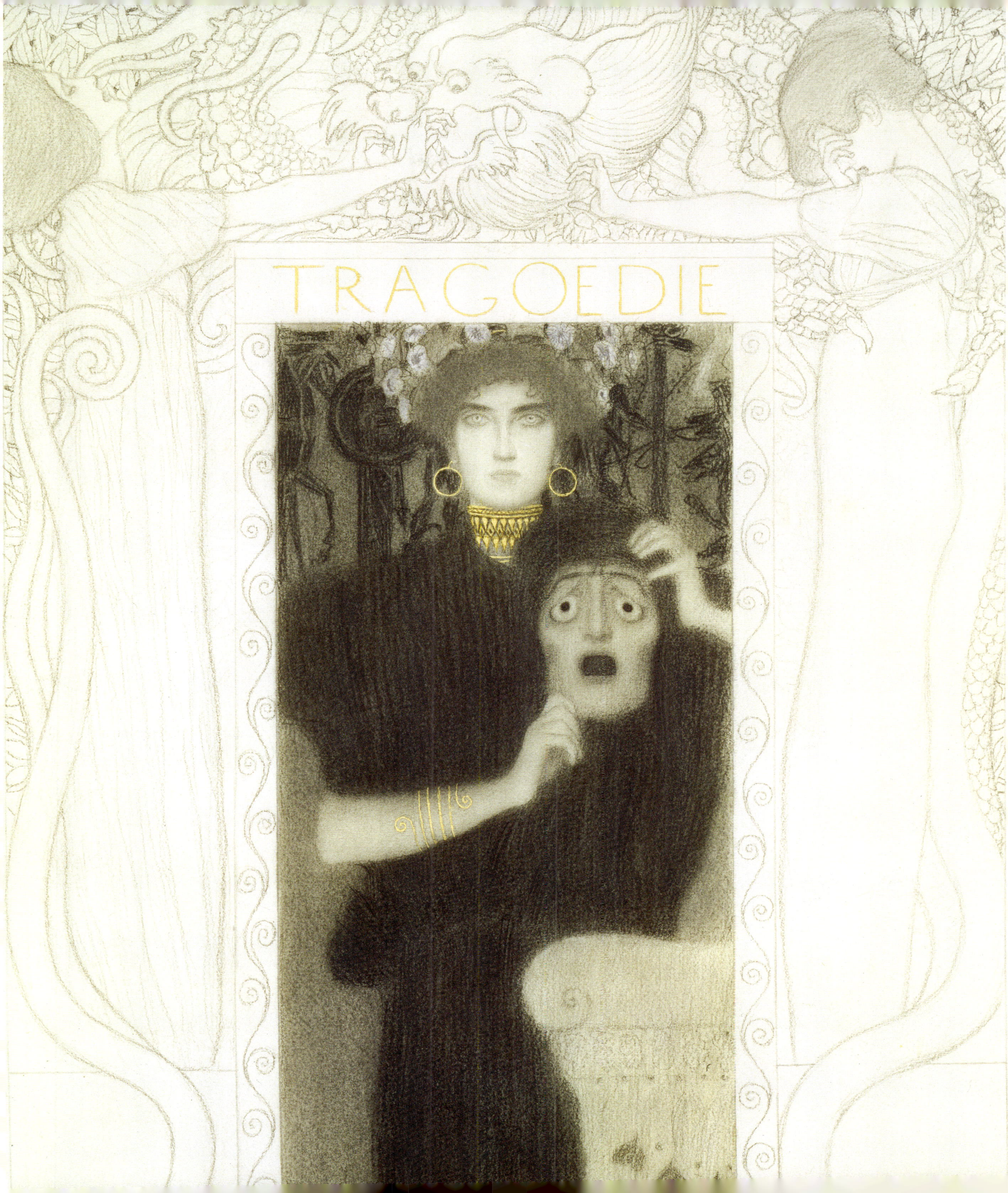
TRAGOEDIE

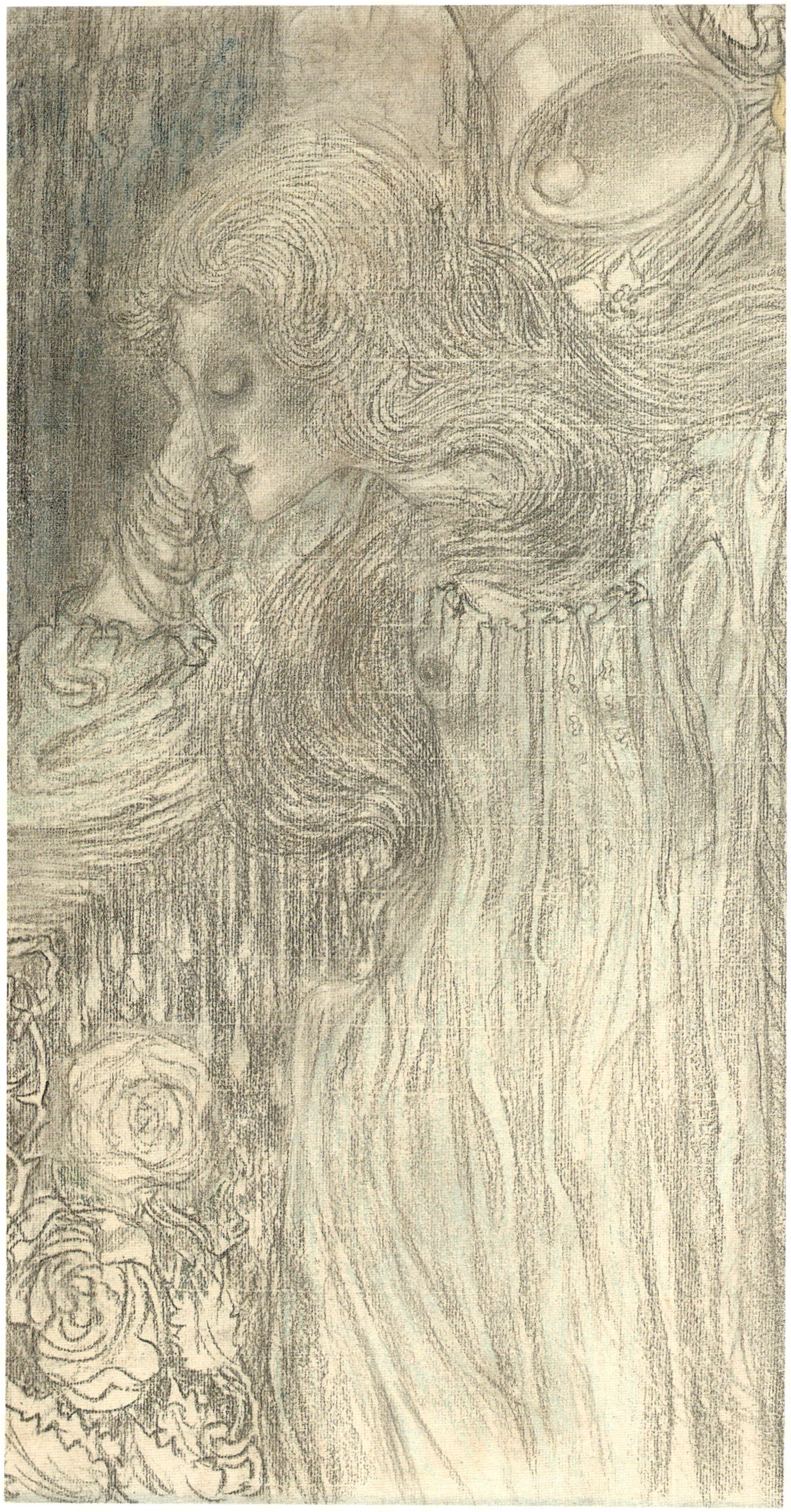

composition in 4:4 or 6:8 time, the pattern in a piece of cloth created a visual rhythm that gave aesthetic satisfaction without the need for any narrative or meaning.

Patterns and Repetition

The same went for Art Nouveau or the *Jugendstil* – whether in the cascading tresses of a 'Mucha Woman' or the tumbling floral forms of a poster by Henri Privat-Livemont (1861–1936). Or, for that matter, in the works of the Glasgow School – for example, in the super-stylized figures (more pattern than picture) lined up in Margaret Macdonald's *The Opera of the Sea* (*c.* 1902, *see* page 59).

In some ways, the applied arts lent themselves particularly well to this sort of patterning, because some degree of repetition was fairly inevitable: hence the patterns we see emerging in the furnishings for a room by Charles Rennie Mackintosh, a banister by Victor Horta (1861–1947) or a piece of jewellery by René Lalique (1860–1945). This also proved the case for Secessionist artists: in a calendar by Koloman Moser or a bracelet or set of dining chairs by Joseph Hoffmann, the same scope for repetition and variation can be found. Music and decoration came together in a stunning cabinet designed by Moser in 1904 for the music room of Dr Hugo Koller. The swirling grain of its black-stained oak panelling was reflected in regular form in the wavy lines of its surround; with a direct contrast between the hammered silver of its ornamented inset plates and the smoothness of white metal and glass.

Building a Brand

Joseph Maria Olbrich got off the mark with astonishing swiftness to build the Secessionist movement's new HQ – on a plot of land paid

LEFT ◆ THE DREAMER, 1897. JAN TOOROP (1858–1928)
OPPOSITE ◆ GERTI SCHIELE, 1909. EGON SCHIELE (1890–1918)

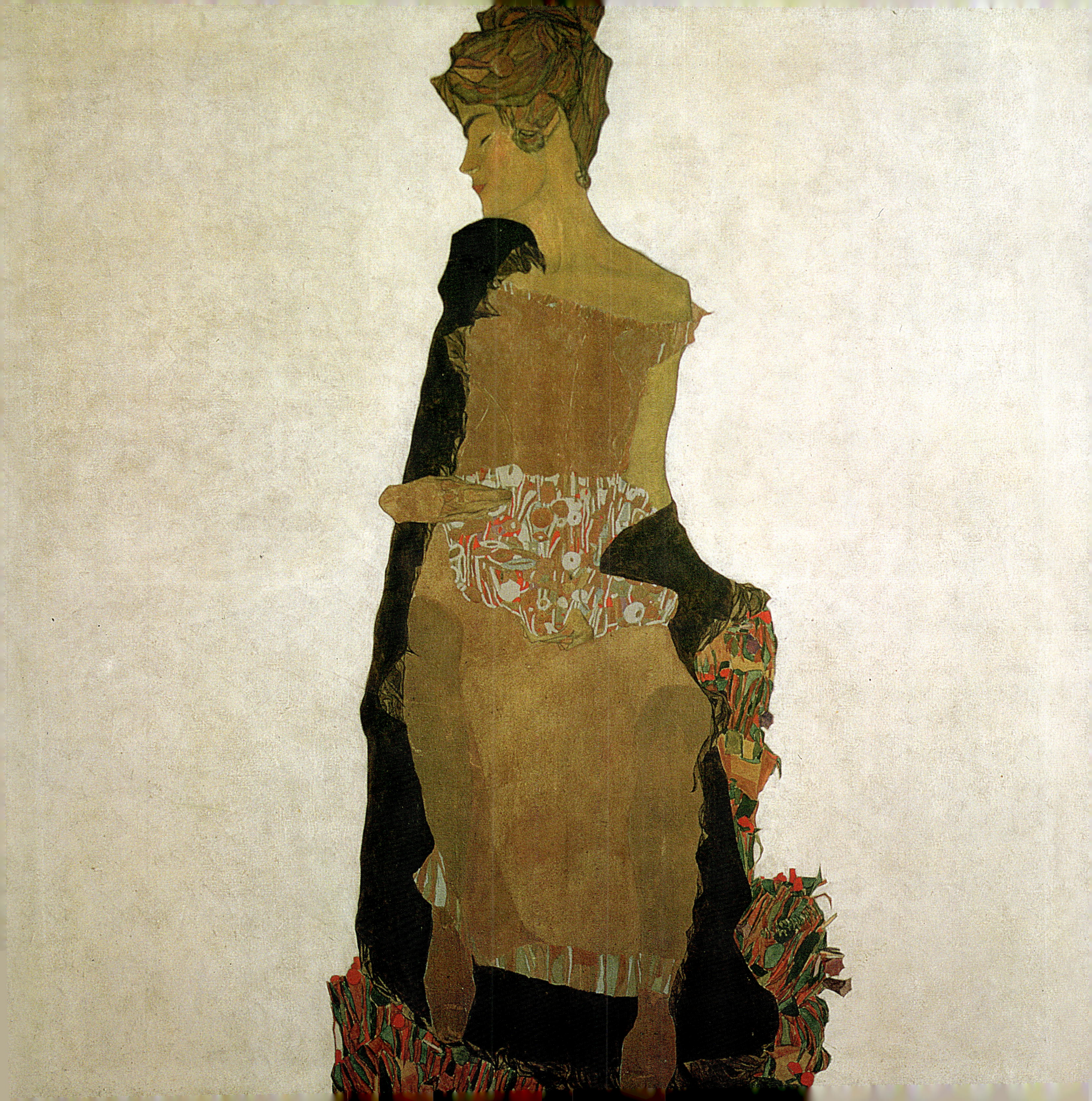

for by the steel magnate Karl Wittgenstein (1847–1913); father of the philosopher Ludwig Wittgenstein (1889–1951). But while it was being built, the Secessionists still needed some means of announcing their existence to the wider world and of advertising what they were about.

Despite its commercial associations, the word 'advertising' is apposite: the Secession was by no means purely aesthetic in its aims. Although the artists involved certainly wanted artistic change, as professional painters and sculptors seeking clients, they were aggrieved at what they saw as the inadequate efforts made by the Austrian Artists' Society on their behalf, and the failings of the Künstlerhaus as a showcase for their work.

Proclaiming their artistic aims wasn't going to be easy, given that as yet these were uncertain and that the Secessionists themselves were such a motley crowd. But this was no reason not to set about raising their collective profile through their new art magazine, or (as we'd now describe it) establishing a 'brand'. And as complicated as publishing a magazine might be, it was likely to be easier and quicker than building a headquarters (though the Secession Building had in fact been completed by October 1898).

Sacred Spring

The first issue of this new magazine, *Ver Sacrum*, appeared in January 1898. Alfred Roller (1864–1935), the magazine's editor-in-chief, himself designed the cover (*see* page 58), showing a tree growing out of a wooden barrel-tub. Above, in the foliage, hang the three shields that in one form or another would adorn all the Secession's publications. Below, the barrel's slats have come apart, burst open in violence by the growing roots. 'God, the tree, will roar out of ripeness,' Rilke wrote around this time in one of the poems destined for his *Book of Hours* (1905),

OPPOSITE • DESIRE AND SATISFACTION, 1893. JAN TOOROP (1858–1928)

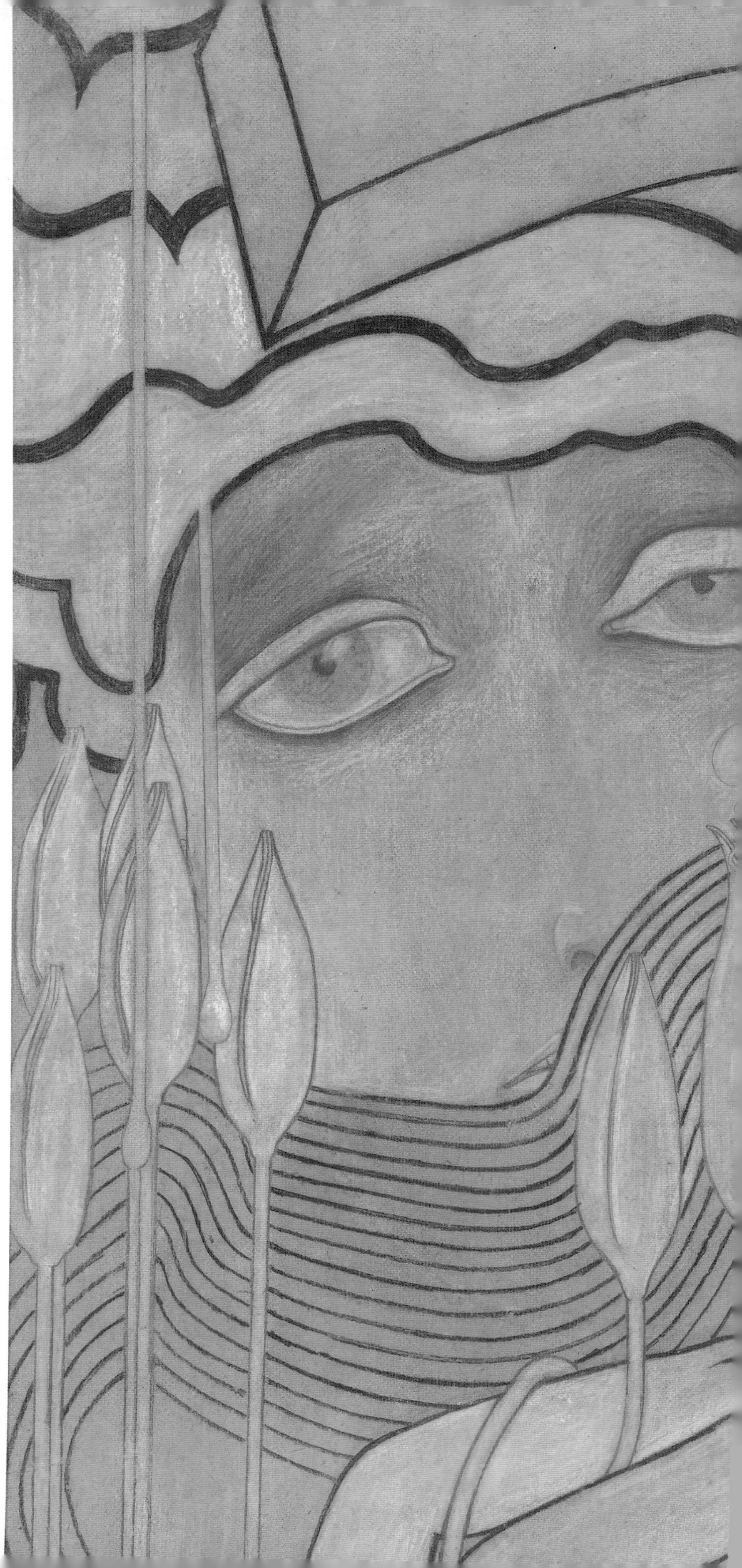

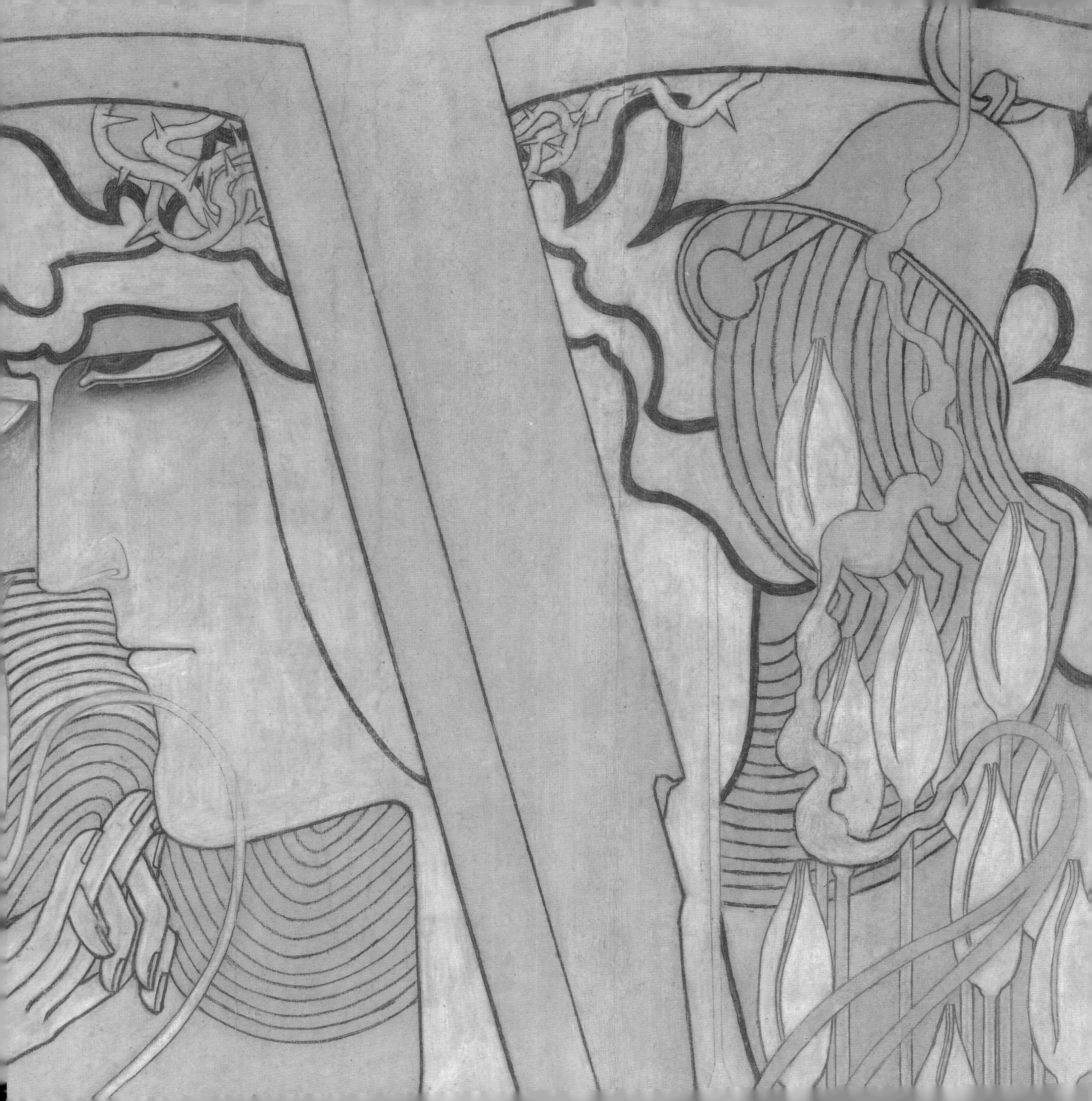

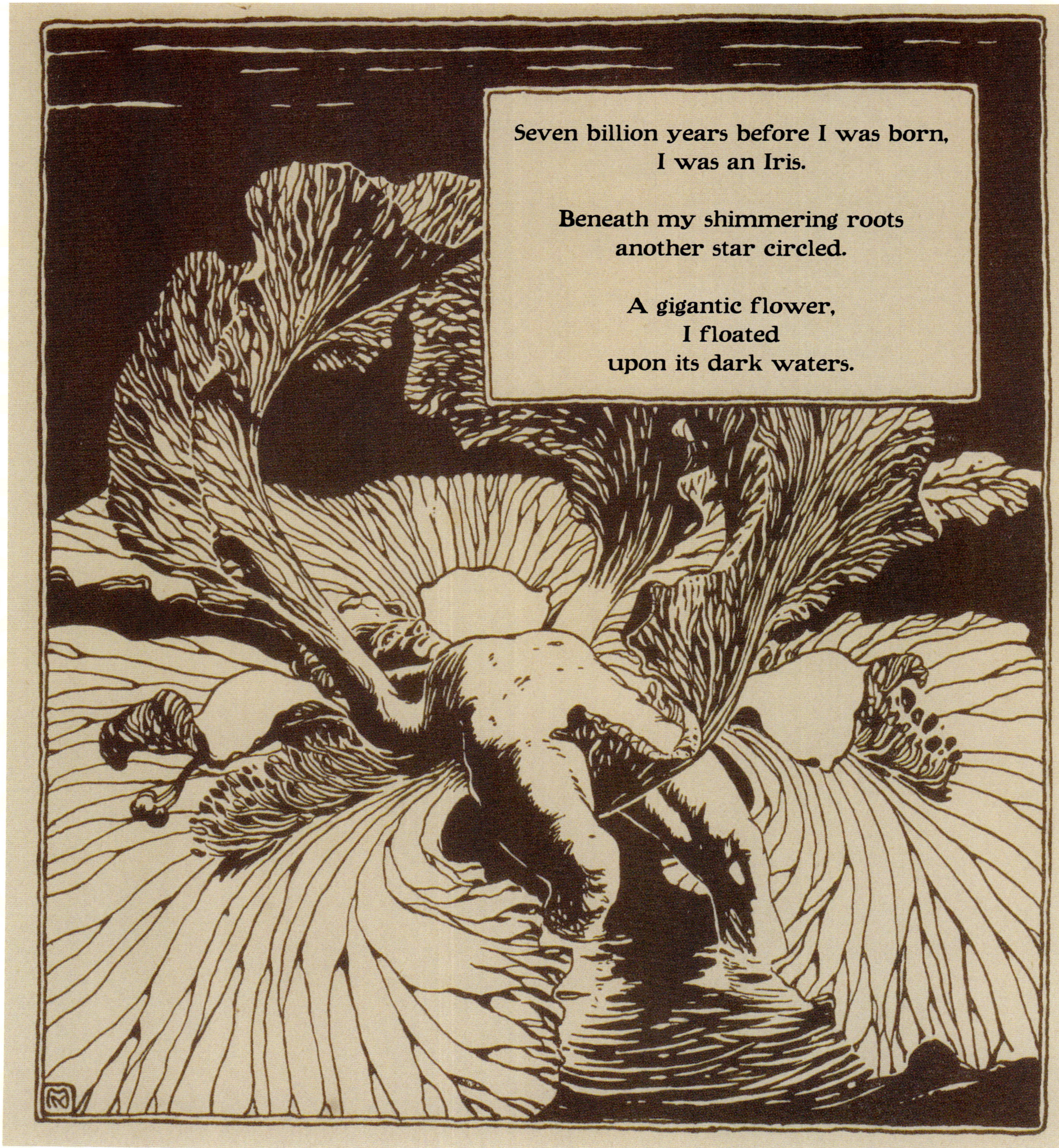
Seven billion years before I was born,
I was an Iris.
Beneath my shimmering roots
another star circled.
A gigantic flower,
I floated
upon its dark waters.

imagining the universe as an explosion of creative growth. 'Where is the outside for this inside?' the poet went on to ask, again suggesting the endless continuity of creation, the boundless interconnectedness of art.

Inside the new magazine, meanwhile, on beautifully laid-out pages, Secessionist luminaries like Koloman Moser, Joseph Maria Olbrich and Josef Hoffmann were represented with designs and picture plates, along with lesser-known names like Albert Hynais (1854–1925), Leo Kainradl (1872–1943) and Adolf Böhm (1861–1927). Moser's contribution encompassed even the level of the typography – his tautly geometric lettering contrasting with the effortless flow of his graphic work. (Images like the (paradoxically square-set) *Round Dance of Trout* from the April 1899 edition took further Moser's fascination with the counterpoint of wriggling curves and strictly square and planar shapes.)

Klimt was included, of course, showing just how extravagantly sensuous and seductive a simple black-and-white drawing of a woman could be. There was also the odd critic, like Ludwig Hevesi (1843–1910), who contributed a piece on the Secession's Honorary President, Rudolf von Alt. The first issue was only a start, and yet it was already clear that – in keeping with the idea of the *Gesamtkunstwerk* – the whole was greater than the sum of its parts.

Further Issues

And it was all only going to get grander, more complex and more impressive as the months went on and the issues accumulated. Roller wrote to his friend Klimt after 1898's April issue of *Ver Sacrum*: 'I am holding fast to the principle that every edition of *V.S.* is a small exhibition, but that *V.S.* as a whole is a large one.'

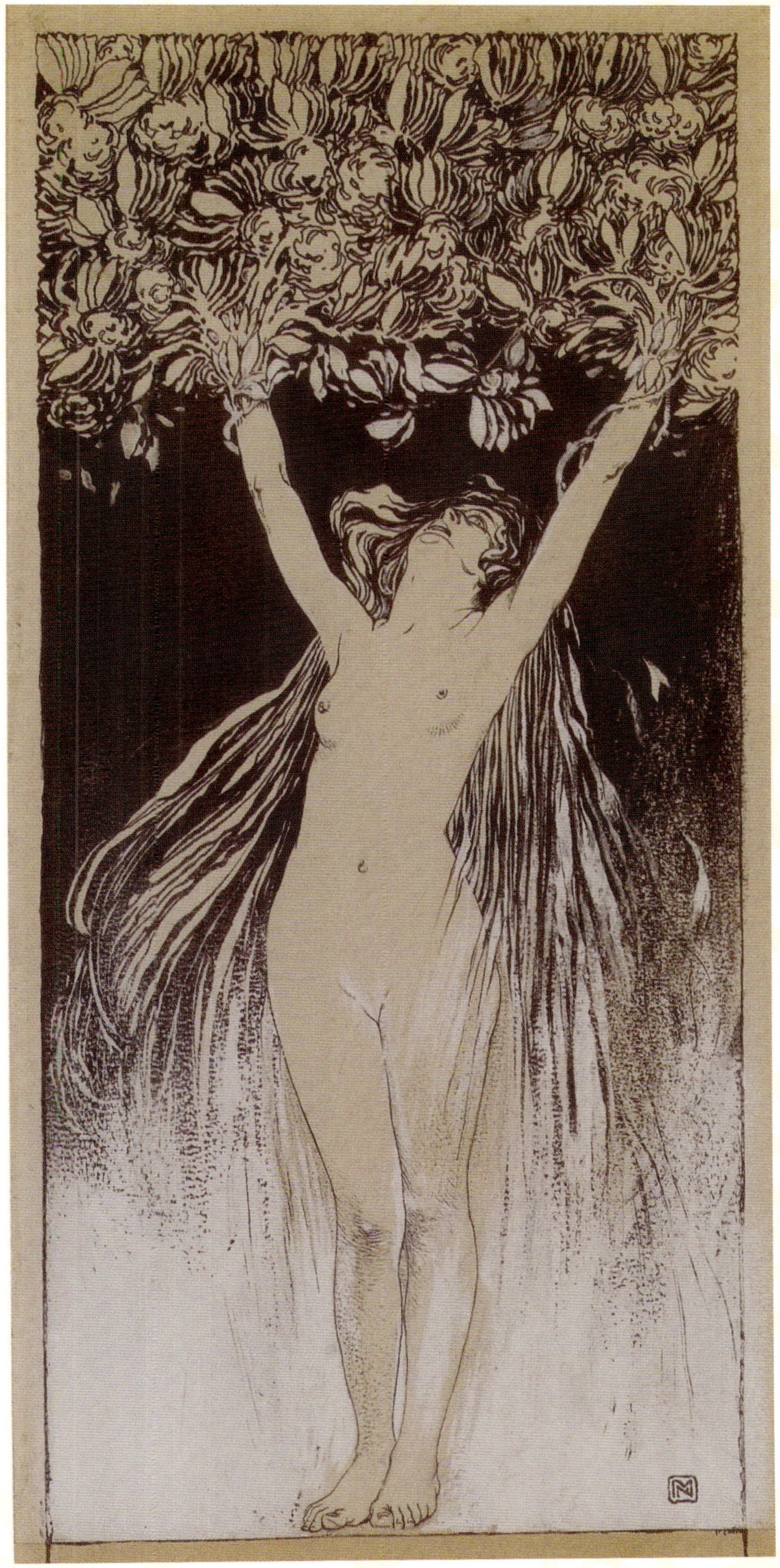

OPPOSITE • ILLUSTRATION FOR ARNO HOLZ'S POEM 'IRIS', 1898. KOLOMAN MOSER (1868–1918)
RIGHT • ALLEGORIE: VER SACRUM, 1897. KOLOMAN MOSER (1868–1918)

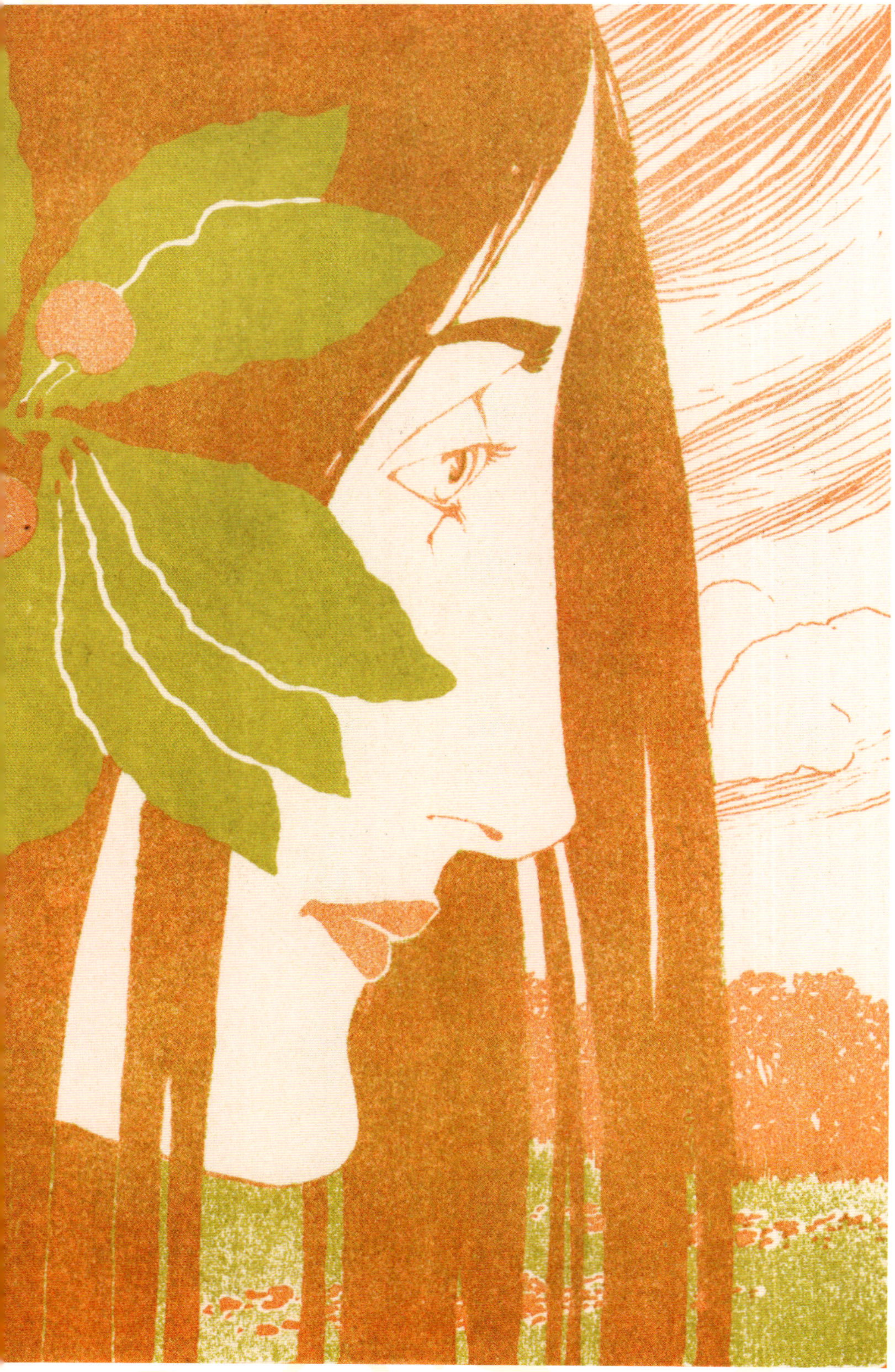

But such stunning artwork was only part of what *Ver Sacrum* was about. The magazine made common cause between early Modernism in writing and the visual arts. *Ver Sacrum* was not so much a gently bubbling spring as a seething cauldron into which some of the finest work of the Secessionists was stirred, together with some of the most interesting and challenging writing of the time; and the results were frequently bewitching.

Modernist Mingling

Rainer Maria Rilke, as we've already seen (*see* pages 6–7), was an enthusiastic supporter of the magazine. A keen student of art history, he contributed several critical reviews over the years, but of course it's for his poetry that he's famous now. Rilke's verse had another airing in the September 1898 edition of *Ver Sacrum*:

Hands intermingled, one within the other;
A lengthy kiss upon the coolness of a mouth.
Then we wander down dazzling white paths
Across the meadow underneath a rain of blossoms,
The day brings us this first kiss –
Far as I'm concerned, we are turning towards God
Who must come towards us across this plain.

It was not, however, just the lovers' hands and mouths that were intermingled: Rilke's words were set amid a stiff and stylized shower of flowers and interwoven stems. Josef Hoffmann's design had the unyielding appearance of black-and-white stained glass, its rigidity contrasting with the much softer imagery of the poem.

Rilke was featured again in the April 1899 issue, which included a series of three short, dramatic prose pieces, *Masks (A Coloured Sketch)*.

ABOVE LEFT ◆ EIN DECORATIVER FLECK IN 'ROTH UND GRÜN'. 1898. KOLOMAN MOSER (1868–1918)
OPPOSITE ◆ PORTRAIT OF A GIRL. 1897. KOLOMAN MOSER (1868–1918)

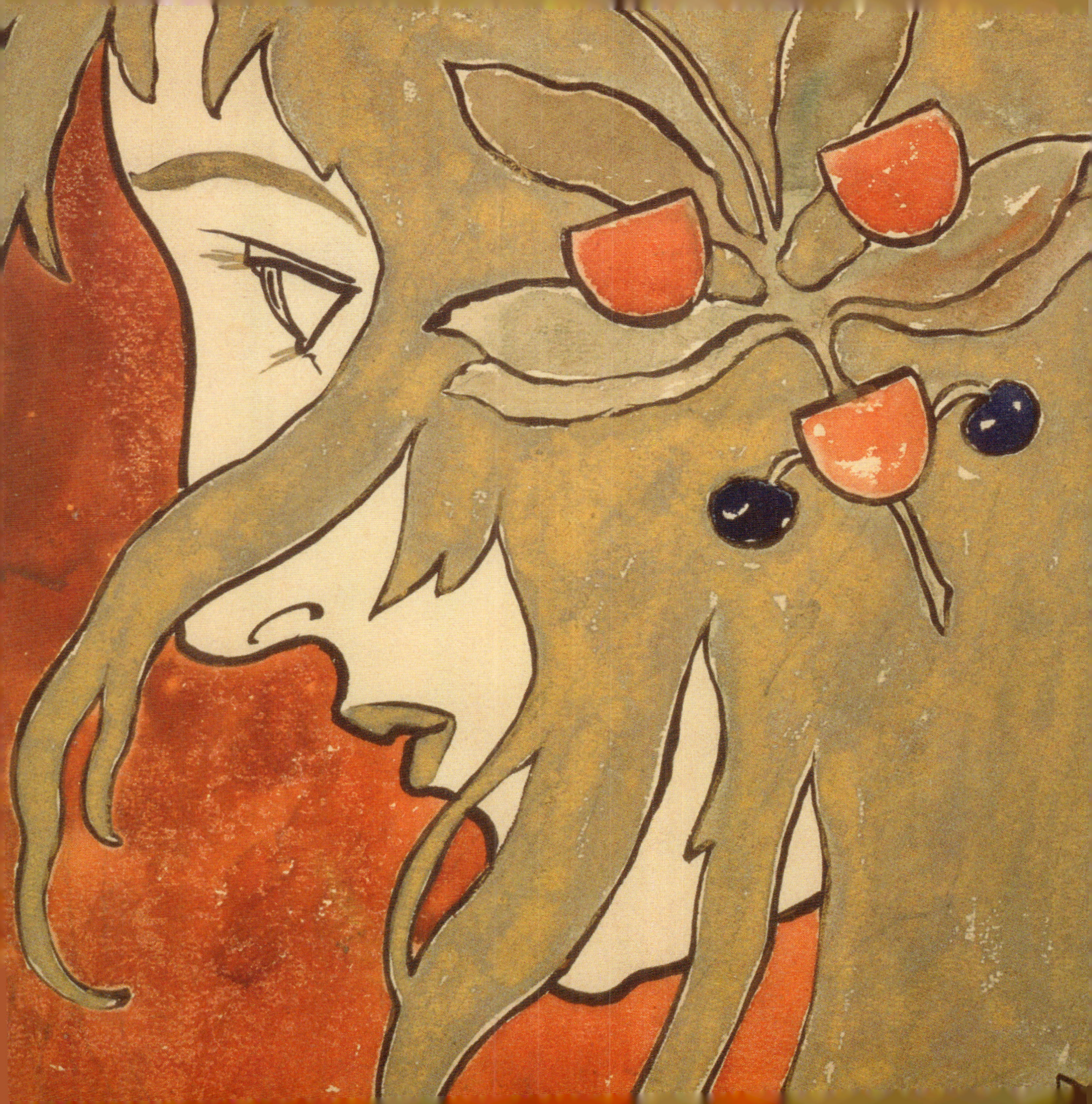

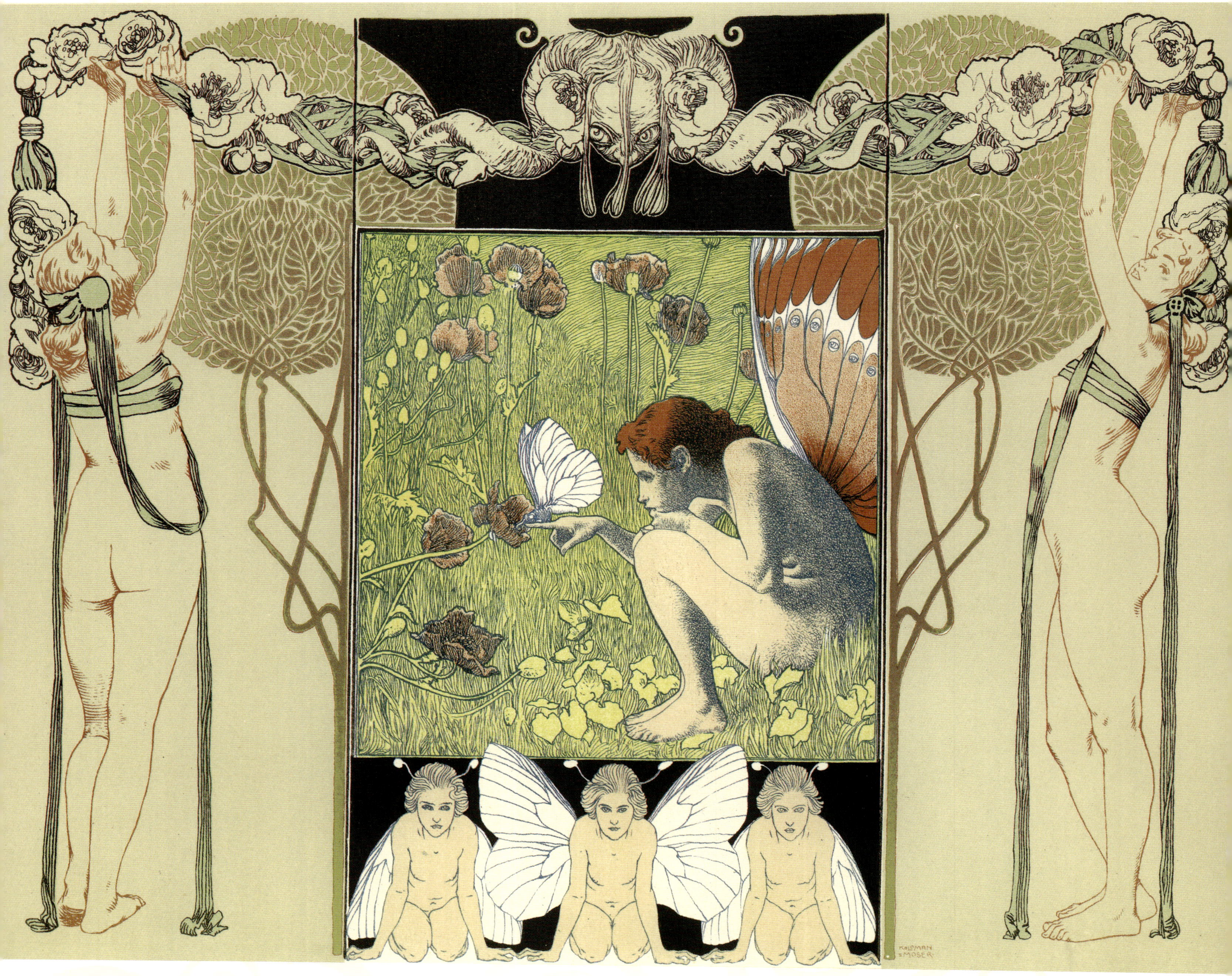

ABOVE ◆ SUMMER. ILLUSTRATION FOR GERLACH'S ALLEGORIES, 1896/97. KOLOMAN MOSER (1868–1918)

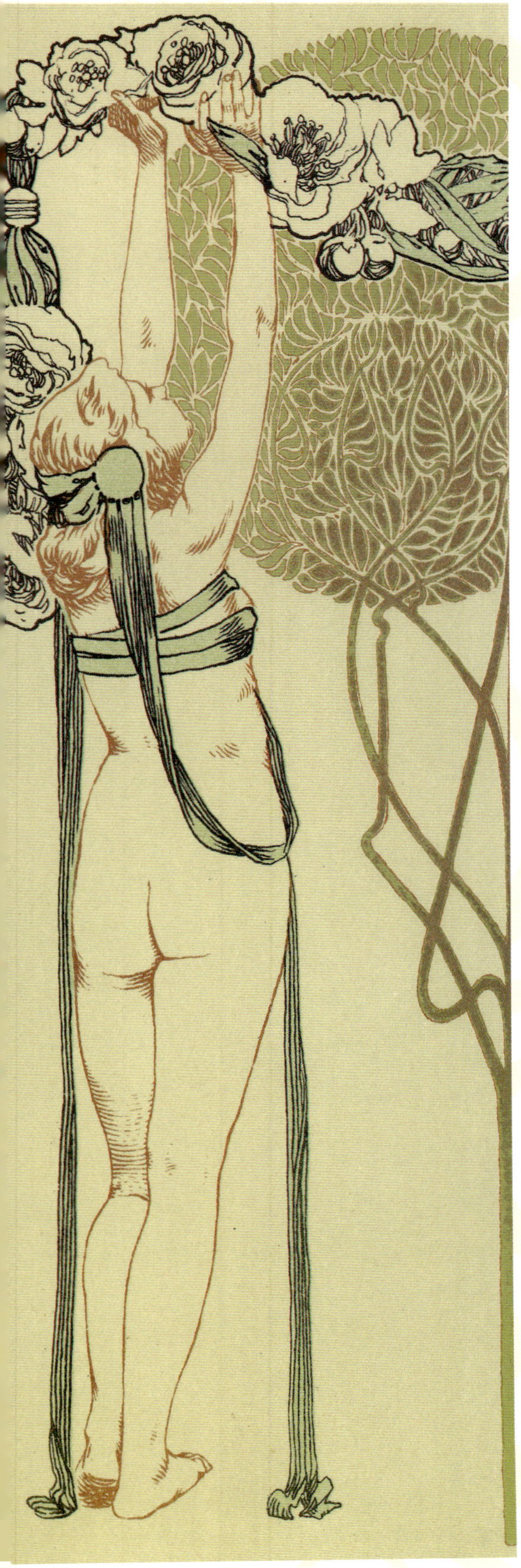

Essentially, this was the account of an episode in the life of the 'Julius Caesar of Austria', an illegitimate son of the Emperor Rudolf II (1552–1612) and his relationship with a poor barber's daughter, with whom he'd become obsessed. A story of degeneracy, madness, murder – and, as the title 'Masks' suggests, hypocrisy – it could be seen as a horrifically unfunny satire on the society of its time. Atop elaborately decorative columns either side of Rilke's text grinned malicious-looking masks, apparently amused by the story they accompanied. Alfred Roller was responsible for these.

Evolutionary Change

The November 1898 issue of *Ver Sacrum* included the first of three important poems by the German writer Arno Holz (1863–1929). Holz was the man of the moment thanks to his shockingly realistic – and deliberately formless – Zola-inspired dramas and the outrageously difficult, unrhyming verse in which (following the natural rhythms of the language) he explored the ideas of Darwinism. 'Seven billion years before I was born, I was an Iris,' he wrote in this poem. 'Beneath my shimmering roots another star circled./A gigantic flower, I floated upon its dark waters.' Koloman Moser illustrated these lines (though again this verb barely begins to do his achievement justice) with a glorious scene of metamorphosis, a human form emerging from the vast veined petals of a flower (*see* page 76).

December's issue was dedicated to the Symbolist painter Fernand Khnopff (1858–1921), who was Belgian-born although of Austrian descent. Khnopff specialized in sensuous and beautiful but enigmatic works that appeared to be allegories although it was never quite clear of what. Nobody appeared to mind. The nine works he sent for inclusion in the Secessionists' first exhibition earlier that year had

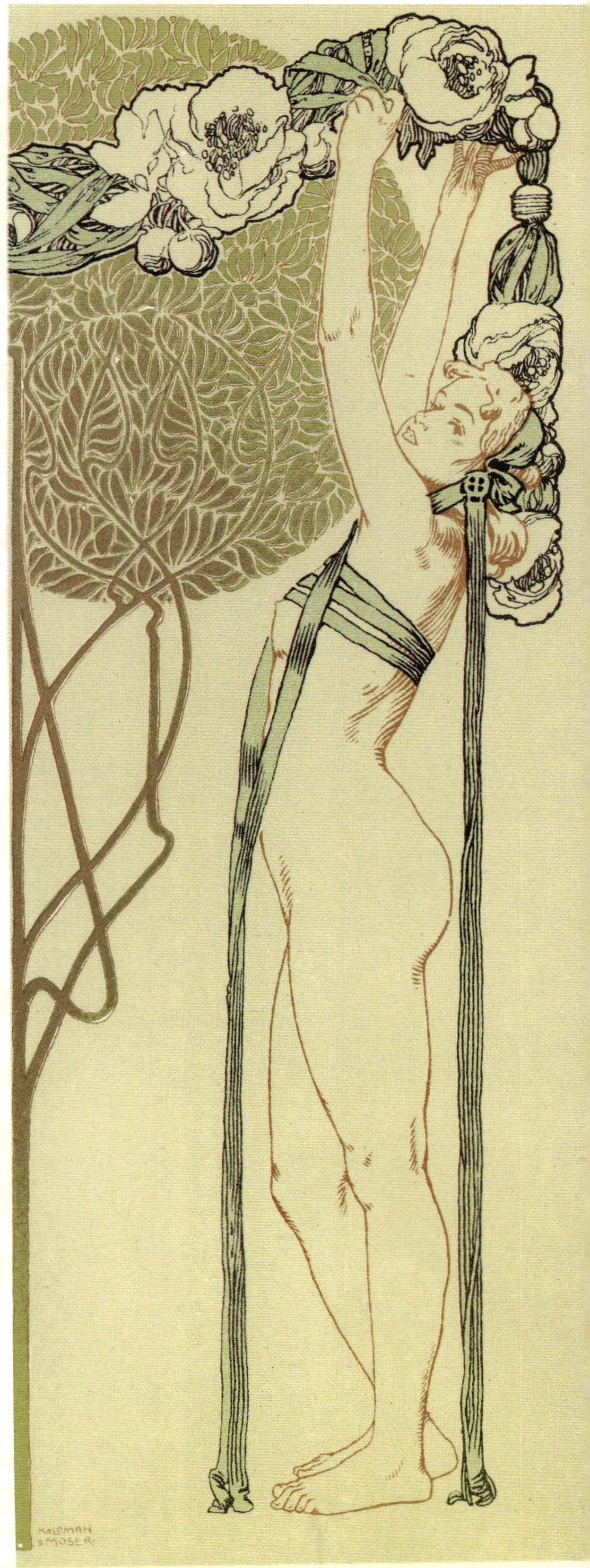

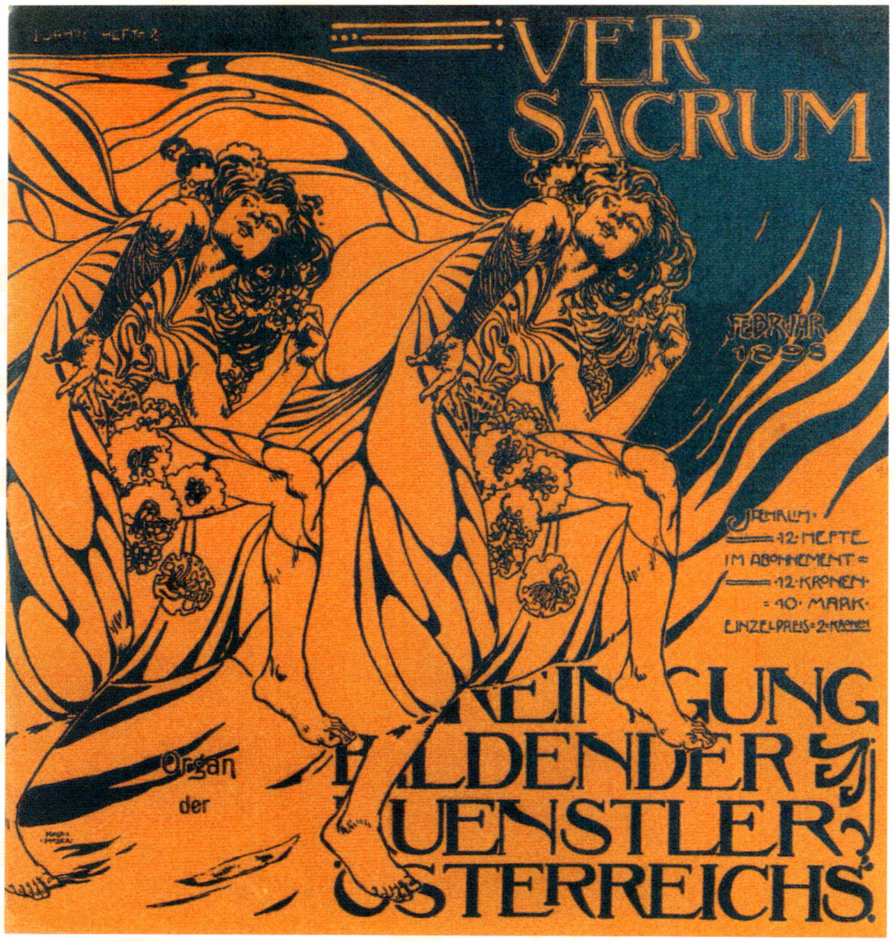

turned out to be the show's main attraction, and his admirers in Vienna included Gustav Klimt.

Symbols and Allegories

In the opinion of Hermann Bahr, Khnopff had in common with Klimt 'that elegance of the soul that would rather not be understood at all than decide to speak out and cause discord'. A series of strange, stiff, inscrutable female figures with masked faces (or expressions) testifies to Klimt's fascination with the work of Khnopff. They include *Tragoedie* (1897, *see* page 71), *Pallas Athena* (1898, *see* page 60) and *Nuda Veritas* (1899, *see* page 49).

Khnopff himself designed the issue's cover, understated and enigmatic, its central image a gloved hand reaching up with a flower stalk towards a ring in which the three-shield symbol of the Secession is set. Inside, the only purpose-drawn pictures were those for a text by his fellow Belgian, Maurice Maeterlinck, the marionette play *La Mort de Tintagiles.* Written two years earlier, in 1896, this play had already formed the basis of a symphonic poem by the German-American composer Charles Martin Loeffler (1861–1935), lending yet another resonance to its inclusion. (Another grown-up play for marionettes, *Interior,* was also reproduced in *Ver Sacrum.* This remains among Maeterlinck's most highly regarded dramas, its puppet characters embodying the helplessness of human beings before an unheeding fate.)

The Masks of Man

An essay on Khnopff's work by Hermann Bahr was illustrated with reproductions taken from the painter's work, including a striking one of the 1897 watercolour *La Défiance.* Determined but utterly unfathomable, this female figure gazes out at the viewer, as though challenging us to understand. She wouldn't make too bad an emblem for Fernand Khnopff and his oeuvre as a whole – or indeed for this edition of *Ver Sacrum.* Like Maeterlinck, Bahr argued, Khnopff saw reality as no more than a mask; the task of the writer or artist was to create what could be no more than inadequate sketches of the eternal verities.

Hugo von Hofmannsthal worried at the same difficulty in his poem 'World Secret'. Like Maeterlinck before him (*see* page 55), he drew an analogy between the evasiveness of language and that of water:

ABOVE LEFT ◆ DANCING GIRLS. VER SACRUM. 1898. KOLOMAN MOSER (1868–1918)
OPPOSITE ◆ SPRING MORNING. FOR GERLACH'S ALLEGORIES. 1896/97. KOLOMAN MOSER (1868–1918)

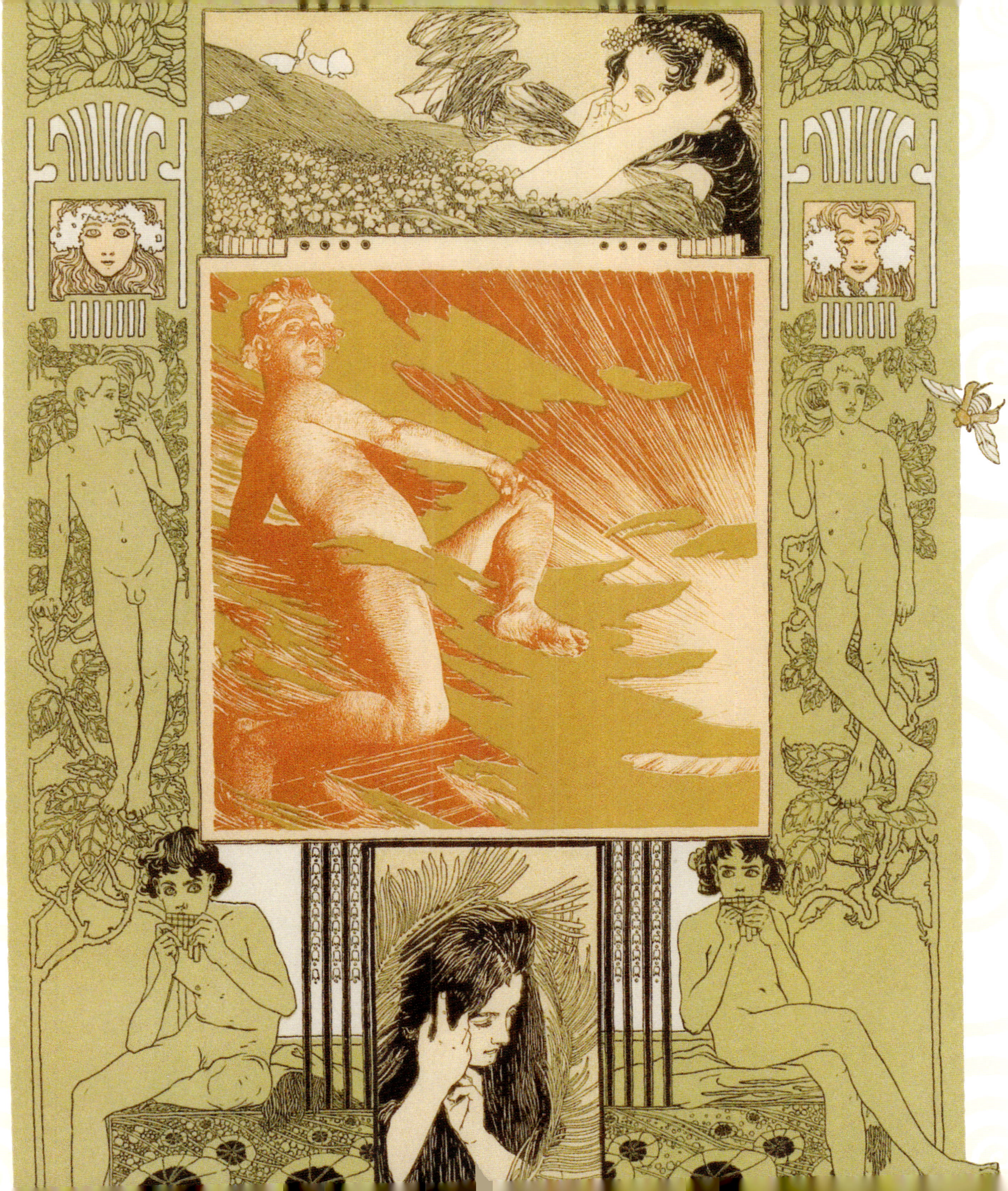

The deep well knows it, that's for sure:
There was a time when all was deep and still
And at that time everyone knew everything.

Like the script a little child recites,
The story flits from one person's lips to another's
Without anybody actually understanding it.

The deep well knows it, that's for sure:
And if he were to lean down into it, a man would understand.
Once he came up again, though, the thought would go …

Like Schopenhauer, Hofmannsthal held that humankind existed in a state of alienation from a universe with which they had once (the time when 'everyone knew everything') lived in a happy harmony they'd been trying desperately to recapture ever since. Khnopff too, Bahr said in his essay in this issue, was always trying to capture the ineffable in his art. One of Khnopff's pictures – an elegantly dressed woman holding up a sword, who seemingly represented *La Solitude* (1891) – accompanied Hofmannsthal's poem.

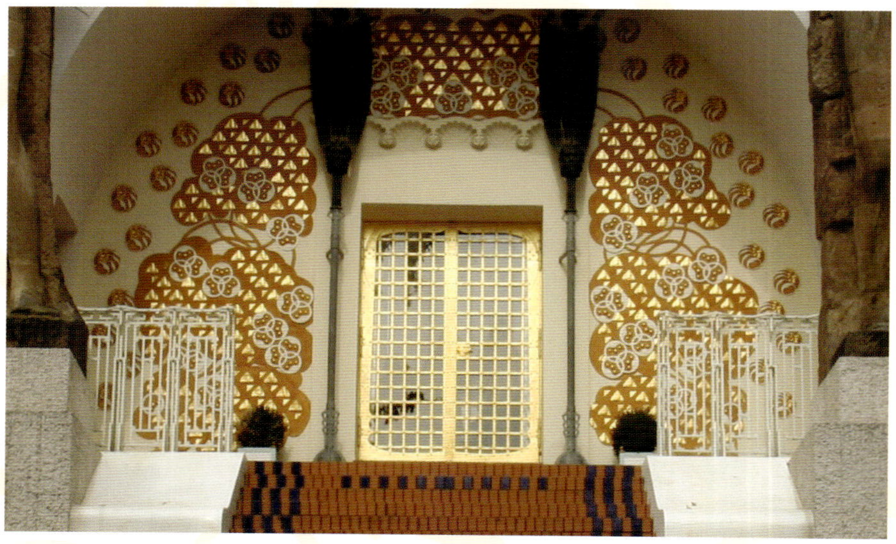

Cultural Relations

The first issue of *Ver Sacrum* in 1899 was largely given over to Olbrich's Secession Building, which had opened its doors the preceding autumn, but along with another essay by Rilke, 'On Art', it also featured several poems by 'Paul Althof'. In reality, this was the pen-name of Alice Gurschner (1869–1944); her husband Gustav Gurschner (1873–1970) was a Secessionist sculptor. The most memorable of the poems – in part on account of being framed by some striking lilies by Koloman Moser – bore the Klimtian title 'The Kiss', and as in the great man's most famous painting, the kiss here had as much to do with death as with eroticism. Powerful stuff, though – especially when on the facing left-hand page, in a sketch by Klimt himself, sprawled a slightly sardonic-looking beauty in black-and-white.

Klimt kept up his connection with the magazine: his literary interests are well attested, although he must also have appreciated the opportunity it gave him to explore other aspects of his art apart from painting. The celebrity of a few great canvases, while in itself richly deserved, has done an injustice to the breadth and complexity of the artist's work. The exploration of the relation of one image with another was a vitally important aspect of what *Ver Sacrum* was about – and, of course, essential to the overall construction of the *Gesamtkunstwerk*. The way 'his' woman here echoed and interacted with Moser's – and, of course, with the poem of 'Paul Althof' – was an example.

Internal Connections

Interrelationships existed between Klimt's own works, both in *Ver Sacrum* and beyond. The painting *Pallas Athena* (1898, *see* page 60)

LEFT ◆ ERNST LUDWIG HOUSE, DARMSTADT, BUILT 1900–01 JOSEPH MARIA OLBRICH (1867–1908)
OPPOSITE ◆ DECORATIVE INLAY, MUSIC HALL, VIENNA, 1898, JOSEPH MARIA OLBRICH (1867–1908)

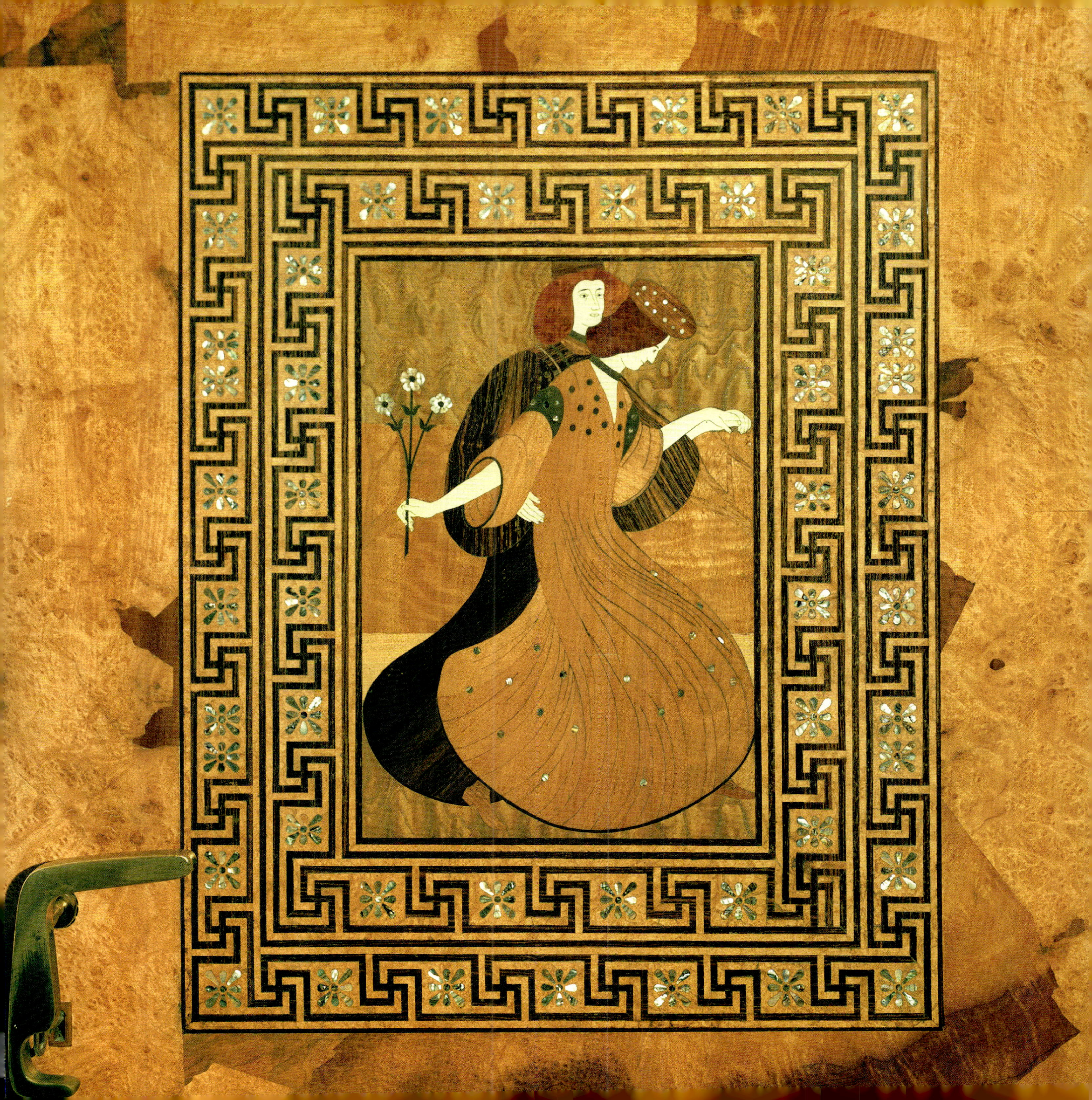

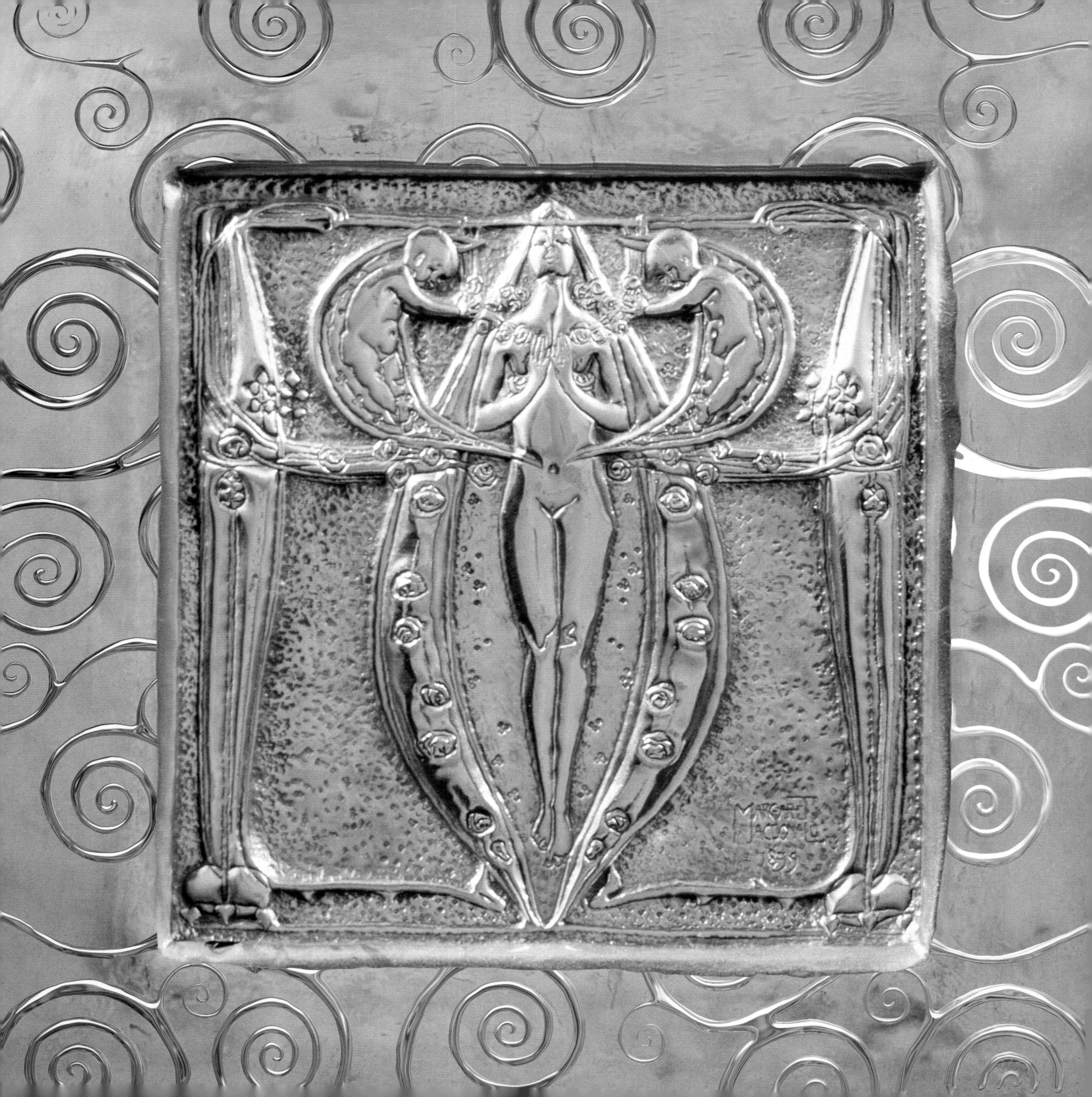

was followed by a brush-and-pen vignette version included in *Ver Sacrum* in 1900 – and also adapted for use as a Secessionist *ex libris* label (*see* page 61). Although his *Nuda Veritas* is most famous in its painted form (1899; *see* page 49), a version had appeared the year before in the March issue of *Ver Sacrum*, executed in black crayon, graphics, pen, and brush in ink (*see* page 25). Here, instead of the painter's shimmering glow, we have an unsparing starkness, and – instead of Goethe – a quotation from the novelist Leopold Schefer (1784–1862): 'Truth is fire. And to speak the truth is to shine and burn'; rather as Lady Veritas does in the following year's painting, it might be thought. But these two visions of Truth don't exist only in relation to each other – any more than Truth can exist in pure abstraction from existence as it is. On the same page as the *Ver Sacrum* version is another allegorical image: that of *Neid*, or Envy, gowned in black and with a serpent coiling round her neck. In this context, we can't imagine one without the other.

Some of Klimt's contributions to *Ver Sacrum* can be seen as preliminary trial runs for later work – though this is a reductive way of regarding what might better be viewed as the progressive exploration of an especially important theme or image. Hence the handsome lithograph, *Music* (1895, *see* page 48) – with a classically-robed woman standing, playing on a lyre – anticipates a similar image in the *Beethoven Frieze* (*see* page 103). It was in the nature of Secessionist art that the image didn't just stand for itself – or for an allegorized 'truth' – but existed in relation to other artworks and to the world.

Travels and Flights of Fantasy

The featured artist in another issue was Johann Victor Krämer (1861–1949), a traveller in the Near and Middle East, represented by striking scenes and portraits from the Arabian Desert and the Greek

OPPOSITE ◆ DECORATIVE PANEL OF BEATEN METAL, 1898–99, MARGARET MACDONALD (1865–1933) (BACKGROUND ADAPTED)

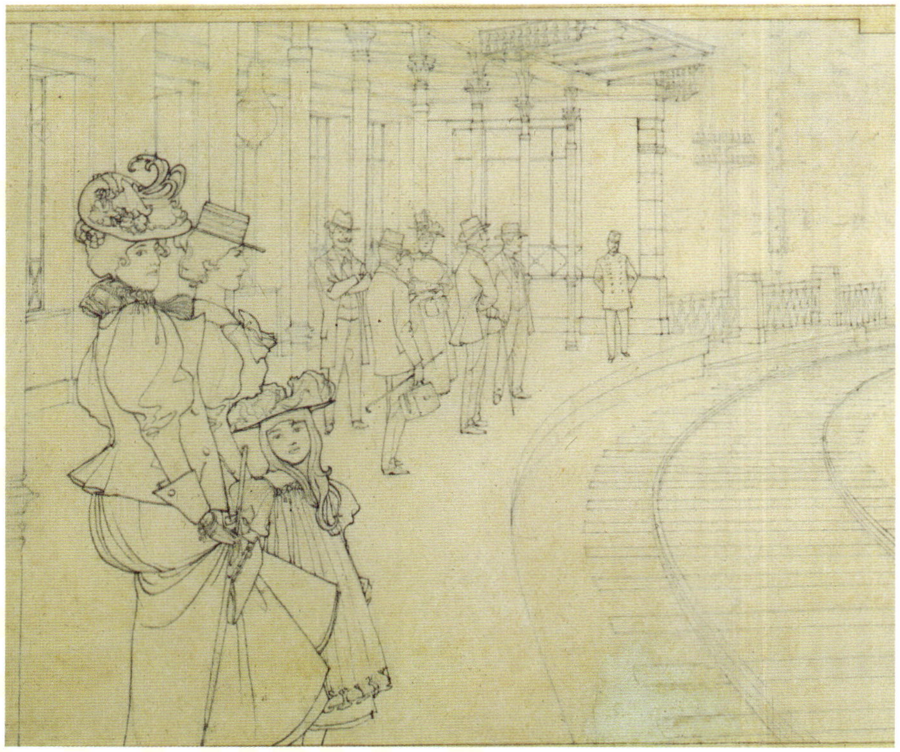

Islands. Along with some bravura studies of Christ's Passion in the Renaissance style, there was a nude personification of Springtime, her alabaster body set off by the burgeoning vegetation by which she was framed, her snowy bosoms picked up by the sprays of white blossom all around.

Ver Sacrum's Midas touch wasn't always infallible. In this same issue, the now-all-but-forgotten Austrian poet Paul Wertheimer (1874–1937) contributed an elegy to the similarly lesser known Swiss poet Conrad Ferdinand Meyer (1825–98). Of more enduring interest was one of those grotesquely fantastical stories for which the German author, architect and illustrator Paul Scheerbart (1863–1915) was celebrated. This one, however, had pictures not by the writer, but by a home-grown Austrian artist of the macabre, Rudolf Jettmar (1869–1939). The winner of 1920's Nobel Prize for Literature, Norwegian writer Knut Hamsun (1859–1952) can hardly be described as 'forgotten' – though the fact that he contributed to *Ver Sacrum* in April 1899 largely has been. His story 'The Son Himself' was given the Koloman Moser treatment, illustrated with the figure of a youth sitting in a tree, one hand holding a branch and the other upraised, with three silver stars rising up from it.

ABOVE LEFT AND OPPOSITE ◆ THE EXTERIOR AND A VIEW OF THE RAILWAY PLATFORM OF THE STADTBAHN PAVILION OF THE VIENNA UNDERGROUND RAILWAY, c. 1894–97. OTTO WAGNER (1841–1918)

Songs and Symbols

Music wasn't forgotten, difficult as it is to imagine a printed journal reproducing music – even song lyrics – to any great advantage. But such scepticism reckons without the full-spectrum Secession openness to every single aspect of artistic creativity. German music, since the days of monastic chant and Bach's chorales, had been quick to combine words and music: the quintessential German genre, the *Lied*, or song, represented the classic coming together of literature and musical composition. Richard Wagner (1813–83), in his operas, had made the first sustained attempt to create a *Gesamtkunstwerk* – a word that he himself coined in 1849.

The celebrated Hungarian composer Franz Liszt (1811–86) had also, with his 'programme music', developed this idea further. In the solo piano pieces of his *Années de Pèlerinage* ('Years of Pilgrimage', 1835–8), for example, he had responded musically to some of Petrarch's sonnets and to paintings by Raphael (1483–1520). The idea of the 'symphonic poem' was his. *Mazeppa* (1851) was a treatment of an 1819 work by the British poet George Gordon, Lord Byron (1788–1824), while *Tasso, Lamento e Triunfo* (1849) was based on a play by Goethe commemorating the Italian Renaissance poet Torquato Tasso (1544–95). Liszt also wrote a *Faust Symphony* that had premiered in 1857, the same year as his *Dante Symphony*. The composer, who saw himself as a 'painter-symphonist', had even

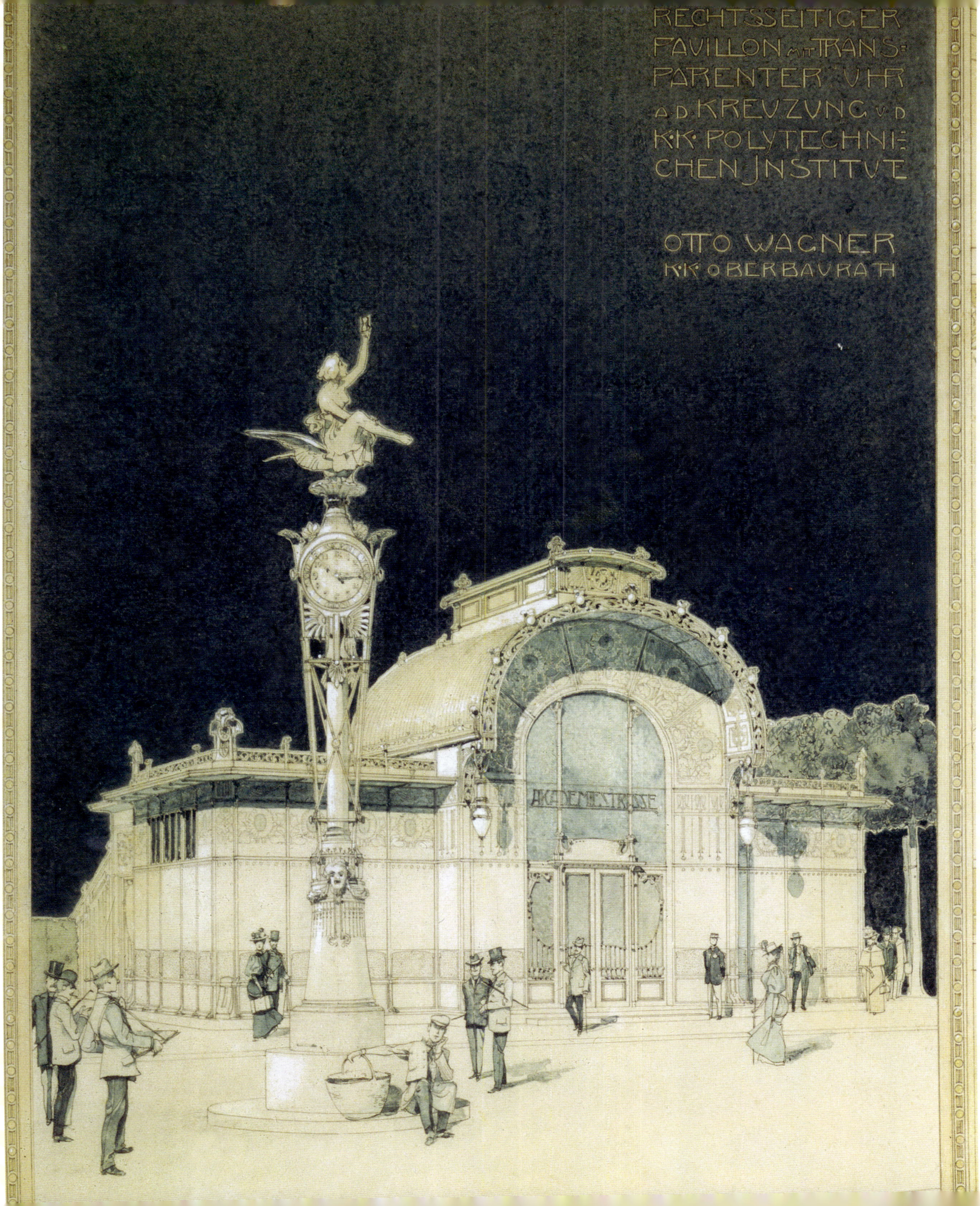
RECHTSSEITIGER PAVILLON MIT TRANS- PARENTER UHR A.D. KREUZUNG V.D. K.K. POLYTECHNISCHEN INSTITUTE
OTTO WAGNER
K.K. OBERBAURATH
AKADEMIESTRASSE

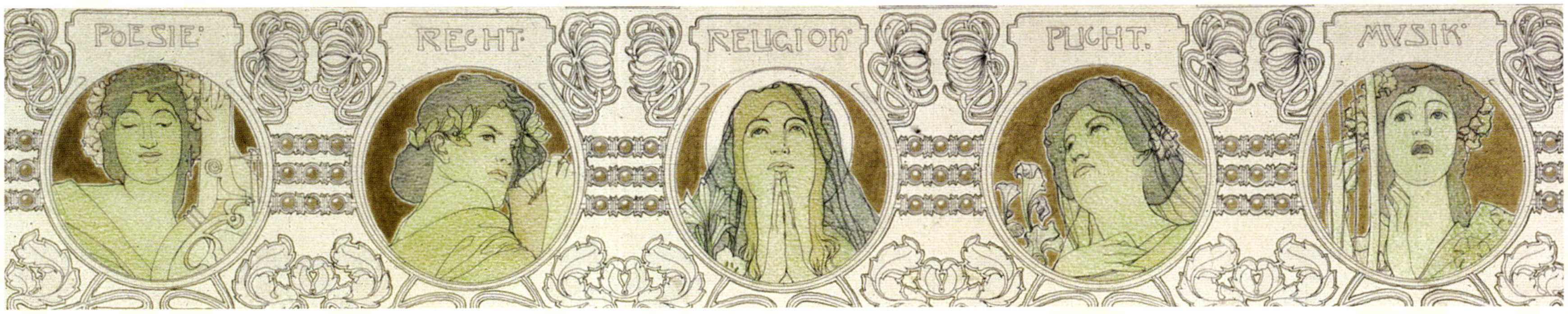

envisaged creating, in collaboration with the German artist Wilhelm von Kaulbach (1805–74) and a poet who hadn't yet been decided on, a massive multimedia *World History in Colours and Tones*.

A Celebration of Composers

It made sense, then, that the Secessionists would want to bring about a meeting between their work and that of the contemporary musicians of Austria and Germany. The December 1901 edition of *Ver Sacrum* was given over to the presentation of recent developments in *Lieder* by composers at this time working in Vienna. Most of these have been forgotten: the one real exception is Hugo Wolf (1860–1903), still highly regarded for his contribution to German-language culture. Though born in Slovenia, Wolf had moved to the imperial capital with his family in boyhood and gone to school and grown up in Vienna. His love for *Lieder* was evident from early on, but his interest in the works of Richard Wagner made him more ambitious in his aims. Along with songs for voice and piano, he created operatic, choral and orchestral works – marked increasingly by dissonance and experimental harmonies. The sound of Wolf's compositions – and those of others like Eugen d'Albert (1864–1932), Conrad Ansorge (1862–1930) and August Stradal (1860–1930) – could not of course be captured in *Ver Sacrum*'s pages, but this didn't mean that they had to be ignored.

ABOVE AND OPPOSITE ◆ DESIGN FOR THE HALL OF HONOUR, ACADEMY OF FINE ARTS, VIENNA, 1898, OTTO WAGNER (1841–1918)

Printed in black, and adorned with glittering silver throughout, this special celebratory issue set out the songs in their staves, with stunningly decorative surrounds. This was an artefact to be treasured: so much so that it was hard to see it – in its silent flatness – as a limitation on the power of music. Rather it was a reminder that song existed in other emotional spaces and aesthetic planes.

Poetry in Harmony

Hugo Wolf's contribution was a setting of Goethe's poem 'Anakreons Grab' ('Anacreon's Grave').

Here, where roses flower and where creepers twine round laurel trees,
Where the turtle-dove coos, and the happy cricket chirps away …
Tell me: to whom does this grave belong, dressed and decorated as
it is by the gods

With beautiful vegetation? Here lies Anacreon
Who lived happily through Spring, Summer and Autumn,
And now sleeps sheltered from Winter's cruelty by this
kind mound.

Anacreon (*c.* 582–*c.* 485 BC) had been a lyric poet, so Goethe was arguably commemorating himself here – as now was Hugo Wolf.

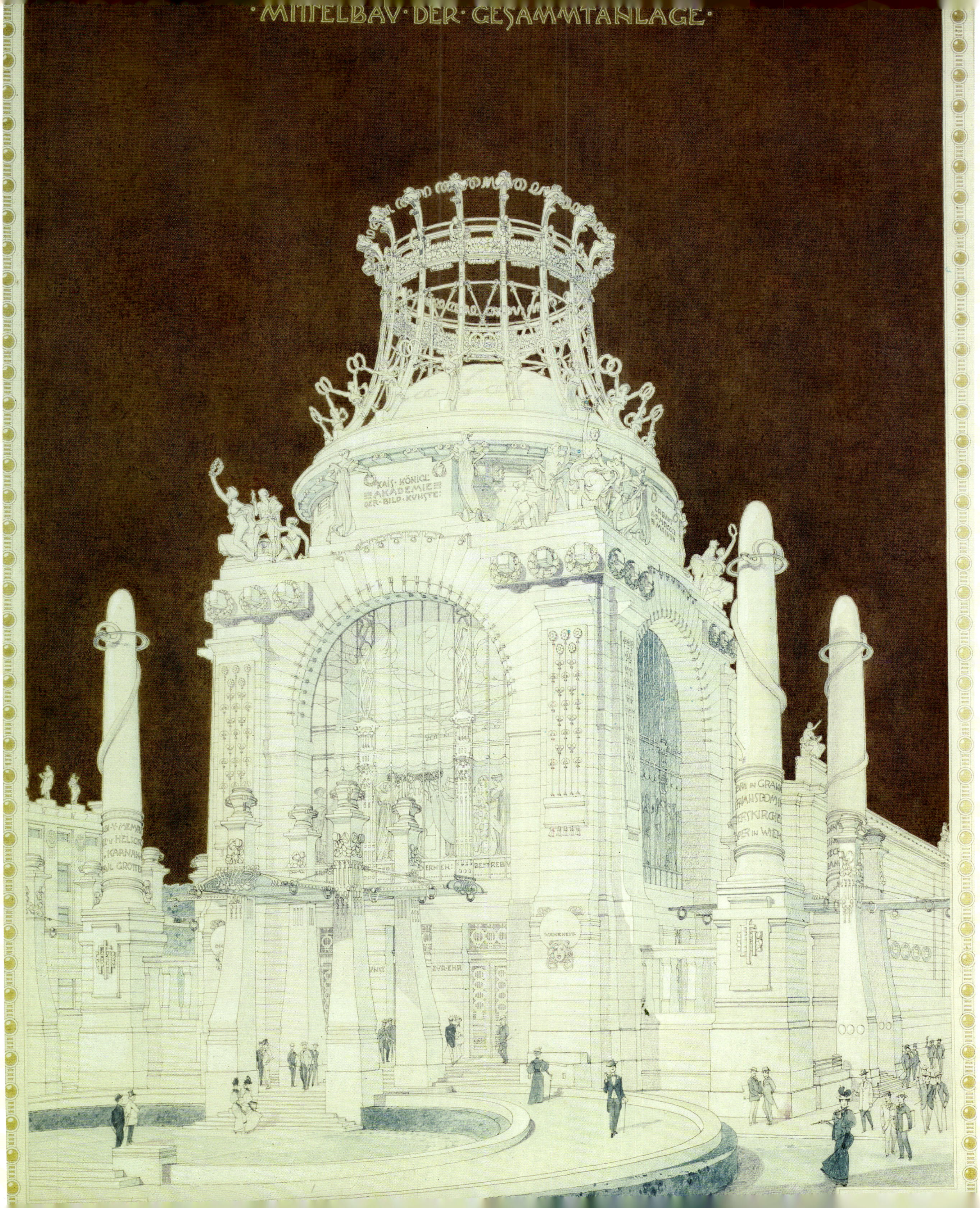
· MITTELBAU · DER · GESAMMTANLAGE ·
KAIS · KÖNIGL · AKADEMIE DER · BILD · KUNSTE ·

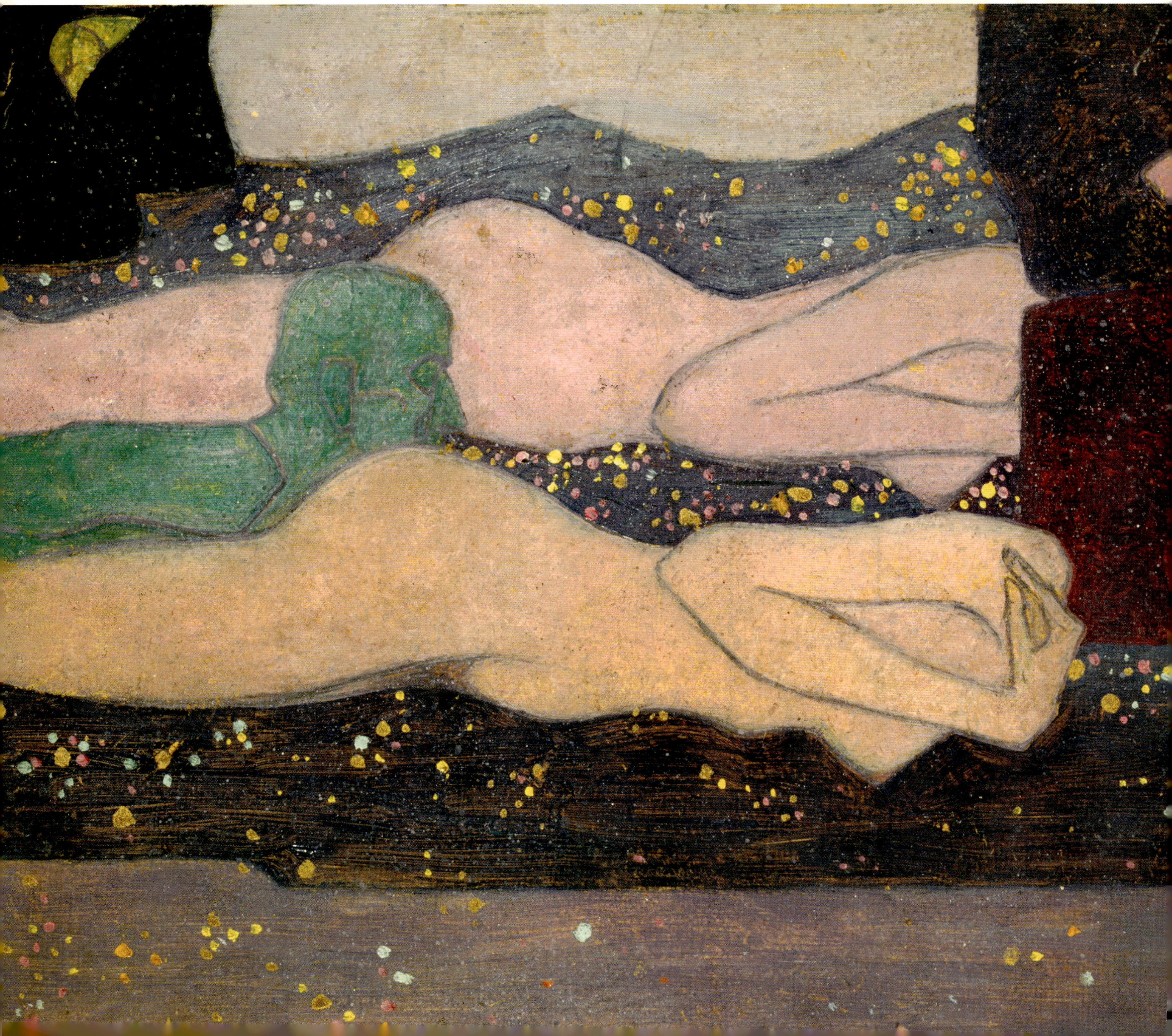

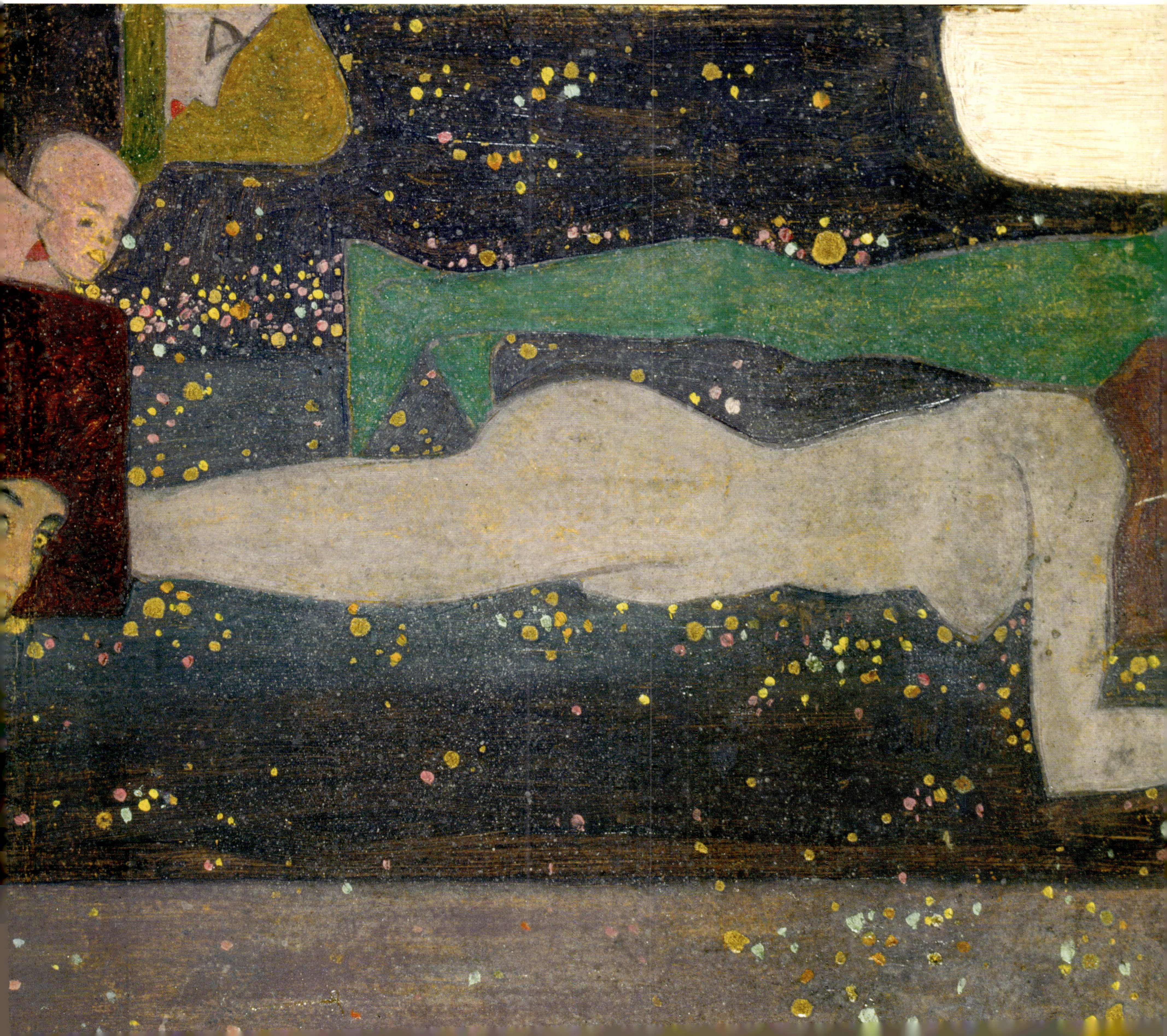

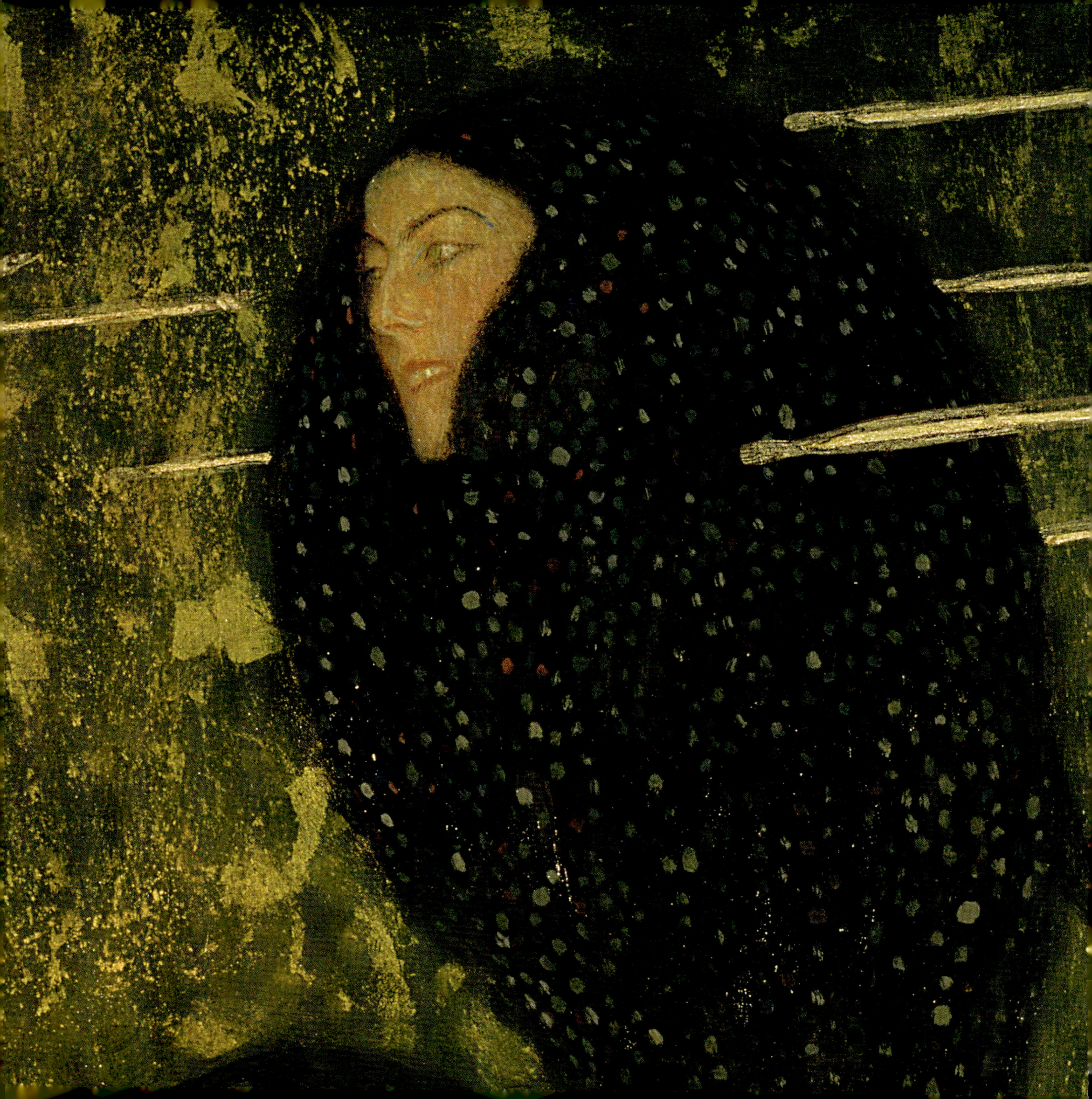

Inscribed on the page as on a gravestone, Goethe's text reads like an epitaph, drawing a line under a life that, at the same time, it immortalized. Wolf's music both breathed new life into the poet's words and was invigorated in its turn: art, music and literature sang in harmony.

All the World's a Stage

In 1888, after offering the city over a century of spectacle and society, Vienna's Burgtheater closed its doors. A new and more modern venue was about to open by the Ringstrasse. Before its unique atmosphere was lost for ever, the city fathers asked Gustav Klimt and his friend Franz Matsch (1861–1942) to record views of the auditorium as it had been on performance nights. While Matsch took the view of the auditorium looking towards the stage, Klimt showed the view from the stage, out across the fine and fashionable audience of the stalls to where the galleries rose in tier after tier to the ornate ceiling above with its dazzling chandelier. As we look, we are at the theatre, but where we might expect to see the actors, instead we see a throng of Vienna's leading citizens.

By the standards of Klimt's later work, *Auditorium of the Old Burgtheater* (1888) seems academic and a bit mundane, but it does capture the sense of occasion, the excited buzz. For, as writer Stefan Zweig later recalled, the Burgtheater had been much more than a place of entertainment: it had been the beating heart of Viennese life. For the Austrian, he insisted, it was 'more than a stage upon which actors enacted parts; it was the microcosm that mirrored the macrocosm, the brightly coloured reflection in which the city saw itself.'

Zweig described how, after the curtain fell on its final night, the theatre's stage had been stormed by souvenir-hunters determined

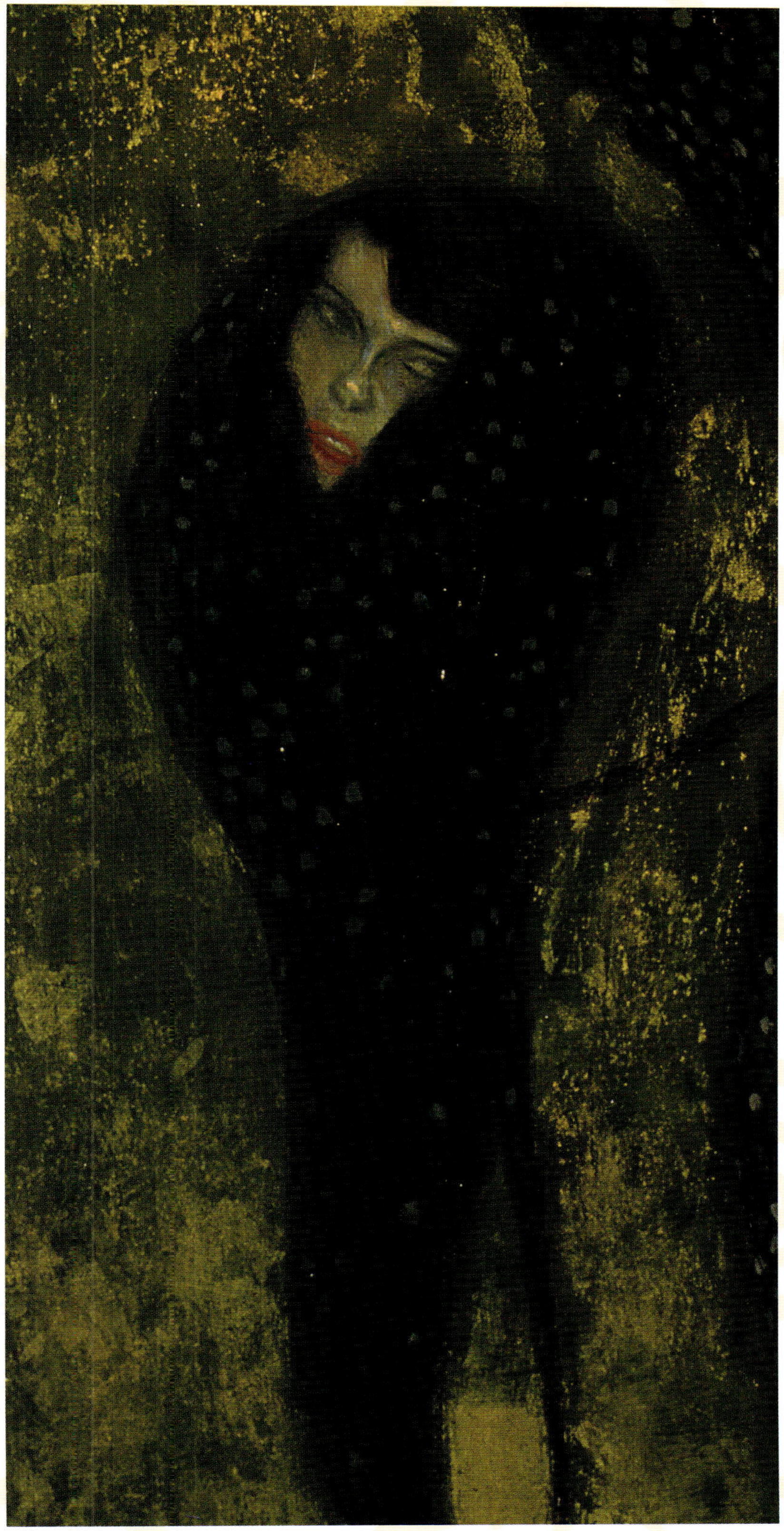

PREVIOUS PAGE ◆ WATER SPRITES, 1907, EGON SCHIELE (1890–1918)
OPPOSITE AND RIGHT ◆ WATER SPRITES, 1899, GUSTAV KLIMT (1862–1918)

'to bring home at least a splinter of the boards which the beloved artists had trod'.

A Tragic Commission

As it happened, Klimt was also to have a stake in the city's new Burgtheater, having been commissioned to paint the ceilings above its main staircases. One showed Shakespeare's Globe in London – its very name a reminder that the world could be a stage. A performance of *Romeo and Juliet* was being enacted, its young hero and heroine lying prone in tragic death: perhaps an oddly downbeat image with which to present the Vienna bourgeoisie as they made their way to their expensive seats.

Well, yes and no: Klimt's picture of 1886 certainly showed that drama might be a matter of life and death, and that the latter might very likely triumph in the end. But it showed as well the scope of art, its ability to encompass everything – and our ability to engage with everything through it. For Klimt didn't just depict Shakespeare's players; he also showed their audience watching spellbound – experiencing, feeling the scene.

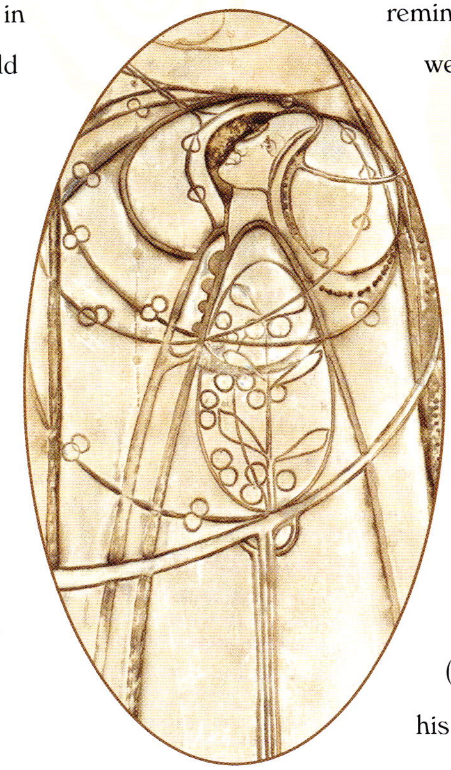

A City on Show

Surviving sketches attest to the trouble Klimt took to do justice to the lifeless Romeo and (especially) Juliet. She certainly looks beautiful in death. That mattered, because as Zweig explained, death was just another stage in a cycle of Viennese existence in which every single stage had a public aspect:

Even funerals found enthusiastic audiences and it was the ambition of every true Viennese to have a 'lovely corpse', with a majestic procession and many followers; even his death converted the genuine Viennese into a spectacle for others.

Klimt's portrayal of Miss *Ria Munk on her Deathbed* (1912, *see* page 63) took this idea to macabre extremes, perhaps, but it reminds us of the extent to which life – and even death – were a performance. The logical conclusion of the quest for the *Gesamtkunstwerk* was that art had no beginning and no end; everyday life became the acting of a part.

This is maybe why many of the most fêted writers of this period were so quickly forgotten. Much of their creativity went into their daily lives. 'Café society' surely existed in all Europe's great cities, but in Vienna, it had an importance all its own. Stefan Zweig, celebrated in his day as one of the world's foremost writers, is now remembered chiefly (in *The World of Yesterday*, 1942) as a chronicler of his time.

Life as Art

Peter Altenberg (1859–1919) was another writer more revered in his day than read in ours: he held court in cafés, dazzling all with his wit, his insight and his aphoristic verses. In hindsight, it's hard to avoid concluding that he dribbled out his talents a coffee, a lunch, a drink, a dinner at a time: perpetually strapped for funds, he had to sing for his supper every day.

ABOVE • INGRAM STREET TEA ROOMS PANEL, 1900. CHARLES RENNIE MACKINTOSH (1868–1928)
OPPOSITE • A CONCORDIA BALL PROGRAMME, 1909. JOSEF HOFFMANN (1870–1956)

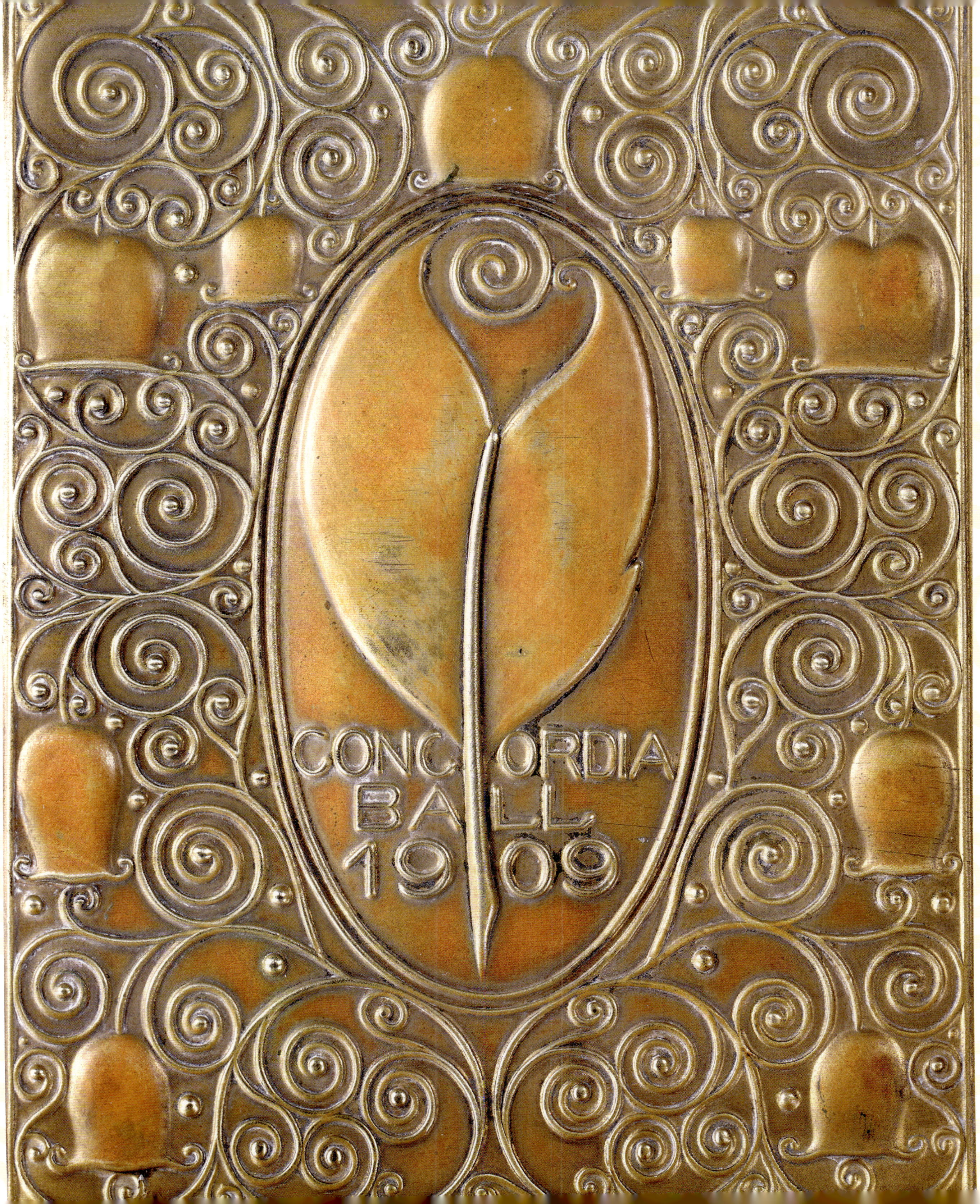
CONCORDIA
BALL
1909

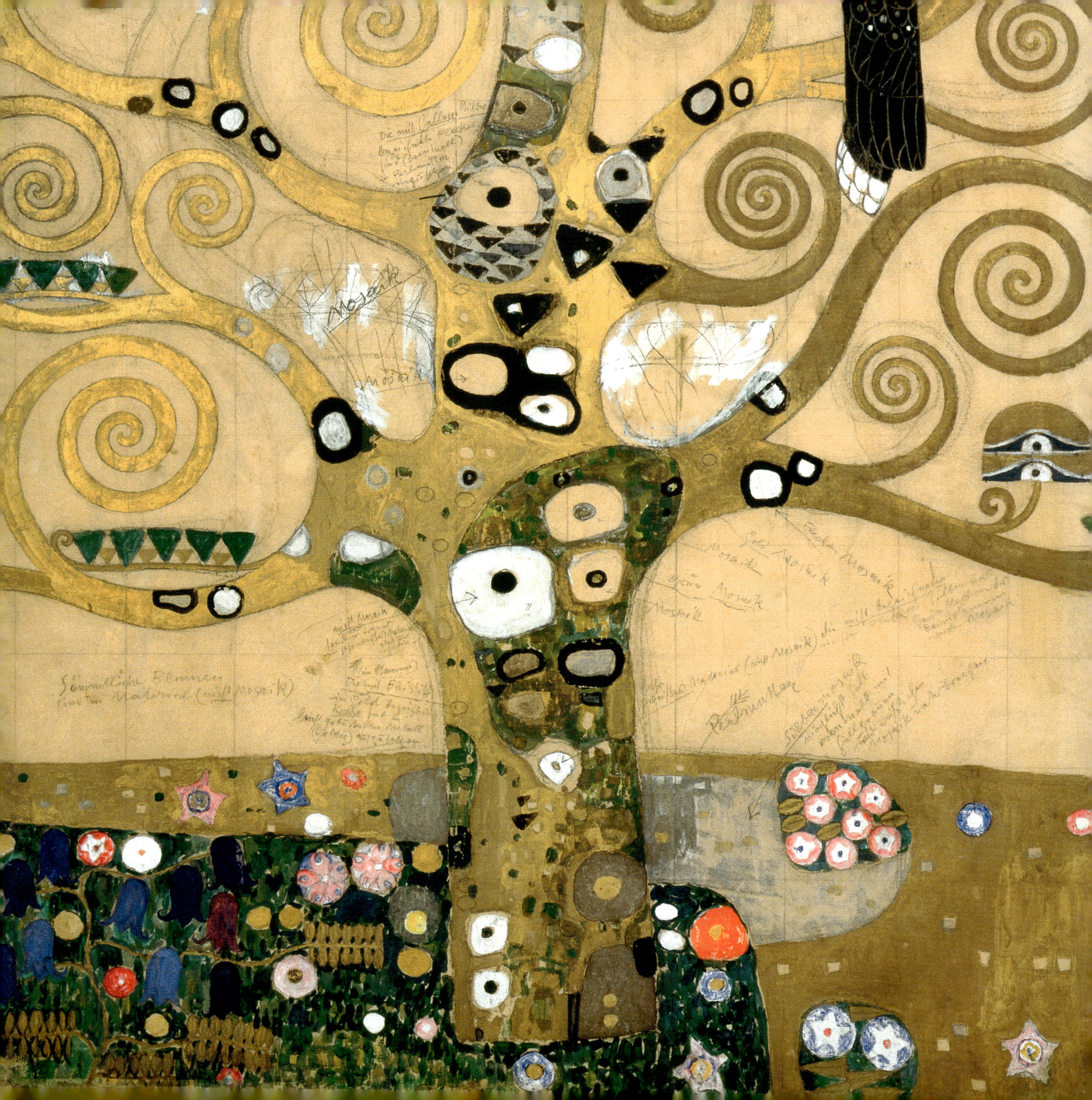
Mosaik

Should we thank his friends for feeding him, or criticize them as exploiters of his talent? The world would never have known of him, after all, had it not been for their good offices. Altenberg's first book, a collection of sketches called *As I See It* (1896), appeared only after the writer and journalist Karl Kraus (1874–1936) and the playwright Arthur Schnitzler culled some of Altenberg's witticisms from his reviews and conversations and sent them off for publication. Even so – and even though a grateful Altenberg went on to publish several more collections of this kind – their intervention may seem overbearing. Like Oscar Wilde, Altenberg put much of his best work into his life.

Gesamtkunstwerk

It says much about his age though, that Altenberg's death was so widely and sincerely mourned: he received obituaries from Hugo von Hofmannsthal, Thomas Mann and many more. But he's now remembered mostly for the words with which he praised his good friend Gustav Klimt: 'As a discerning painter, you are also a modern philosopher, an entirely modern poet!' There was for Altenberg, as for the Vienna Secession generation as a whole, no difference in category between these titles, these walks of life.

A poem, a play, a picture, a book (or decorated bookmark), a conversation, an opera, a walk down the street, a sitting room, a sculpture: all these could and should be works of art. Or rather, ideally, aspects of a greater *Gesamtkunstwerk* in which each part exists both in itself and in relation to the other parts around it – and so on, and so forth, ad infinitum. Seen this way, the Secession wasn't so much a breaking-away from anything as a joining, a signing-up to something: an enlistment in the wider world of art.

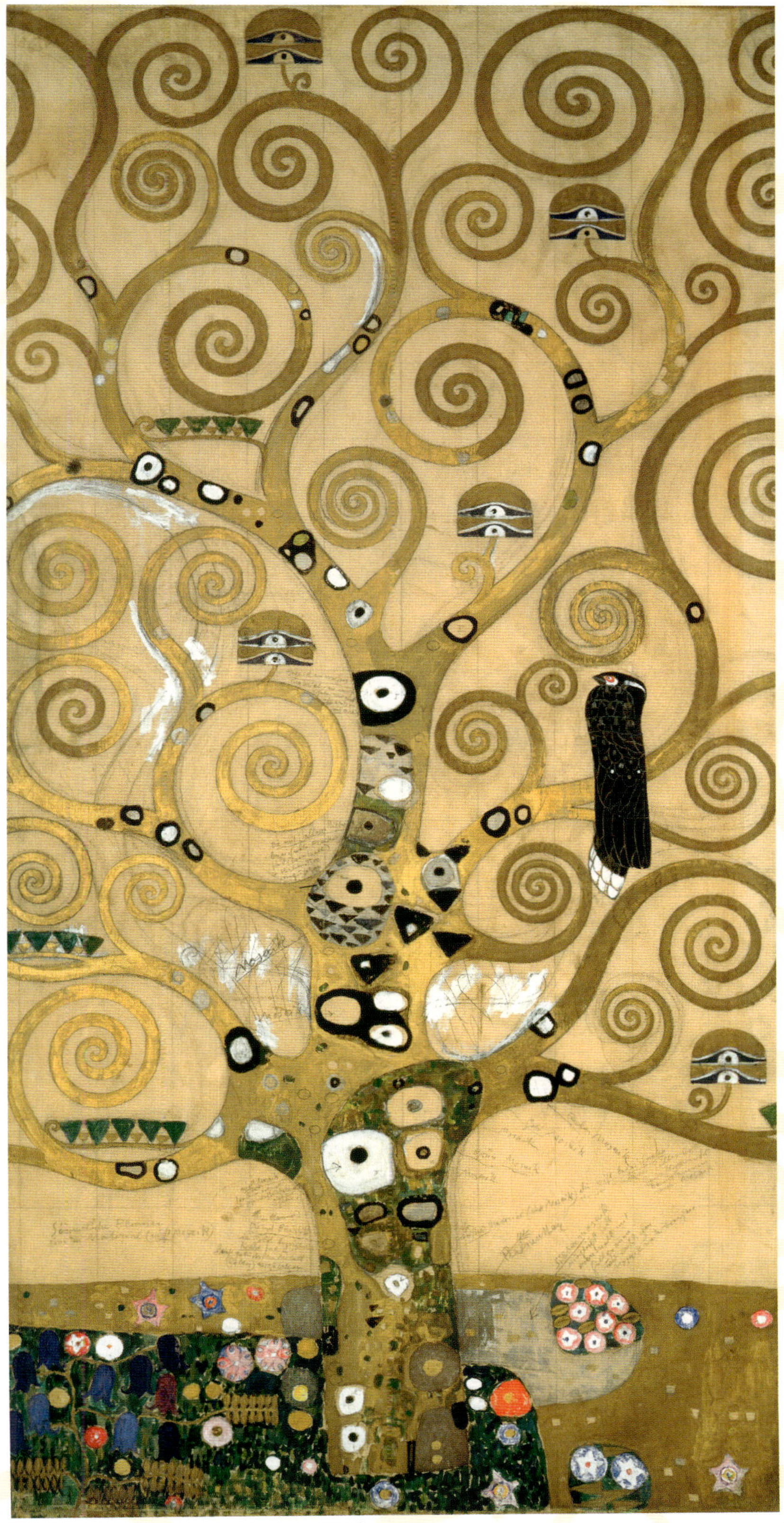

OPPOSITE AND RIGHT ❋ THE STOCLET FRIEZE: THE TREE OF LIFE, c. 1909
GUSTAV KLIMT (1862–1918)

GUSTAV KLIMT & THE BEETHOVEN FRIEZE

THE MAJESTY, POWER AND RADICAL INVENTION OF KLIMT'S MASTERPIECE IS THE QUINTESSENTIAL WORK OF SECESSION

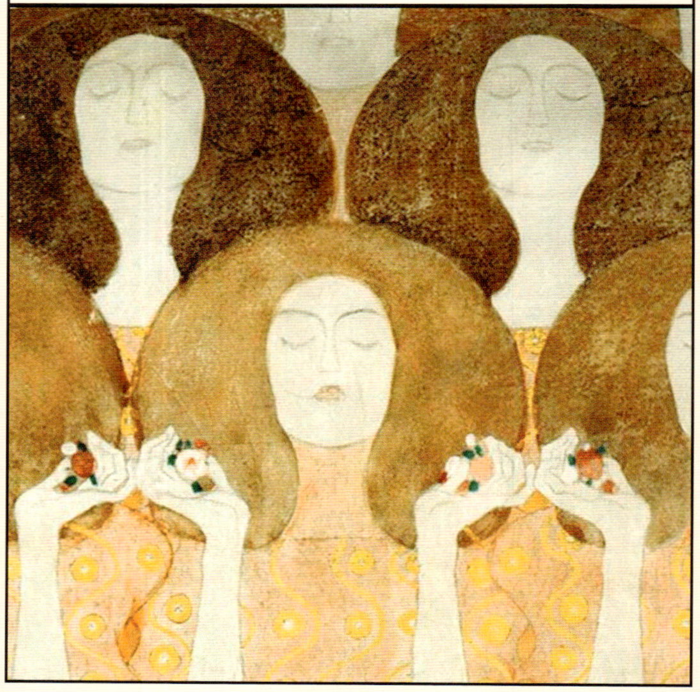

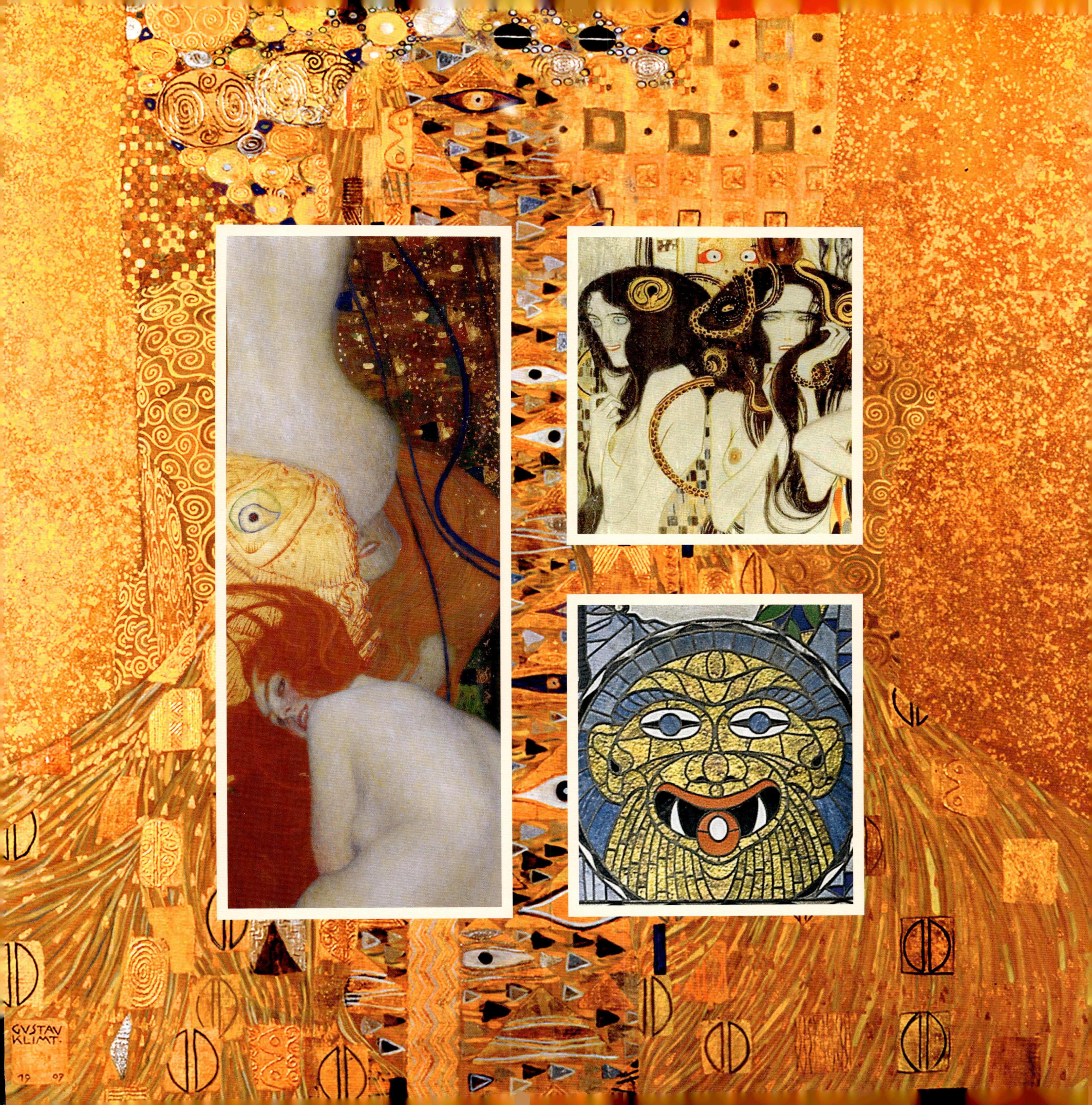
GVSTAV
KLIMT.

THE 14th Vienna Secession Exhibition, held in 1902, was dedicated to Beethoven. Created especially for this exhibition was a frieze by Gustav Klimt. A powerful vision of the human longing for happiness amongst suffering, this masterpiece of the Secession celebrates the beauty of art, love and music.

On 9 November 1989, months of mounting crisis in the Iron Curtain countries came to a head: large crowds besieged the military checkpoints along the Berlin Wall. East and West Berliners danced together atop the hideous concrete construction that had divided their city for so many years. Its full-scale dismantlement didn't come until the following year, but within a week, it was looking distinctly ragged. Not so badly damaged as the structures of the Socialist state, however – let alone the legitimacy of what had called itself the 'German Democratic Republic' – but tatty enough to be emblematic of these things. A few weeks later, to celebrate Christmas, a concert was held beside the Wall, with the American-Jewish conductor Leonard Bernstein presiding over an orchestra of East and West. Musicians and singers from both Germanies, the United States, the USSR, Britain and France came together in a rousing performance of Beethoven's Ninth Symphony – what else?

A Symphony for All Seasons

So much symbolism. So much self-conscious construction of history, of national destiny – things that, in practice, generally work themselves out without regard to the human will. But since its premiere in 1824, Beethoven's Ninth has been the work of first resort for those who have wished to see the symphony – and especially its Finale, a choral setting of Schiller's 'Ode to Joy' (1785) – as an affirmation of what the 'human spirit' can achieve.

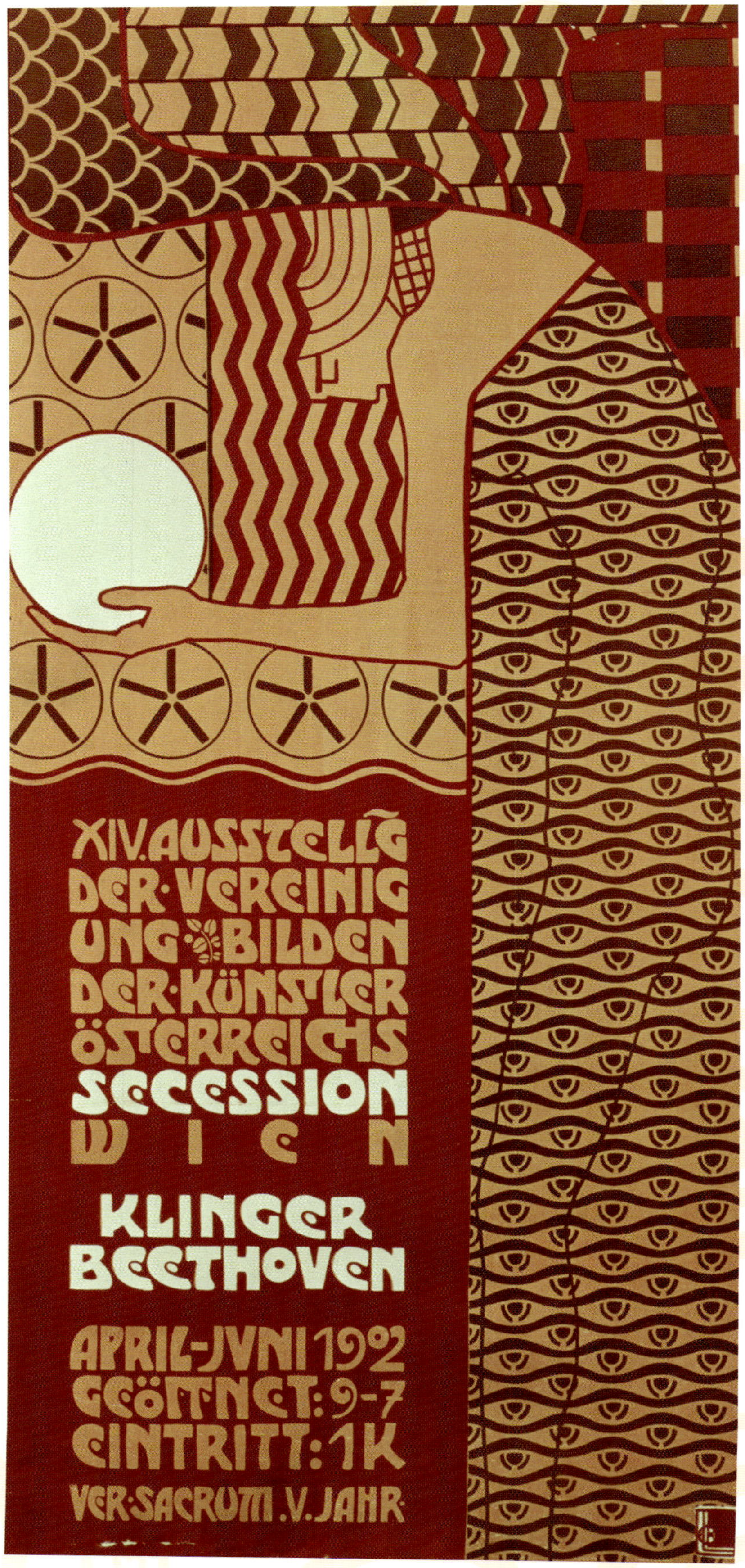

RIGHT ◆ VIENNA SECESSION 14TH EXHIBITION POSTER, 1902. ALFRED ROLLER (1864–1935)
OPPOSITE ◆ THE BEETHOVEN FRIEZE: POETRY, 1902. GUSTAV KLIMT (1862–1918)

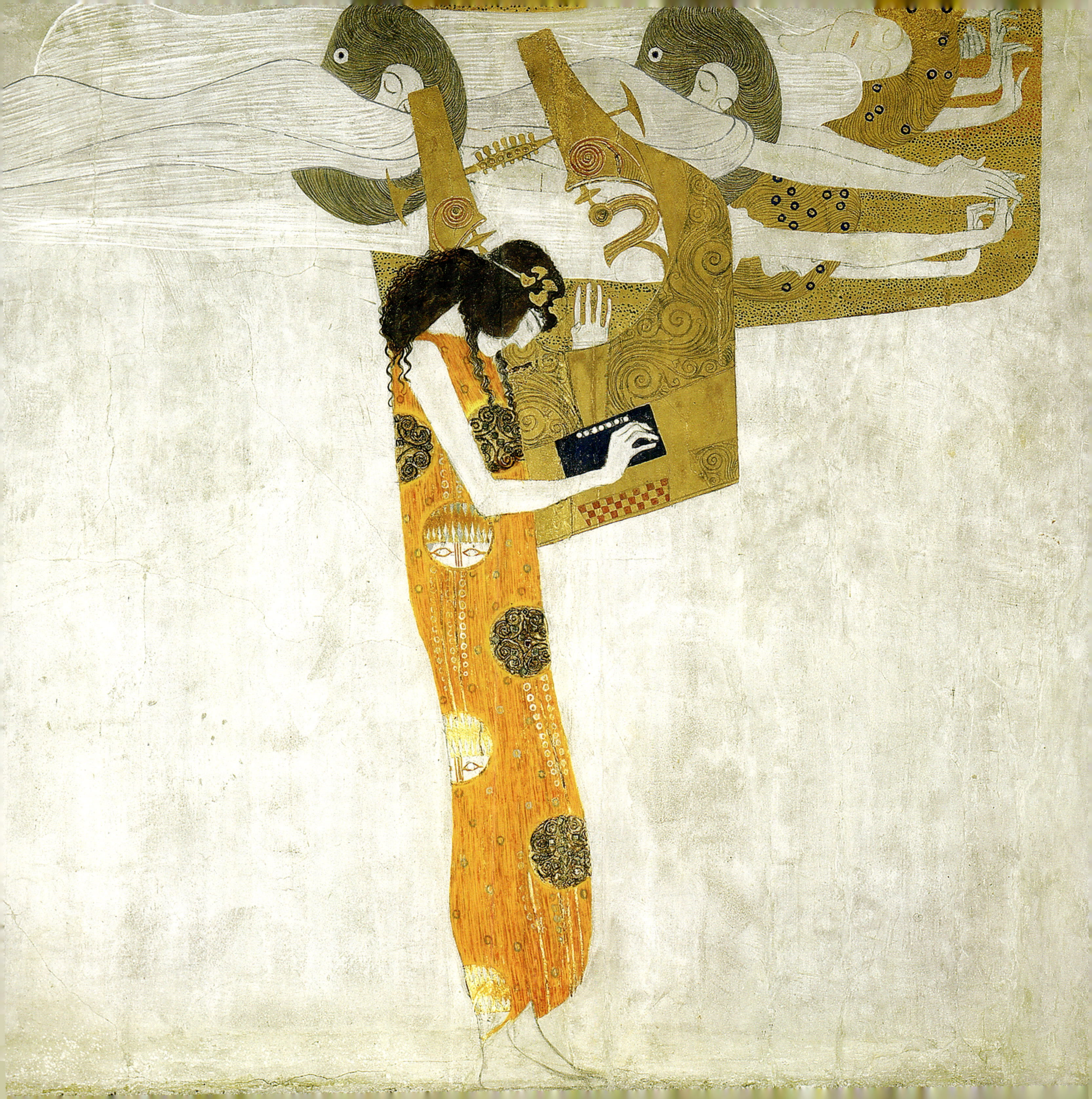

As Nicholas Cook has shown in his fascinating history of Beethoven's Ninth and its reception, it's been just about all things to all ideologies. For the Third Reich in the 1930s, Schiller's exhortation that all men be brothers represented the need of the individual to subsume himself into the triumphant march of the Aryan people; for the Germans' Communist contemporaries, it was more about social fraternity. As the anthem of the European Union in the post-War period, it was to celebrate the spirit of partnership between democratic trading nations; for Leonard Bernstein, it represented the end of totalitarianism. So strongly did he feel about this that he changed the wording of Schiller's script for his 1989 concert. Instead of crying out 'Joy! Joy!', his choir acclaimed 'Freedom! Freedom!' This despite the fact that Schiller's lyric had gifted him the lines 'Your magic brings together/ What fashion has sternly divided' – an affirmation of the human will to reunite.

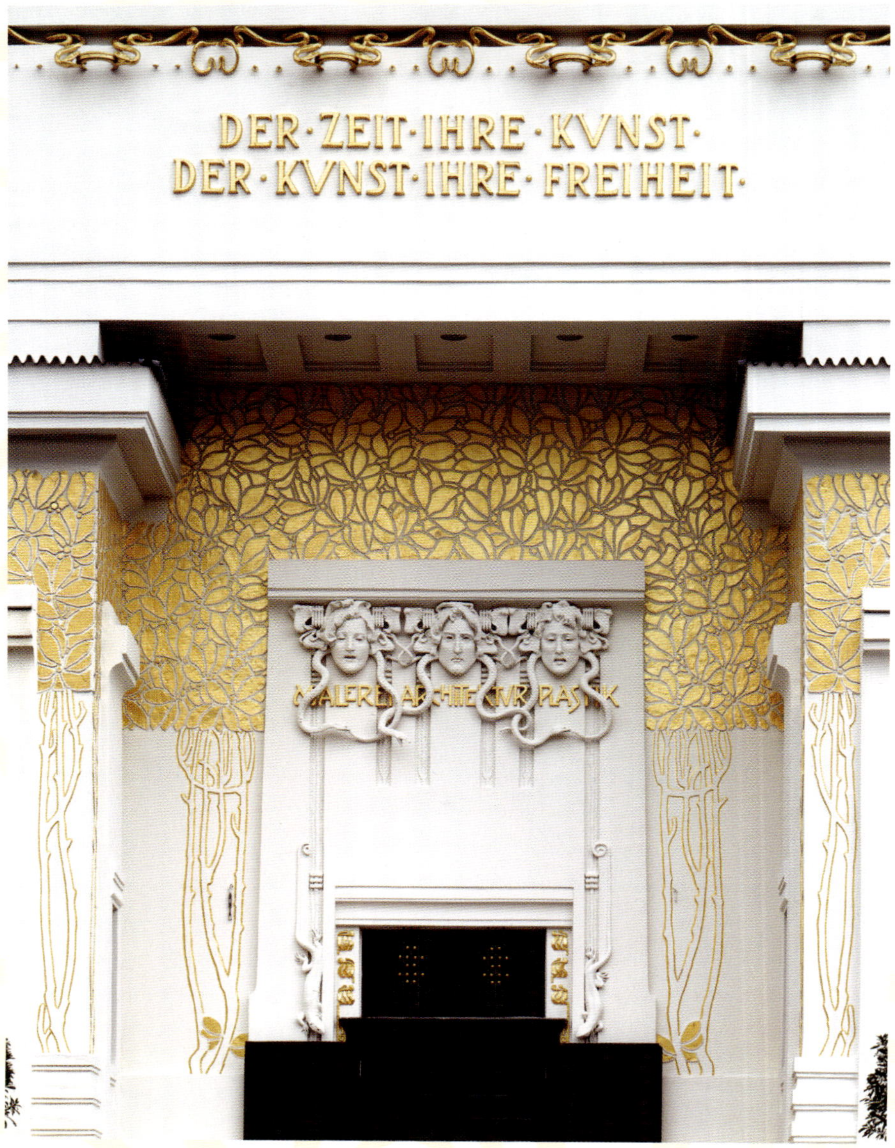

Of course Beethoven is not to blame for the fact that his Ninth Symphony has emblematized so many different things, some of them quite ugly; nor does this detract from the greatness of the work. In the rich complexity of its associations, indeed, Beethoven's Ninth can be seen as emblematic of all that's involved in the very idea of artistic greatness; that is, all that people mean when they enthuse about an important work of art and the impact they believe it has on human life.

A Rare Kind of Reverence

It was to this piece that Nietzsche naturally turned when (in *Human, All Too Human*, 1878) he wanted to evoke the sort of sensations that might be experienced by the listener to a great concert work:

> *At a certain place in Beethoven's Ninth Symphony … he might feel that he is floating above the earth in a starry dome, with the dream of immortality in his heart; all the stars seem to glimmer around him, and the earth seems to sink ever deeper downwards.*

Simultaneously vivid and vague, this observation is fairly typical of the sort of sentiment sparked by Beethoven's Ninth – and by Beethoven in general – in the nineteenth century. What musical historians refer to, without the slightest hint of irony, as the 'Beethoven Cult' became pretty much universal across the self-consciously civilized world. Concerts given by London's Royal Philharmonic Society were

LEFT AND OPPOSITE ❋ STUCCO ON WALLS OF VIENNA SECESSION BUILDING, 1897–98
DESIGNED BY JOSEPH MARIA OLBRICH (1867–1908)

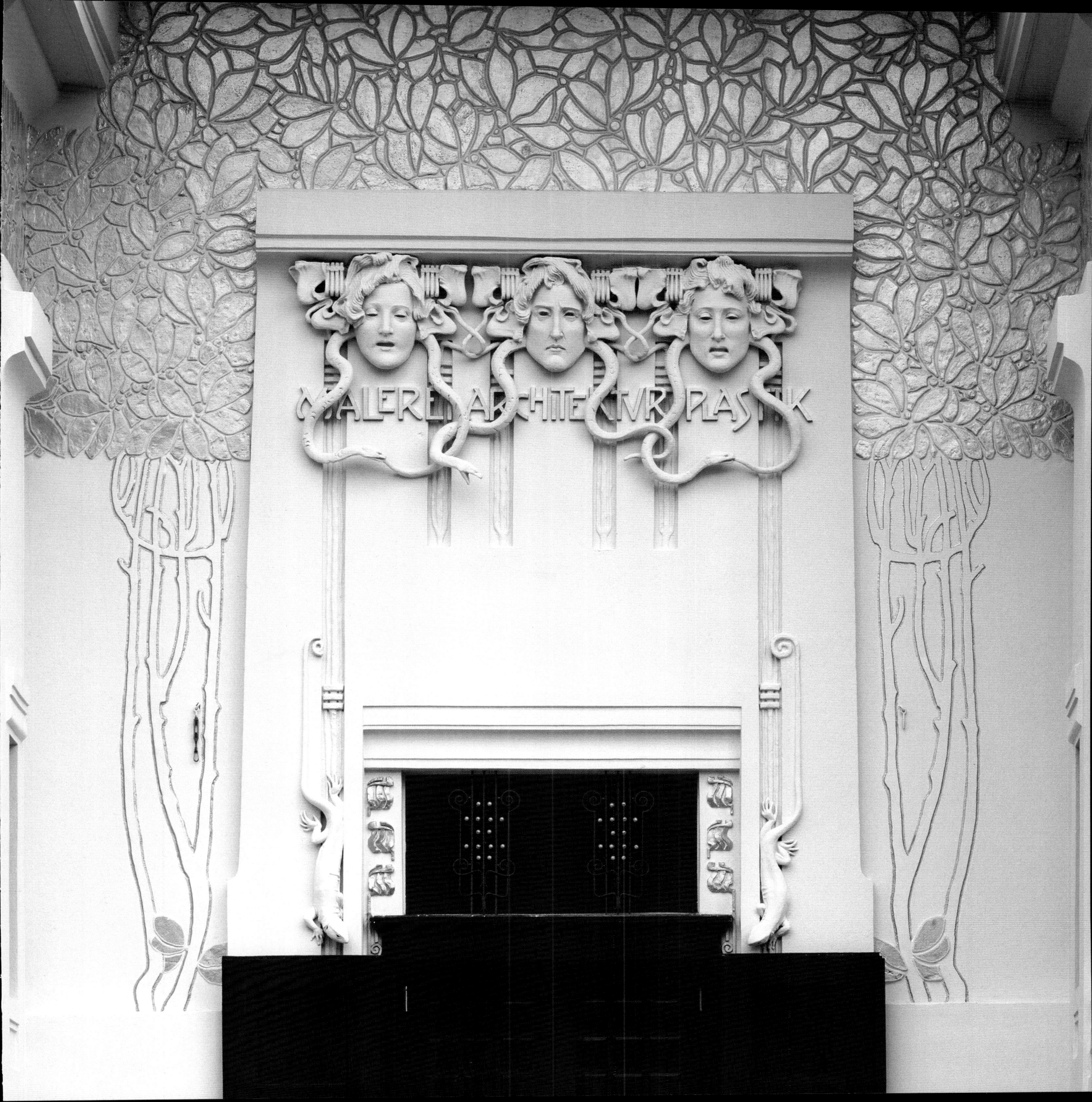

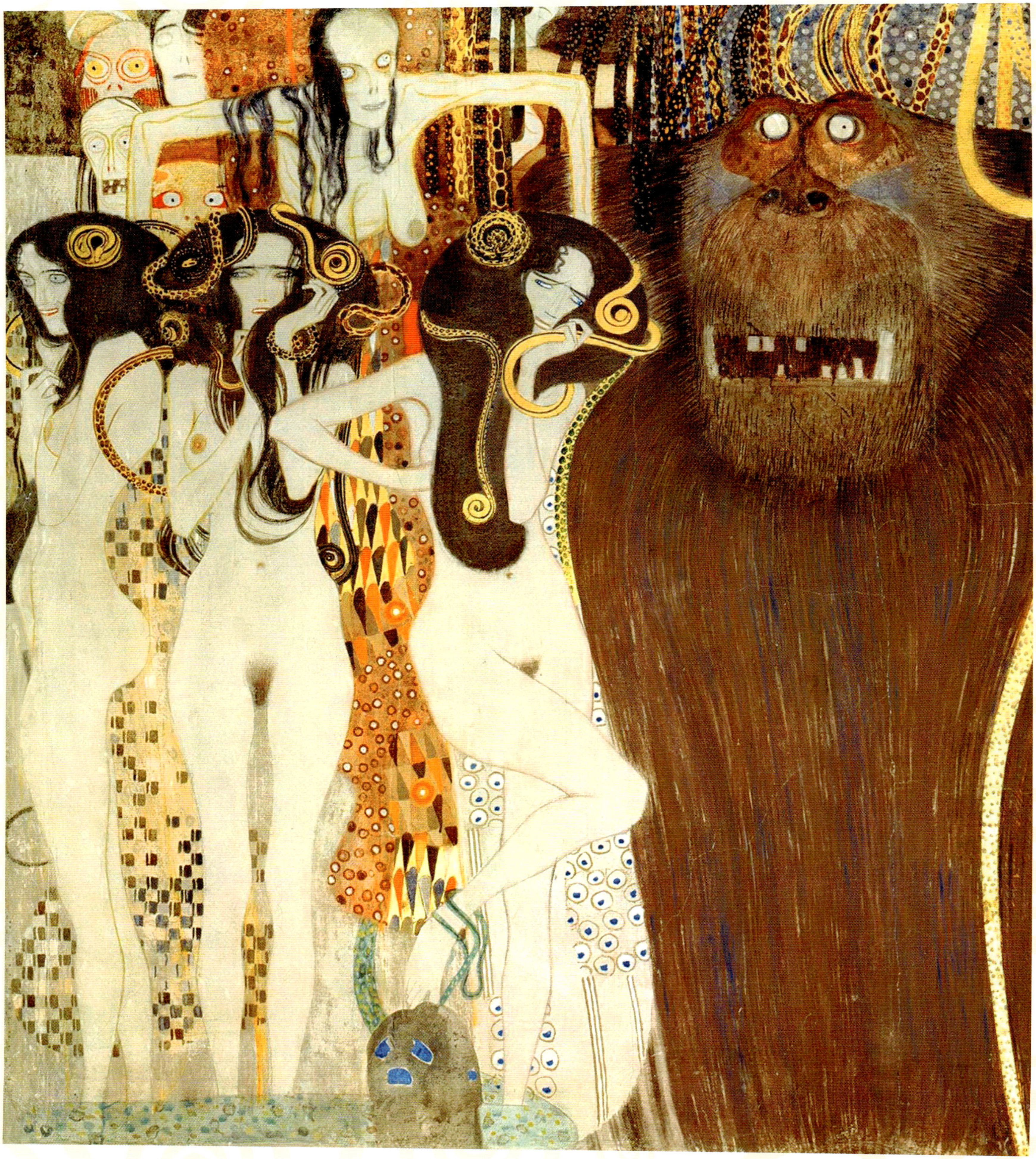

attended not just by fashionable audiences, but also by a bust of Beethoven, brought on to the platform to oversee proceedings.

In other words, the bust was like the idol in some ancient pagan temple – and indeed some enthusiasts didn't flinch from describing Beethoven as a god. The more orthodox were content to see him as a man whose special talents gave him a special closeness to God; a great spirit who partook of the divine in his artistic genius, but whose works were the ultimate expression of something called 'humanity'. In his portraits, busts and statues, the great man was just about inevitably represented as frowning – so heavily did the weight of the world rest on his shoulders.

Austrian Ambitions

The artists of the Vienna Secession had, like everybody else, inherited this view of Beethoven as universal hero, if not demigod – with the special edge of pride that German speakers (understandably) felt. The more so because they had no place politically in the greater Germany that Otto von Bismarck (1815–98) had built and, since 1871, made the dominant power in Europe. The Austro-Hungarian Empire, with its Habsburg monarchy, may have had a glittering and sophisticated society, but in the age of the modern nation-state, it didn't seem to have history on its side. Even at the beginning of the twentieth century, no one better exemplified the New German spirit more perfectly than Beethoven did at the beginning of the nineteenth. Austrian artists wanted both to show their appreciation and to claim their share.

Hence the Secessionists decided that in 1902 they would stage an exhibition, which would be dedicated to the great composer and to what he meant to them. But there was more to their enthusiasm than thwarted nationalism; more even than the desire to pay homage to a

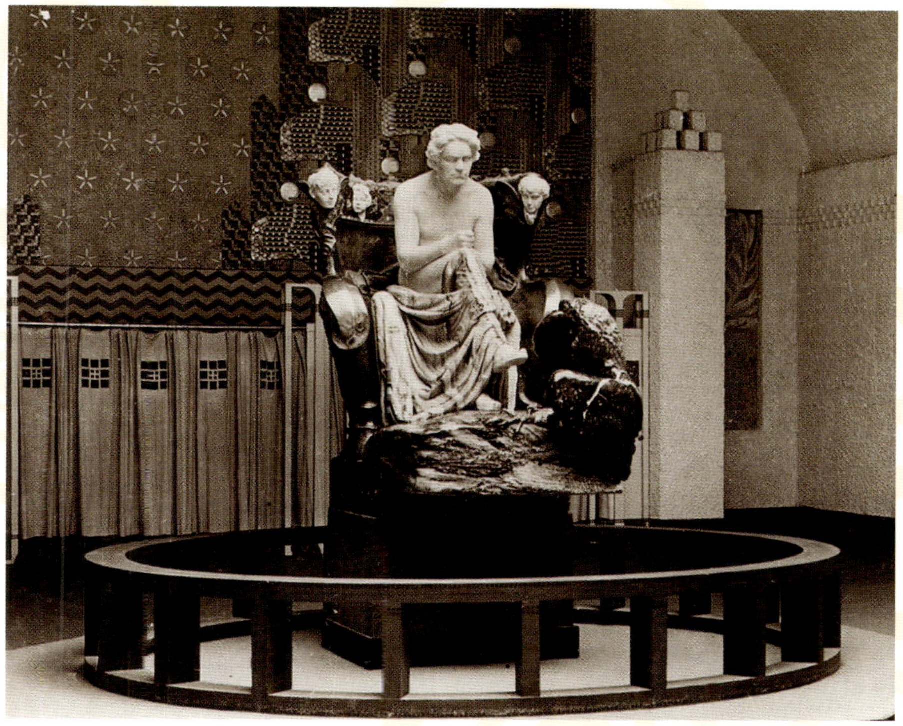

figure generally revered as the ultimate heroic artist: Beethoven had also arguably ushered in the age of the *Gesamtkunstwerk*. And it was with the Ninth Symphony that he had done this. The setting of Schiller's verses in the Finale combined the power of orchestral harmony, the human voice, the rhythms of rhetoric and the colour of verbal imagery to create an exhilarating assertion of all that art could do.

Mixed Feelings

The practice of doubling up on the woodwind and brass sections for performances of the Ninth Symphony – so that the whole thing, quite literally, made more noise – had, in recent years, made this assertion the more emphatic. This practice had in fact been introduced in Vienna by the young conductor and composer Gustav Mahler (1860–1911). That he was Jewish was paradoxical, given that he'd

ABOVE RIGHT • MAIN HALL AT THE 14TH VIENNA SECESSION EXHIBITION, 1902
OPPOSITE • THE BEETHOVEN FRIEZE: HOSTILE FORCES, 1902, GUSTAV KLIMT (1862–1918)

become celebrated as the pre-eminent interpreter of Richard Wagner's works, themselves important mileposts in the march towards the ultimate *Gesamtkunstwerk*. Wagner's anti-Semitism was not only legendary: it had been well to the fore in his discussions of his music, and so by implication in the operas themselves.

In Mahler's case, though, this contradiction in some ways only added to the interest of a Viennese culture that was coming to be characterized by a certain gamy, even sordid quality. As we've already seen (*see* pages 29–30) Viennese love was a curious cocktail: there was the play of 'pure' chastity and 'dirty' sexuality; of tender love and cruel, rapacious lust. By the same token, Viennese society was at once conspicuously cosmopolitan and shot through with the darker undertones of racism and hatred. This of course is one of the things that makes the Vienna of the turn of the twentieth century so fascinating – uncomfortable as it must have been for a great many of those who had to live there. Nowhere else has the full complexity of human nature, in both its light and its darkness, been more nakedly displayed than it was in this particular place and time. In parallel with the quest for the *Gesamtkunstwerk*, the total artwork, this extraordinary culture seemed bent on both consciously exploring and unconsciously displaying the totality of human feeling and morality.

The Music Man

Bohemian-born Gustav Mahler trained in music at the Vienna Conservatory (where he became a close friend of the future composer Hugo Wolf). In 1897, though already well-established as his country's greatest conductor, he had to convert to Catholicism to take up a post heading up the Vienna Court Opera – though this didn't shield him

OPPOSITE ✱ THE BEETHOVEN FRIEZE: THE LONGING FOR HAPPINESS, 1902
GUSTAV KLIMT (1862–1918)

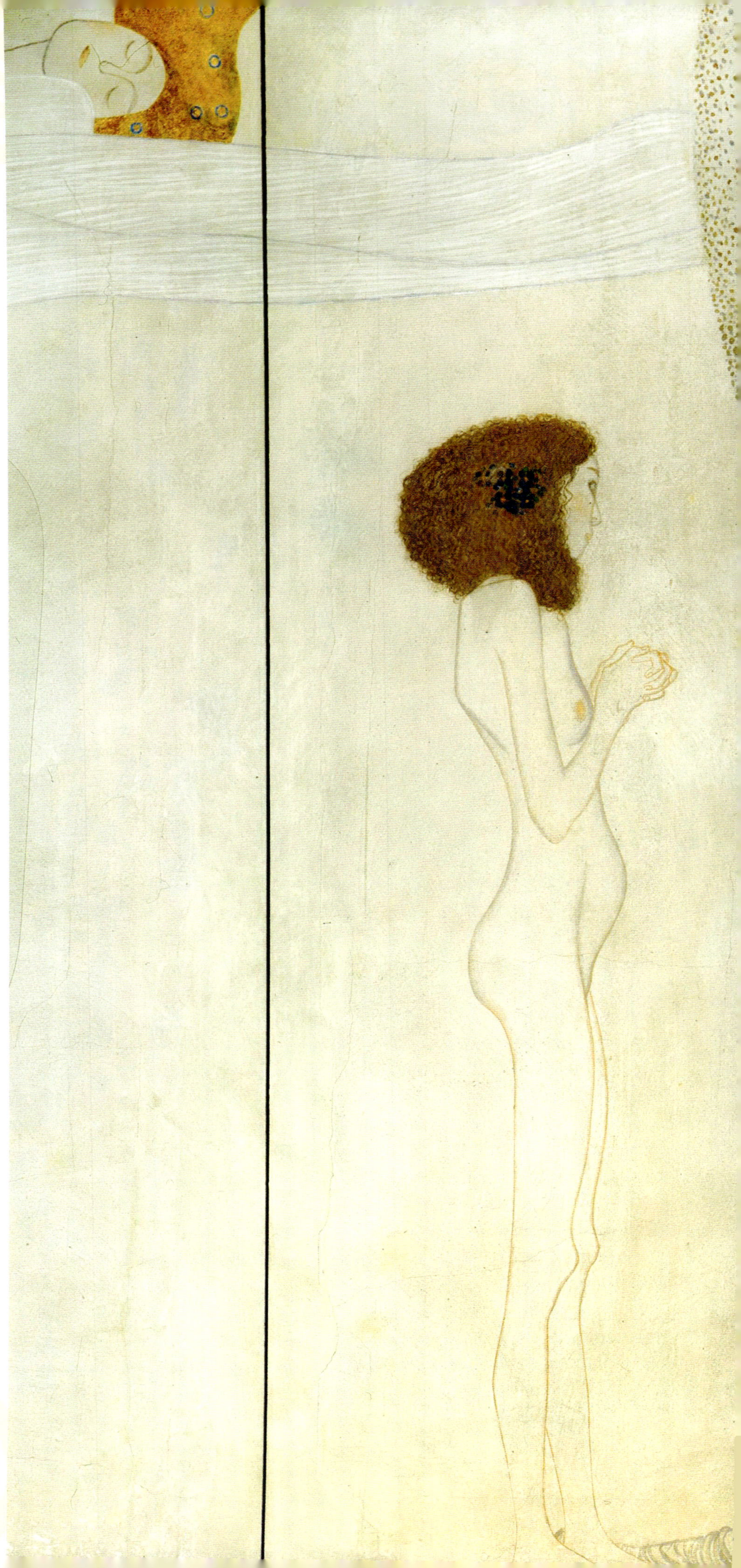

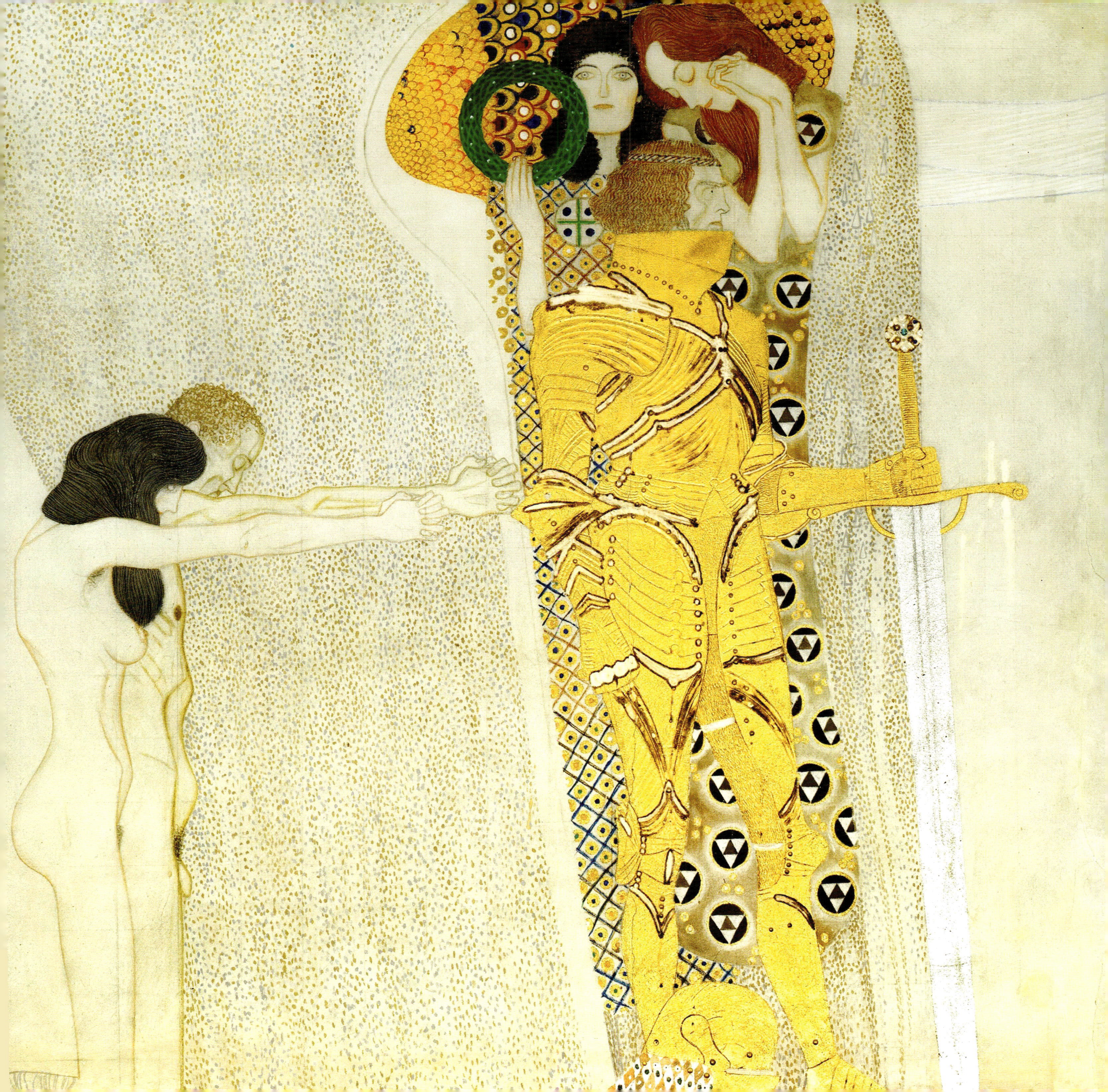

from anti-Semitic abuse from the local press. Nor did it prevent – and this was much more important to a man who ate, slept, breathed and generally lived his music – sullen unco-operativeness from his orchestra and its officials. But this did not deter Mahler from espousing all that was modern and forward-looking in music, whether in performance or in composition, or in the arts in general – he was a keen supporter of the idea of the *Gesamtkunstwerk*.

Although a natural ally of the Secessionists, Mahler had no obvious link with their lives or their artistic activities until he started courting Alma Schindler (1879–1964). Though the daughter of the landscape painter Emil Jakob Schindler (1842–92), her mother had remarried and Alma was now the stepdaughter of Secessionist Carl Moll (1861–1945). A renowned beauty and bluestocking, Alma frequented all Vienna's most fashionable salons, including that of Adele Bloch-Bauer, where her flirtations with Gustav Klimt excited remark. She met Mahler in late 1901, and as their relationship deepened, he inevitably found himself drawn into Secessionist circles. Her now-husband had, Alma admitted later:

> *no native feeling for painting; his mind was too much under the dominion of literature. Yet by degrees, through much looking and an exorbitant desire to know all that was to be known, he began to derive pleasure from pure painting and the ability to judge it. Moll, Klimt, Roller and Kolo Moser disputed the right to be his teacher.*

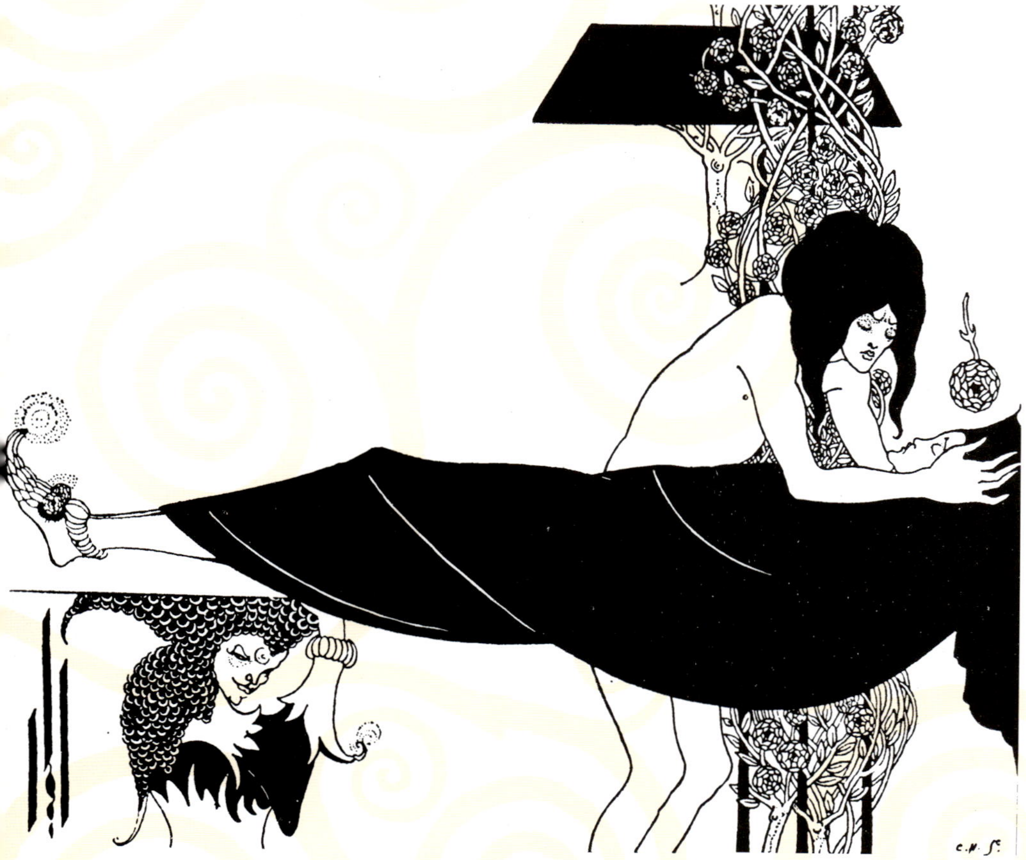

Staging Beethoven

Alfred Roller quickly forged another important connection with the great conductor, working with him as the designer and creator of painted stage sets. This was all, of course, a natural fit with both men's yearnings to pursue the *Gesamtkunstwerk* project, developing Richard Wagner's ideas in the operatic field.

So when the idea of a Beethoven Exhibition for 1902 was mooted, Gustav Mahler was thrilled to be involved – and was ideally placed to organize the musical dimension. (At least he should have been ideally placed: in the event, making a not entirely convincing claim of over-commitment, the Vienna Court Opera orchestra refused to co-operate. The intended full-scale performance of the Ninth Symphony therefore had to be scaled down radically, with Mahler arranging extracts for a small chorus and wind ensemble.) The music was of course to be just the start: the sounds of Beethoven's harmonies and Schiller's words were to be heard against a fully imagined and carefully executed visual background of art and sculpture in an utterly overwhelming experience of 'total art'.

LEFT ◆ THE PLATONIC LAMENT, FROM 'SALOME', 1894. AUBREY BEARDSLEY (1872–98)
OPPOSITE ◆ LIFE IS A STRUGGLE (THE GOLDEN KNIGHT), 1903. GUSTAV KLIMT (1862–1918)

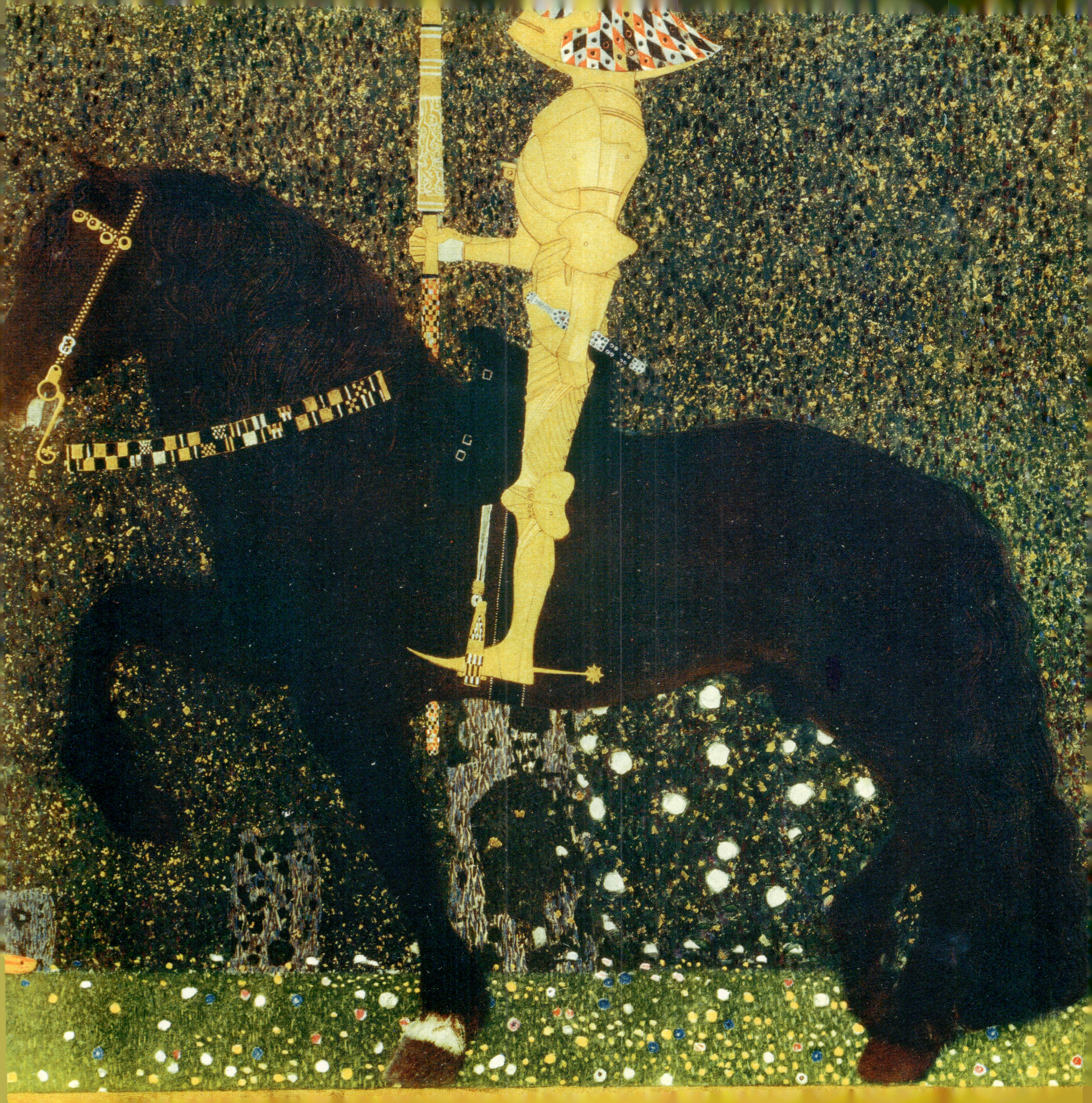

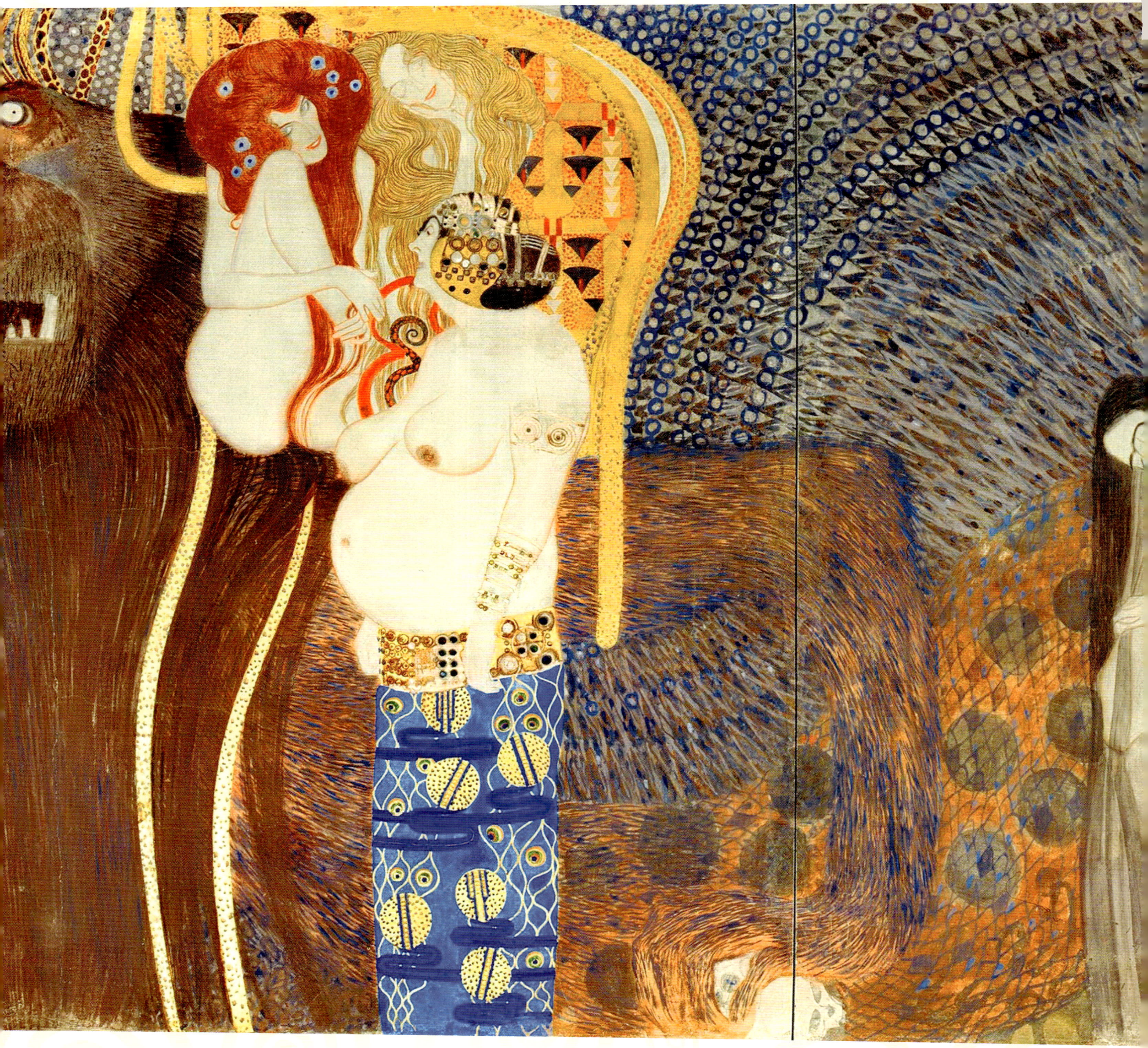

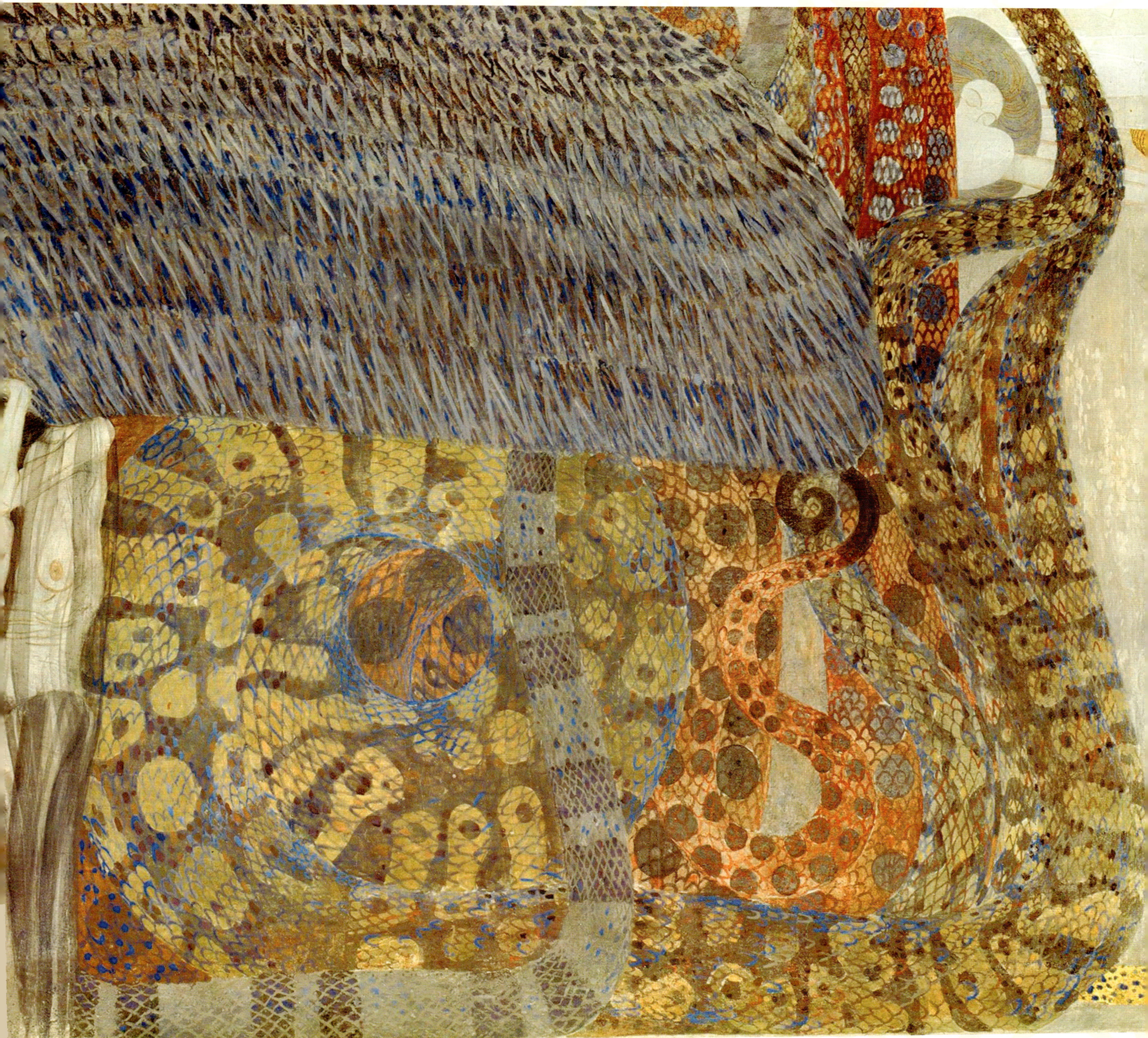

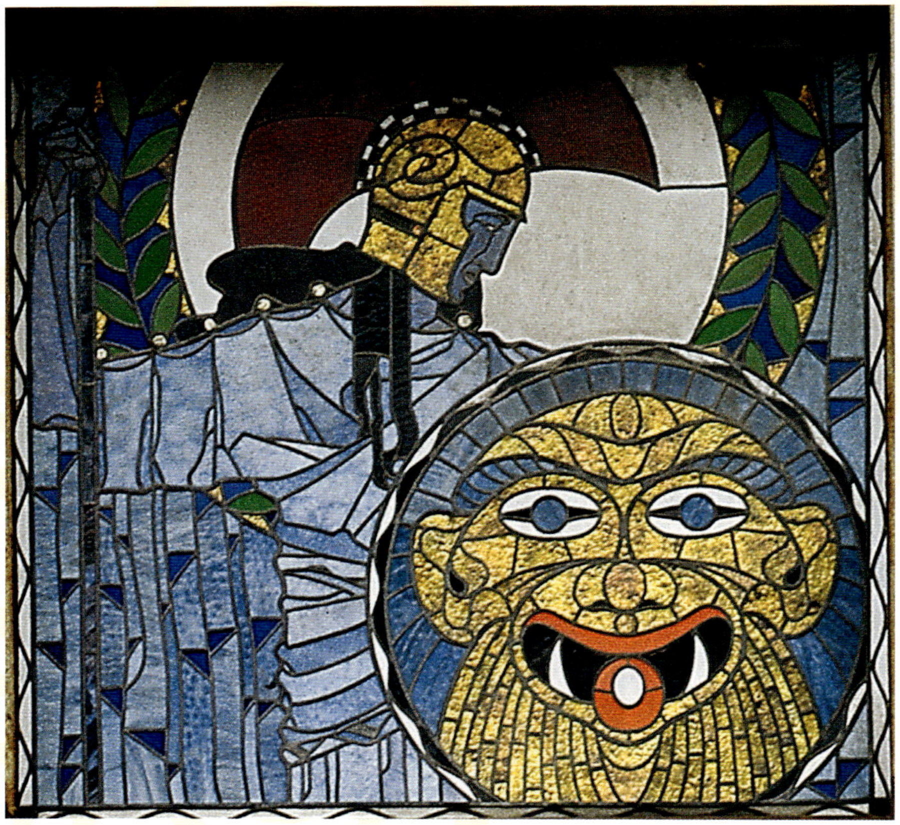

A Worthy Venue

Joseph Maria Olbrich's Secession Building was of course conceived as an example of *Gesamtkunstwerk* principles at work; as the fitting background against which the full range of modern art and sculpture might be displayed. The inscription above the door read 'To every age its art, to every art its freedom', which a cynic might say was having its Secessionist cake and eating it. Insisting on the one hand on the artist's liberty to experiment, to rebel, to reject all precedents, it subtly suggested on the other the legitimacy conferred by so many centuries of artistic tradition. In fairness though, the question of how the artist was to relate at once to the present and to the past (not to mention posterity) was practically as old as art itself.

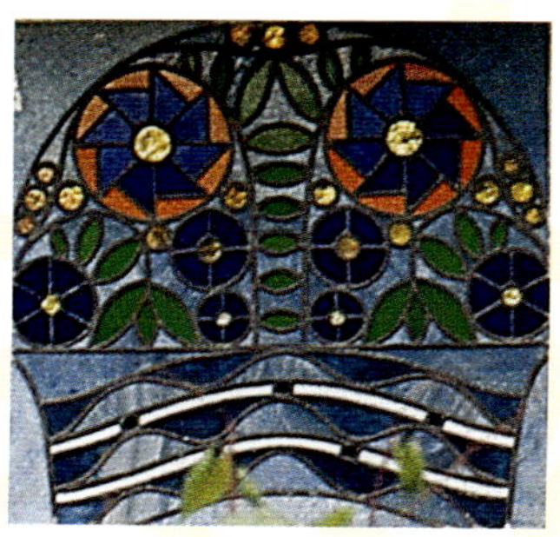

LEFT AND ABOVE LEFT ◆ DETAIL OF MOSAIC FROM VILLA WAGNER 1912–13. KOLOMAN MOSER (1868–1918)

Below this inscription, a trio of Gorgon faces looked down, their twisting serpent-hair intertwining (*see* page 104). One represented art, one architecture, and one sculpture: a mixed aesthetic message, to say the least. Metaphorically, because the mythic Gorgons were so scary that they turned the beholder into stone – were these sisters here to frighten off the old conventions or new visitors? A mixed aesthetic message more literally because their snake-tresses clearly connected the different disciplines. Here, art, architecture and sculpture were to come together.

The three disciplines were to be joined by music – as well as by the literature of Schiller's verse – at the Beethoven Exhibition of 1902. While Mahler would bring the music and the chorus, Max Klinger (1857–1920) had created a statue of the seated Beethoven that seemed on the point of snapping, so strong was the sense of the composer's internal tensions. But this symbolic intermarriage of the arts was to be ceremonially sealed by the unveiling of an utterly original and breathtakingly ambitious painting: a new *Beethoven Frieze* by Gustav Klimt. Its subtitle was 'This Kiss to the Whole World', a famous quotation from the 'Ode to Joy'.

Sequence and Space

As explained in the carefully-written catalogue notes – which visitors were urged to follow – this exhibit was intended to be looked at in strict sequence, since it represented a sort of progression: part narrative, part logical. The frieze, which was painted directly on to the wall, ran around three sides of the exhibition room. Although each wall comprised a separate scene inspired by a quotation from Schiller's poetry, the work as a whole was designed to lead and prepare the visitor; to get them into the

OPPOSITE ◆ STUDY FOR THE BEETHOVEN FRIEZE. c. 1901–02. GUSTAV KLIMT (1862–1918)
PREVIOUS PAGE ◆ THE BEETHOVEN FRIEZE (DETAIL). 1902. GUSTAV KLIMT (1862–1918) SEE PAGE 188

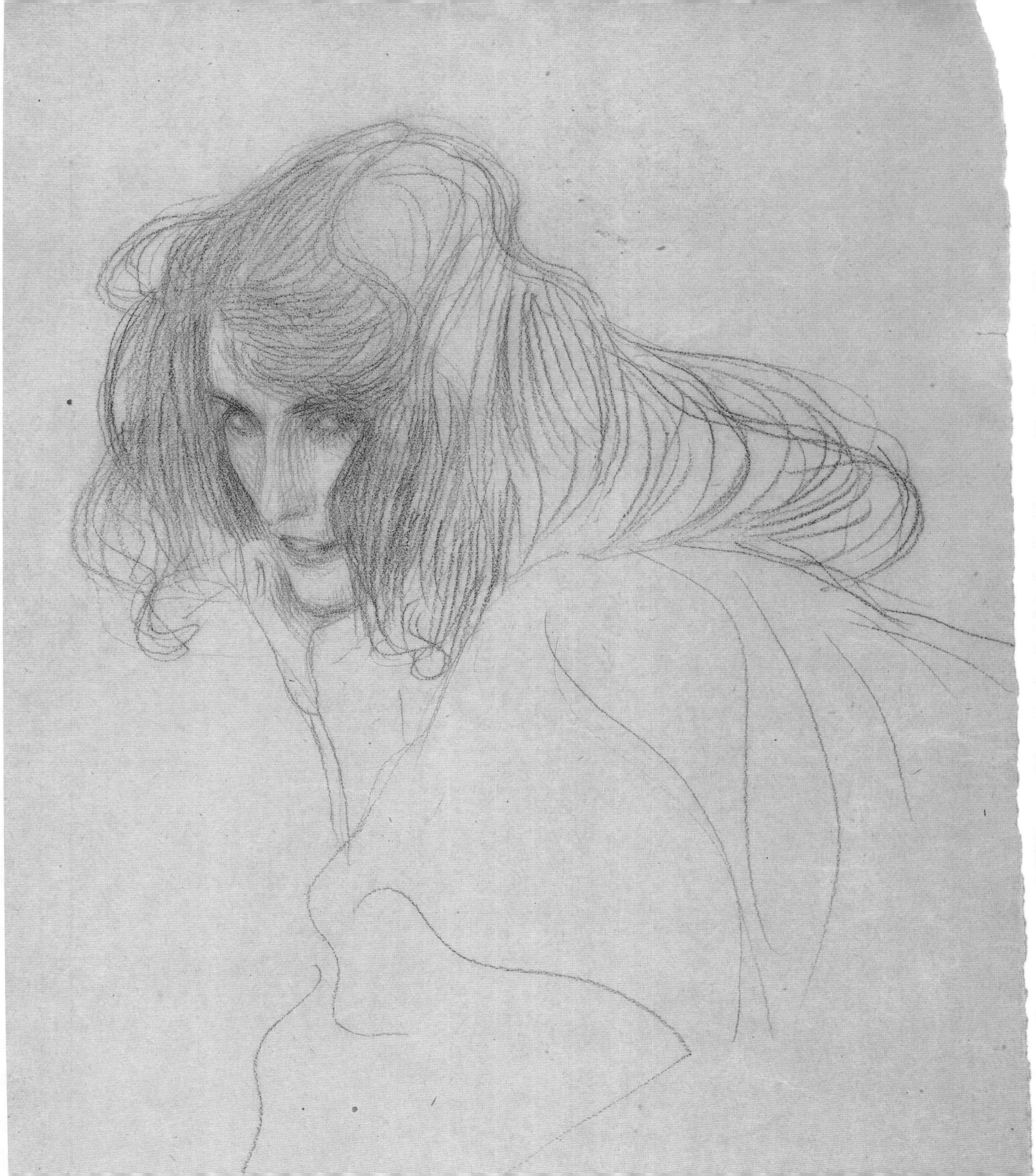

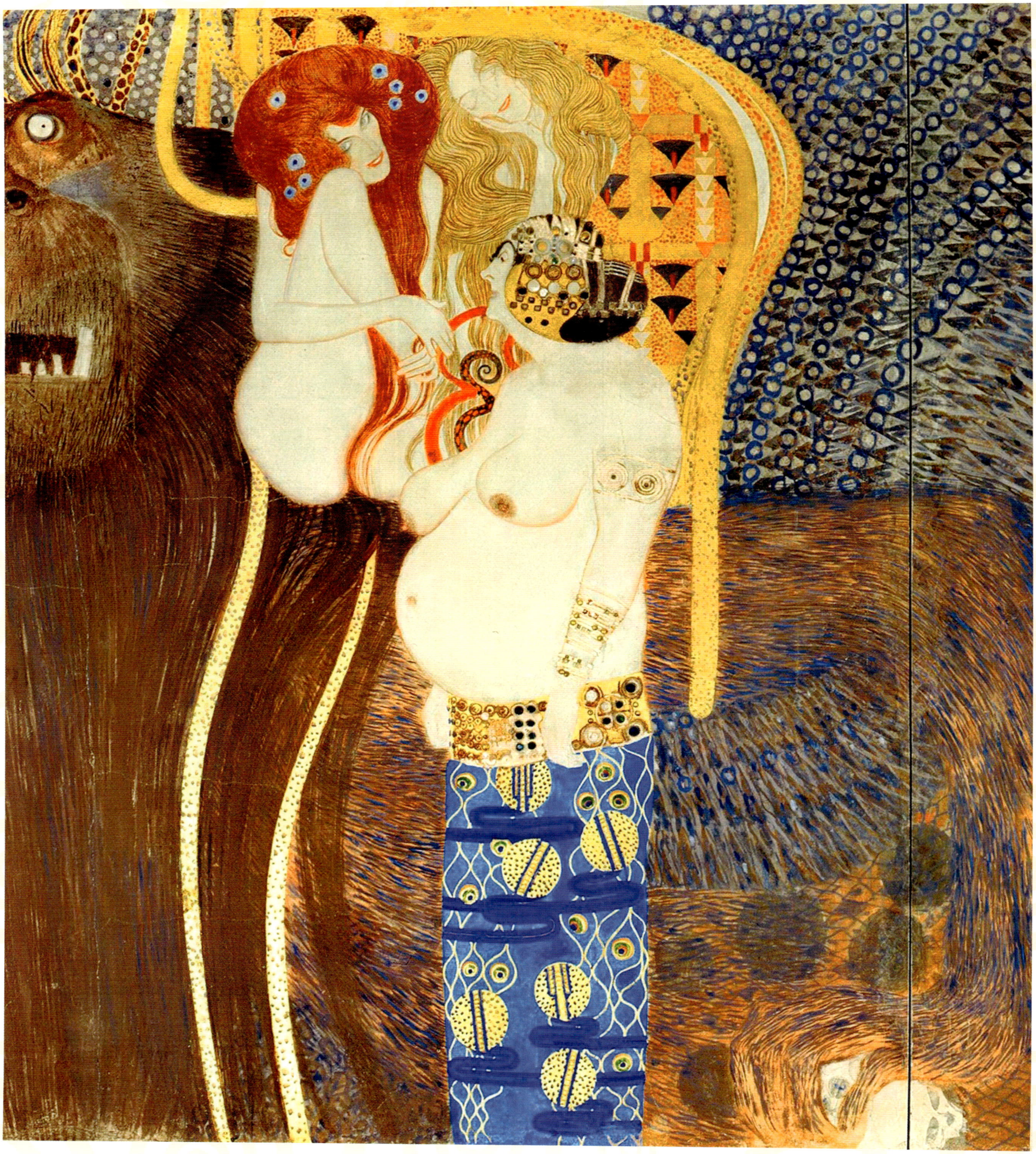

appropriate frame of mind for that final, culminating moment when they gazed upon the image of genius, in the form of Klinger's statue of Beethoven (*see* page 126).

But for the visitor who set foot in the exhibition room, the most striking feature of the frieze was that there was less of it than might have been expected: it occupied only a relatively thin strip along the upper section of the wall. It also had an 'incidental' air. We see the frieze nowadays in a sort of splendid isolation, which was never Klimt's intention. He imagined that it was created for the duration of this one exhibition, after which it would be destroyed. (In the event, the Secessionists decided to hold on to the frieze for one more year while a retrospective of Klimt's work was being planned. After that, it was decided that it might as well be salvaged. It was carefully removed and then remounted in the basement.)

So the blazing white space now below the frieze – like (some commentators have noticed) the audacious space found amid the black lines of an Aubrey Beardsley picture – wasn't actually there when it was viewed in 1902. Other works were mounted in the space – 21 different artists were represented in the exhibition as a whole, not counting Beethoven himself. But a bold use of blankness *was* a feature within the frieze itself. Its first section is largely blank – but grey, not white. 'Floating genii' – female figures, heads haloed by their long hair and dressed in long, diaphanous white robes – fly or float in a dream across the upper part of this open space, their arms upraised, reaching out – seemingly yearning for whatever happiness this world can yield. The grey space below them is interrupted only some 12 metres into the frieze, where we see the figure of a golden-armoured knight (*see* page 119).

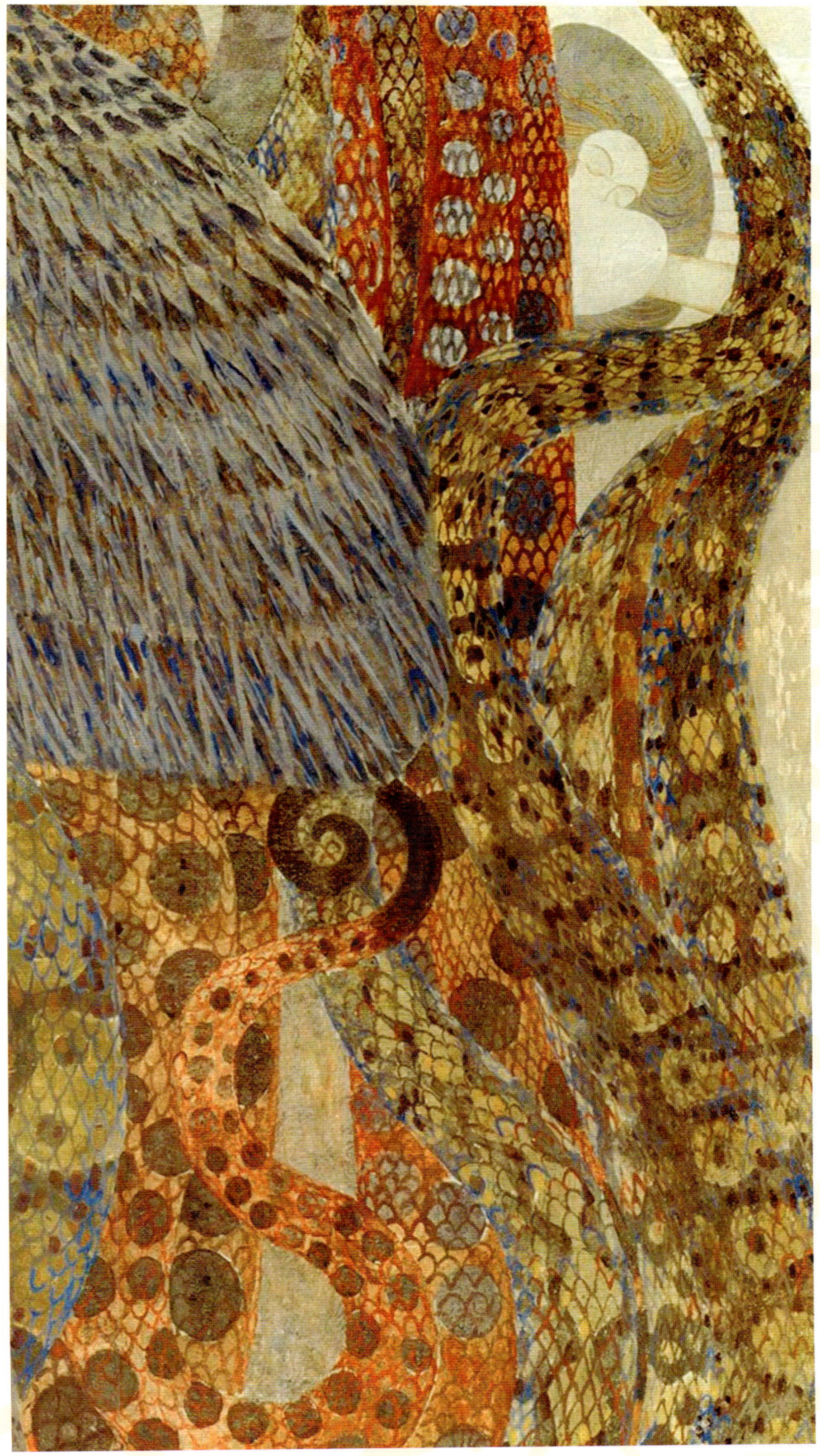

RIGHT ◆ THE BEETHOVEN FRIEZE: GNAWING SORROW, 1902. GUSTAV KLIMT (1862–1918)
OPPOSITE ◆ THE BEETHOVEN FRIEZE: HOSTILE FORCES, 1902 (DETAIL). GUSTAV KLIMT (1862–1918)

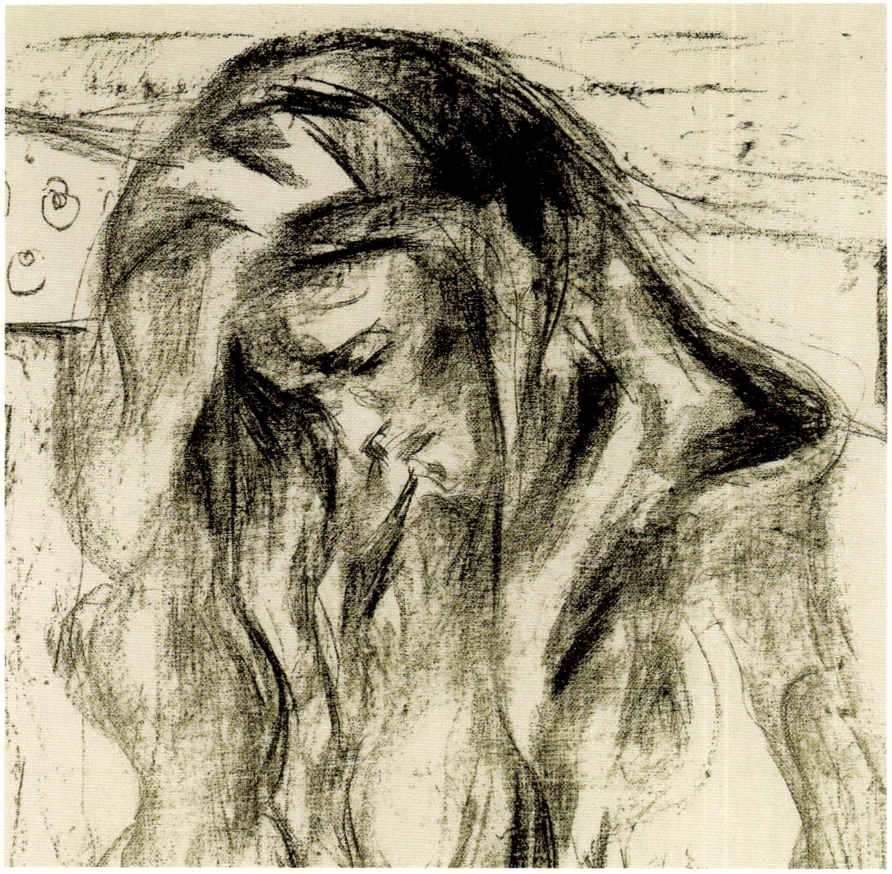

Champion of Beauty

This scene references Schiller on the 'ideal realm' of art: 'Yearning for happiness,' the extract reads:

> *The sufferings of weak mankind; mankind's appeal to the strong one in armour as the outer force and to compassion and ambition as inner forces make men take up the fight for happiness.*

The artist, then – or Art personified, perhaps (or both) – fights the good fight for idealism on humankind's behalf; the chivalric knight rides to the rescue of the damsel in distress. Two fair maidens are seen behind him, one seemingly swooning away in alarm and admiration; the other preparing to crown him with a hero's laurel wreath. The real distress we see displayed here though, is in the naked male and female forms kneeling at the knight's left in supplication, their lanky, skinny bodies those of a humanity bereft.

There's no doubt though, that it's this stunning knight at arms who steals the show. His armour stands out – quite literally, for it's painted on strips of wood elaborately fastened to the wall, which are then plastered over in their turn. The blade of his sword is silver; its hilt and his armour is glittering gold, set off by mosaic patterning of semiprecious stones and fragments of mirror, mother-of-pearl and glass. He has a golden helmet at his feet.

Hostile Forces

Crowded into the end-wall of the room – only six metres or so in breadth – is the frightening, malevolent throng of 'hostile forces' (see pages 112–13). There's barely an inch of blankness here. Instead, the whole surface seems to heave with horror, ugliness and menace in dramatic counterpoint to the lovely scenes we've seen so far. Klimt, the catalogue made clear, had followed Schiller closely in this passage:

> *The hostile forces. The giant Typhoeus, against whom even the gods fought in vain; his daughters, the three Gorgons. Disease, madness, death. Sensuality and lechery, intemperance. Gnawing sorrow. The yearnings and longings of mankind fly over them.*

So it is in the painting on the wall before us – we start out at the far left with the three Gorgons with their serpent hair (*see* page 106).

ABOVE ✦ THE BEETHOVEN FRIEZE: HOSTILE FORCES, 1902 (DETAIL). GUSTAV KLIMT (1862–1918)
OPPOSITE ✦ CRYING GIRL, 1920. EDVARD MUNCH (1863–1944)

We may recognize these hellish sisters not only from the front of the Secession Building, but also from the allegory of *Jurisprudence* at the University. Seen here in colour (unlike in the other painting, long since lost), they cut startling figures, their pubic hair as shocking in its stark abruptness now as it was in its indecorousness in its day. Like little black fangs, these triangular slashes of black pick up the angularity of what 'should' be more rounded, feminine outlines. The only real curves here are in the sinuous sweep of these women's hair – and of course in the serpents coiling within it.

At the bottom, beneath the triangle made by the crooked knee of the Gorgon on the right, a looping anklet echoes the snaking forms above. Below that, we see a wailing mask of sadness. Above the Gorgons' heads, meanwhile, further female heads line up to menace us: visages of madness and disease (of syphilis?); cadaverous near-skulls. Behind, receding into the distance, we see staring, fainting, impassive faces, which echo the words of Dante: 'I had not known death had undone so many.'

Disease and Deadly Sins

Immediately to the right of this group looms 'the giant Typhoeus' (*see* page 116), a dark and hairy ape, his mouth more gaps than teeth; his expression all but vacant – one eye with a pinprick pupil, the other quite blank. Less is more in this representation of horror: typhoid was an unspectacular killer; like cholera and consumption, it went hand in hand with poverty in the nineteenth-century slums of Vienna, as in the other great cities of the world.

Like lianas in the jungle, golden ropes curve down to the right of Typhoeus's crouching form. Her body contorted in keeping with the

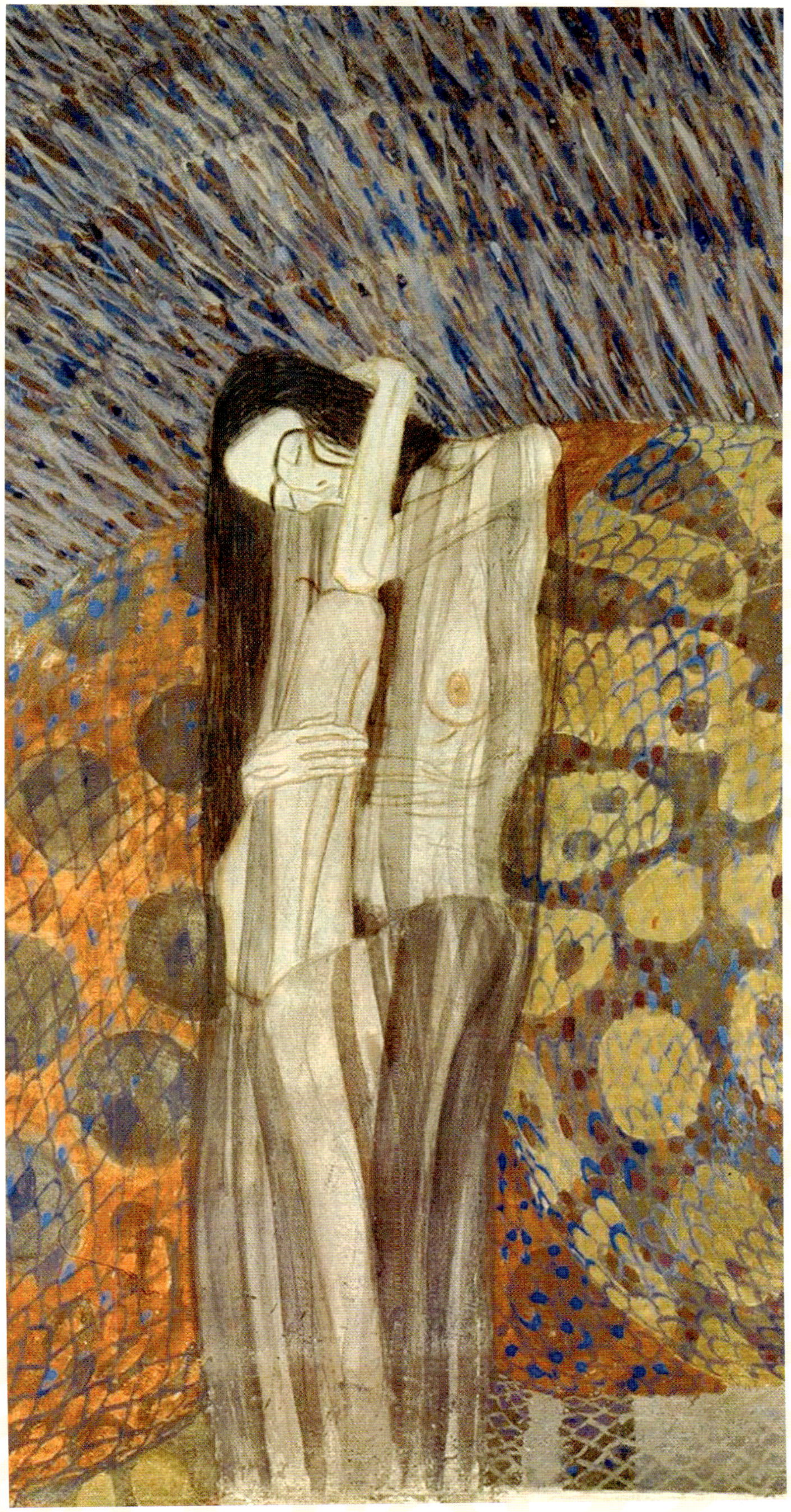

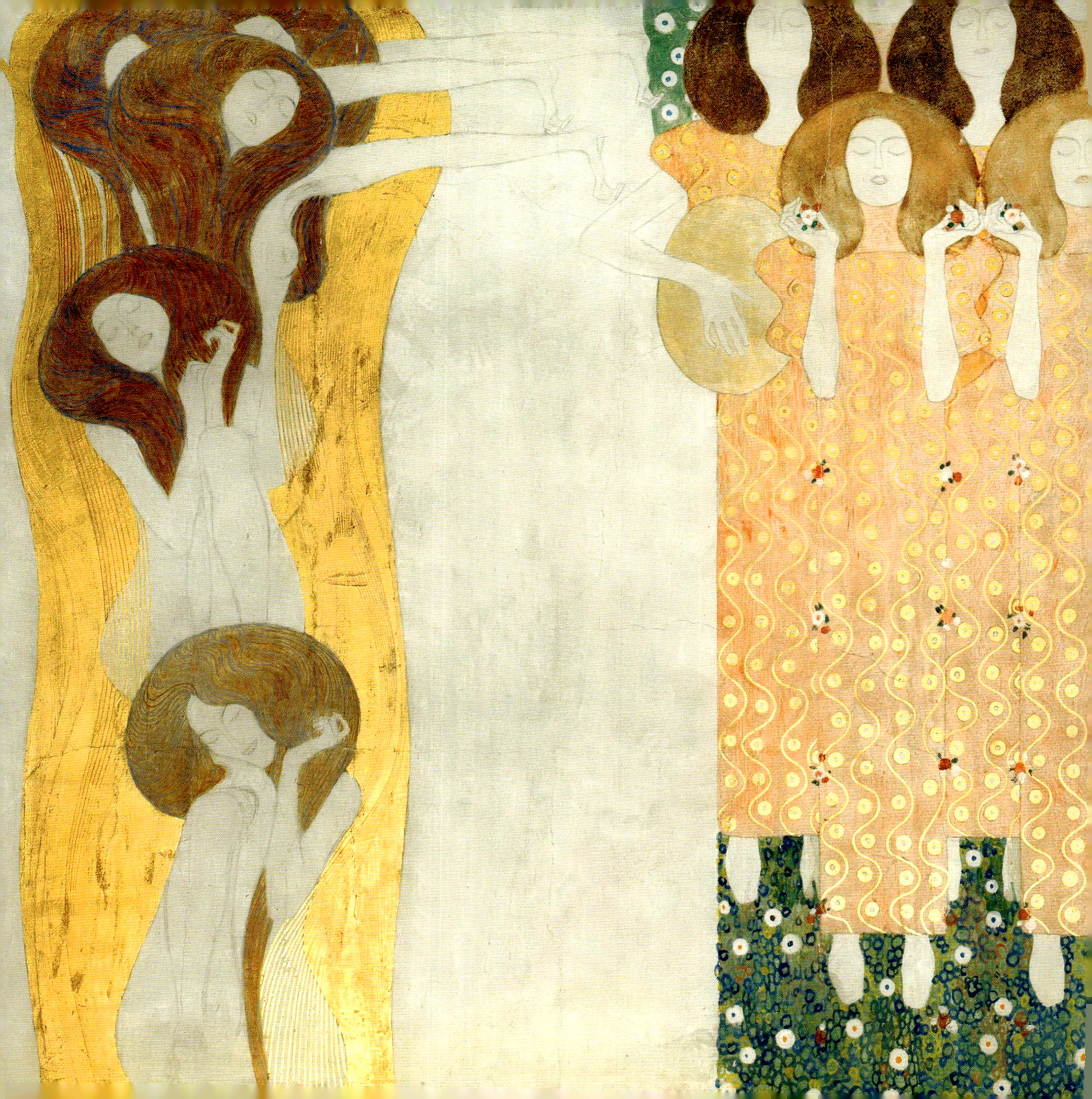

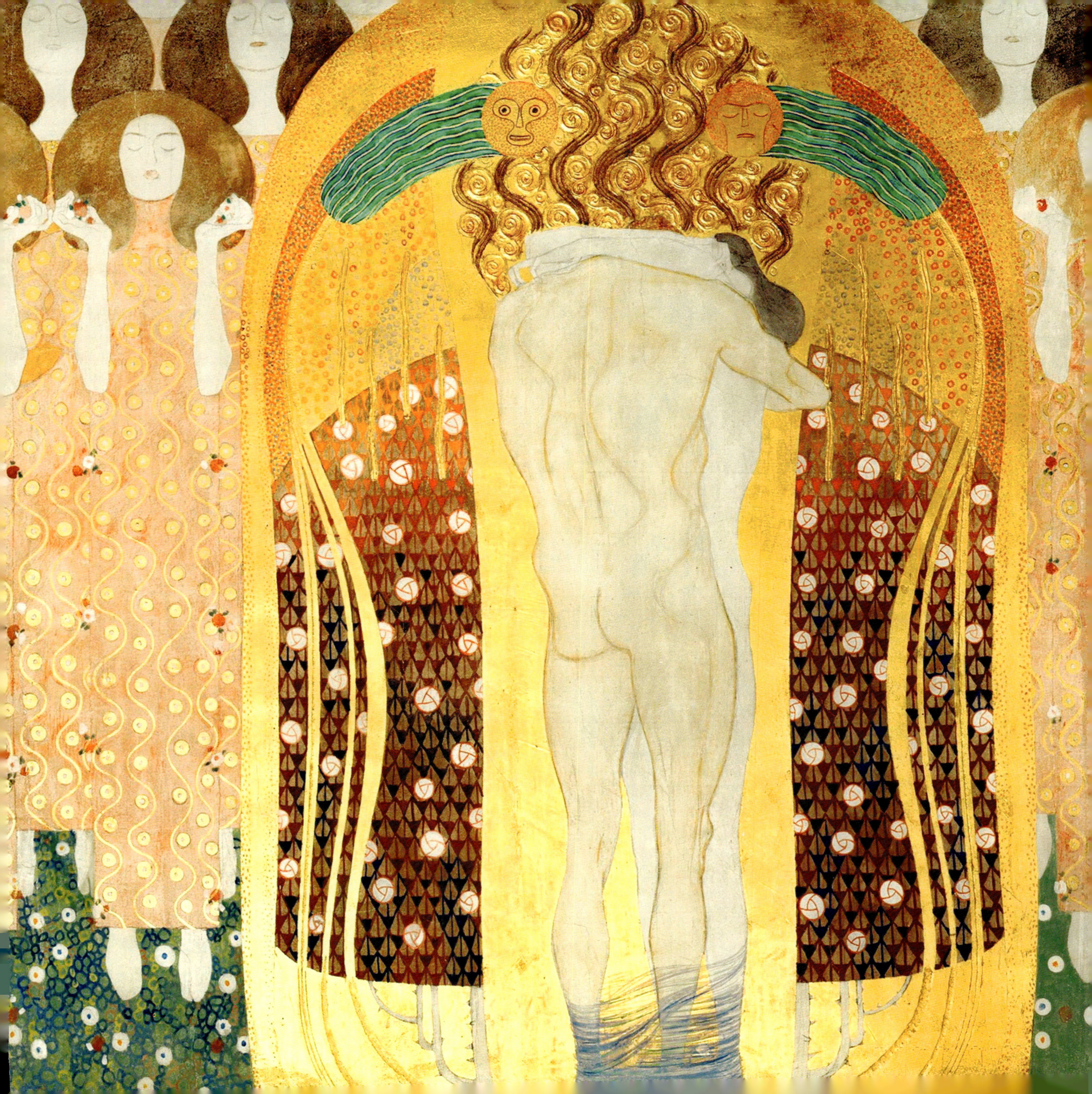

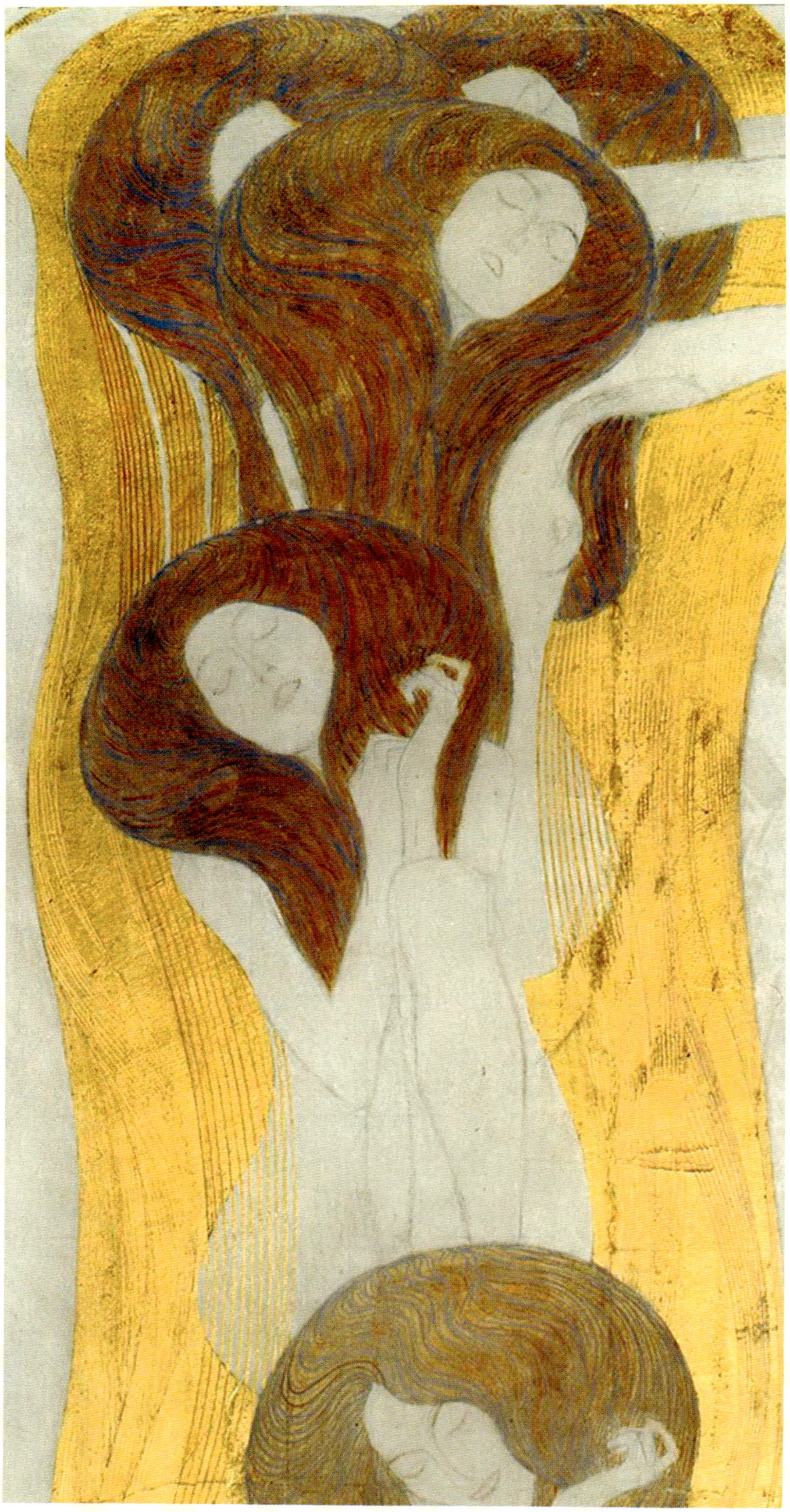

perversity of her desires, the female figure of Lust eyes us hungrily from above. Beside her, eyelids luxuriously lowered, Voluptuousness keeps her company above the standing figure of Intemperance, with her loud, bright skirt, her richly-decorated headdress and the spangled circlets round her arms. But all this adornment can't begin to conceal the essential ugliness of one who's given herself up to gluttony and drunkenness – her paunch, her sagging posture, her drooping breasts.

Sorrow and Poetry

Here, Klimt's vision of evil is as uncontainable as beauty and desire were to be in later 'golden-phase' paintings like *Portrait of Adele Bloch-Bauer I* (*see* page 189). Although we see Typhoeus crouching semi-upright to the left of this trio of sins, we also see what we can only imagine is his body stretching away behind him (and them) like a quadruped's, all the way into the next section of the frieze; here, if we look closely, we can see hindclaws clutching a human skull. And then, arcing away behind to the right, we see what might be an upscaled continuation of the Gorgons' writhing snakes – or it might just be scaly patterns, spiralling into an enfolding infinity of coils. At their centre sits Sorrow (*see* page 117) – visibly gnawed away by her sufferings, her head bent; her scanty, skinny form draped with a darkening gauze.

On the other long wall, more floating genii drift above more grey open space until – moving to our left – we finally encounter a solitary woman: the figure of Poetry (*see* page 119) who, gowned in orange, bends her head over an outsized lyre. In the black patterning on her dress, the decorative meets the representational, as so often in Klimt's work: while some rosettes are geometrical, others resemble faces with stylized (but clearly staring) eyes.

PREVIOUS PAGE • THE BEETHOVEN FRIEZE: THE ARTS, CHOIR OF ANGELS AND HERE'S A KISS TO THE WHOLE WORLD, 1902. GUSTAV KLIMT (1862–1918)

Longing and Fulfilment

By way of explanation, the catalogue gave a further quotation from Schiller: his jotted thoughts upon the 'ideal realm' of art. Here we've clearly seen how – again – the 'longing for happiness finds relief in poetry'. Next in his musings, the great Romantic poet went on to point out that: 'The arts transpose us into the ideal realm, the only source for us of pure joy, pure happiness. A choir of angels in paradise sings an Ode to Joy' (*see* pages 124–25).

And so indeed they do: first the arts (*see* page 122), maidenly muses stand and sway in inspiration and enjoyment, their nakedness to some extent covered by their flowing hair. Or is this rather a crowd of souls rising up to an artistic heaven? (They also resemble – in much more benign form – the column of forms in the Vienna University Philosophy scene. They could well be rising to heaven, given that beyond them ranks of angelic figures in ornately copper-coloured vestments sing in joy. Eyes down in concentration, they hold their hands upraised in spiritual exultation, letting bright flowers fall to the verdant ground below (an image reminiscent of Rilke's 'meadow underneath a rain of blossoms'. Beside them, clinched in their ultimate fulfilment amid a stylized burgeoning of vegetal ornamentation and an explosion of gold, a naked man and woman cling together (*see* page 123). The waves of gold around them 'rhyme' with the swaying forms of the souls or muses to the left.

Quite a Kiss

This scene, the 'Kiss to the Whole World' referred to in Klimt's subtitle to the *Beethoven Frieze*, is obviously about human sexual love, but it's also just as clearly about spiritual transcendence. We see the male

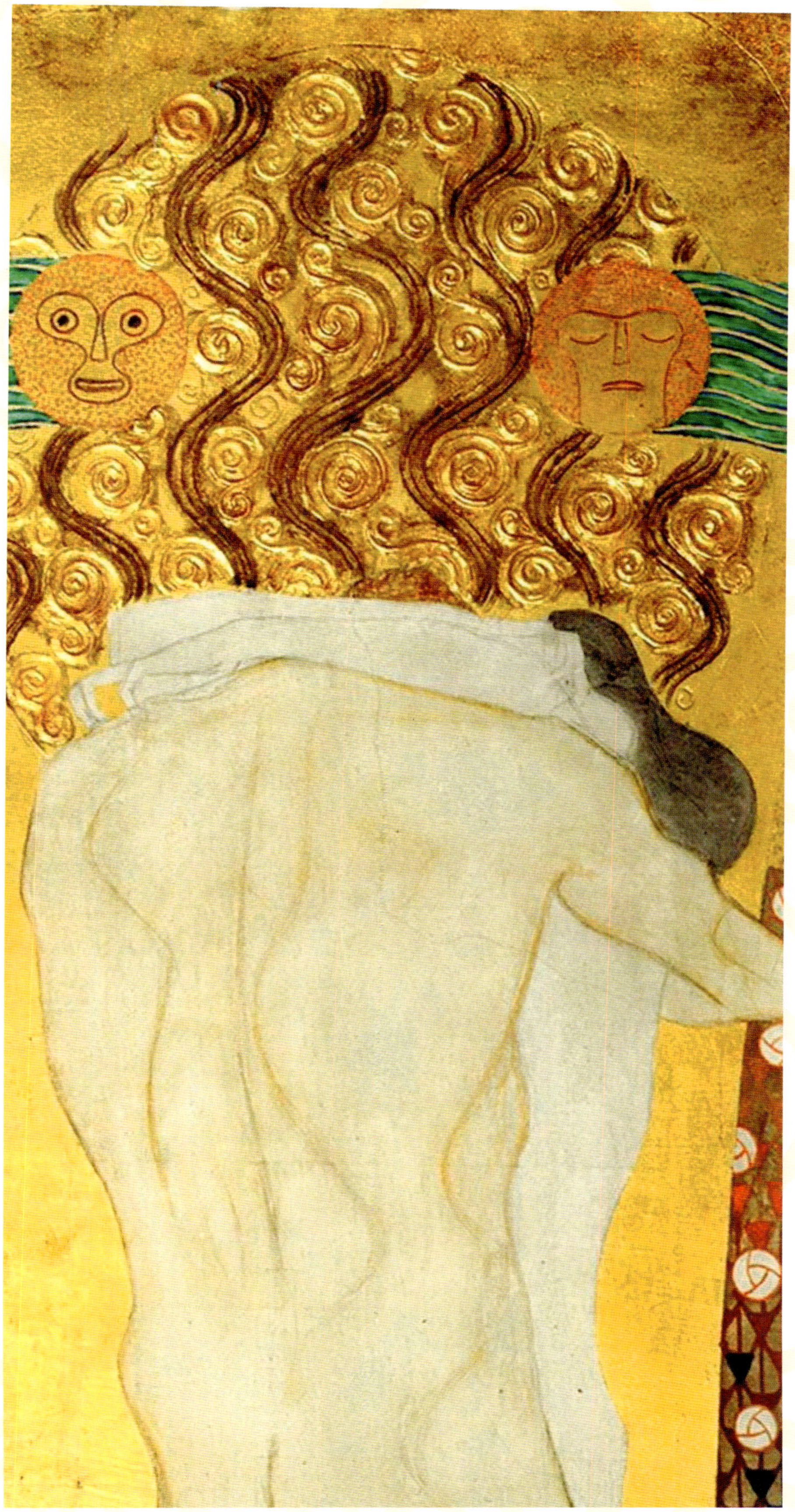

OPPOSITE ◆ THE BEETHOVEN FRIEZE: THE ARTS, 1902. GUSTAV KLIMT (1862–1918)
RIGHT ◆ THE BEETHOVEN FRIEZE: HERE'S A KISS TO THE WHOLE WORLD, 1902. GUSTAV KLIMT (1862–1918)

figure from behind, his face – and indeed his whole head – concealed by his broad shoulders as he bends down to kiss his partner. At the literal level, this shows us the ardency of his embrace; more symbolically, it shows us a passion that has overruled the intellect, a couple thinking with heart instead of head. Of the woman's body we see only the odd curving contour; of her head no more than a tress of tumbling hair.

Where we might expect to see the man's head, we see instead a glittering gold effulgence – like the canopy of a magic tree for which the bodies below would make a trunk. While its swirling ornamentation matches the waves of gold on either side (and the rippling waters of life around the lovers' feet), it also makes a playful allusion to the 'golden cabbage' upon the Secession Building's roof.

God and Man

We too easily forget that Klimt's great frieze wasn't originally intended as the main attraction here, though it doesn't seem that the artist himself, with all his ego, let it slip his mind. The wide white spaces on the Secession Building's basement walls; the expansive bands of grey above; the decorative texture of the painting … it's difficult to appreciate this when we've gone specifically to see it, but Klimt's work here actually keeps itself to itself. The frieze certainly did nothing to upstage the statue of Beethoven by Max Klinger – a work that was every bit as extraordinary in its way.

And it was every bit as shocking. As reverential as nineteenth-century denizens had come to feel towards its cultural idol, it was still a shock to see Beethoven represented as a Greek or Roman god. Not because his divinity was really doubted, but because – as classical gods were traditionally represented in a state of semi-undress – it was startling to

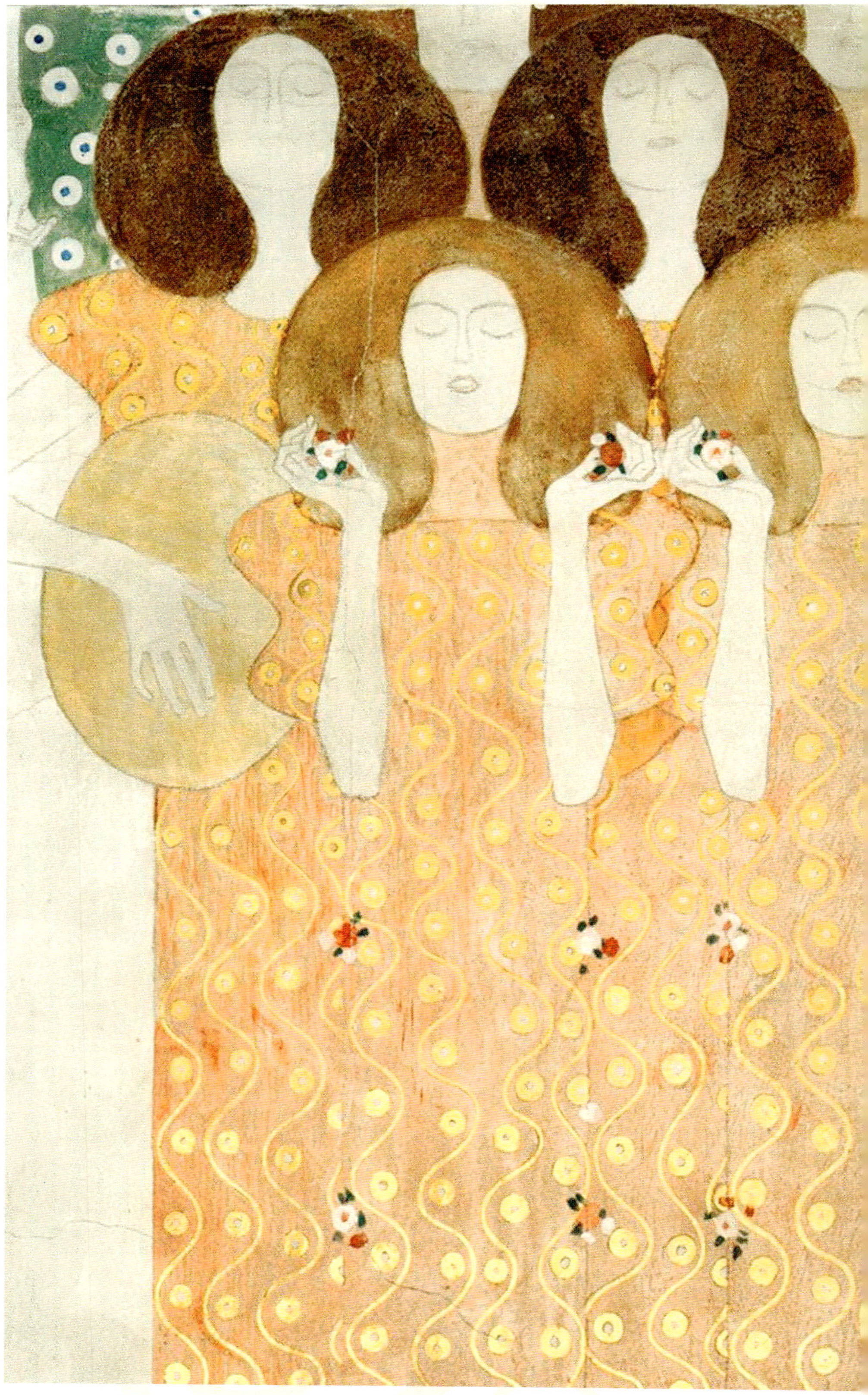

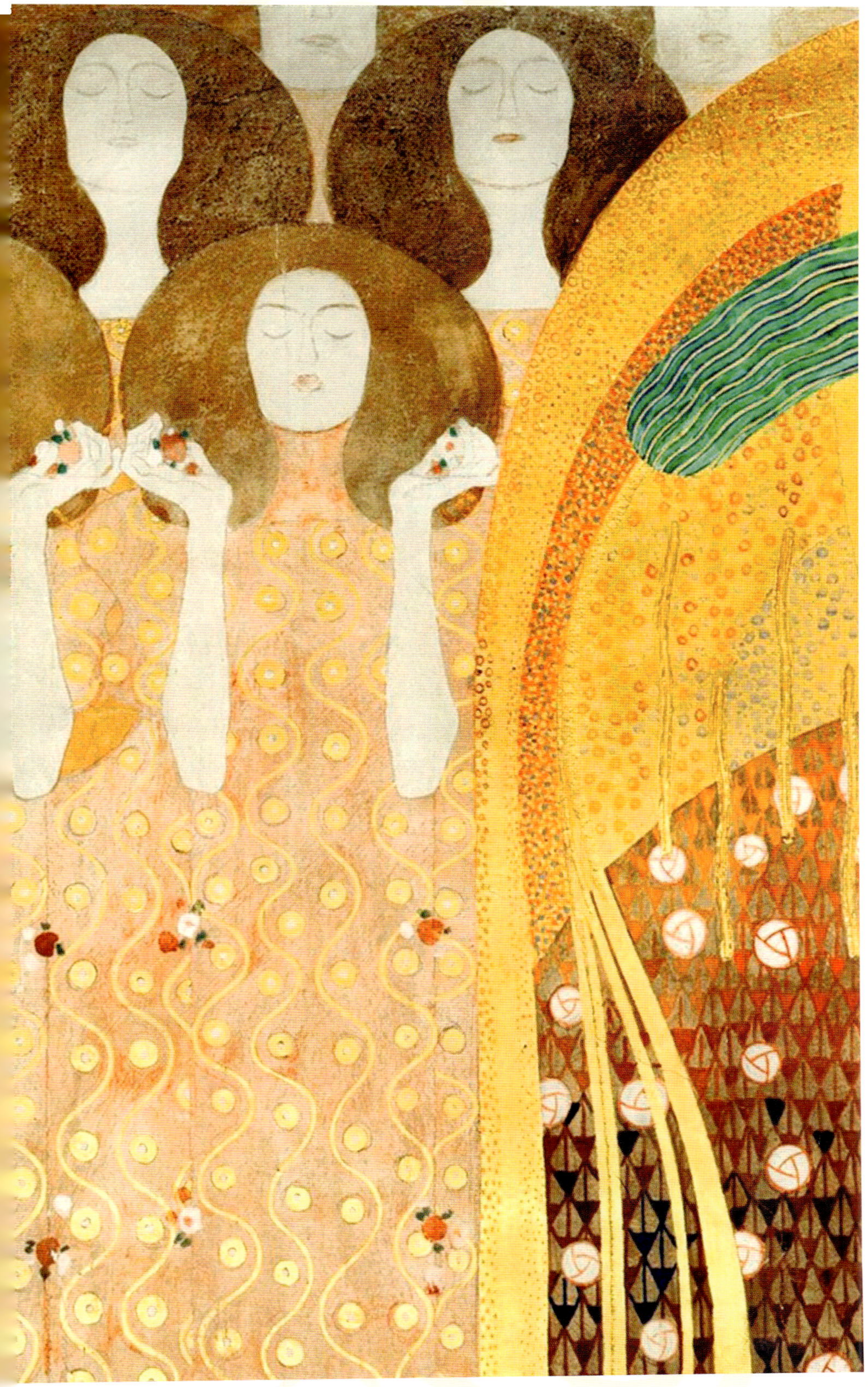

ABOVE • THE BEETHOVEN FRIEZE: CHOIR OF ANGELS, 1902, GUSTAV KLIMT (1862–1918)

see the great man without his frockcoat. And although, his head tilted intently forward, Klinger's composer frowned in the approved manner, in just about every other respect, he broke the mould. His snow-white body bare and buff from the waist upwards, his lower parts were covered by a toga or cloak of coloured marble. At his sandaled feet sat an eagle, the emblematic bird of Jupiter or Zeus.

Christians and Pagans

So much for modern culture's line of descent from the civilization of its classical pagan past. Klinger's Beethoven was seated on an ornate wooden throne that formed part of the sculpture, and whose decorative designs referenced more Christian ideals of godhead and redemption. Around the back and sides were scenes in cast bronze, gold leaf and mosaic of many different materials, representing scenes from the Fall of Man; the Expulsion of Adam and Eve from Eden; and – finally – humanity's redemption by Jesus Christ.

The Crucifixion is also shown, as if witnessed by Christ's cousin, John the Baptist – whom Klinger seems to have confused not just with St John the Evangelist but John the Divine, supposed author of the Book of Revelation. But more shocking to bourgeois Vienna's self-appointed custodians of moral decency was the juxtaposition of *any* such scriptural figures with pagan deities like Zeus/Jupiter or Prometheus, Titan bringer of the gift of fire, or – even worse – with Aphrodite/ Venus, ancient goddess of love.

A Work of Redemption?

What had Beethoven to do with any of this? A good question, and one that no attempt was made explicitly to answer. The viewer was left with a vague feeling that works like the Ninth Symphony had somehow

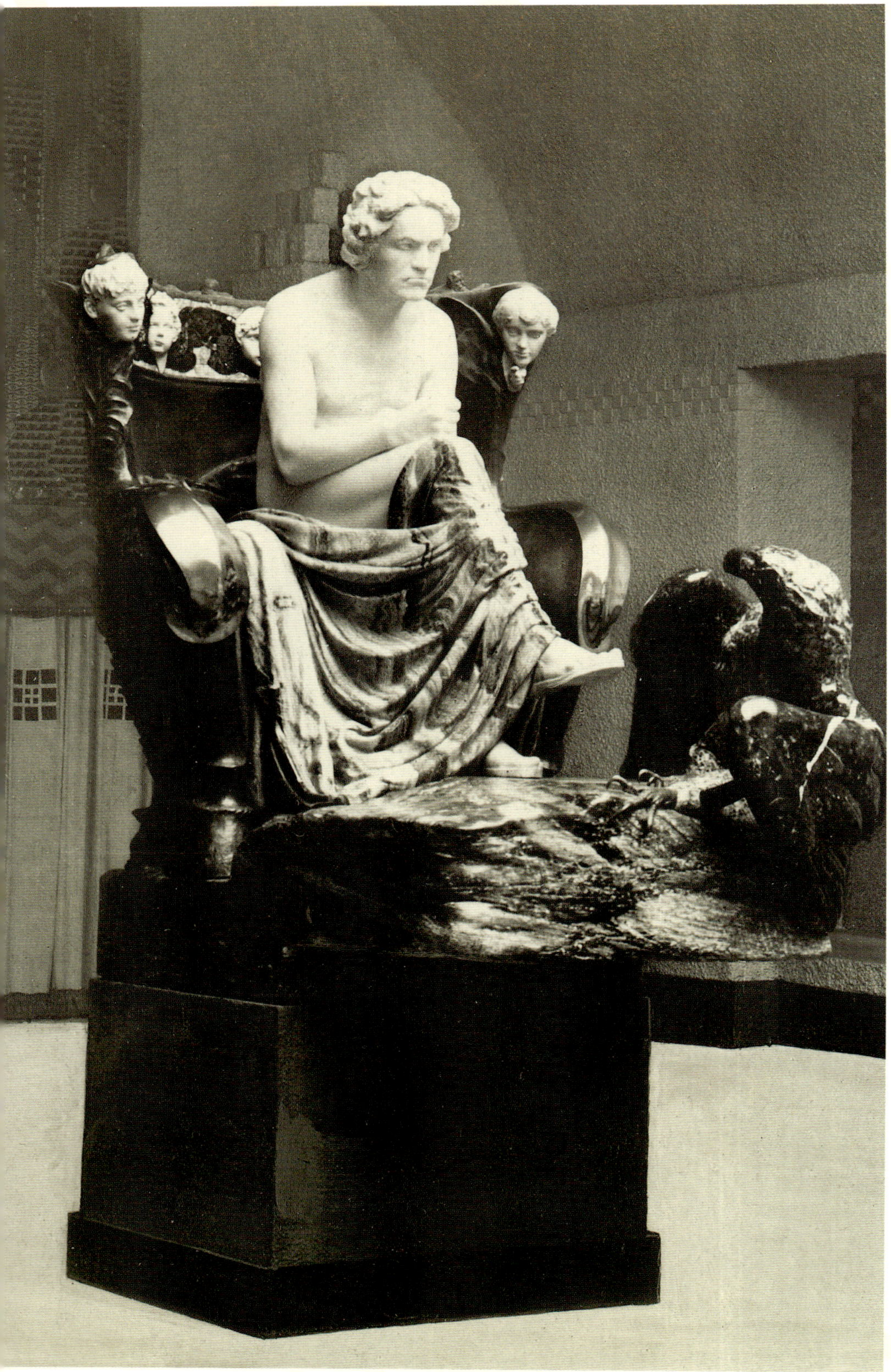

ABOVE ◆ STATUE OF BEETHOVEN IN THE SECESSION BUILDING, 1904. MAX KLINGER (1857–1920)
OPPOSITE ◆ GOLDFISH, 1901–02 (DETAIL). GUSTAV KLIMT (1862–1918)

helped redeem us – just as Jesus had with his death and resurrection and ancient Athens and Rome had with their art and learning. The values embodied in the classics, and the Word made flesh in Christ, had seemingly become word again (and sound, and form, and colour and so forth) in more modern works of heroic human creativity.

Great sculptors have always made exciting paradoxical play with the unyielding character of the material they work with: think of the floppy Christ in Michelangelo's *Pietà* (1498–99), or Bernini's *Ecstasy of St Teresa* (1647–52) – that panting passion captured in cold stone. In the case of Klinger's *Beethoven*, now to be seen in the art museum of the artist's native Leipzig, the complexities are to be found more in the problematic iconographic relation between the principal figure and the subsidiary scenes on his throne, and between the work as a whole and the artistic traditions from which it springs. Once we take these factors into account, the unarguable hardness of the statue seems to dissolve into fluidity, its intractable certainty into ambiguity and doubt.

Dusk, Dawn and Death

On the wall above, behind his head, Beethoven was backed by another great wall painting: a vast creation by Alfred Roller, entitled *Nightfall*. Above a regimented line of panels, decorated towards the top with 'windows' of coloured squares, great banks of colour swept away to either side of a starlit space. Viewed more closely, the spaces to either side turned out to be filled with a repeated female figure – collectively, a crowd: the Daughters of Elysium, bending as they offered up little moonlike spheres of silver light. This mural was 'answered' from the facing wall by *Daybreak*, a work by Adolf Böhm (1861–1927). This showed Eos, the Greek goddess of the dawn, supervising the golden fire from which the light that would bring the day was to be taken.

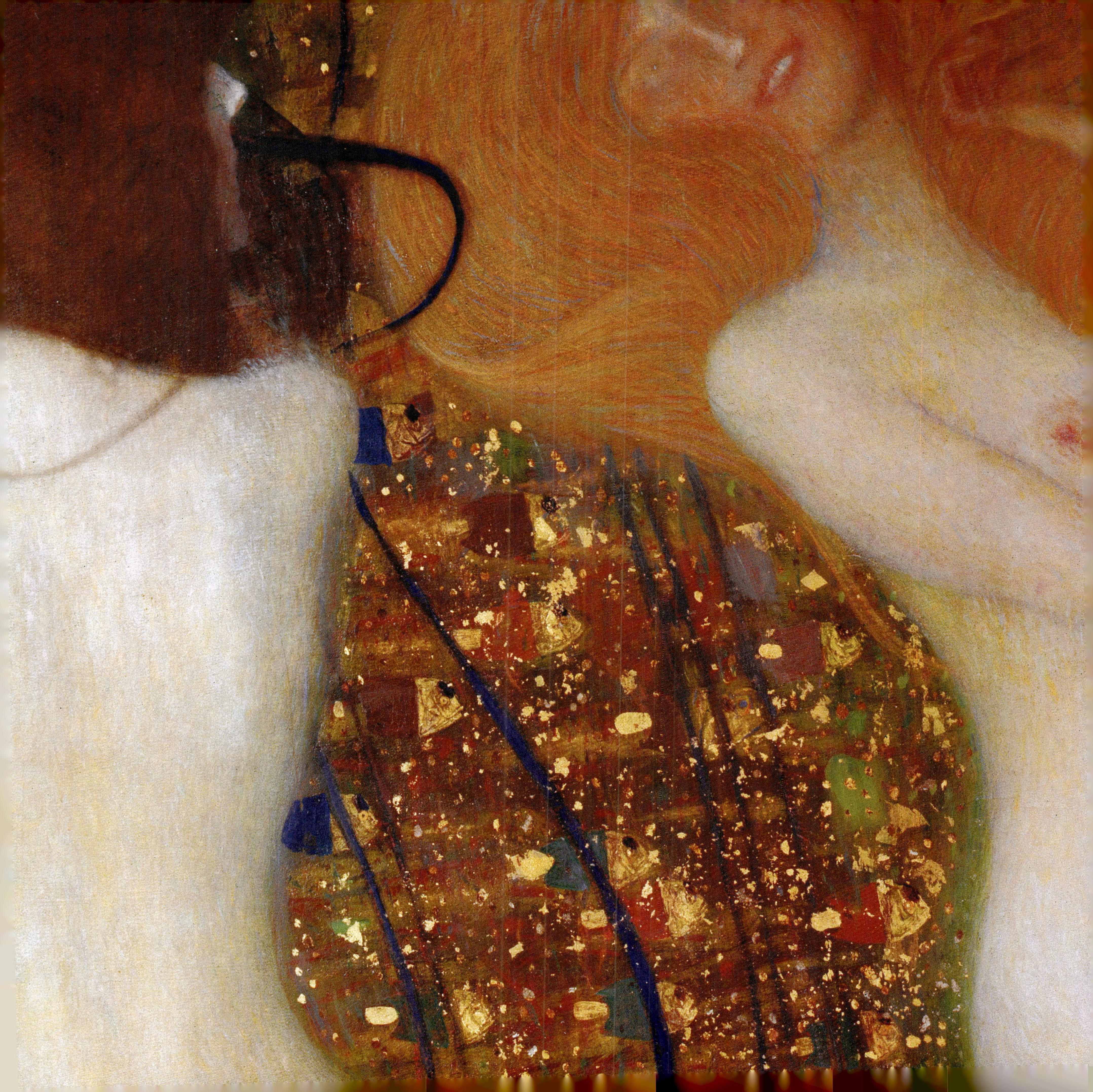

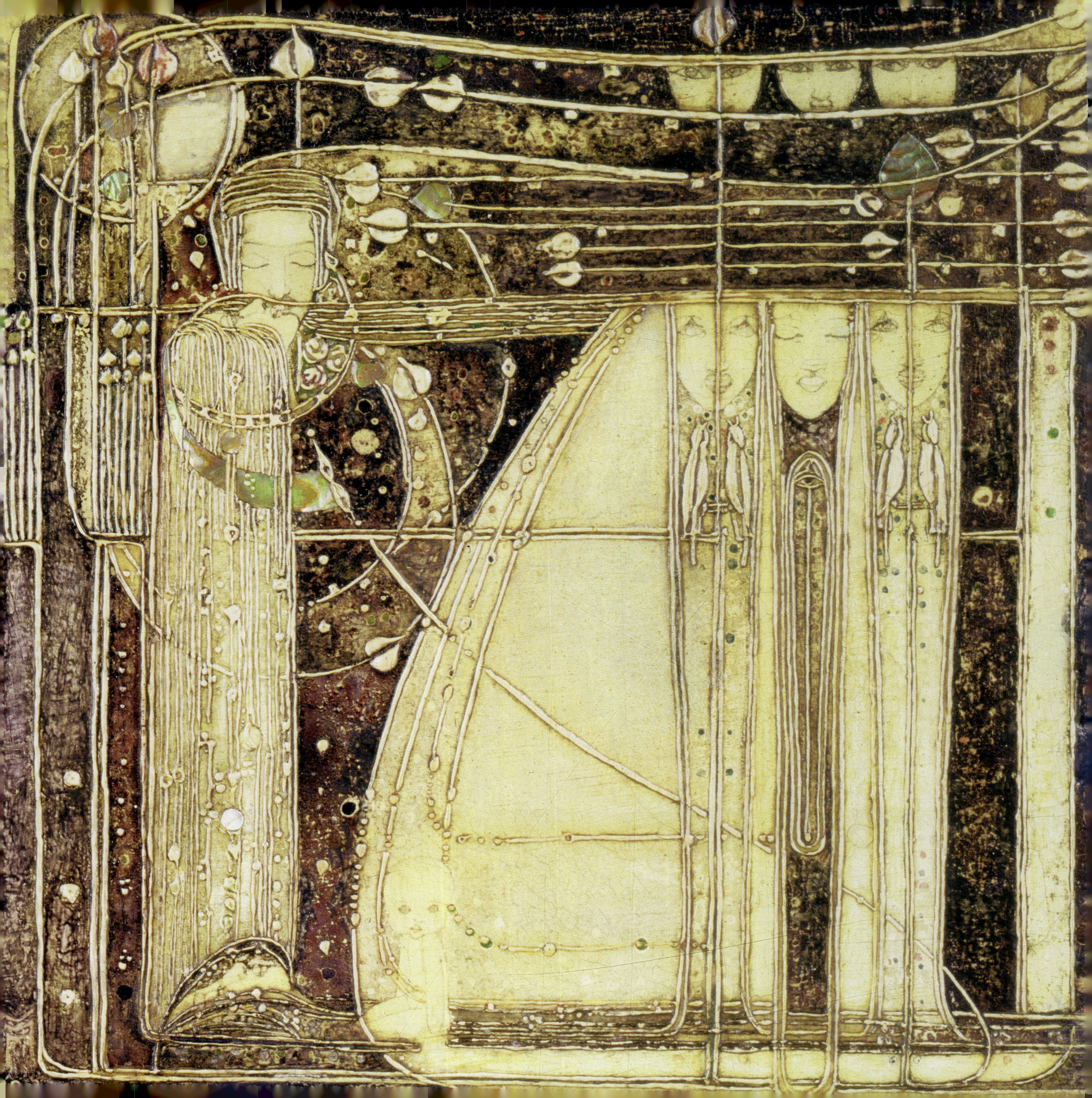

Sunlight, fire and life were obviously a major theme of the exhibition. A stunning sculpture in beaten copper by Friedrich König (1857–1941) showed the Titan Prometheus (already of course featured on Beethoven's throne), chained to a rock by the jealous gods of Olympus, angry that he has given humanity the gift of fire. The connection with Schiller's verse as used by Beethoven was made explicit in a major mural by Josef Auchentaller (1865–1949), *Joy, the Beautiful Spark of the Divine* (a direct quotation from the 'Ode to Joy') and by *Manly Courage and the Battle for Joy* by Ferdinand Andri (1871–1956). This was an epic account of Zeus and his Olympians' fight to vanquish the earthbound Titans and to usher in an age of Joy in heaven.

Artistic Opposition

The opposition of earth and heaven had echoes in the Christian scheme, of course: these were evoked in Koloman Moser's rich mosaic of angels flying. Both Ernst Stöhr (1860–1917) and Friedrich König contributed panels on which maidens floated upwards over stylized plants – not unlike the 'floating genii' of Klimt.

Opposition was indeed at the artistic and intellectual heart of an exhibition which, although obviously in one sense centred on Beethoven and on Klinger's statue, still promoted Secessionist ideas of art as something infinitely multiple, complex and self-transcending.

So symbolically, phallic serpents and blazing suns could be seen as counterpointing feminine mists and moonlight, just as sculpture and decoration complemented painting. And Elena Luksch-Makowsky's Russian folk-art-inflected *Sadko Selects a Bride* found a reply in the female figure of mortality as a cadaverous scythe-wielding peasant woman in another of her works, *Death and Time*.

OPPOSITE ◆ THE OPERA OF THE WIND, c. 1902. MARGARET MACDONALD (1865–1933)
RIGHT ◆ GOLDFISH, 1901–02. GUSTAV KLIMT (1862–1918)

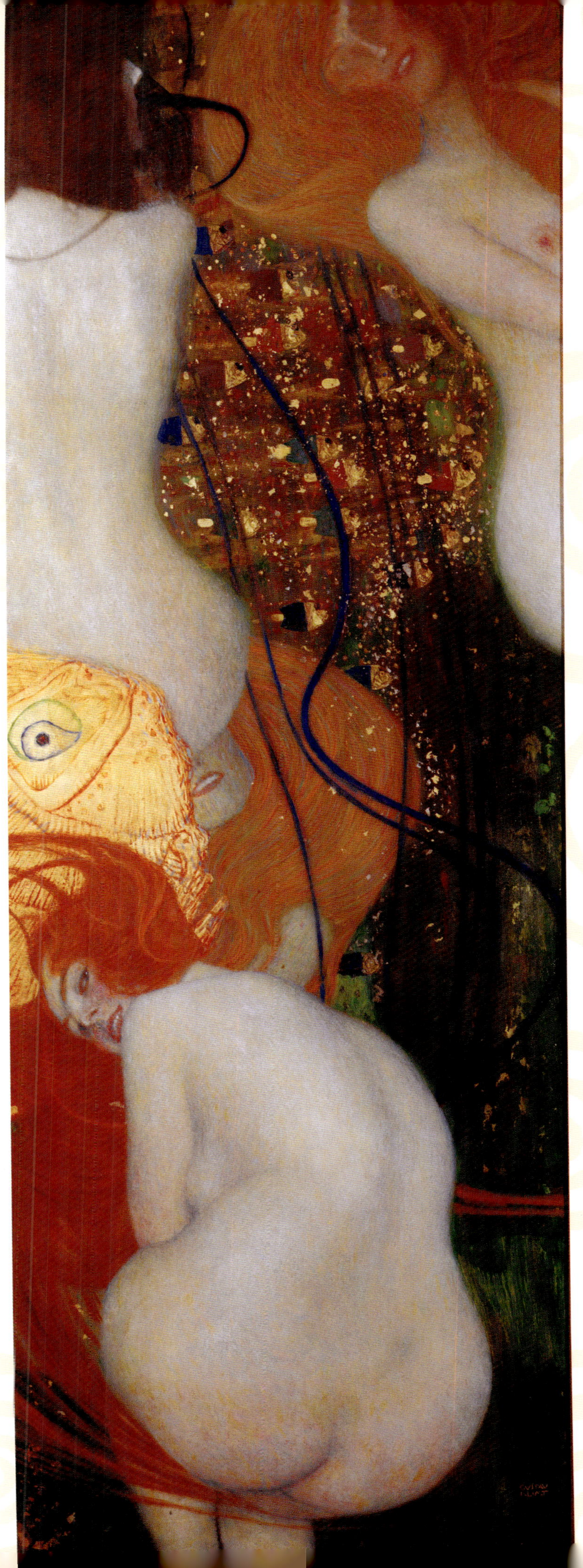

EXHIBITIONS

VIENNA SECESSIONISTS CELEBRATED EXCITING AND INNOVATIVE ART FROM ALL AROUND THE WORLD THROUGH THEIR EXHIBITIONS

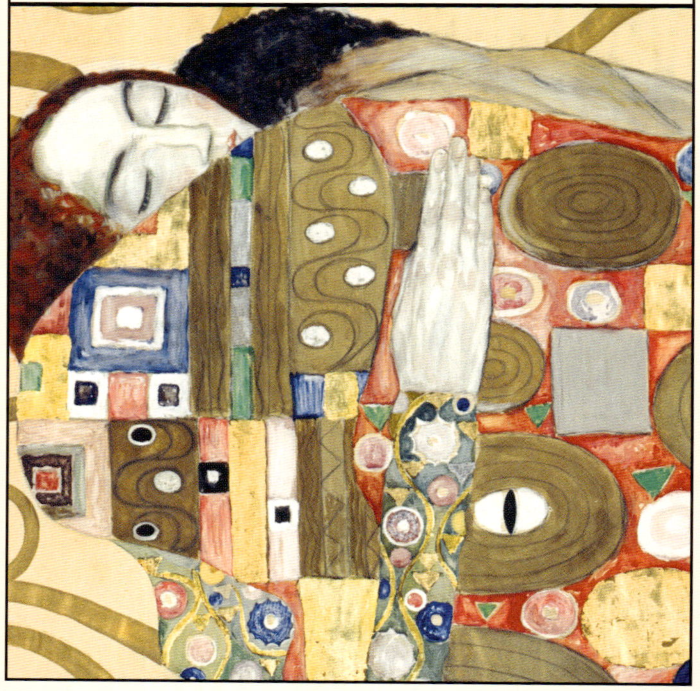

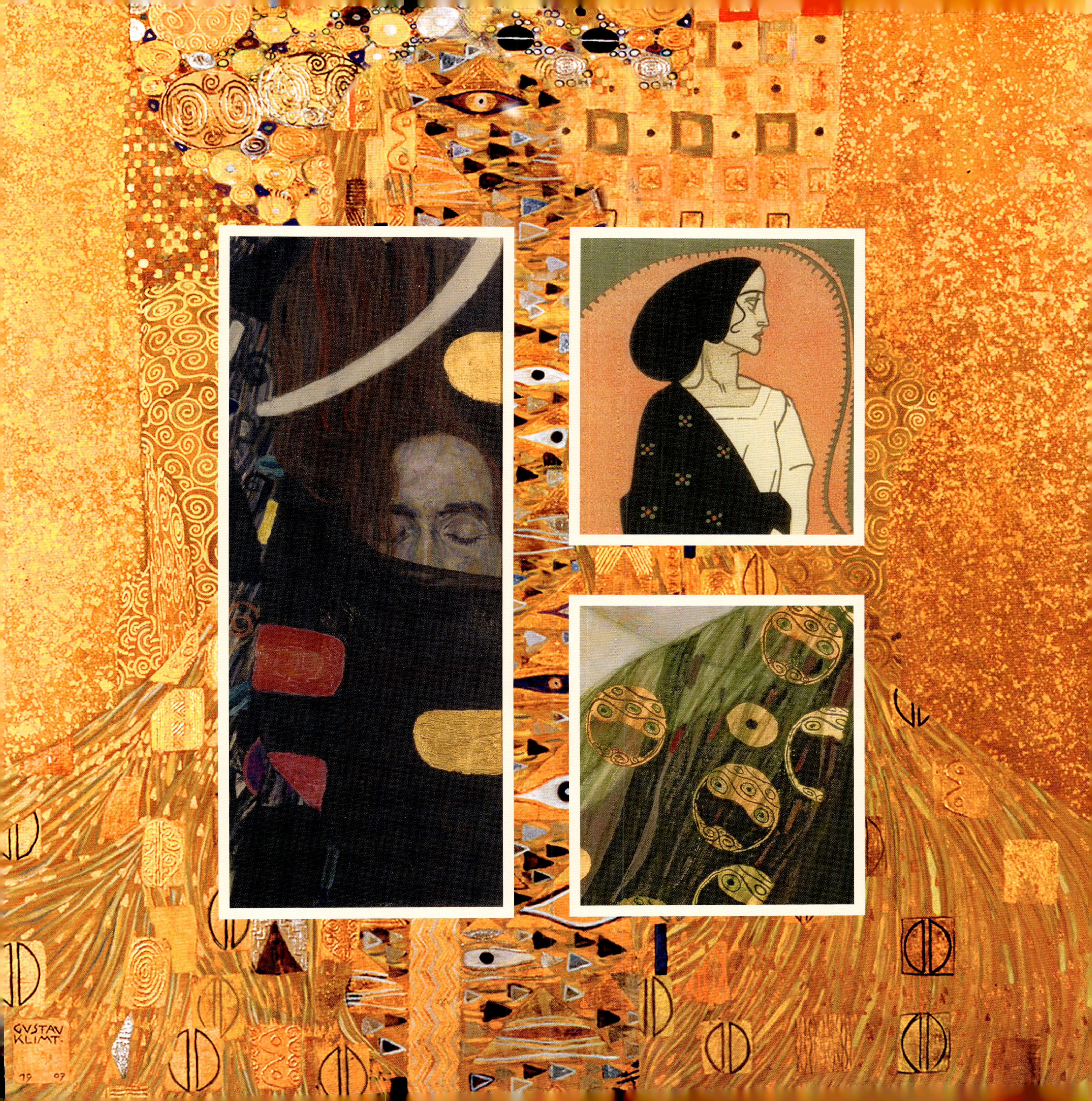
GVSTAV
KLIMT.
19 07

THE Vienna Secessionists held their first exhibition in 1898. As time went on and exhibition succeeded exhibition, all the while bringing in new talents and styles from outside Austria and revealing the innovative creativity of homegrown artists, the Secession was constantly renewing itself, expanding its breadth of reference, pushing back the boundaries of its art.

The success of the Beethoven Exhibition of 1902 did not of course come out of nowhere. It did not even come out of the studios of the Vienna Secession artists – at least not entirely. As we've seen, the Secessionist aesthetic, though highly individualistic in its instinctive recoil from any form of prescriptivism, didn't believe that the individual artwork should exist in isolation. Just as Beethoven's music provided an aural 'accompaniment' for the paintings of Elena Luksch-Makowsky, the panels of Ernst Stöhr and the *objets d'art* of Koloman Moser; just as these in turn created a context for Alfred Roller's *Nightfall* and Adolf Böhm's *Daybreak*; and just as Böhm's sunshine helped to cast new light on Klimt's great frieze, which in its turn illuminated Klinger's special statue; so all these works, taken together, revealed new possibilities and opened up new interpretations – of Olbrich's building, of Vienna's cityscape, of art itself.

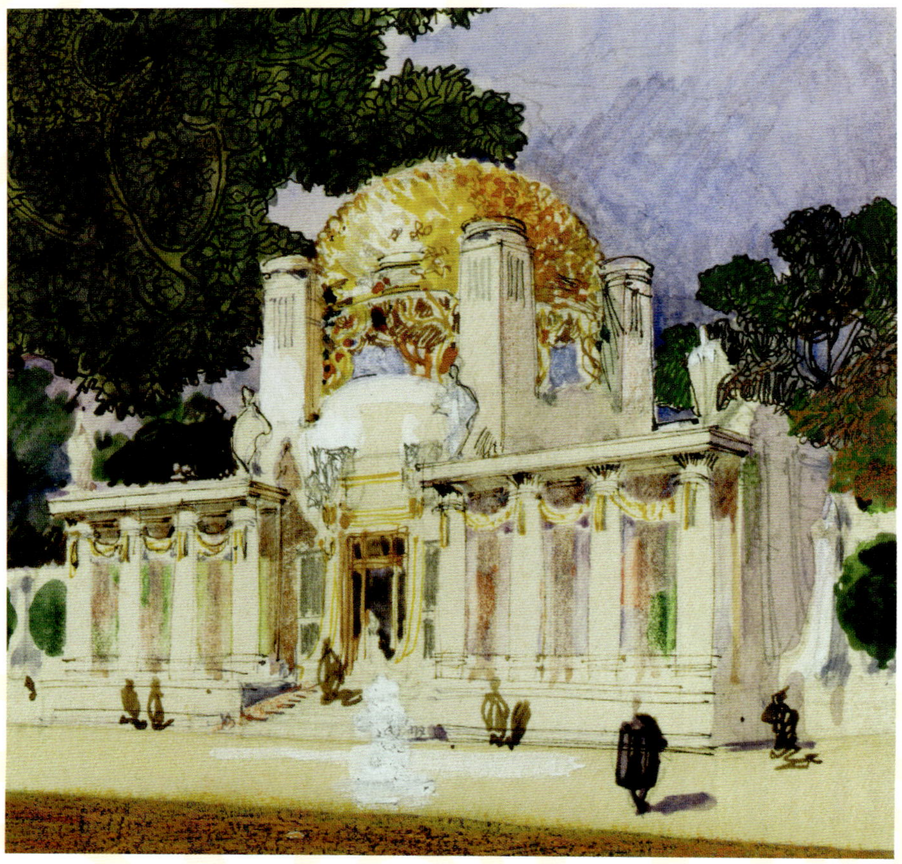

Promotion and Creation

It was also – if we may for a moment go from the sublime to the banal – selling sculptures, promoting pictures and persuading moneyed members of the public that they wanted this or that decorated mirror (or this or that complete home redesign). As we saw in Chapter 2, the Secessionists' stand from the start was, at least in part, a matter of marketing: they had to shape new tastes if they were to be able to keep creating new forms of art. Those who signed up with the Secession (oxymoronic as this may sound), agreed to exhibit exclusively with the movement: their commercial ties were in some ways stronger than their artistic bonds.

Another point which should be borne in mind is that, by the time the Beethoven Exhibition was held in 1902, the Secession – though only five years old – had already held no fewer than 13 exhibitions in that time. Accordingly, they were good at it; had acquired experience; developed skills and insights that had come to seem instinctual. They knew what they were doing – they hardly had to try.

First Principles

But there wouldn't have been a Vienna Secession had not an important element in the artistic community already been growing impatient of the established conventions by the 1890s; nor would Klimt and his

LEFT ◆ SKETCH FOR THE SECESSION BUILDING, VIENNA, 1897, JOSEPH MARIA OLBRICH (1867–1908)
OPPOSITE ◆ OWLS, FAÇADE OF THE SECESSION BUILDING, ATTRIB. TO KOLOMAN MOSER (1868–1918)

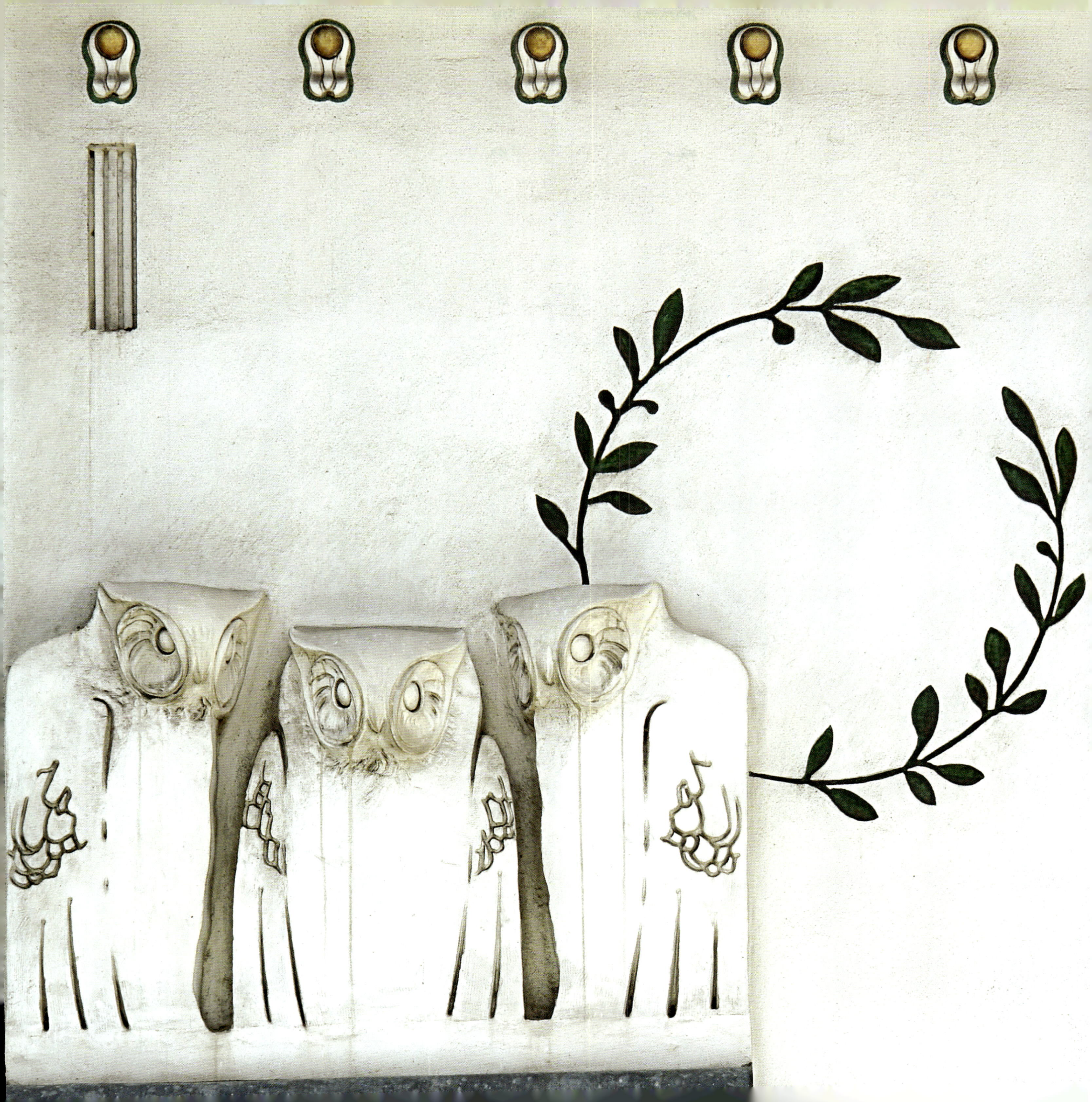

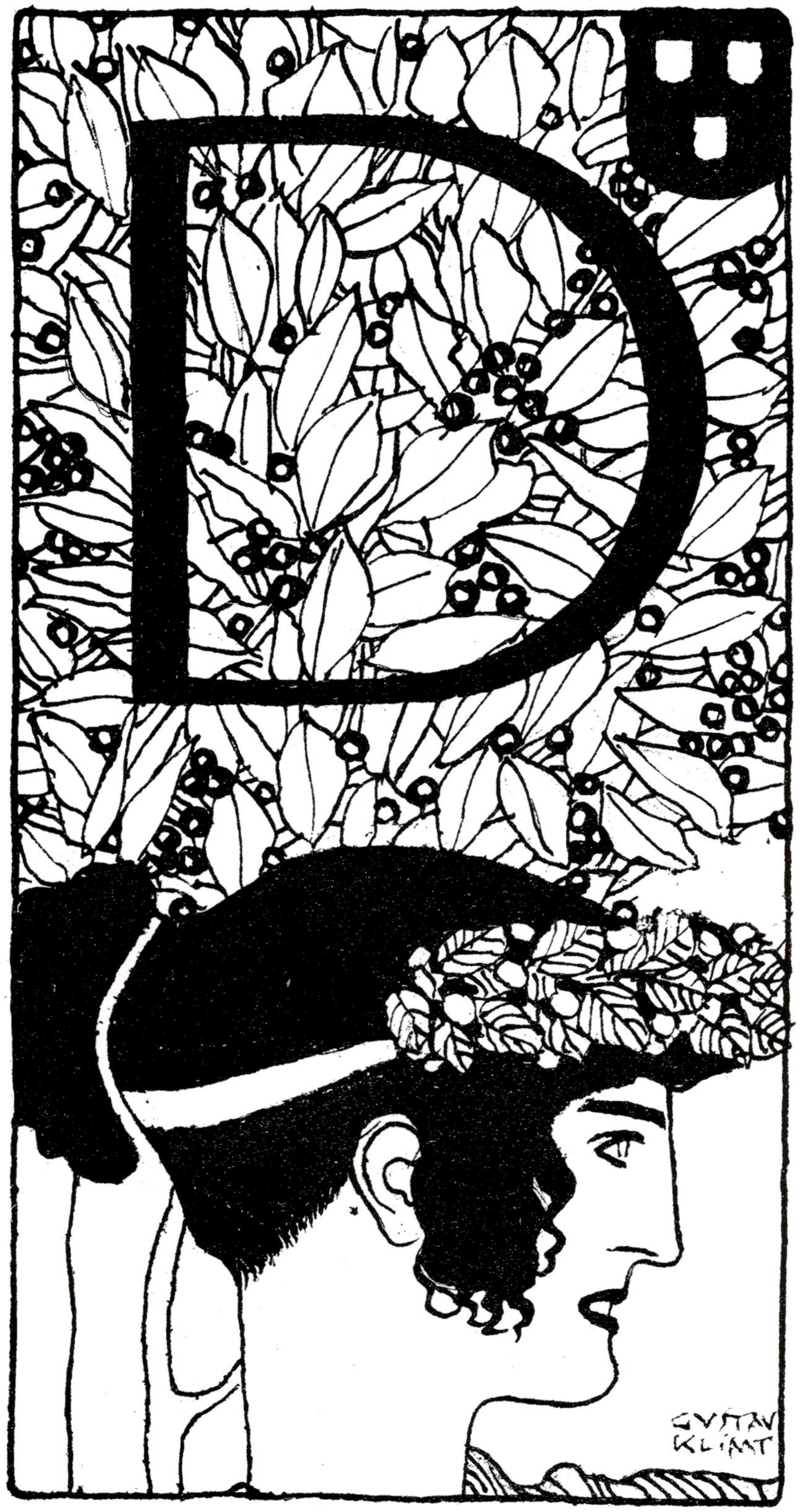

contemporaries have staged their walkout if they hadn't already been eager to find new ways of exhibiting their work – a sticking point in their discussions with the Künstlerhaus from the first. So although time and experience surely developed these interests, then, the sensibility that was ultimately to give rise to the Beethoven Exhibition was already there when the Secession took place in 1897. It was certainly in evidence by the time the first exhibition of the new group was staged, at the end of March, 1898.

The Secession Building did not yet exist, though an eager and ambitious meeting of young artists had already agreed and announced their intention of building it. But Joseph Maria Olbrich, the man who was to undertake the design of the 'Assyrian public lavatory', had agreed to take charge of the arrangements for this first show. It was to be held in the pavilion of the Royal and Imperial Association of Horticulture, at the heart of Vienna's central Stadtpark.

Poster Boy

Klimt's poster for the event (*see* page 135) was largely Beardsley-esque blank space, echoed later by the (controversial) flatness of so much of the Secession Building's outside walls. The empty space of the poster was framed above and to the right by mythology-inspired designs – though these seemed calculated more to tease the beholder with their mystery than to advertise. But the allegorical meaning was there when you thought about it a little: in the legend, the Minotaur was kept by King Minos in a labyrinth beneath his royal palace at Knossos. In thrall to the Cretan tyrant, the city of Athens was forced to send a selection of young men each year to be eaten by the monster. In slaying the Minotaur, Theseus had been liberating youth.

LEFT ◆ INITIAL 'D', USED IN THE THIRD ISSUE OF 'VER SACRUM', 1898. GUSTAV KLIMT (1862–1918)
OPPOSITE ◆ VIENNA SECESSION 1ST EXHIBITION POSTER, 1898. GUSTAV KLIMT (1862–1918)

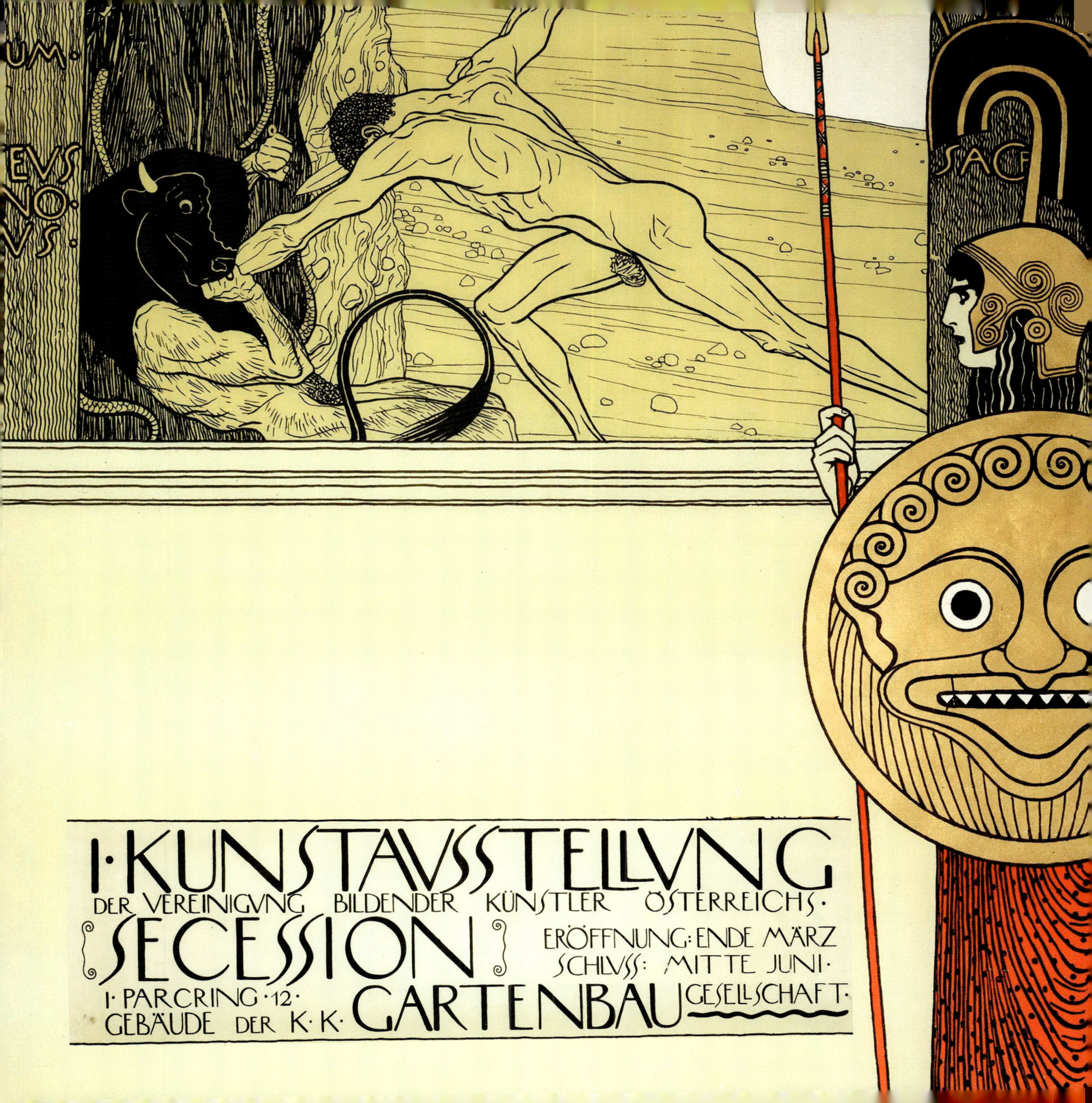
I·KUNSTAVSSTELLVNG
DER VEREINIGVNG BILDENDER KÜNSTLER ÖSTERREICHS·
SECESSION
ERÖFFNUNG: ENDE MÄRZ
SCHLVSS: MITTE JUNI·
I· PARCRING ·12·
GEBÄUDE DER K·K· GARTENBAU GESELLSCHAFT·

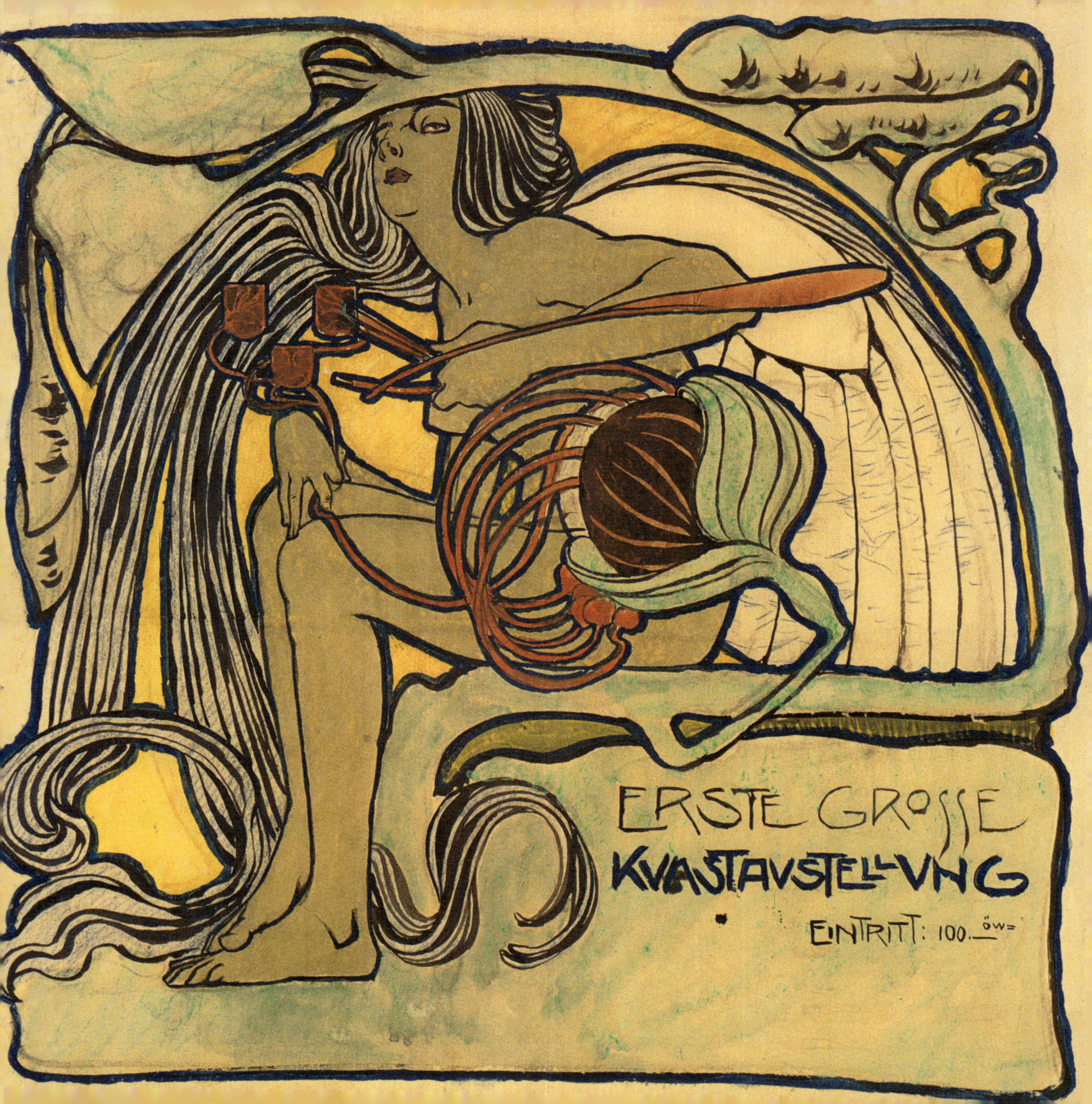
ERSTE GROSSE
KVNSTAVSTELLVNG
EINTRITT: 100.– ÖW=

Whether his public managed to grasp this meaning or not, Klimt's strategy seemed to work, and on the appointed opening day of the exhibition, it was an excited crowd that thronged and jostled in the walkways of the park, waiting impatiently until the pavilion opened its doors. When they were finally able to push their way inside, they found that – as though in some late-nineteenth-century episode of Ovid (*see* page 50) – the place had been changed utterly, whilst at the same time retaining traces of its original nature as the headquarters of a gardening society. Plants and flowers ('specially cultivated and bred in the nursery of the Sophienbad') were everywhere, visitors remarked.

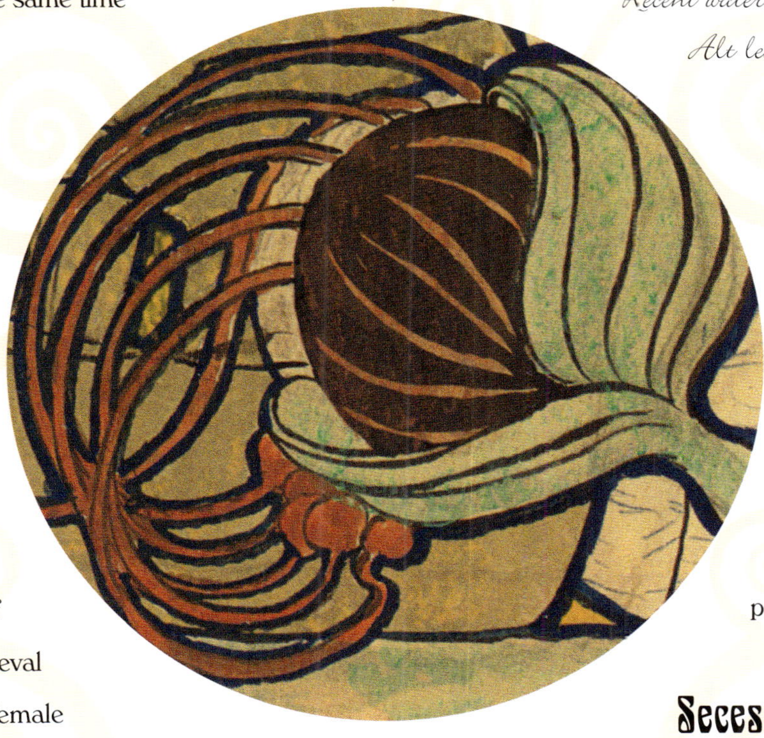

Growth and Abundance

Plants became something of a theme: the picture postcards Koloman Moser designed for sale as souvenirs at the exhibition were conceived of in a range of different styles, from Arts-and-Crafts Medieval to Japonist. But more or less all showed female figures accompanied by symbols of vegetal growth to suggest the idea of artistic rebirth. Even Klimt had adopted the floral theme, presenting his first (and least stylized) landscape at the exhibition: a charming scene of *After the Rain* (1898, *see* page 143).

One reviewer described his impressions on arriving at the exhibition – already clearly sensing that it had to be experienced as a whole:

> *Blunt obelisks flank the entrance; on the pedestals stand exquisite metal and marble sculptures ... decorative plants surround uniquely appealing furniture after English patterns with ornamental vessels and bibelots, while the frieze above shows a fantastical aster motif ... The vaulted ceiling is transformed into a light tent roof; a frieze of golden foliage, luxuriantly growing over the portal arch, marks the upper boundaries of the taupe-coloured walls at a moderate height. Recent watercolours by Honorary President R. v. Alt lean against easels.*

The sense of a spilling-over of creative abundance is as evident in the excitable haste of the writer's syntax as it is in the description of a ceiling that becomes a 'light tent roof'; a frieze of foliage overhanging arches over doorways; or the 'recent watercolours' – seemingly randomly positioned about the place; as yet unframed, like works in progress, still 'against easels'.

Secessionist Success

The Secessionists' favourite, Fernand Khnopff; Giovanni Segantini (1858–99), the Italian landscape artist – now experimenting with Symbolism – as well as a final-period James McNeill Whistler (1834–1903) were among the foreign painters represented at the show. Amongst the sculptors were Auguste Rodin (1840–1917) and Sir George Frampton (1860–1928), an Englishman, whose influence at the head of London's 'New Sculpture' movement had, however, been strongly influenced by the work of the exiled French sculptor Aimé-Jules Dalou (1838–1902).

OPPOSITE AND ABOVE RIGHT ◆ POSTER DESIGN FOR THE FIRST MAJOR ART EXHIBITION OF THE SECESSION, 1897. KOLOMAN MOSER (1868–1918)

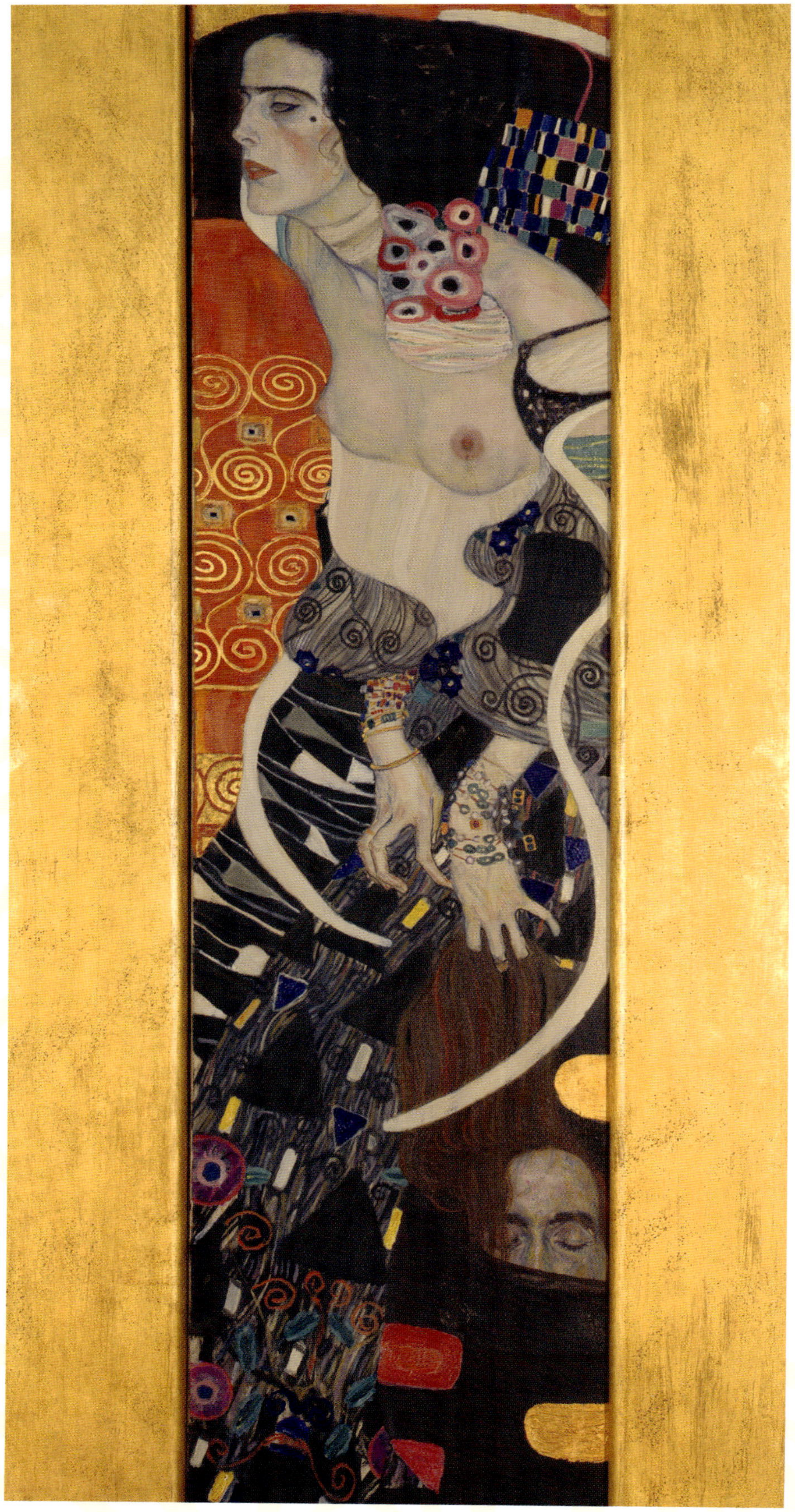

There were also works of decorative art by the Belgian designer Henry van de Velde (1863–1957) – a leading figure in Art Nouveau whose free and easy way with a curved line had made him an important influence on everything from furniture to fabric design. Josef Flossmann (1862–1914) had come from Munich – a man with first-hand experience of staging his own secession, having been involved in events in his home city six years before. The work of these outsiders was juxtaposed within the exhibition with the creations of the Secessionists themselves though, as the critic Ludwig Hevesi (1843–1910) pointed out: 'The various works of an artist are united in a group so that his art is presented in an organic context.'

The wall coverings provide advantageous backgrounds; pictures in pale colours develop their full atmospheric potential in front of pleated white fabrics; walls sprayed in calm dark red or dark green appear lighter than smoothly whitewashed ones.

Most important of all, Hevesi noted, pictures were hung at a sensible height, and in sufficient space, not stacked up one above the other, as in the cluttered galleries of old. All in all, he concluded: 'the arrangement of the exhibition … is in itself already a work of art in the modern taste.' Josef Hoffmann had taken charge of the arrangements for a separate room dedicated to *Ver Sacrum* – once again, artistic and commercial considerations dovetailed nicely.

An Emperor Joins the Crowds

In the end, over 57,000 visitors came to this first exhibition – including the Emperor Franz Joseph I, as conservative as they came in his attitudes to art, but a fan of Klimt since seeing his *Old Burgtheater* 10 years before. The importance of the Emperor Franz Joseph's seal of

LEFT ◆ JUDITH II, 1909. GUSTAV KLIMT (1862–1918)
OPPOSITE ◆ THE ARTS: SKETCH OF A ROUND WINDOW, 1897. KOLOMAN MOSER (1868–1918)

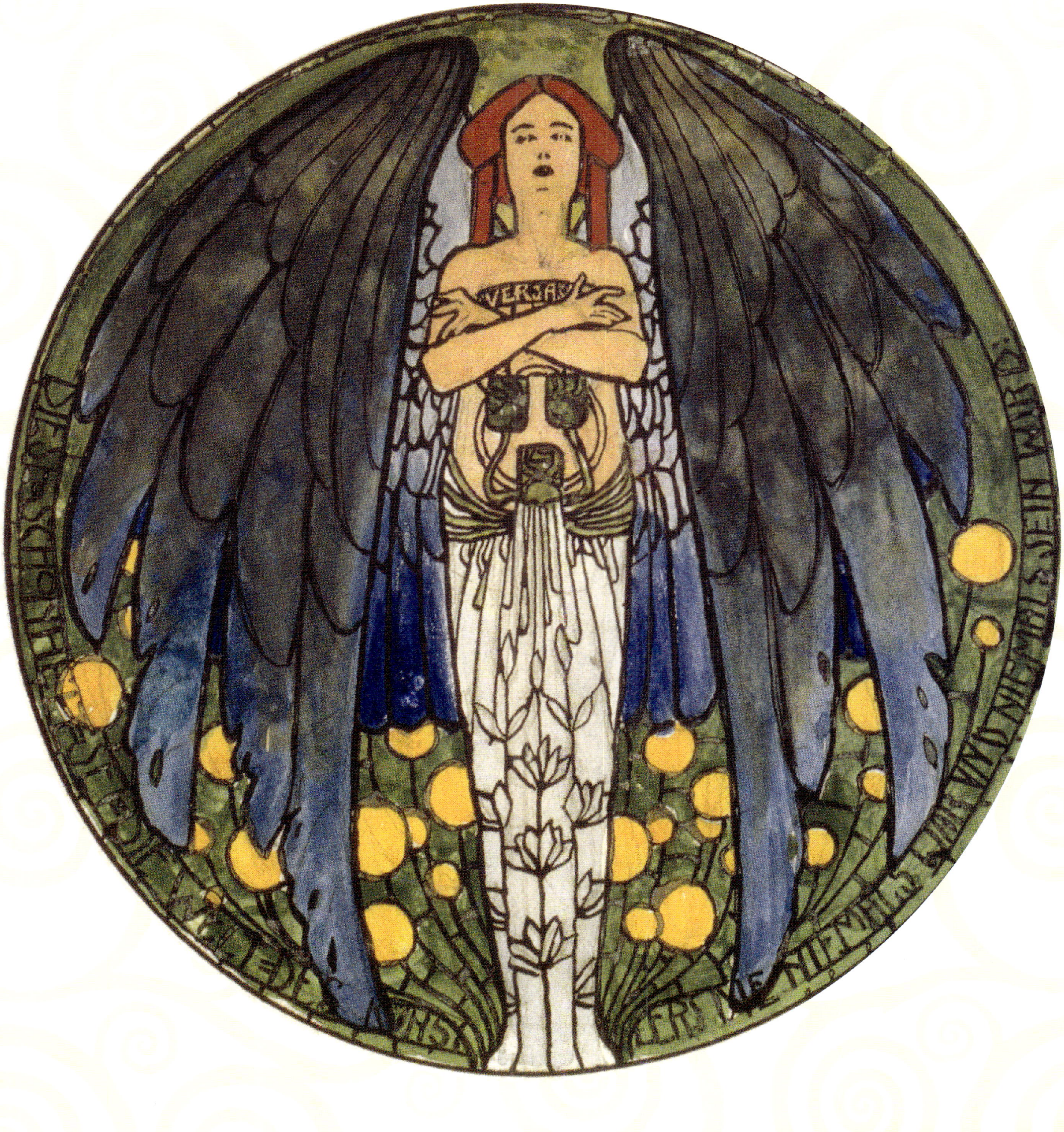

imperial approval can hardly be overstated – especially for young artists and craftsmen who, however aesthetically rebellious, still hoped to sell their works. And sell them they did: more than 200 items were sold in all – a resounding success as far as the Secessionists were concerned.

As at a prestigious art exhibition today, moreover, there was a brisk sale in tie-in merchandise, from picture postcards to copies of *Ver Sacrum*. Indeed, the money raised by the artists at this first exhibition contributed significantly towards the costs of Olbrich's Secession Building, which – though at the centre of his thoughts for months – hadn't yet made it beyond the drawing board. The building could not have been erected without Karl Wittgenstein, but the exhibition money was still vital – not just economically, but in giving the artists a sense of proprietorship. Within a few weeks of their exhibition ending, work was going forward: on 28 April, 1898, the foundation

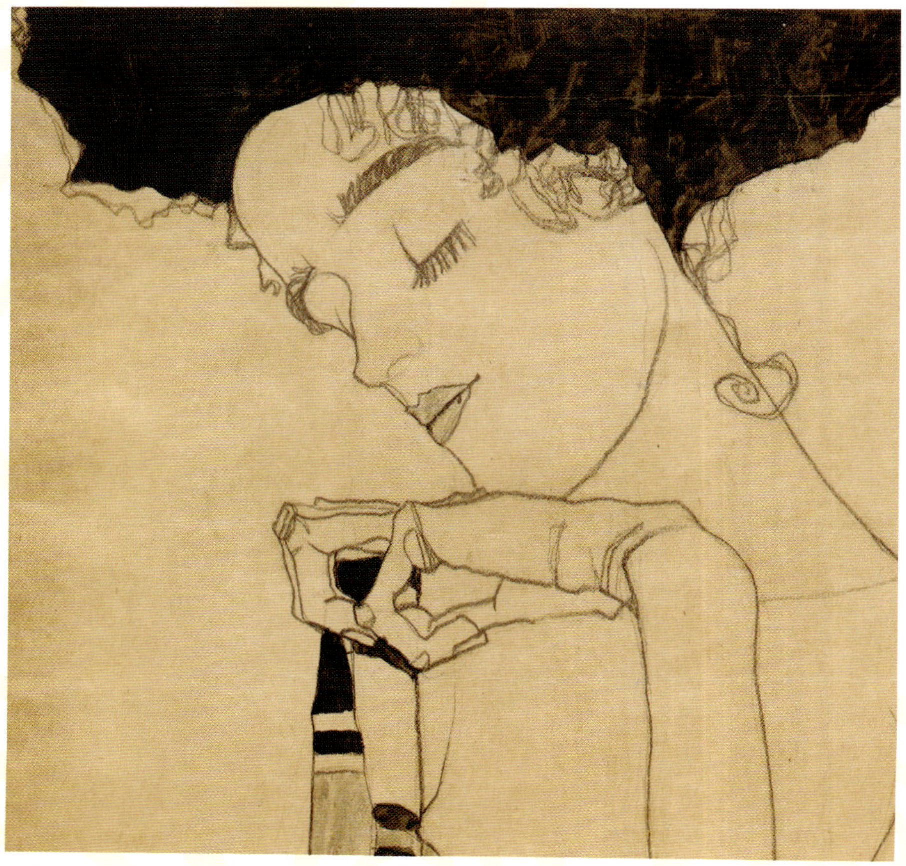

stone of the Secession Building was laid. Construction was then completed in just six months, and the building was ready to open on 28 October, 1898.

From Laughing Stock to Landmark

Ludwig Hevesi described the Secession Building's construction in terms of transformation – not just of an empty site to a museum, but of a source of derision into an impressive artistic centre. 'The white house on the River Wien is finished,' he wrote:

> *The young artists have succeeded in erecting in six months a great new building … And for all these months the Viennese passed the strange building daily. They shook their heads, laughed and were scandalized … soon there were jokes: some called it the Mahdi's tomb, others a cross between a greenhouse and a blast furnace … others, again, went as far as to call it an Assyrian public lavatory. There was general perplexity, but it gradually dawned on people that it was no joking matter.*

The 'cabbage' dome, he said:

> *is a bower crowned by a gigantic laurel tree painted in gold-leaf: 3,000 leaves …. 700 berries, an enchanting sight. And through the gaps you can see the sky above and the townscape beyond.*

This point about perspective, about being able to see through the 'dome' to the sky and the city, was of course yet another example of the Secessionist insistence that 'art' and 'the world' should not be separate spheres. 'Hermann Bahr's words around the exhibition hall run thus …', Hevesi concluded:

LEFT ◆ STANDING GIRL, c. 1908–09 (DETAIL), EGON SCHIELE (1890–1918)
OPPOSITE ◆ VIENNA SECESSION 5TH EXHIBITION POSTER, 1899, KOLOMAN MOSER (1868–1918)

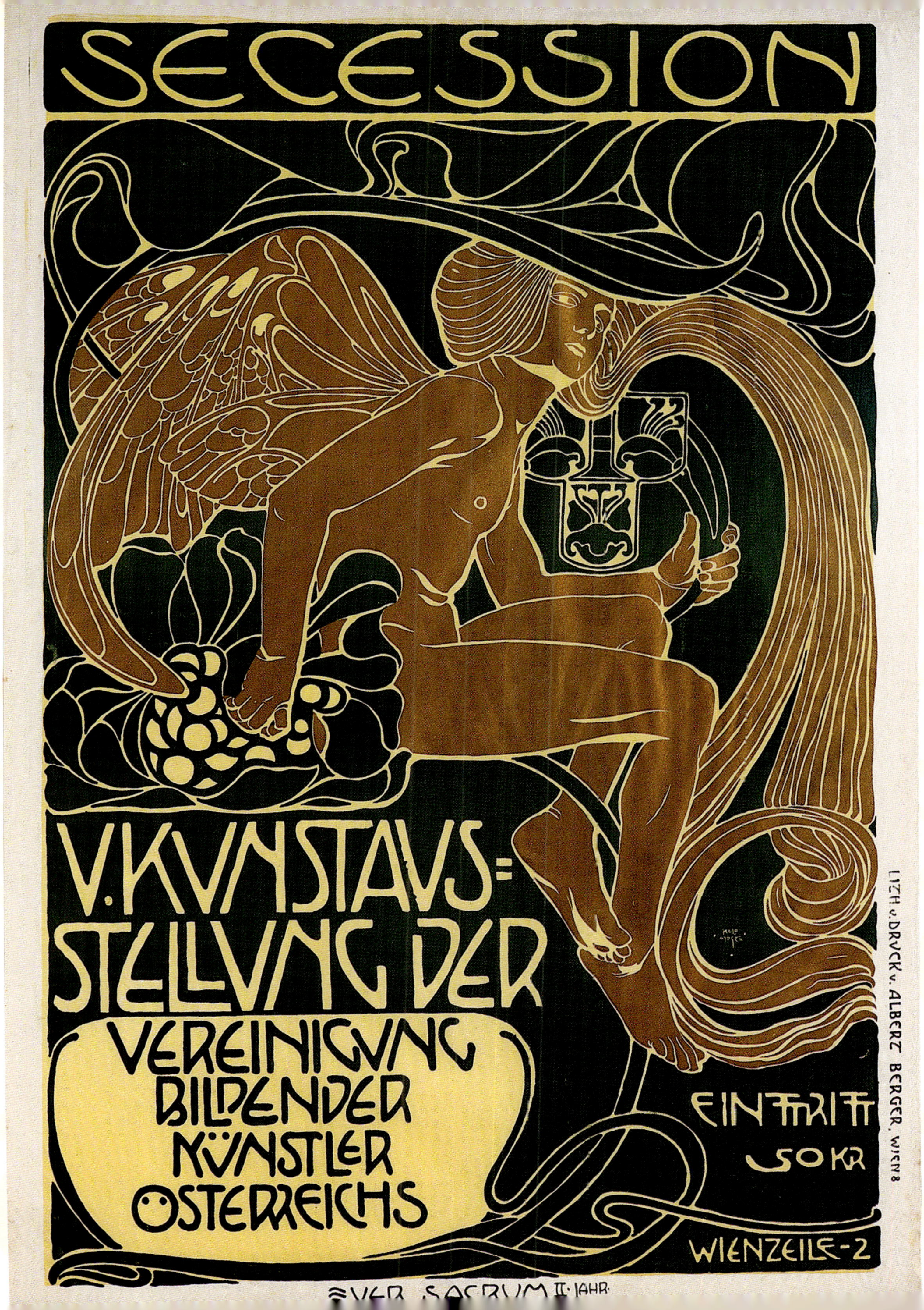
SECESSION
V. KUNSTAUS=
STELLUNG DER
VEREINIGUNG
BILDENDER
KÜNSTLER
OSTERREICHS
EINTRITT
50 KR
WIENZEILE-2
LITH. v. DRUCK v. ALBERT BERGER, WIEN 8
VER SACRUM II· JAHR·

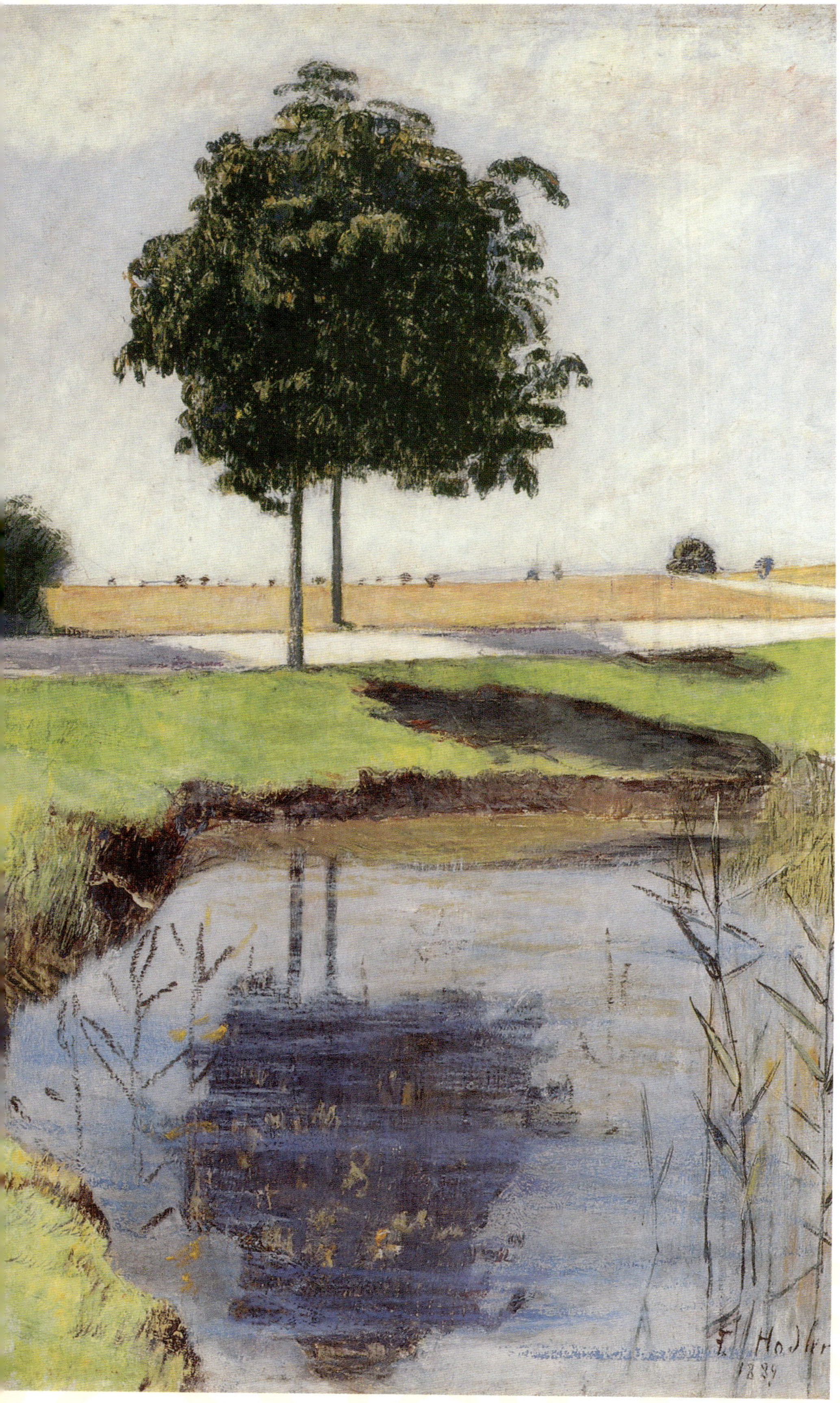

'Let the artist show his world, the beauty that was born with him, that never was before and never will be again.'

Art, in short, was at once of all time and – emphatically – of its own time.

A Room of Art's Own

Not surprisingly, the Secessionist champion Hermann Bahr was having no truck with those who claimed that Olbrich's building looked like a public convenience or its cupola like a cabbage. But he knew that the Philistines were bound to have their say:

I suspect that there will be a great outcry and the foolish people will rage. That is why I want to say the most important things right now, while I am calm and dispassionate. Polemics will come later.

Maintaining that impressive air of unruffled poise, he promptly invited his reader on a walking tour of what he saw as a great boon for his home city:

Let us go into the building. First, we enter a room that is meant to put us into a ceremonial mood. Almost like a propylaeum.

A propylaeum was the imposing ceremonial gateway to some sacred complex – the original had stood at the entrance to the Acropolis in Athens. So it was to be in Vienna's Secession Building:

And that is its sole purpose: it is an atrium where one can cleanse oneself from the mundane, look to the eternal, lay down the worries and vagaries of daily life and prepare for devotion. You could almost call it a silent cloister for the soul.

LEFT • THE CHESTNUT TREES, 1889, FERDINAND HODLER (1853–1918)

If the Graeco-Roman terminology ('propylaeum', 'atrium') suggests a mischievous dig at those who felt that an art museum *had* to be classical in its conception, Bahr's religious imagery here is more unexpected. And it perhaps suggests a certain defensiveness on his part, that he's maybe protesting too much about the artistic resonance of Olbrich's work. Indeed, in the self-same essay, Bahr observed that Olbrich's building 'does not pretend to be a temple' – just a 'space which allows works of art to develop to their greatest effect'. But he's clearly reluctant to relinquish the idea that secular art is in some sense sacred.

Spirit and Dignity

As well he might be: Olbrich himself had written of his aims in designing the Secession Building in all but ecstatically spiritual terms. 'The walls shall be white,' he'd said:

> *shining, sacred and chaste. Solemn dignity shall pervade everything. Pure dignity as it seized me as I stood alone, shuddering, in front of the unfinished temple in Segesta!*

That said, the Secessionist desire to demystify art had never really been about bringing it 'down' to the level of ordinary life: rather, it had been the reverse; a desire to elevate the quotidian to artistic heights. And even as Olbrich engaged in flights of artistic piety, he was planning with the utmost practicality an exhibition space more pragmatically adaptable than had ever yet been seen. With its blank walls and its cunning construction (such that only six pillars were needed to support its roof), it permitted the free use of movable partition walls so that no two exhibition layouts had to be the same.

RIGHT • AFTER THE RAIN, 1899, GUSTAV KLIMT (1862–1918)

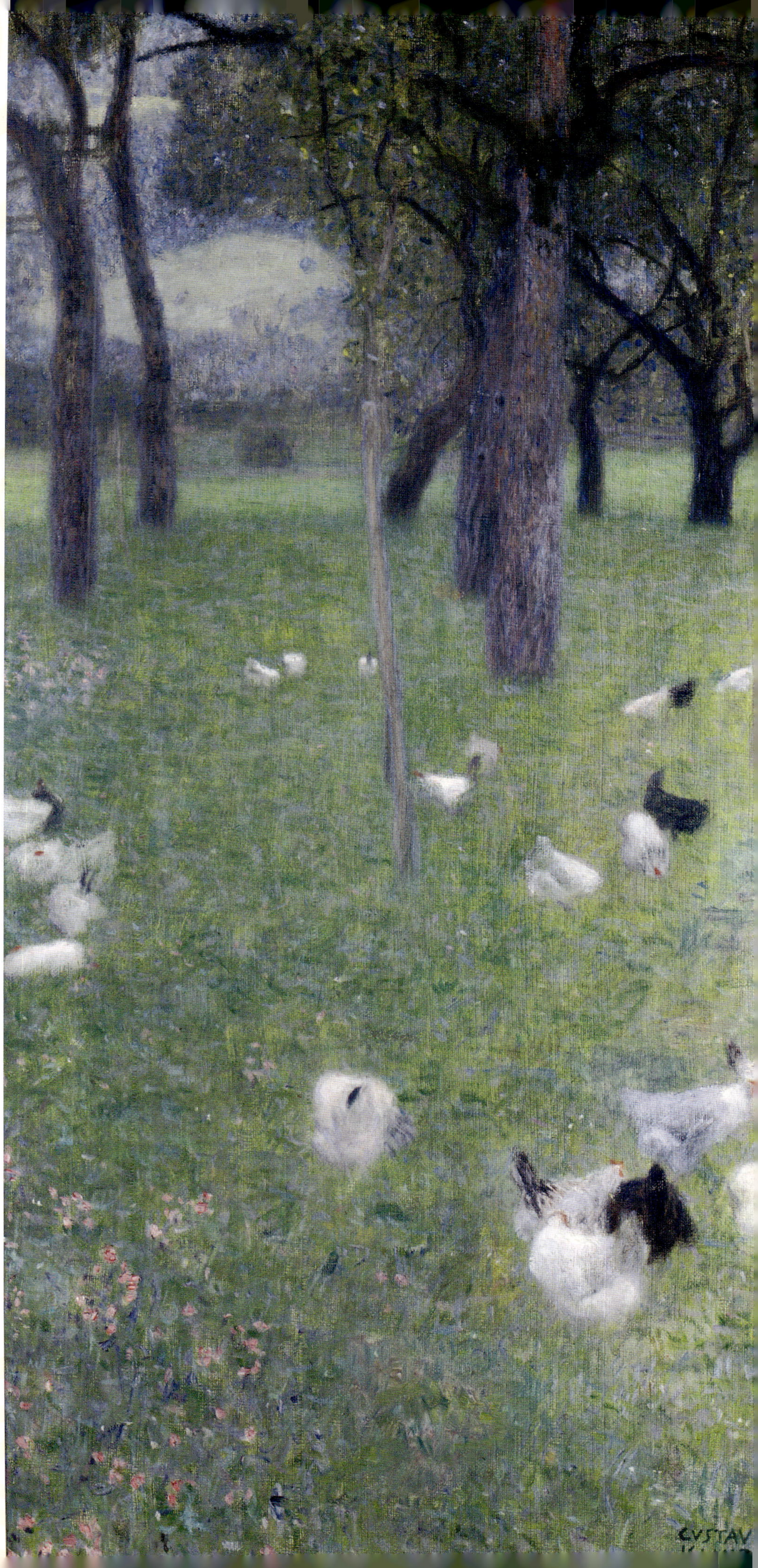

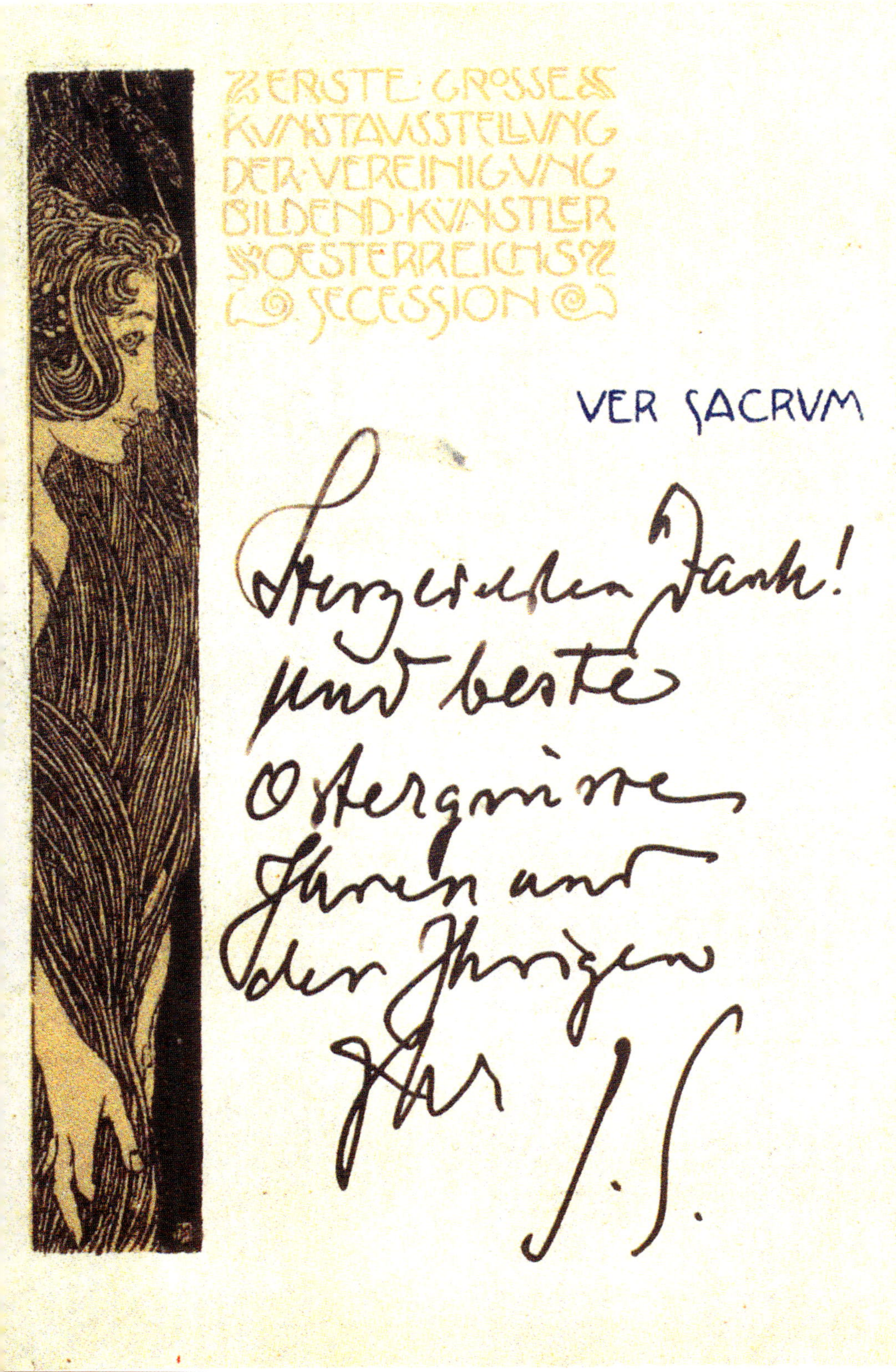

Guided Tour

Bahr's walking tour continued:

> *After leaving the first room, we enter the building itself. Everything is functional here. There is no frivolous attempt to boast, or to blind with pomp. The house of the Secession does not want to be a palace or a temple but rather a room that is able to arrange works of art to best effect possible. The artist did not ask himself 'How can I design this so that it looks the most impressive?' but rather 'How can this serve its purpose, its new mission, our needs?'*

Now came the Secessionist message, loud and clear – and, as ever, straight out of the promptbook established by the Arts and Crafts movement some years before:

> *The object has dictated the purpose: as the object wills it, was the sole law of design. It was created the way a wheel is created: with the same precision, geared towards purpose, not concerned about anything else and determined to look for true beauty that unravels in function. ... Everything has been done with utmost dedication to purpose. Nothing is superfluous, nothing needs to be added, nothing needs to be re-thought; everything is necessary and natural.*

Like It or Not

Warming to his theme, and apparently emboldened, Bahr now upped the level of insistency – without, however, abandoning his measured tone:

ABOVE LEFT AND OPPOSITE ◆ VER SACRUM POSTCARD FEATURING GREETINGS FROM THE ART HISTORIAN JULIUS VON SCHLOSSERHOPE, 1898. KOLOMAN MOSER (1868–1918)

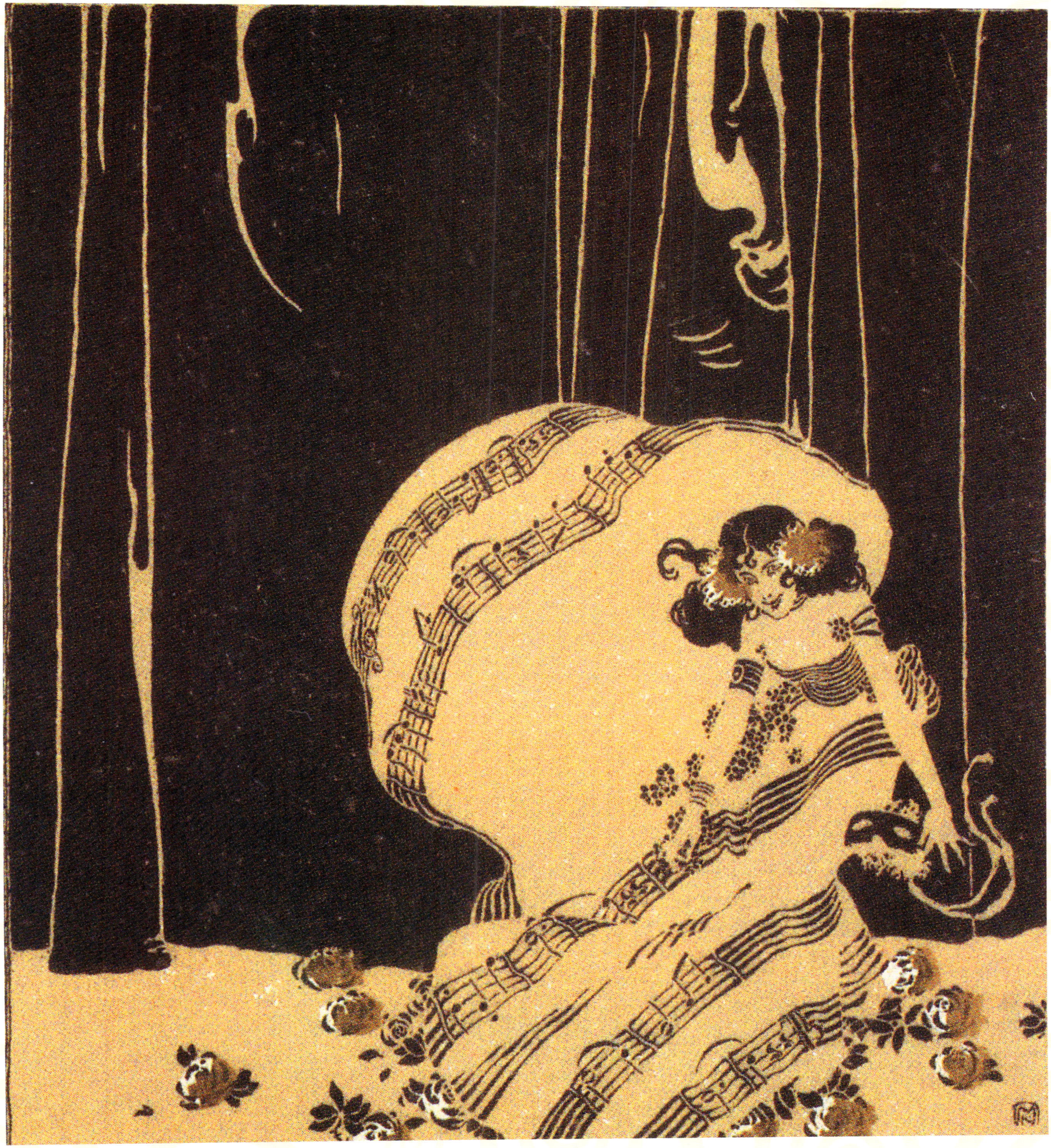

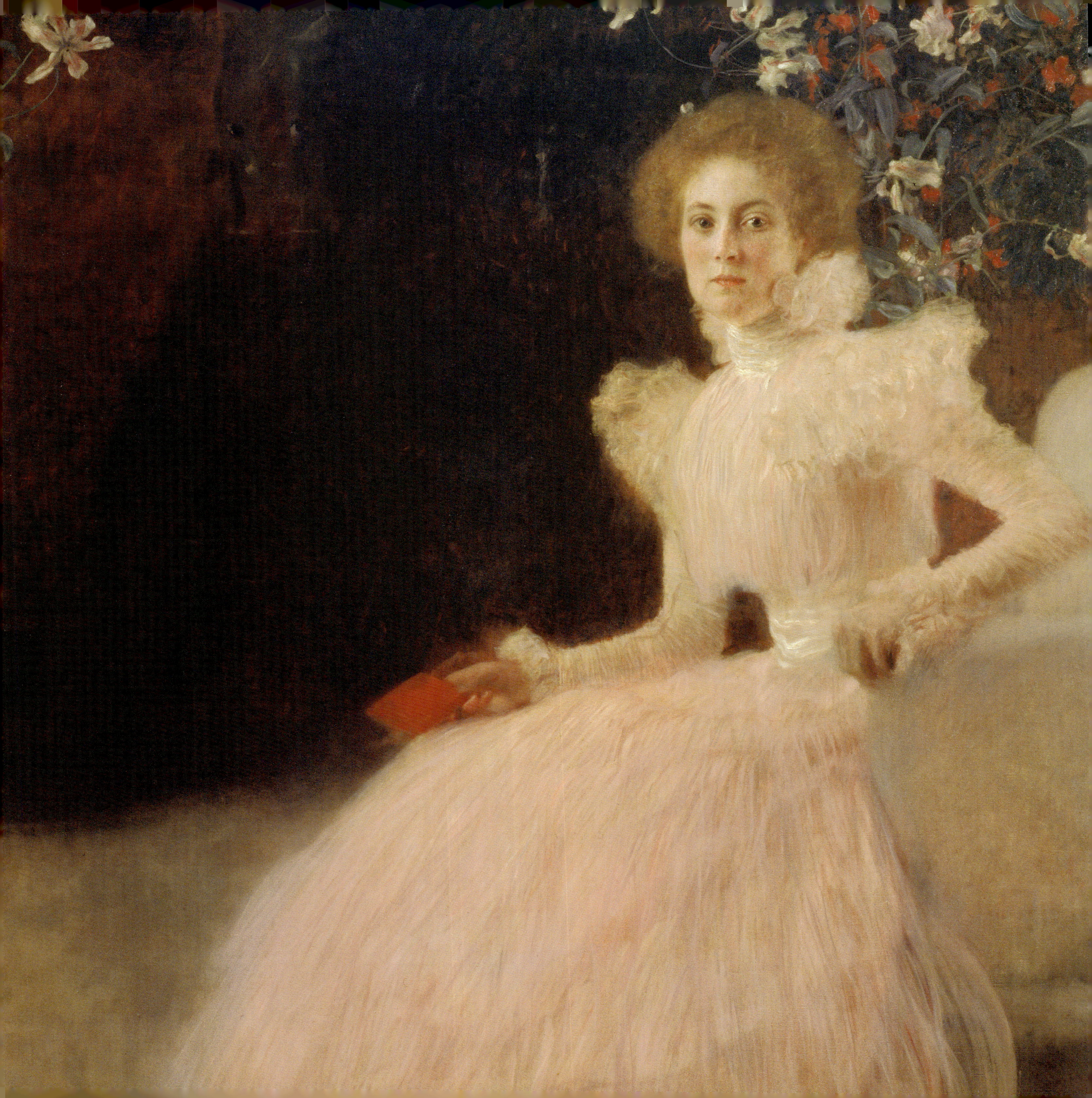

Let us consider the ideals of the Secession for a moment, take into account the resulting requirements and convert them into fixed parameters. The result is, as in a calculation, a certain sum. This sum is what the designer expressed artistically. One cannot say 'I like it' or 'I don't like it': this is not about preference or non-preference but a matter of right or wrong.

So no petit-bourgeois pussyfooting about with thoughts of 'subjectivity' or – still less – 'taste', then. 'The accomplishment of our young architect':

is to have seen the truth, and the way truth expresses itself, its only and irreplaceable expression, and consequently to have rendered this expression tangible.

Few architects – few artists of any kind – could claim to have created their works the only way they could 'truly' have been created. Olbrich was quite some talent, that was clear.

He'd certainly thought of everything. At the end of his tour, Bahr took his reader through a final room that he explained was a sort of aesthetic decompression chamber. This room, he said:

exhibits the same serious and ceremonial architecture that characterizes the atrium, the first room. Before we return to daily life again, we can contemplate the emotions of art, behold it once again and calm down afterwards. We want to preserve its reverberations in us. After this we can leave.

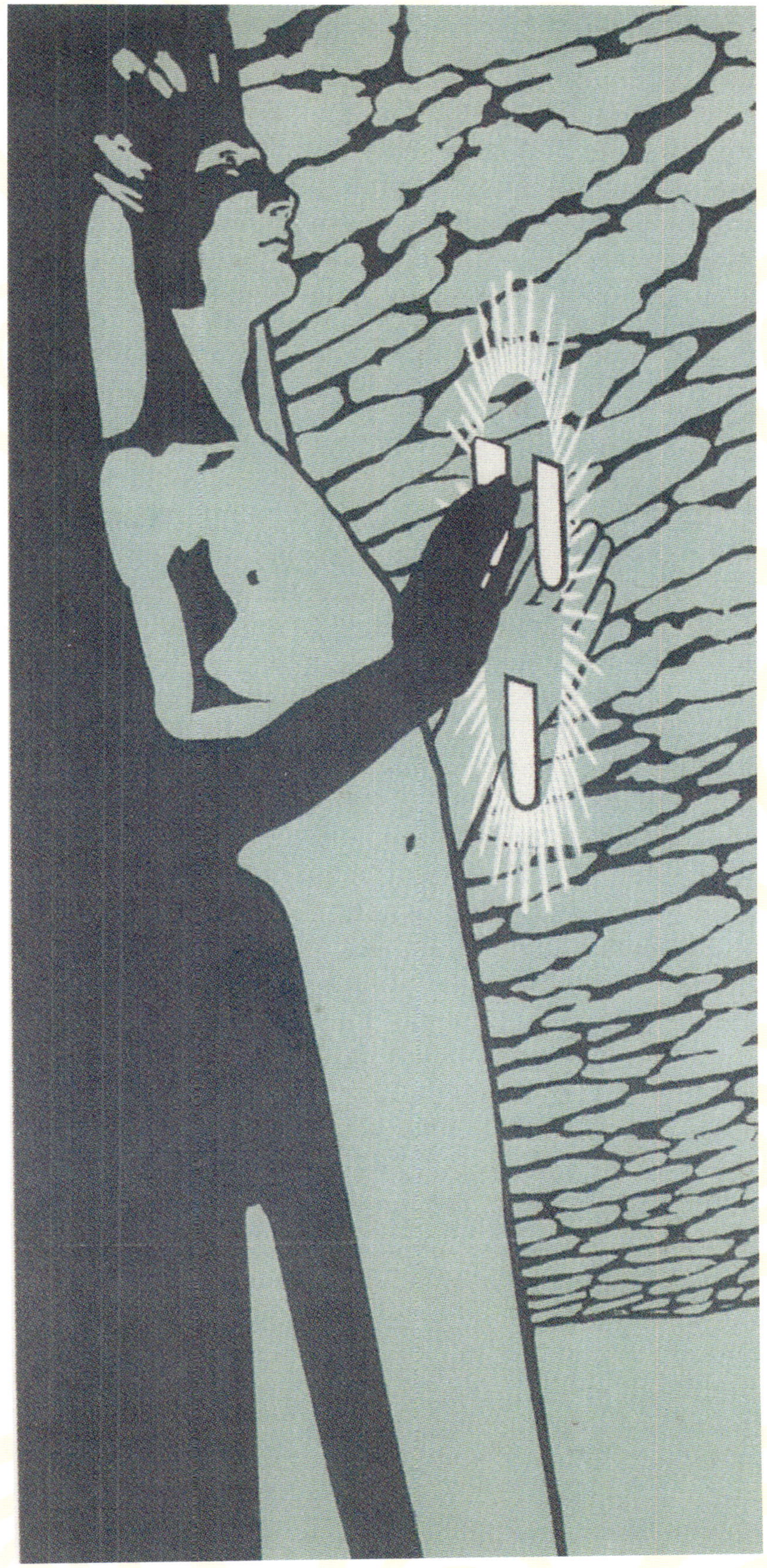

OPPOSITE ◆ PORTRAIT OF SONJA KNIPS, 1898. GUSTAV KLIMT (1862–1918)
RIGHT ◆ VIENNA SECESSION 9TH EXHIBITION POSTER, 1901. ALFRED ROLLER (1864–1935)

A Home for Art

The building's exterior, Bahr argued, demonstrated the same qualities of truthfulness. 'The very first glance tells the observer about the interior and purpose: this can be nothing else than a home for paintings,' he insisted. If 'home' seems an odd word for Bahr to have used here, it quickly became clear that he did so advisedly, for he had some severe words for his public on how they viewed their own places of residence and employment:

> *All of this naturally seems alien and strange to us, spoiled as we are. Our houses for living look like palaces for boasting; our workplaces look like they were rather made for festivities. Houses conceal their true nature. We have completely forgotten what a façade is meant to be. We are used to the idea that it is a mere game with pillars, beams and ornaments. We will have to remember first before we can truly recognize the truth of the Secession Building.*

Home was where the art was, then, in Olbrich's design. Bahr was right of course in that, in far too many public building projects of the time, classical colonnades and other similar accoutrements had come to be the merest 'trimmings' to works of the most crashing mundanity and banality; silly frills and furbelows in solid stone. To this extent, he was justified in suggesting that Olbrich's Secession Building showed integrity – but some intrinsic, unalterable 'truth'? That surely went too far…

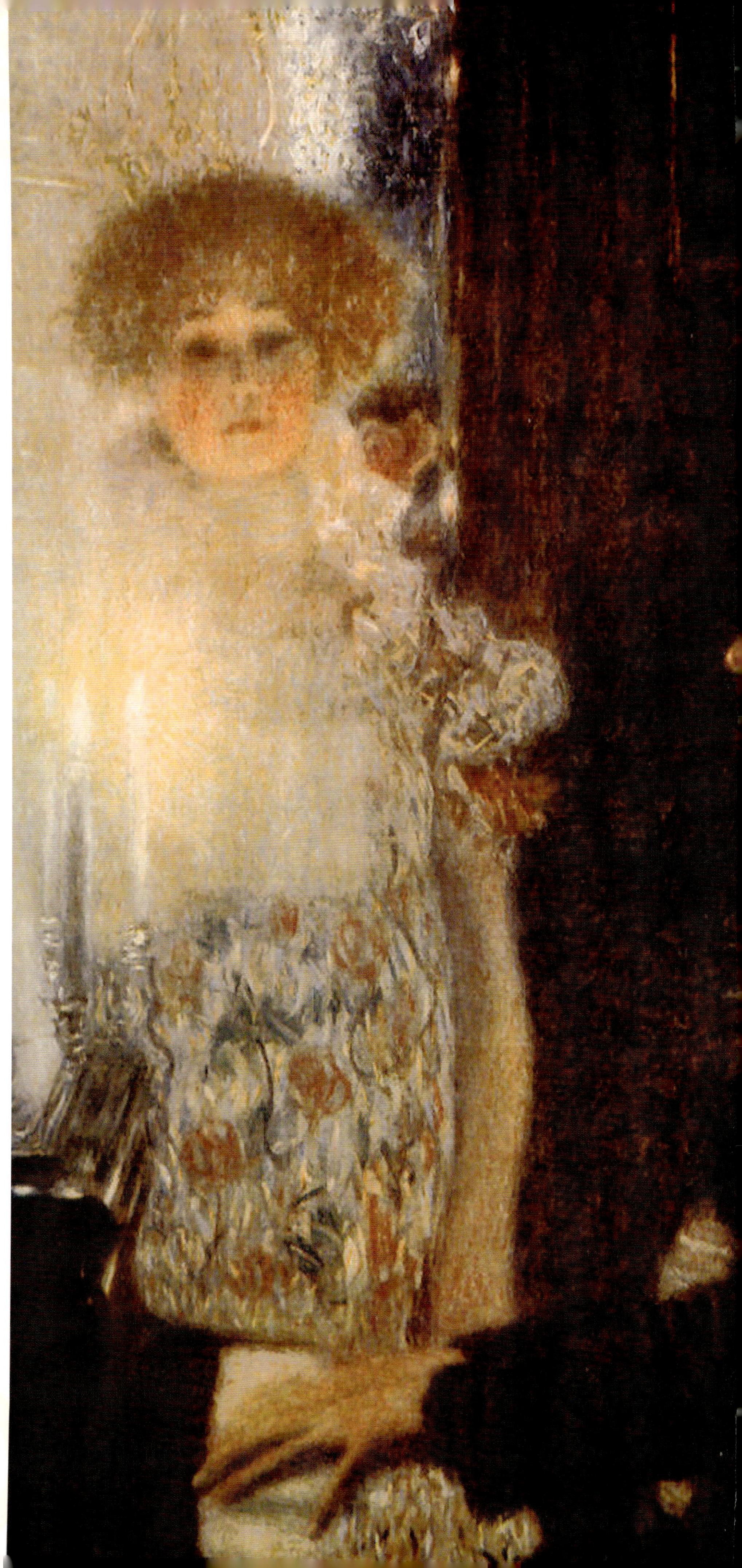

OPPOSITE ◆ SCHUBERT AT THE PIANO, 1899, GUSTAV KLIMT (1862–1918)

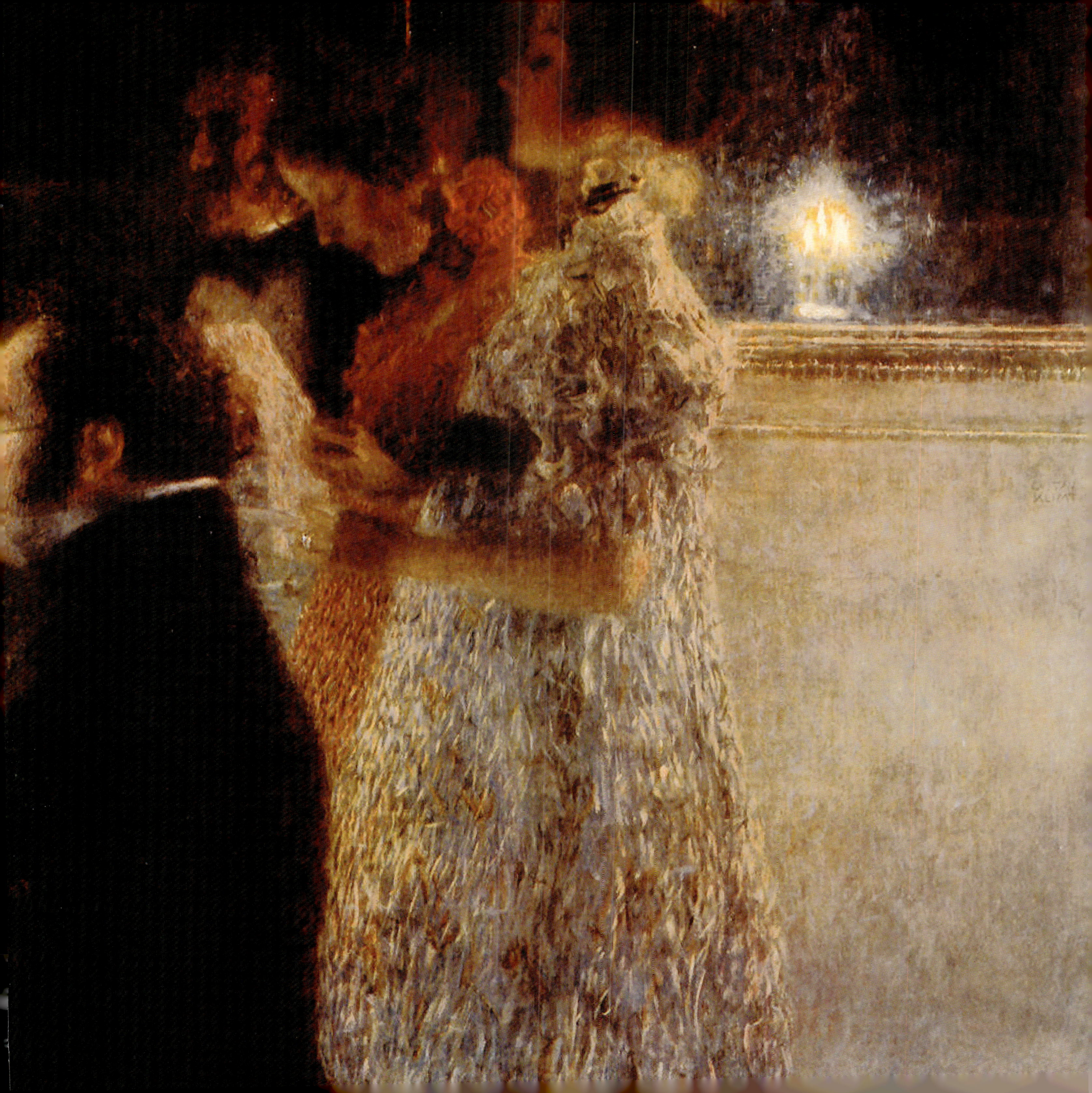

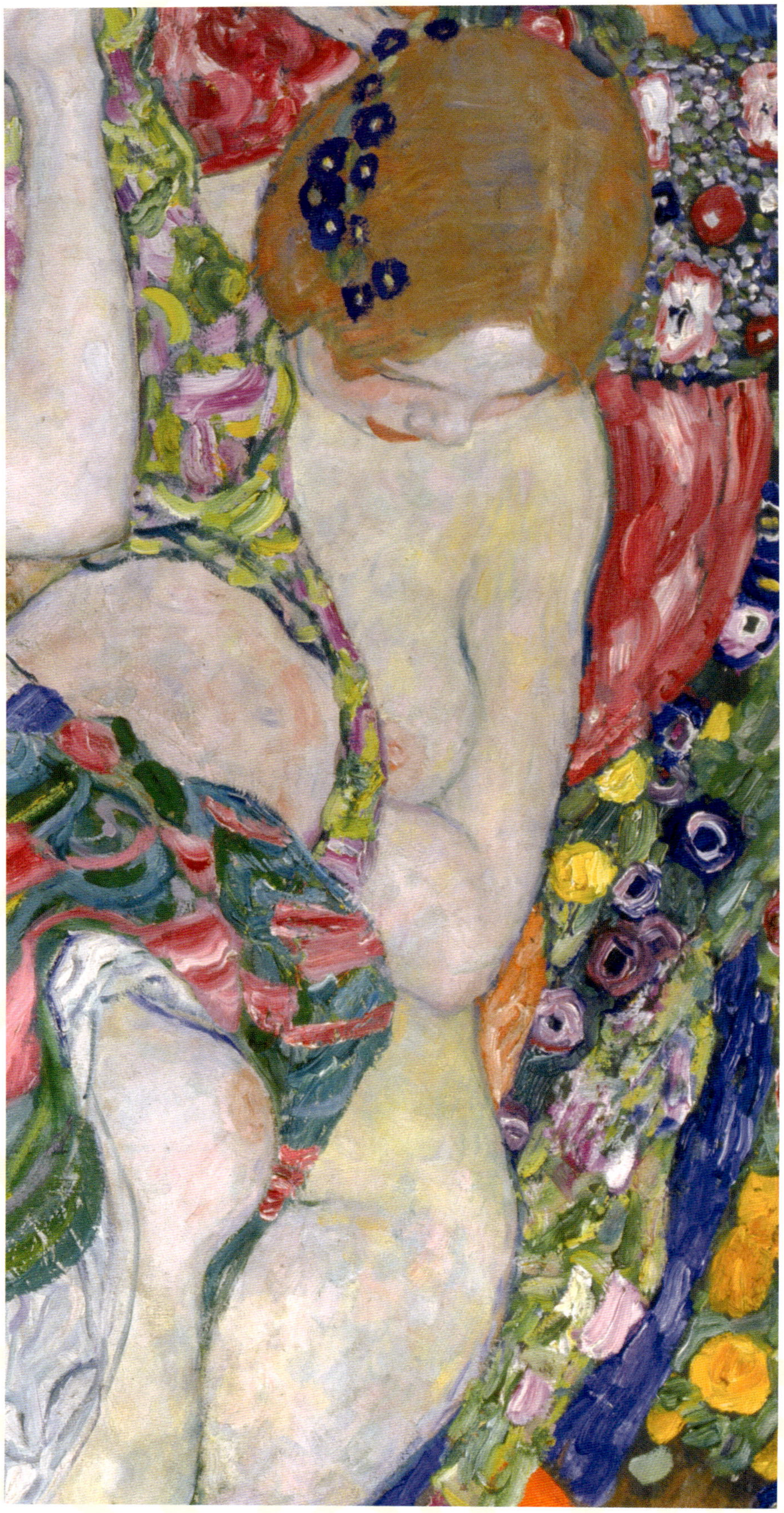

Art for Life

November 1898 saw the unveiling of both the new Secession Building and the movement's Second Exhibition. Olbrich designed the exhibition's poster, and – fittingly – it depicted his new monument. As, self-referentially, did the exhibition, which made the Secession Building itself its star attraction, and pushed 'things', rather than paintings or 'pure' sculptures, to the fore. Highlights included wallpaper – and an entire interior stained-glass window – by Koloman Moser as well as a great many other examples of applied art by Secession craftsmen.

Hermann Bahr's view of the Building as a 'home' for art makes more sense when seen in conjunction with Henry van de Velde's exhortation that he and his Secessionist friends should work to 'impress beauty on every aspect of our lives, that the artist should no longer simply paint pictures, but rather create whole rooms, or even whole dwellings, with wallpapers and furniture as well as paintings.' Or, as Josef Hoffmann put it:

> *It just isn't enough to buy paintings, however wonderful they are. As long as our towns, our houses, our rooms, our furniture, our utensils, our clothes and our jewellery, our language and our feelings do not reflect – elegantly, simply, and beautifully – the spirit of our own time, we are living at a level far beneath that of our forefathers and no equivocation can disguise these weaknesses.*

There was of course a commercial as well as an aesthetic logic at work, here, but both were in keeping with the feeling of the Secessionists and with the spirit with which the Second Exhibition had been planned.

LEFT AND OPPOSITE ❖ THE VIRGIN, 1913, GUSTAV KLIMT (1862–1918)

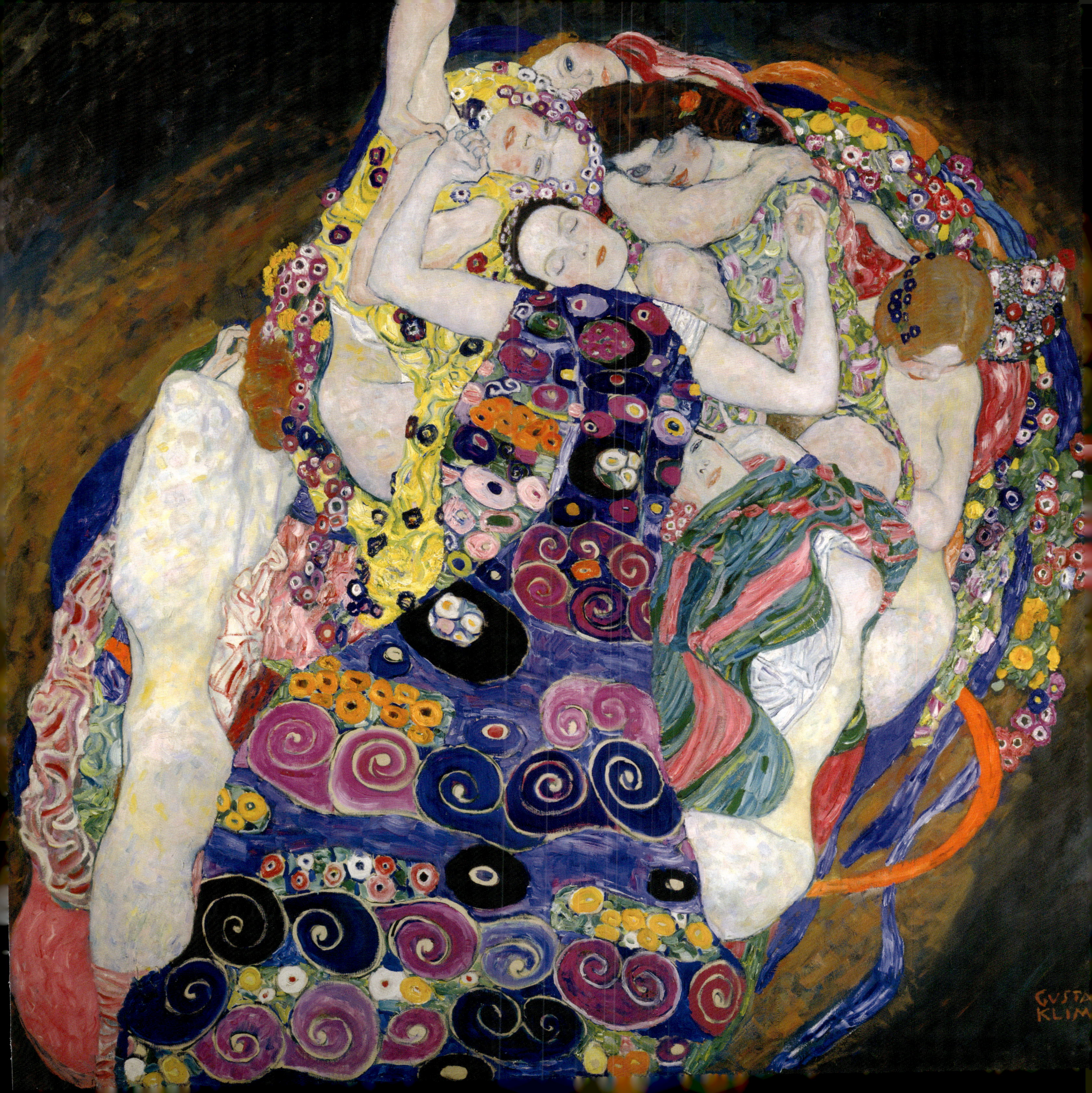
GUSTA
KLIM

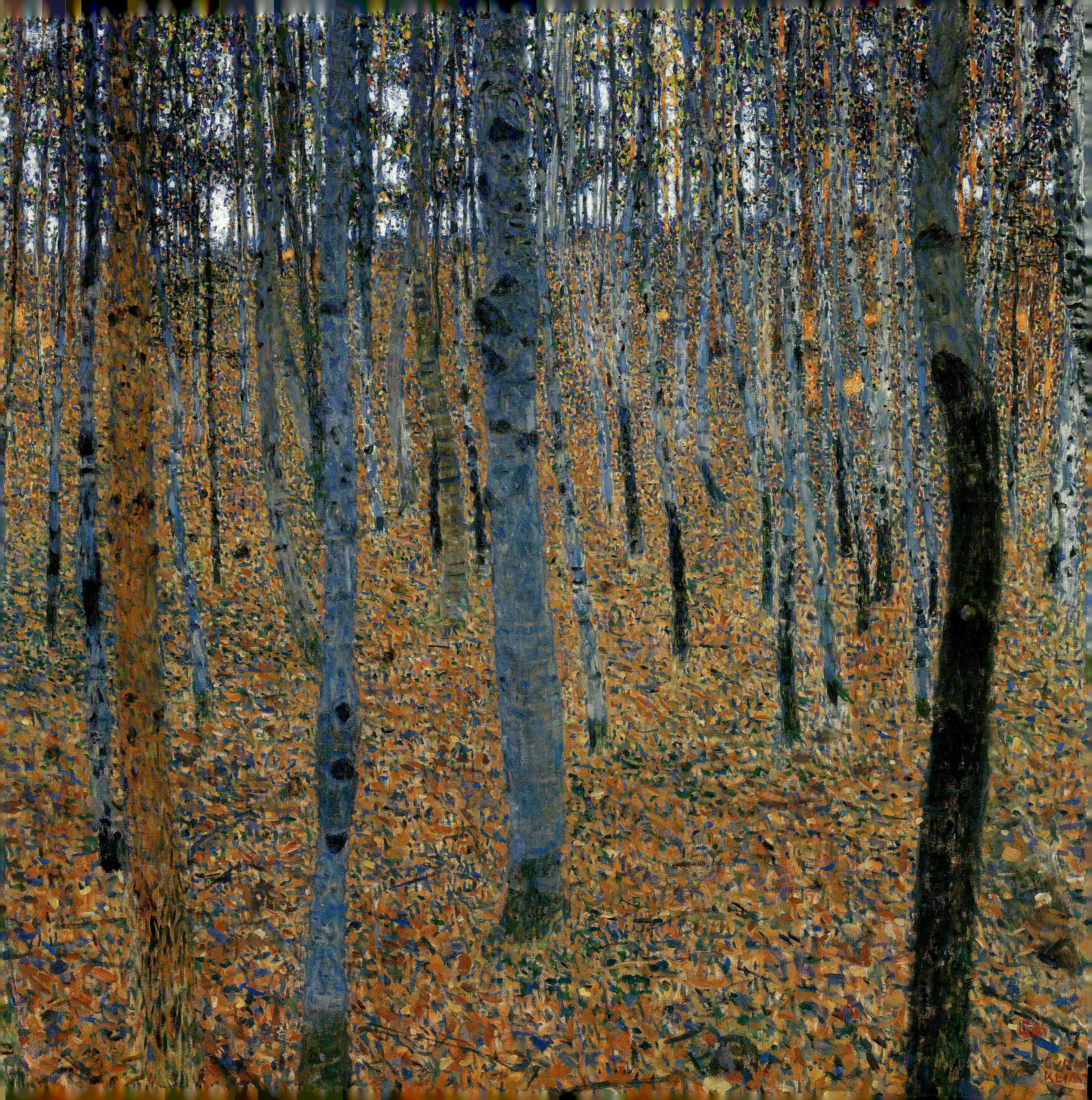

Art Without Paintings

'Such an exhibition has not been before,' enthused Hermann Bahr, 'an exhibition that did not feature one single painting.' And this was fair enough, assuming that by 'feature' he meant 'make a special feature of' – because there were indeed a fair few paintings on display. In fact, one of the comments most often made by the exhibition's visitors was that the pictures had been sensibly set out at eye level, for more comfortable viewing. And a show that included such works by Klimt as *Pallas Athena* (1898, *see* page 60) and *The Portrait of Sonja Knips* (1898, *see* page 146) could hardly be said to have lacked important paintings.

As usual though, Bahr was more concerned with continuing his feud with the self-appointed guardians of his country's cultural heritage – and its art market:

> *It is an exhibition that shows that we have people in Austria who can rise up and compare themselves to the very best of the European artists. A miracle! And a good joke moreover: It has been proven that you can make money with art, with pure art. That must come as a shock to the mercantilists of the Association.*

Glad of the chance to have his above-commercialism cake and eat it, Bahr tore into those of the academic old-guard who had doubted that the public would buy real and innovative art:

> *The Viennese, Your Viennese … whom you thought you knew so well, flock in crowds to the exhibition to buy art, to buy Khnopff.*

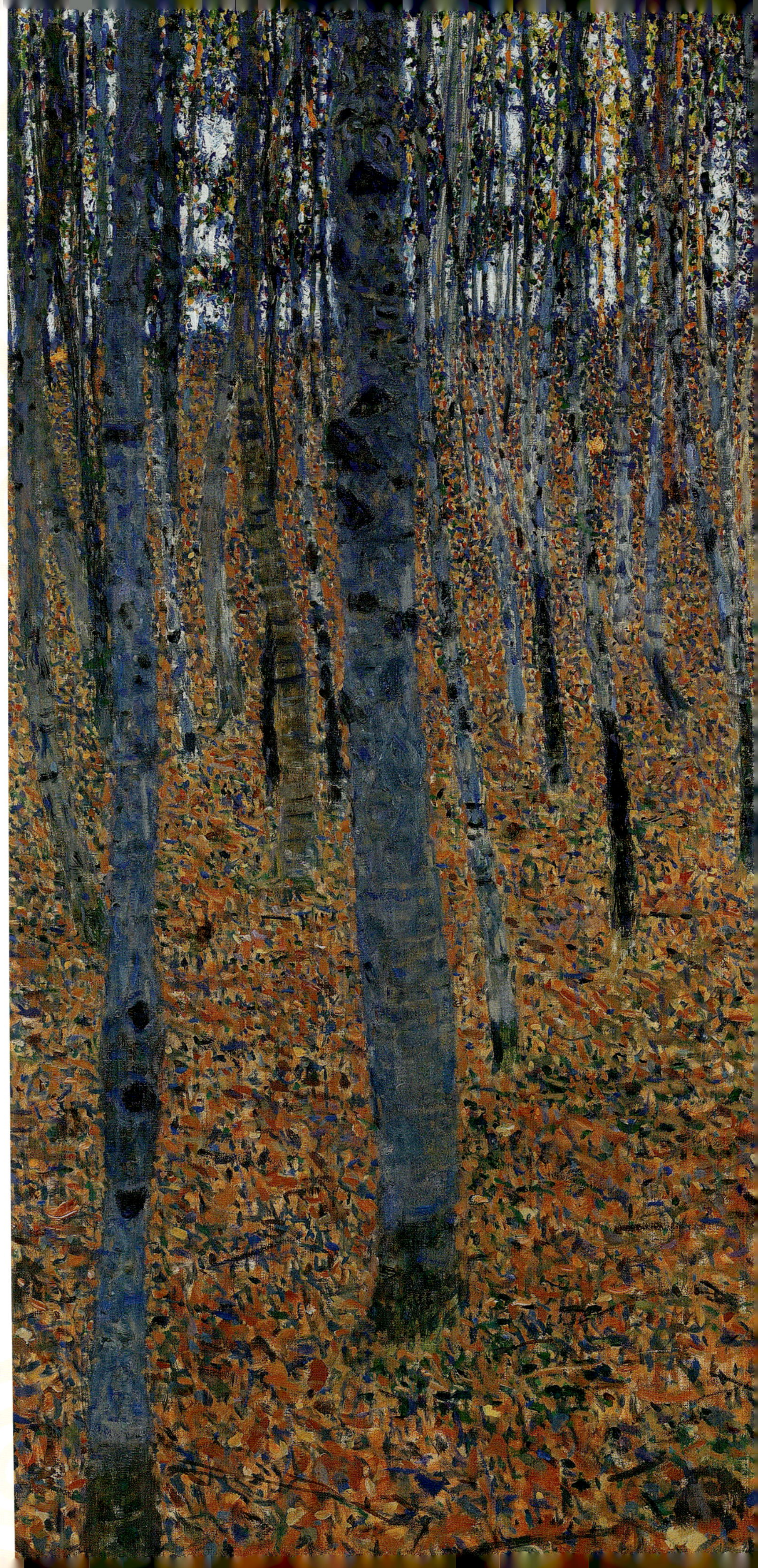

OPPOSITE AND RIGHT ◆ BEECH FOREST I, 1902, GUSTAV KLIMT (1862–1918)

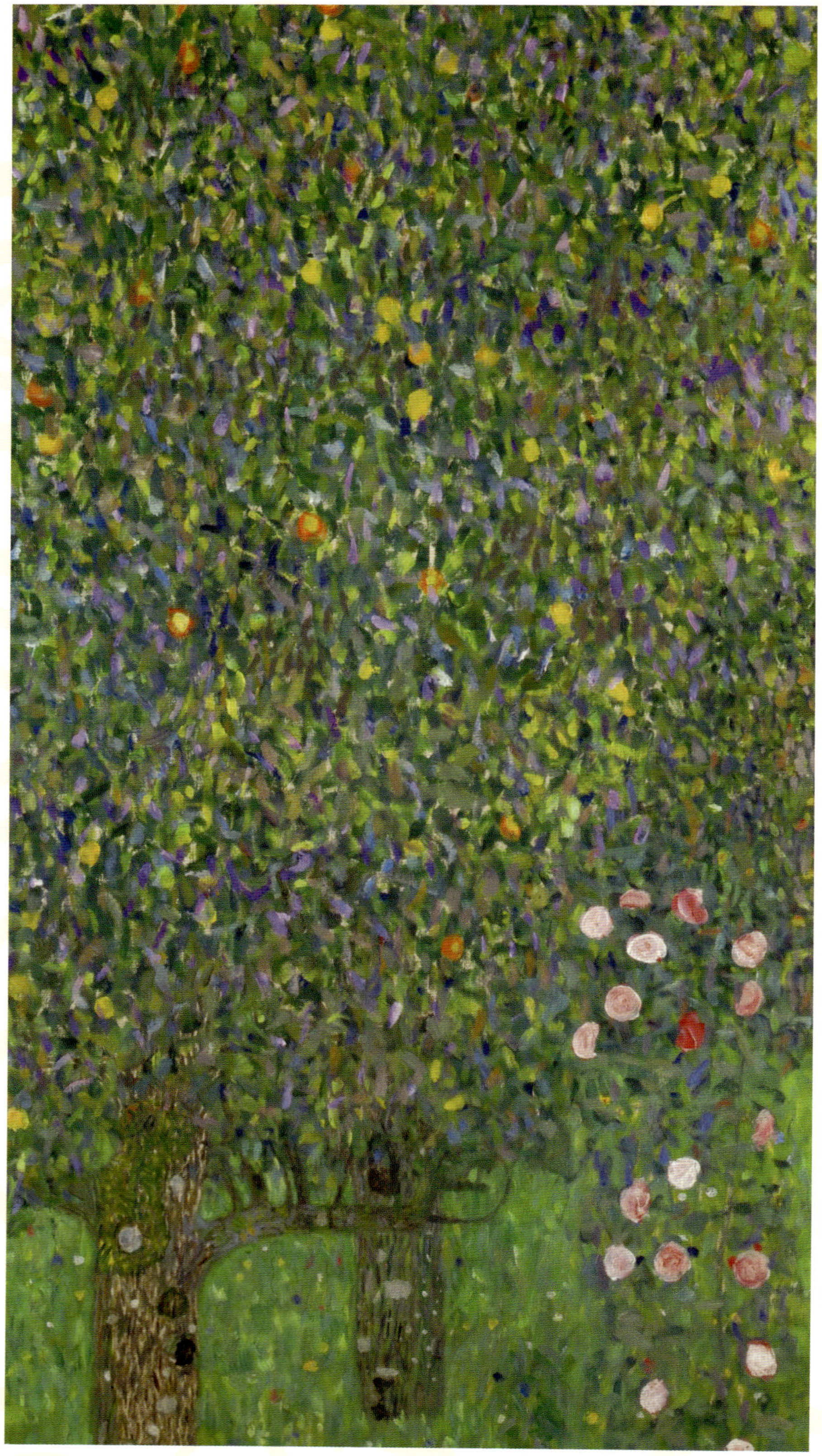

Any Publicity ...

And it wasn't just Khnopff's works that they were buying, of course. The buzz the Secession's exhibitions were creating in Vienna had given a boost to the Austrian art scene as a whole. In Olbrich's Secession Building, local artists had found the perfect showcase – the controversy around its construction had, in hindsight, only helped. Gustav Klimt may have been a master artist, but he was also (and in the best sense) an exhibitionist of genius; few of his contemporaries had his gift for self-promotion.

Painters like Max Kurzweil, Carl Moll or Maximilian Pirner (1853–1924), worthy as they were, could never have created this kind of splash with their works alone; still less could a sculptor like Richard Luksch have made such an impact. Those graphic artists whose work took them to the outer edge of the sort of art that was deemed 'fine' had found it even harder to reach a receptive audience. For people like Josef Maria Auchentaller and Maximilian Liebenwein (1869–1926), the chance to show their work in a gallery context was a godsend.

It's hard to imagine men of Josef Hoffmann or Koloman Moser's talents not making a mark of some sort in their own time. But it's equally hard to imagine them having won their enduring fame without the world of opportunity the Secession brought their way. Otto Wagner was already an architect of distinction when the Secession took place: he didn't need the impetus for his career. But there's no real doubt that his ability to place himself and his work at the leading edge of architectural reform in a radically modern artistic movement was the making of what was to be his lasting fame.

LEFT AND OPPOSITE ◆ ROSES UNDER TREES, 1904. GUSTAV KLIMT (1862–1918)

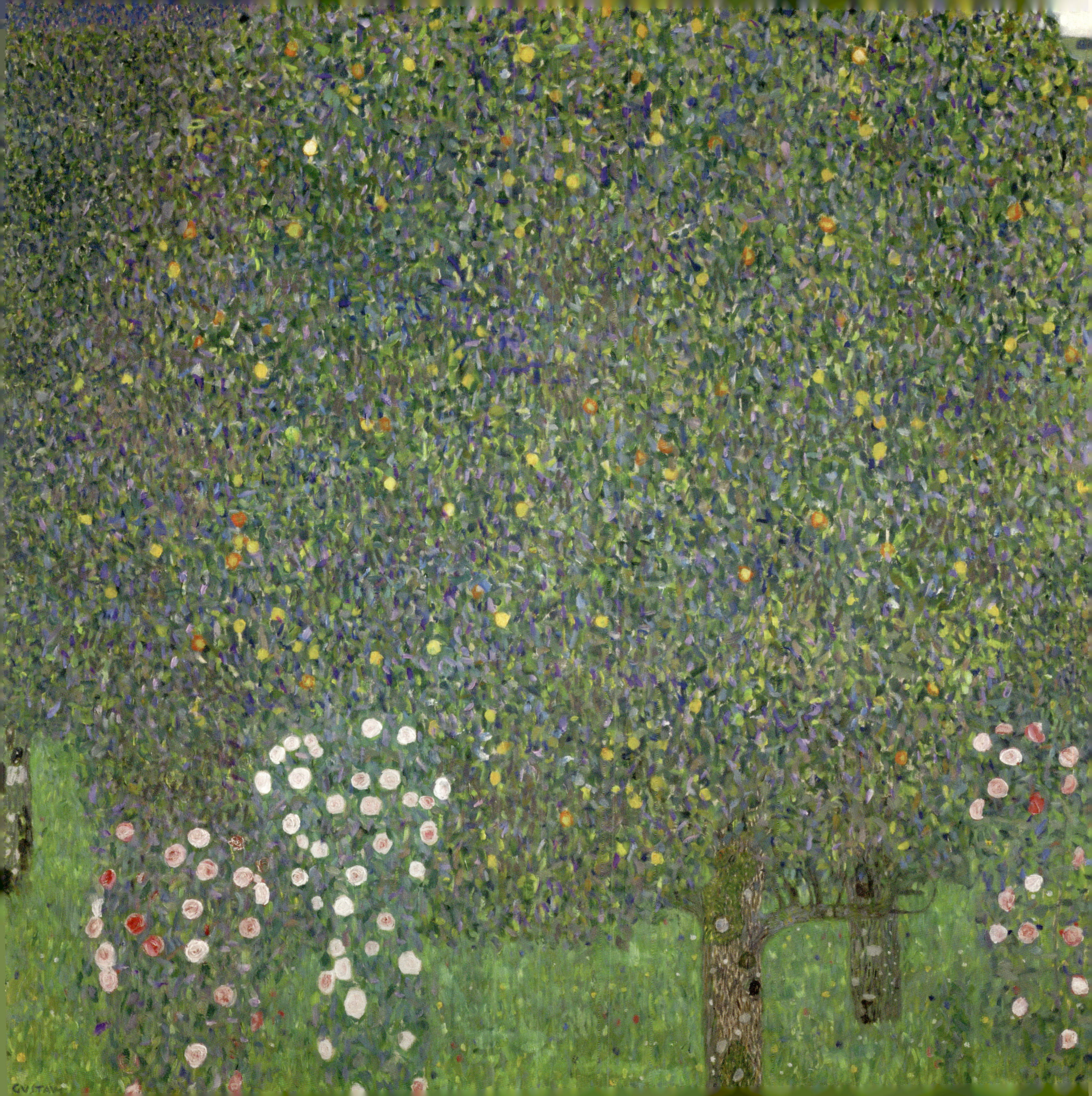

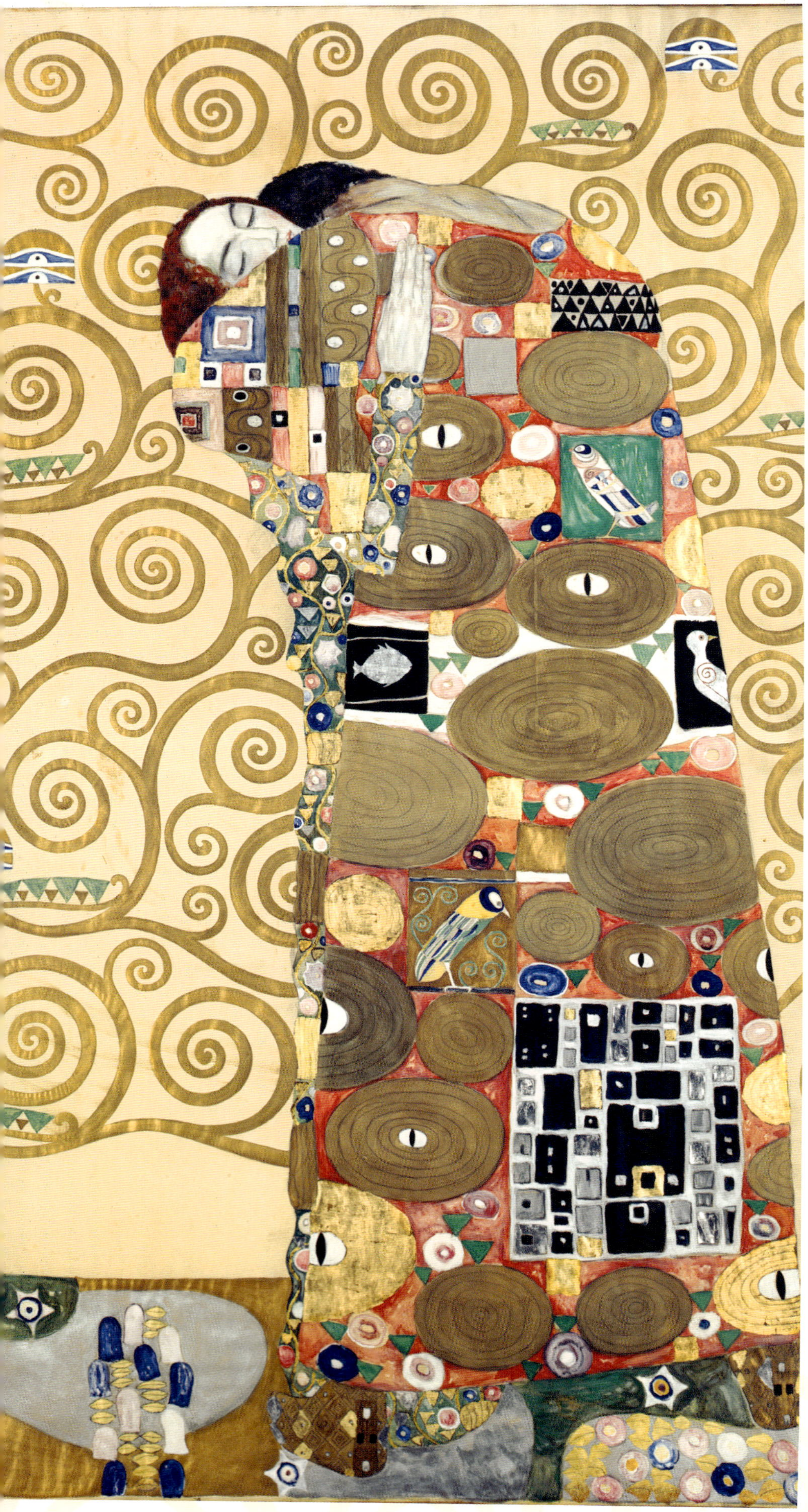

A Place for Women?

Women too were creating opportunities for themselves in the Secessionist ferment – though it would be an exaggeration to suggest that any great breakthrough for equality was made. Radical as it may have been, the Secession was by no means revolutionary in any wider sense. We've already seen that it was in many ways quite conservative, indeed, with a wary eye on the realities of an art market that was inherently respectable and bourgeois, however open-minded Klimt and the others were training it to be. The Secession's success – and its sexism – arguably even helped damp down the acclaim already earned by the Vienna-based Russian sculptor Teresa Ries, by now an international celebrity. But other women, like Elena Luksch-Makowsky and Broncia Koller-Pinell (1863–1934), undoubtedly gained a great deal from the opportunity to exhibit among their artistic peers.

Conservatism, Counsel of Despair

Others still shook their heads, however. Hermann Bahr's polemical energy – intemperate as it was at times – shouldn't blind us to the fact that he sometimes seems to have understood the old-guard better than they did themselves. There's surely at least a grain of truth in Bahr's suggestion that what they saw as a justified conservatism contained an element of old-fashioned cultural 'cringe':

What vexes them the most has been the enormous success our young Viennese had with their new exhibition. That's something no one expected. Because the Viennese just doesn't want to believe that another Viennese can be skilled and able: he doesn't have any self-confidence. You'll hear it all the time at the

LEFT ◆ THE STOCLET FRIEZE: FULFILMENT, c. 1905–09 . GUSTAV KLIMT (1862–1918)

Association. 'What? You want to invite foreigners? You want to show the Viennese the experiments of the French? Do you know what will happen? That will be the death of us! No one will be interested in us any more. Just think! Once the people have grown accustomed to such sophistication, what is going to become of us?

There was really no doubt that, for better or worse, the Secession's exhibitions were dragging a conservative, provincial – and yes, arguably 'backward' – Vienna into modernity, and out into a wider, more exciting world. As the Czech-Austrian art historian Hans Tietze (1880–1954) was to put it, such shows 'brought a thousand strange impulses into the closed-off Viennese atmosphere' to challenge a collective genius that had become complacent and hidebound. Seeing such works reminded the Austrian artist that there was more to creativity than endlessly recycling old ideas, and taught Austrian art buyers to admire the inventive and the new. Change can always bring discomfort, and the Secession exhibitions were no exception, but they did make it clear that innovation could be exciting and appealing.

Home Comforts, Naked Truth

A Third Exhibition, held in the Secession Building in January and February of 1899, was remarkable mainly for giving each contributing artist their own room. The Fourth Exhibition, from March to May the same year, stretched pretty much to breaking point the idea that the Secessionists were all enlisted together in a collective cause: the show was (inevitably) overshadowed by two contributions by Klimt, *Schubert at the Piano* (1899, *see* page 149) and the (painted) *Nuda Veritas* (1899, see page. 49). The former work was absolutely enchanting in its

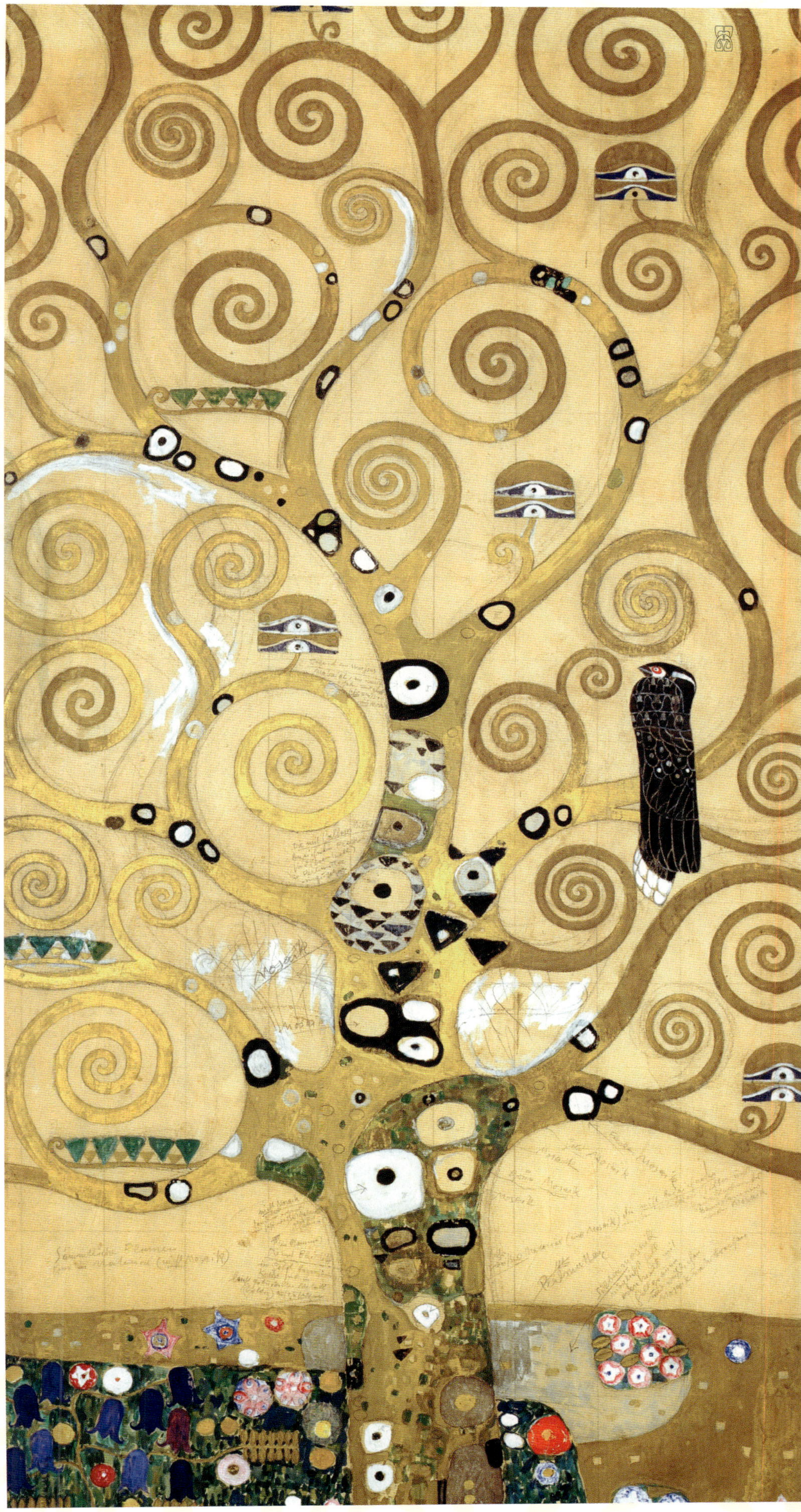

RIGHT ◆ THE STOCLET FRIEZE: THE TREE OF LIFE, 1905. GUSTAV KLIMT (1862–1918)
NEXT PAGE ◆ THE PUNISHMENT OF LUST, 1891. GIOVANNI SEGANTINI (1858–99)

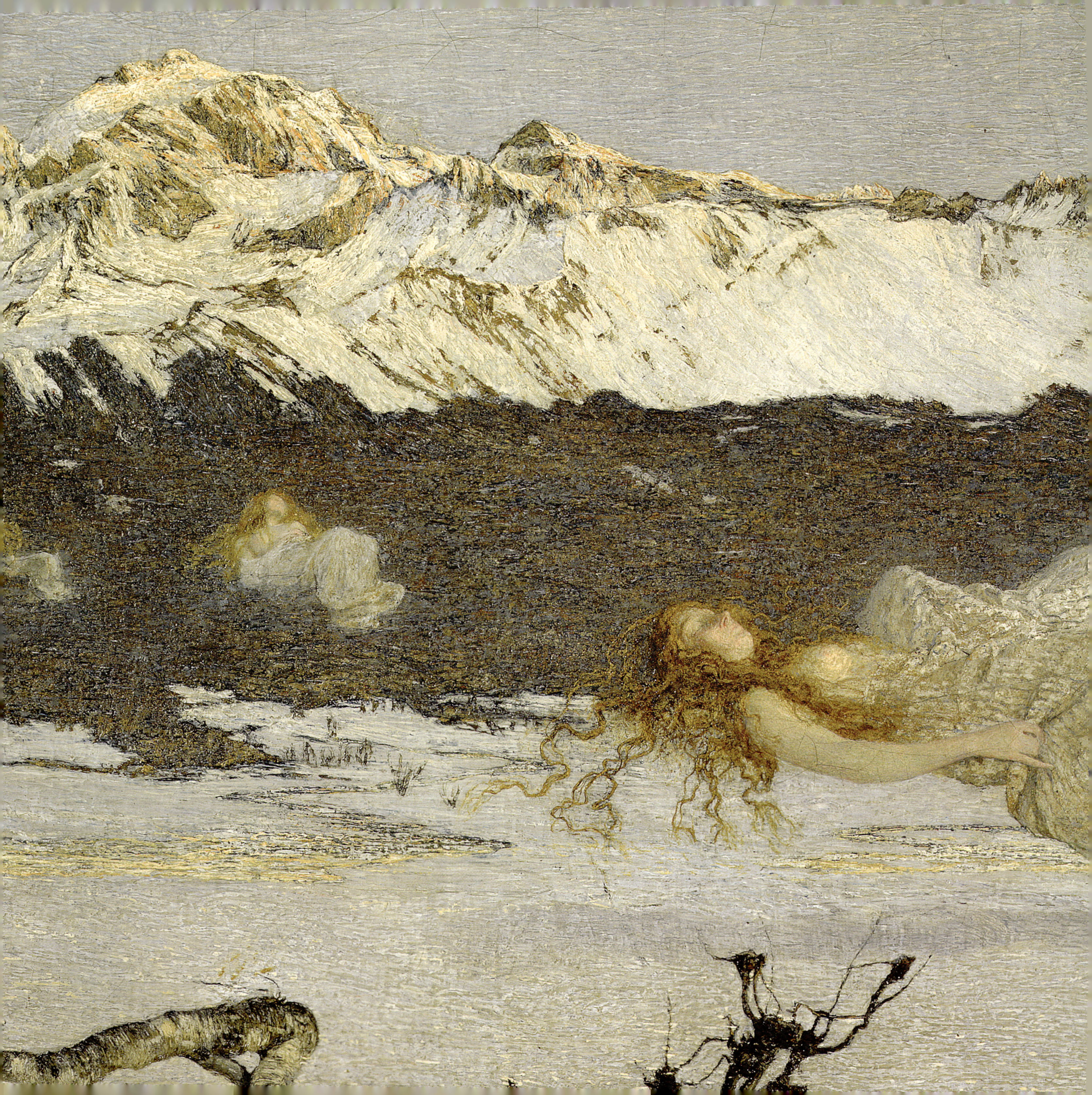

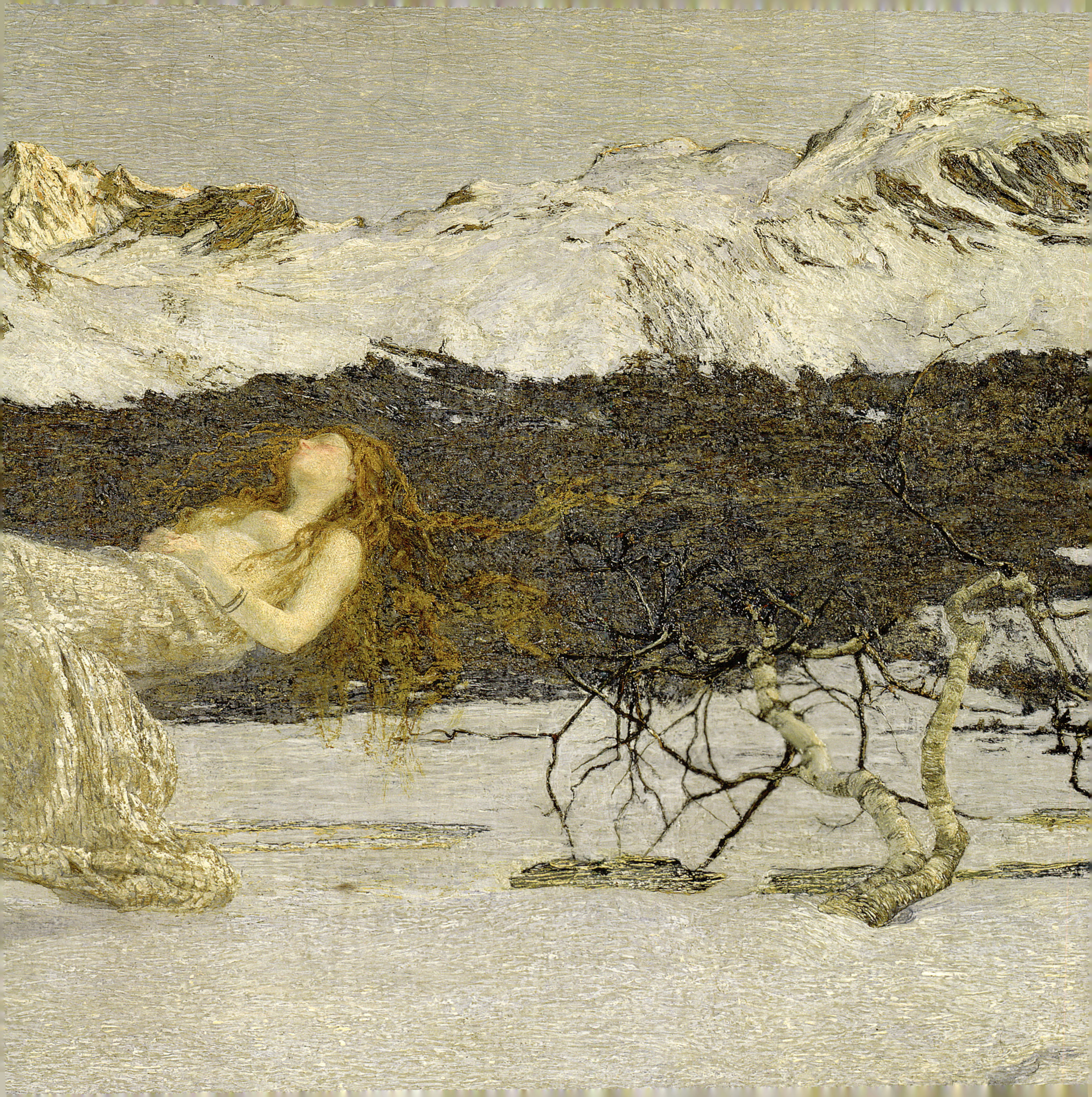

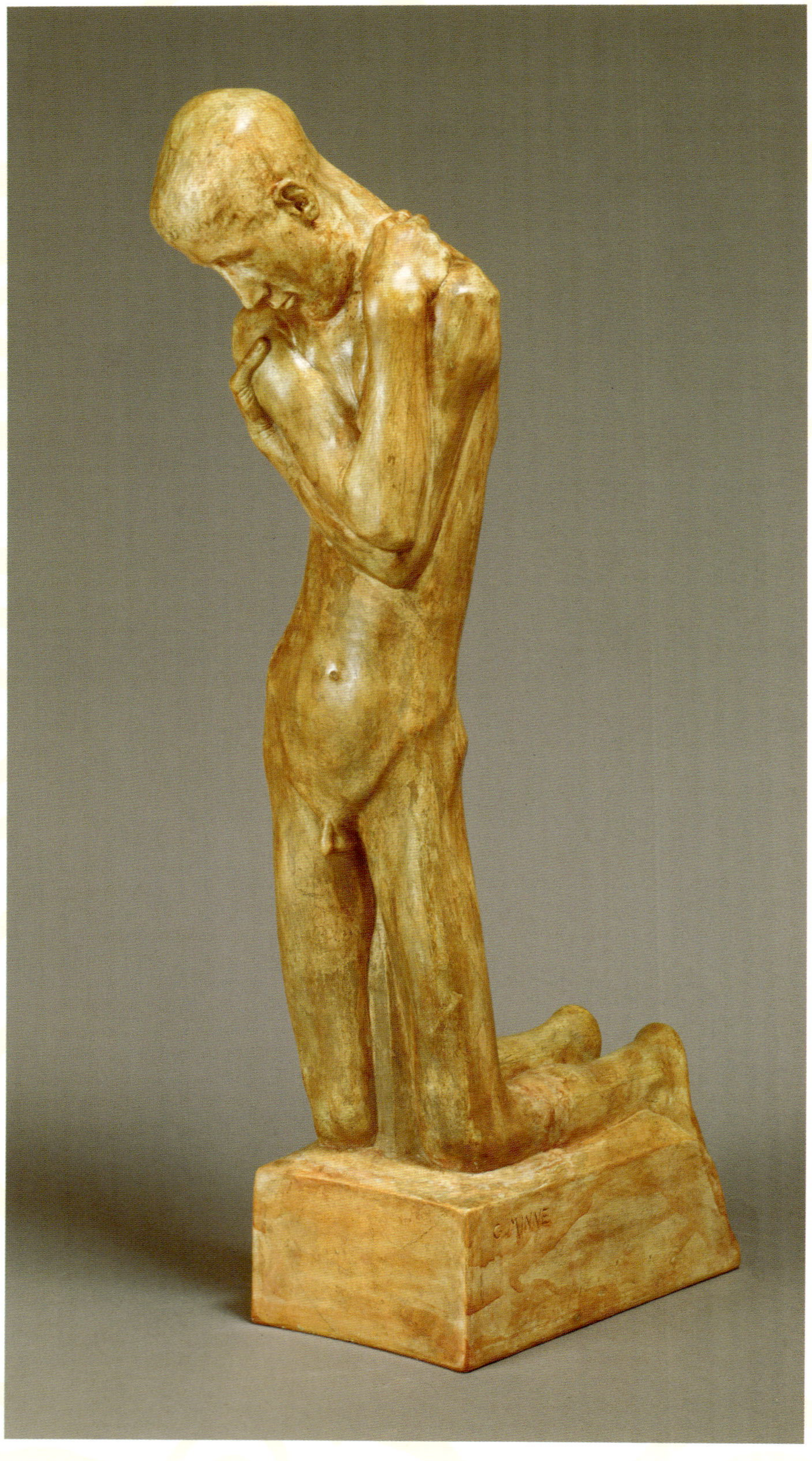

ABOVE ✱ KNEELING YOUTH, 1898. GEORGE MINNE (1866–1941)
OPPOSITE ✱ HYGIEIA, DETAIL FROM MEDICINE, 1900–07. GUSTAV KLIMT (1862–1918)

warmth and luminosity: it showed the composer (and Austrian – this was in its own way a patriotic work) Franz Schubert (1797–1828). Peter Altenberg was one of many Viennese visitors who fell in love with a work that contrived to suggest both high artistic beauty and *heimatlich* ('homely') conviviality. 'Over my bed', he told a friend:

> *hangs a colour reproduction of Gustav Klimt's **Schubert** painting, in which Schubert and three young girls are singing at the piano by candlelight. Underneath, in my handwriting: 'One of my gods! Men created their gods in order to bring to life their own hidden and unfulfillable dreams.'*

For Hermann Bahr, *Schubert at the Piano* was 'the finest painting ever done by an Austrian'. And he was anxious to make the point that it was specifically as an Austrian – not as a German – that he himself loved this work. How, he asked, did one define 'Austrianness'? By looking at this painting, he answered himself:

> *This tranquillity, this softness, this radiance, this domestic simplicity – therein lies our Austrian nature.*

Be it ever so humble, he implied, there was no place like the Austrian home – and it wasn't actually so humble, after all:

> *Here we have our Austrian creed: that every human being, be he ever so small, has in him a flame that no storm can extinguish. Each of us has his own holy sanctuary, and no destiny can crush it. Whatever the turmoil, we can come to no ill, the flame cannot blow out, no one can deprive us of our inner worth. It is this that I mean by the Viennese feeling for life.*

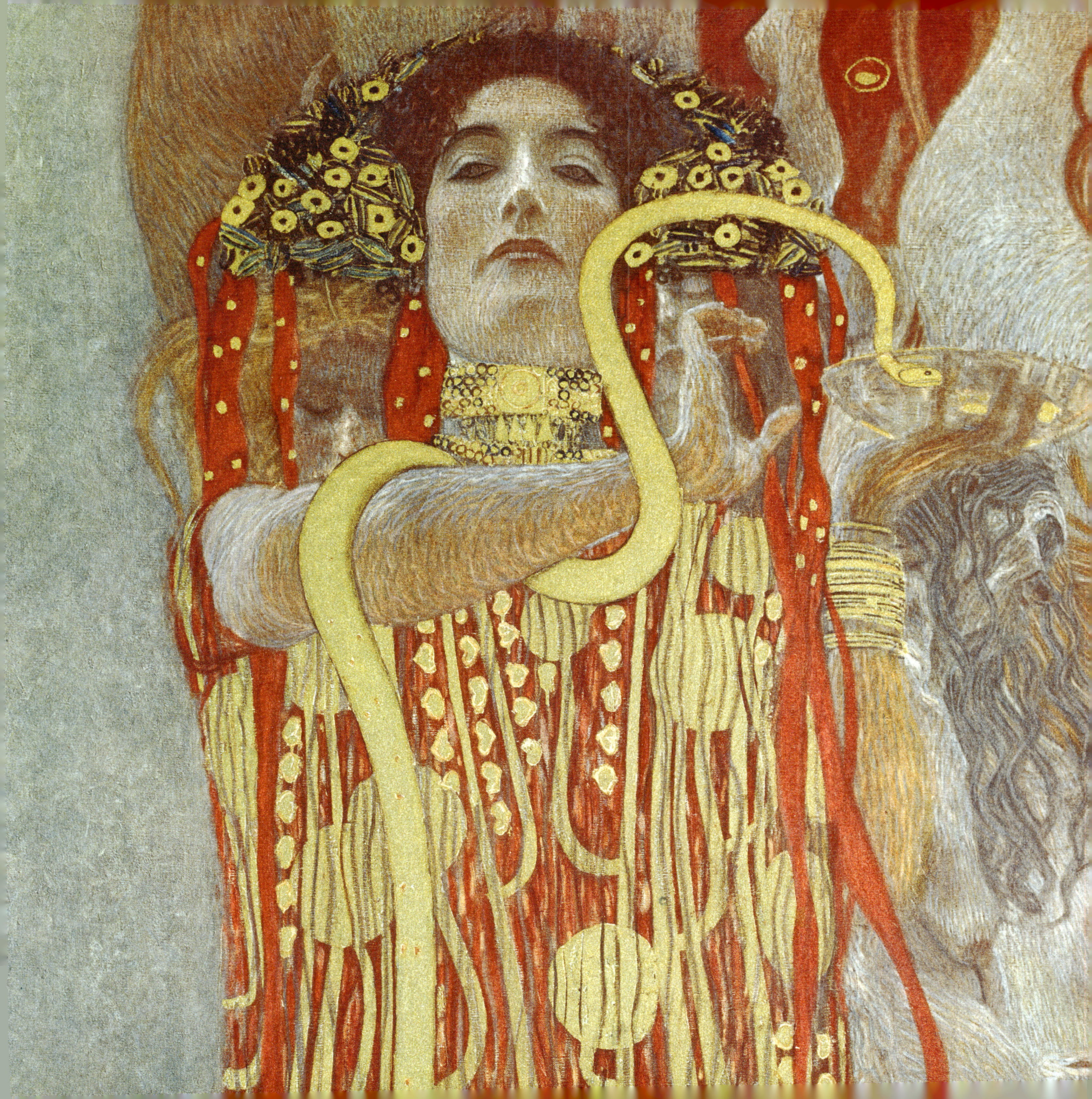

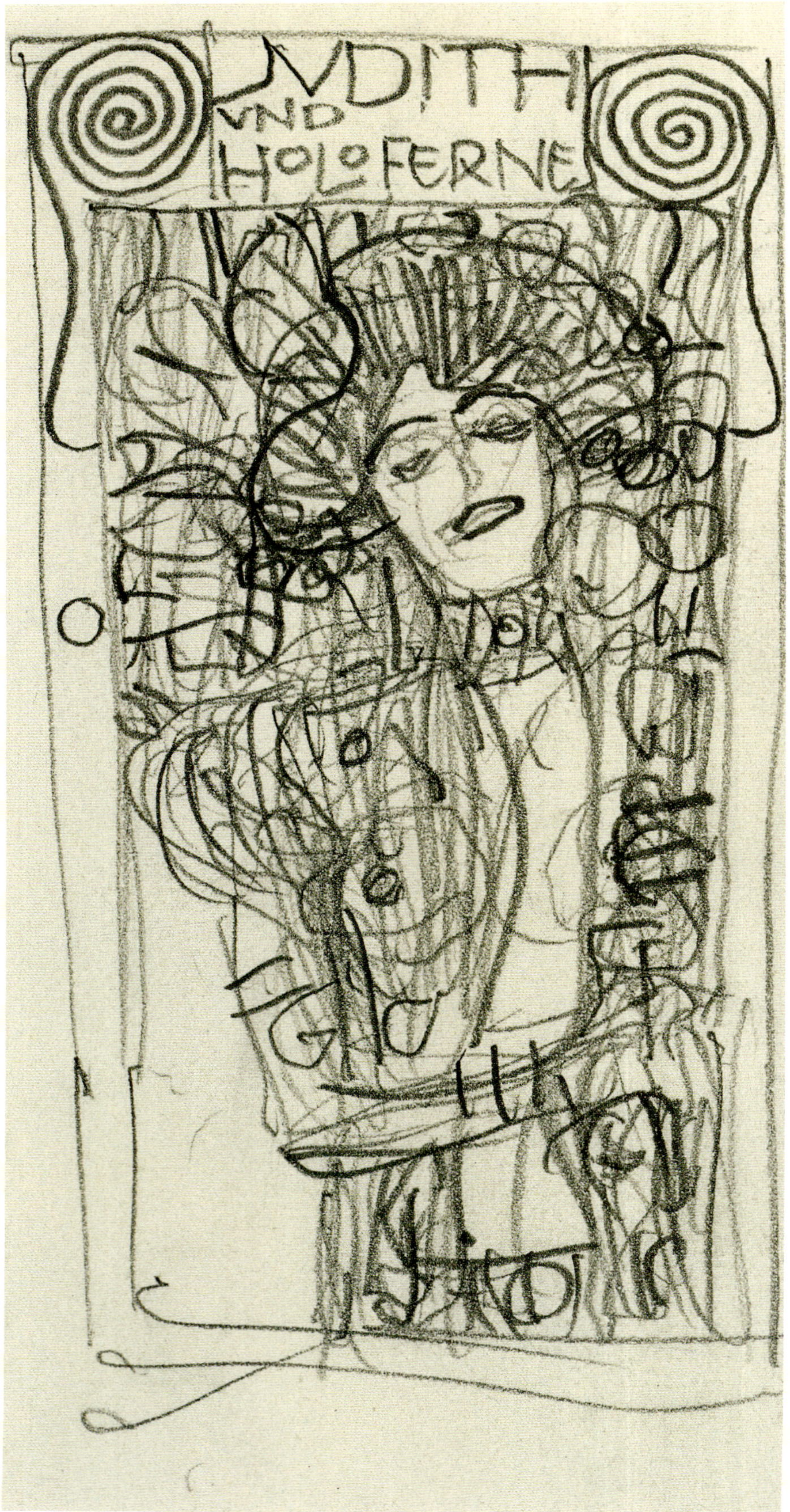

The Power of Truth

It's worth spelling out the intensity of the impact *Schubert at the Piano* had, given that for us today, there's a danger of its seeming a little obvious or underwhelming – even twee. *Nuda Veritas*, however, needs no introduction, nor has its emotional impact – or even its capacity to startle – appreciably diminished with the passing of the decades. And although *Schubert* doesn't come out of the comparison too well, in its way – as contemporary commentators like Altenberg and Bahr made clear – it was every bit as radical a work.

None of which of course is to diminish the importance of ***Nuda Veritas.*** *The way this picture incorporated both written statement and visual artwork, not to mention its avowed dedication to the idea of art as 'truth', made it a fitting manifesto of Secessionist values, and as such it was enthusiastically received. With his customary self-contradictory brio, Bahr (who bought the painting himself) was later to write that it 'has no need of words':*

for it shows us what bliss there is in seeing; it affirms the eye's elemental experience – that moment of revelation connecting seer and seen – in an experience so powerful that we forget to inquire into its meaning and value.

The inscription from Schiller; the serpent of wisdom/temptation/fertility/phallic force; the mirror affirming that art's reflection of life is a true one … It's hard to see how anyone looking at this work could conceivably 'forget to inquire' into the 'meaning and value' of artistic 'bliss'. Yet what this description lacks in meaning, it makes up for in a rightful rapturousness: this is certainly a forceful attestation of the power of art.

LEFT : SKETCH FOR THE PAINTING JUDITH I, c. 1899. GUSTAV KLIMT (1862–1918)
OPPOSITE : JUDITH AND THE HEAD OF HOLOFERNES (JUDITH I), 1901. GUSTAV KLIMT (1862–1918)

A Window on the World

The Fifth Exhibition (September 1899–January 1900) was dedicated to the graphic arts, and included a wealth of French contributions – from Impressionists like Pierre-Auguste Renoir (1841–1919) and Camille Pissarro (1830–1903) to Symbolists and proto-Modernists like the recently-deceased Puvis de Chavannes (1824–98). Also on show were works by Eugène Carrière (1849–1906) and a young Spanish artist who had clearly been much influenced by him: Pablo Picasso (1881–1973). The applied arts weren't neglected though, whether those from France, like the works of the print- and woodcut-maker Félix Vallotton (1865–1925), or works of local talents like Moser and Hoffmann.

The overriding theme of the Sixth Exhibition, following soon after, between late January and February 1900, was Japanese art. This, though arguably a miscalculation (by Secession standards to date, the event had dismal attendance figures), was nevertheless important if the Secession were to maintain its programme of presenting its own aims and educating the public taste. Japonisme was by no means new: Japanese art had first appeared in Vienna as long ago as 1873, at that year's International Exposition, and it had caught the imagination of the more modern-minded right away. Japanese work, in everything from painting and graphic arts to porcelain and textiles, appealed to modern artists in its clean, spare lines, its uncluttered content and its striking use of colour. Lovers of crafts also admired Japanese artists' respect for natural materials.

And of course another reason for admiration was the oriental culture's underlying assumption – so fundamental as not to need explicit statement – that artistic considerations extended into every area of life.

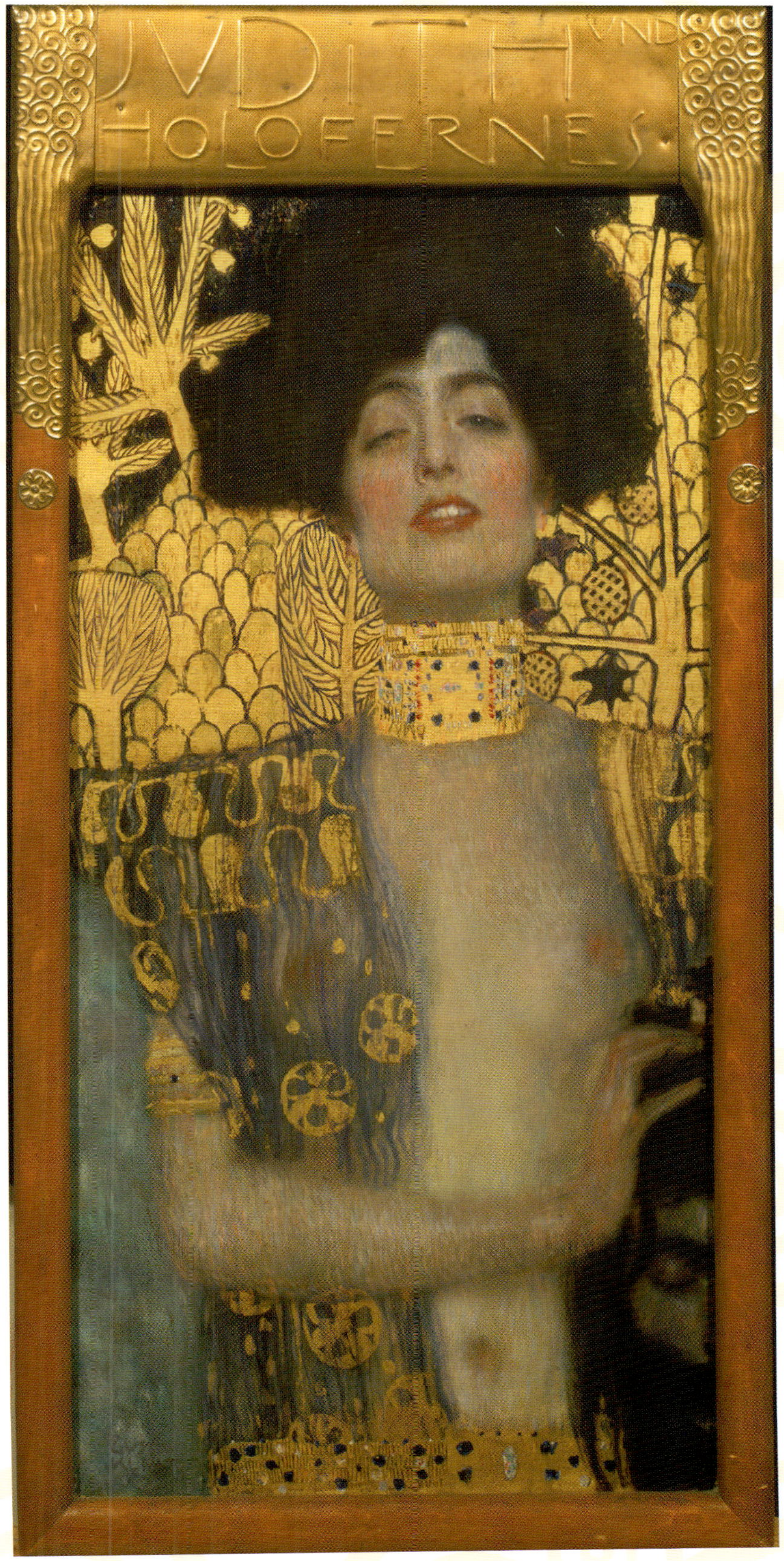

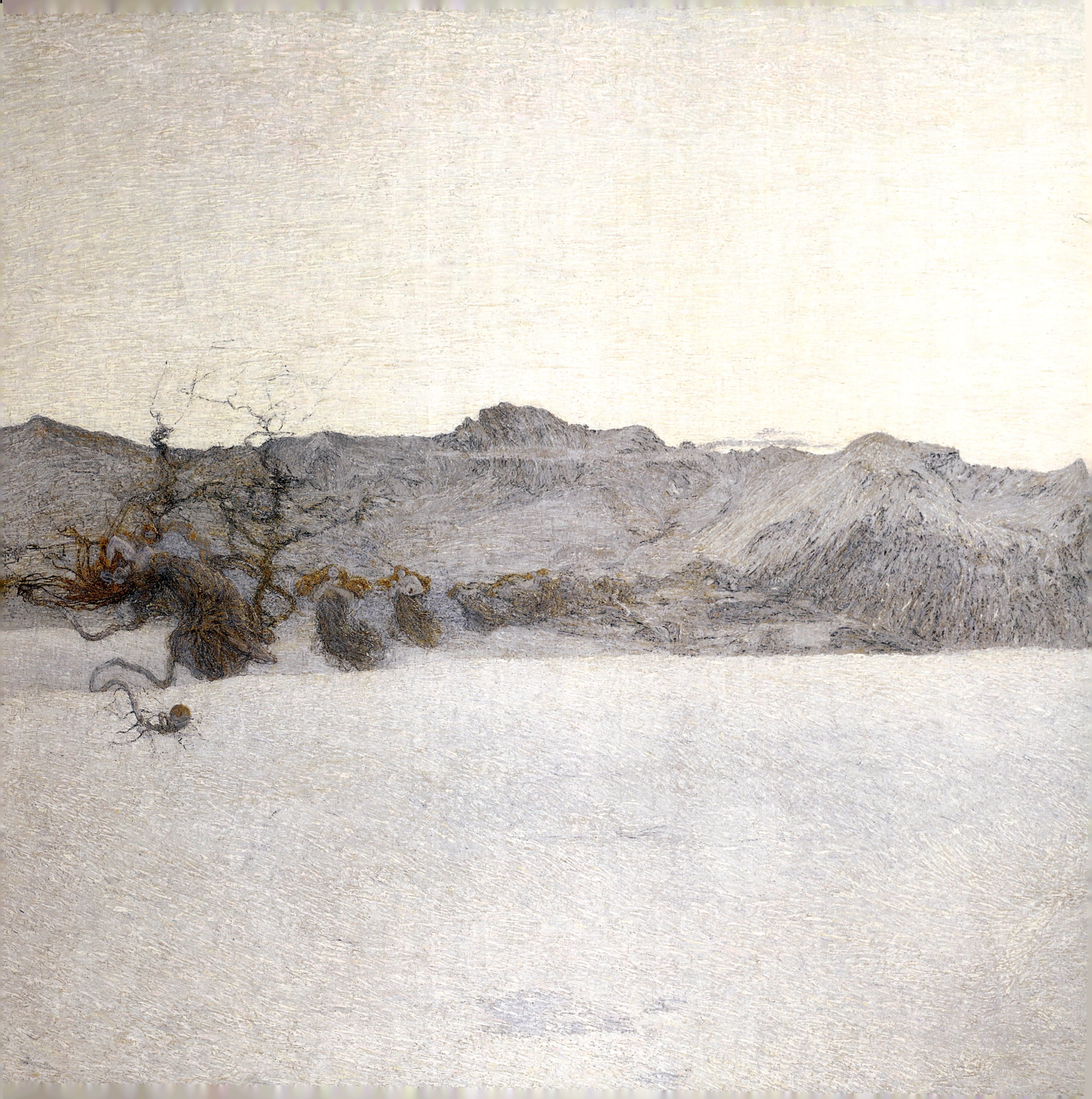

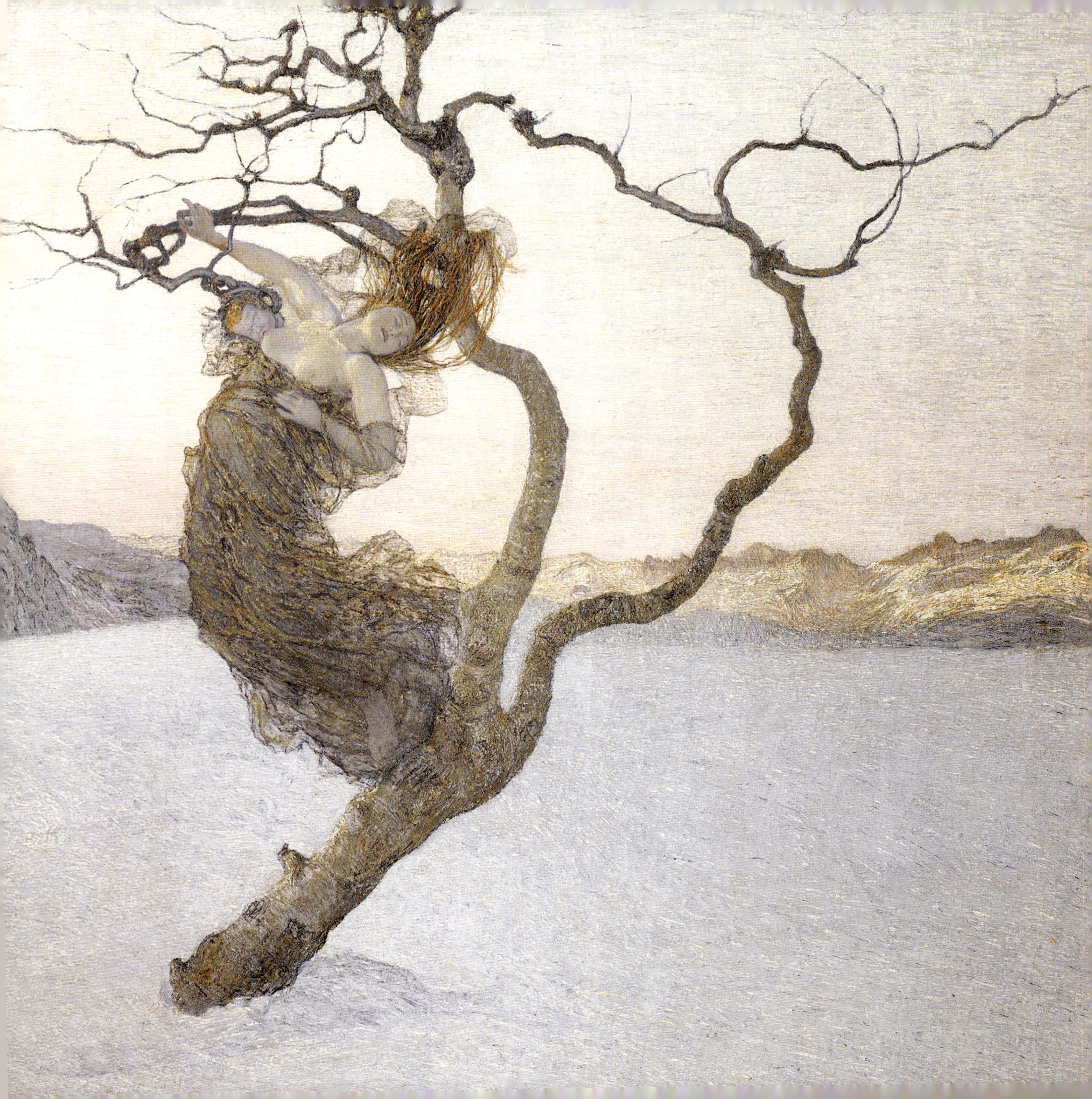

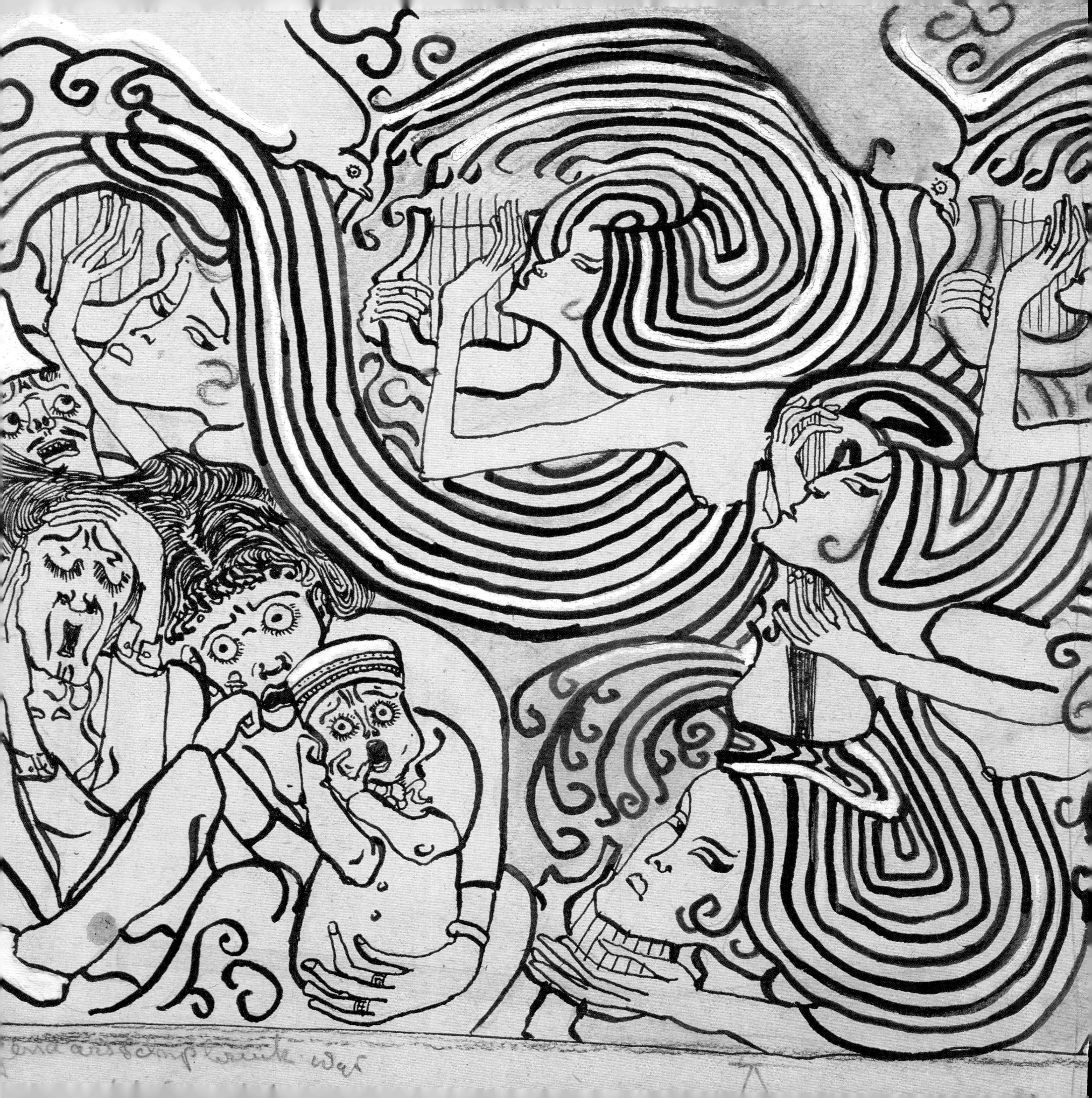

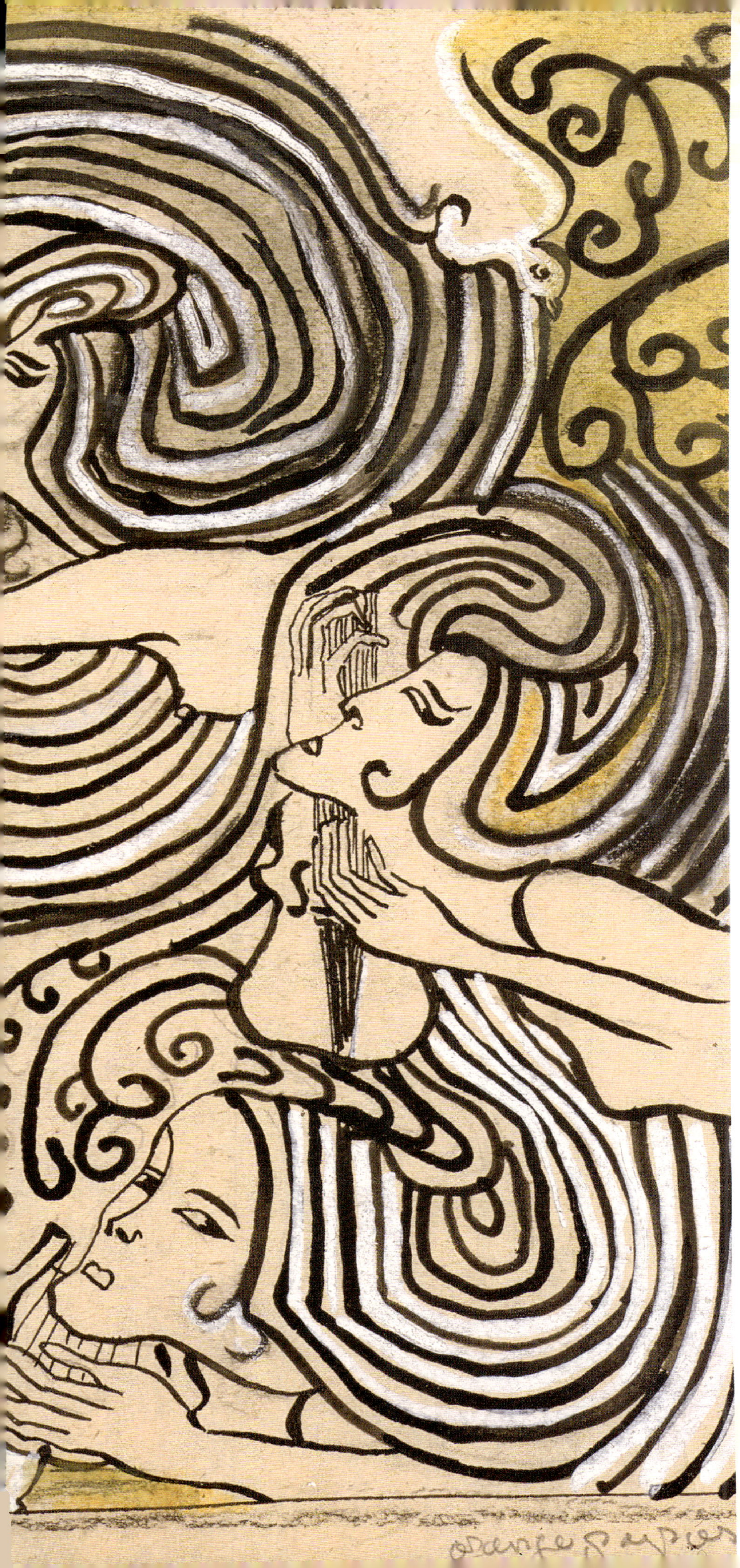

Oriental Ideals

Klimt's love of Japanese and oriental art is well-attested; and he became an avid collector of everything from fine paintings to porcelains. A young Egon Schiele left Klimt's studio dumbfounded. There were, he said:

> *Japanese woodblock prints and two large Chinese pictures … and, in the corner by the window, there was a black and red Japanese suit of armour … [and] a large built-in cupboard containing the most beautiful Chinese and Japanese costumes.*

This love is also echoed everywhere in Klimt's art, from the exaggerated verticality of the formats he used in many of his *Ver Sacrum* sketches, reminiscent of that to be seen in so many *bijin-ga* (Japanese 'beautiful women' prints), to the decorative inlays used in later paintings like *The Kiss* (*see* page 51), *Portrait of Adele Bloch-Bauer I* (*see* page 189), and in paint in still later works like *The Girls* (1912–13). In the *bijin-ga* too, we frequently see the decorative motifs of a woman's kimono, fan or hairpins vying for visual impact with her (equally artificial) made-up face – and both with the strokes and with the forms of a highly-stylized landscape background.

Turning Japanese

And again, there's the question of where life leaves off and art begins – with the implicit suggestion that they continue one another. Klimt is also known to have been influenced by the artists of the Japanese *Rinpa* school – their liberal use of gold leaf is only the most obvious influence in his work. Just as important are their dismissal of 'depth' in favour of a flat perspective, their ease with blank space and the jewel-like delicacy

PREVIOUS PAGE • THE BAD MOTHERS, 1894. GIOVANNI SEGANTINI (1858–99)
OPPOSITE • SHIPWRECK, 1895. JAN TOOROP (1858–1928)

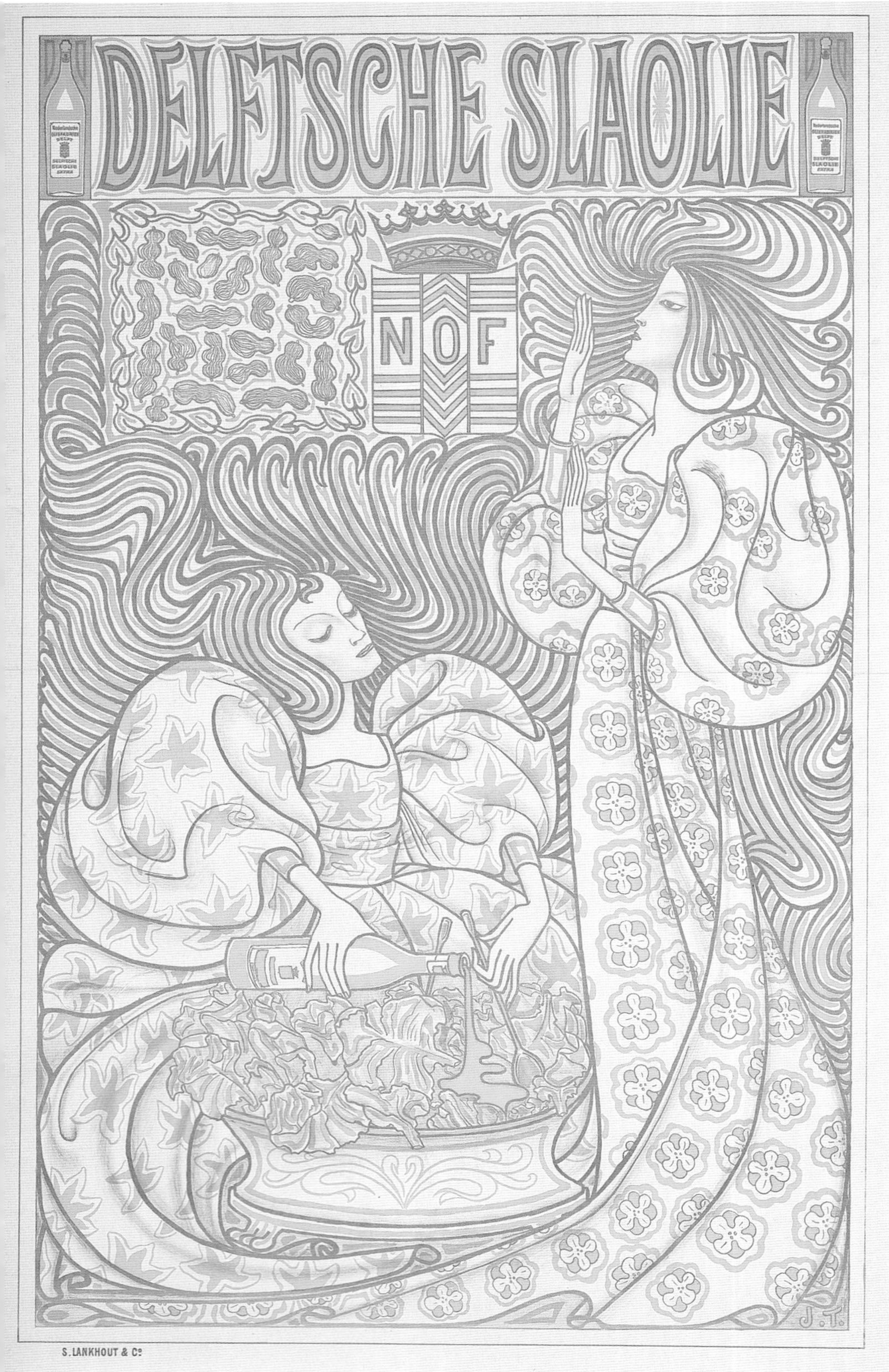

ABOVE ◆ ADVERTISING POSTER FOR DELFT SALAD OIL, 1894. JAN TOOROP (1858–1928)
OPPOSITE ◆ PORTRAIT OF FRITZA RIEDLER, 1906. GUSTAV KLIMT (1862–1918)

of the bright little berries and blossoms to be seen in their landscape paintings. These influences can perhaps be seen in landscapes like *Beech Forest I* (*c.* 1902, *see* pages 152–53), *Roses Under Trees* (1904, see pages 154–55) or *Garden Landscape (Blooming Meadow*, *c.* 1906).

Some critics though, find Klimt at his most 'Japanese' in the mosaic friezes he did from 1907 for the Stoclet Palace in Brussels, Belgium. Josef Hoffmann designed this impressive home for the industrialist and art collector Adolphe Stoclet (1871–1949). Given free rein, Hoffmann called all his Secessionist and *Werkstätte* friends together and told them to make the whole place a walk-through *Gesamtkunstwerk* – and they certainly succeeded.

By comparison, the Sixth Exhibition of the Secession was understated. Adolf Fischer (1847–1914) lent selected items from his collection. These offered a fascinating cultural counterpoint to Western works, whether avowedly Japonist or not, even if this time, the Vienna public stayed away in droves.

The Calm Before the Storm

Far more people turned out for the Secessionists' Seventh Exhibition (March–June 1900), which featured works by Fernand Khnopff (of course), Jan Toorop (1858–1928) and paintings and watercolours by the Neo-Impressionist Paul Signac (1863–1935).

Once again though, the show was stolen by Klimt, with a couple of works that made it clear why his work was so beloved on the one hand and so outrageously controversial on the other. In the former category came *Calm Pond in the Park of Schloss Kammer* (1899),

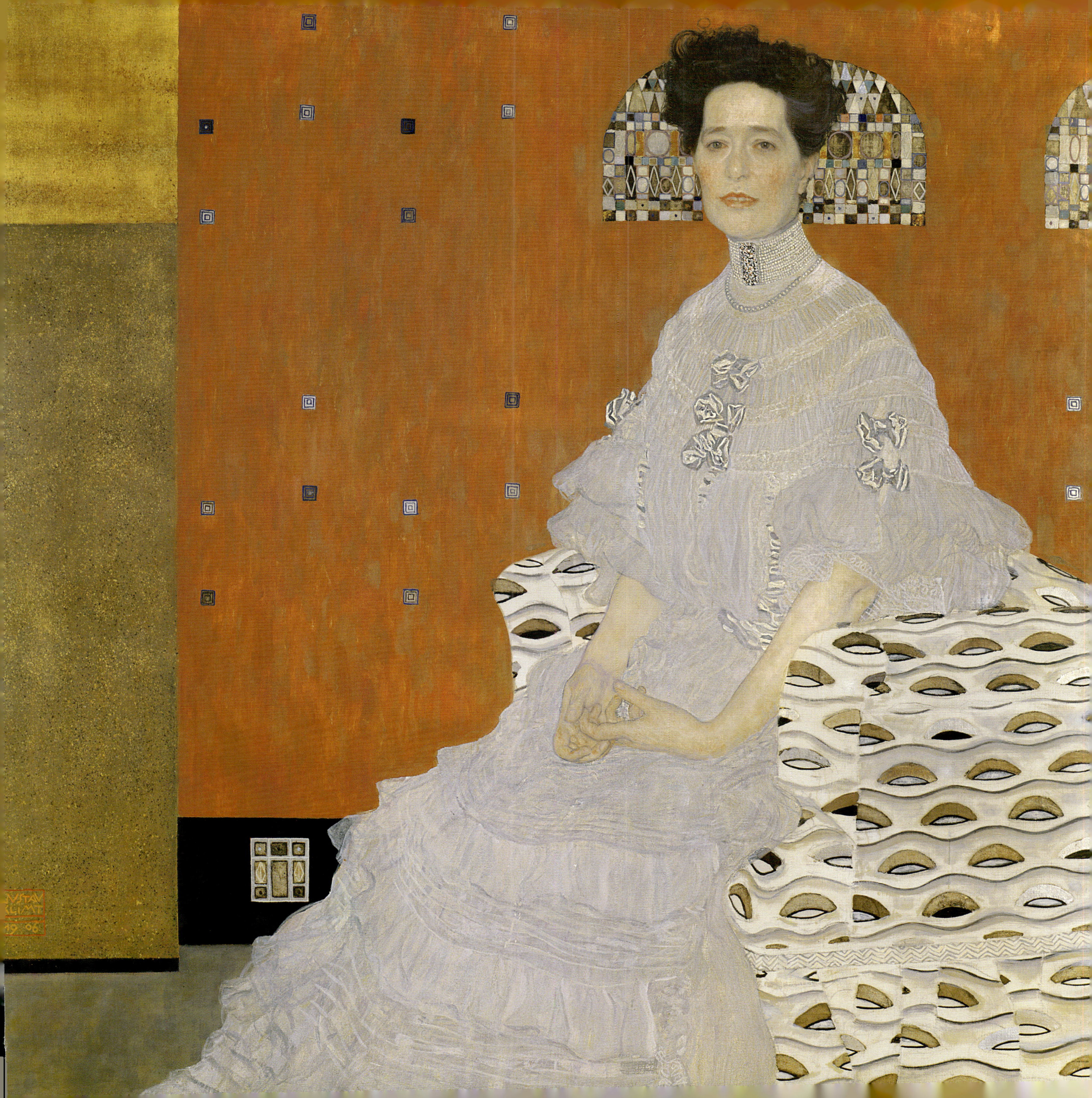
1906

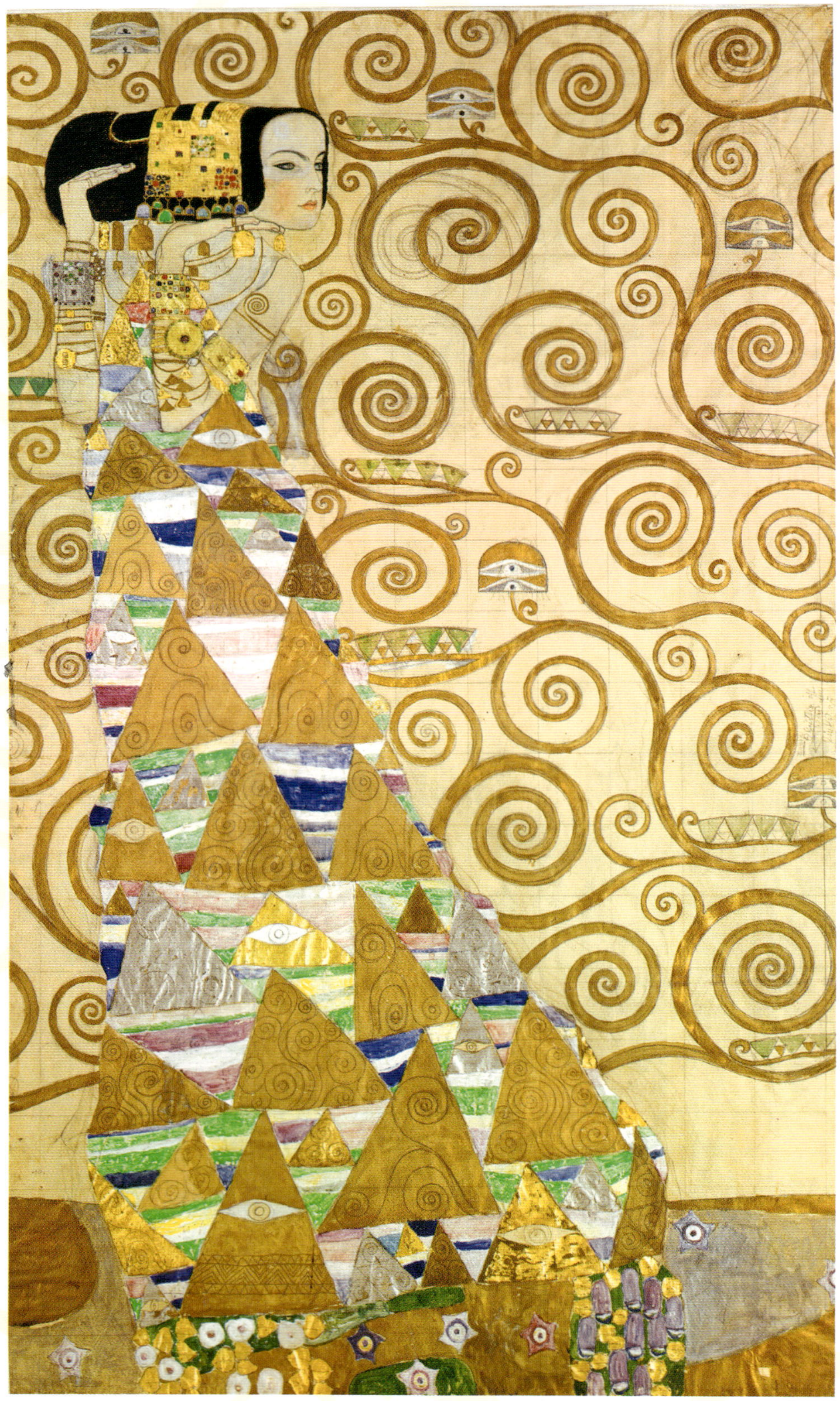

which – calm indeed – made an Impressionist-like use of light and colour to present an extremely pleasing scene. At least it did at first glance: those who stood and studied it a little longer saw – in the shadowy reflection of the trees on the far shore looming forward from stage-left – an atmospheric, even ominous quality; a sense of still waters running very deep.

Philosophical Furore

The other work, we've already encountered: Klimt's ceiling painting for the University, *Philosophy* (*see* page 46), had been commissioned to celebrate 'The Victory of Light over Darkness', but for so profound a painter, this was far too fatuous a theme. It mightn't have mattered so much if the resulting work had simply been impossibly obscure. Unfortunately, unfathomable as it was for the most part, it was just intelligible enough for it to be evident that it came close to representing the victory of darkness over light. 'On the left', in Klimt's own words, was 'a group of figures, the beginning of life, fruition and decay.' But this beginning was not, it seemed, to get too far. 'On the right', Klimt's account continued, 'was the globe as mystery. Emerging below, a figure of light: knowledge.' All the required boxes were ticked, then – reason, knowledge, thought – but the 'light' provided no illumination. Men and women floated hopelessly, like lost souls.

Philosophy's frank eroticism didn't help, of course; nor were Austrian conservatives in any way mollified by being told that this painting had earlier in the year been the toast of the World Exhibition in Paris. On the contrary, it seemed, this damned it as an impossibly difficult, diabolically dirty work.

LEFT • THE STOCLET FRIEZE: EXPECTATION, c. 1905–09. GUSTAV KLIMT (1862–1918)
OPPOSITE • : DANAE, 1907–08. GUSTAV KLIMT (1862–1918)

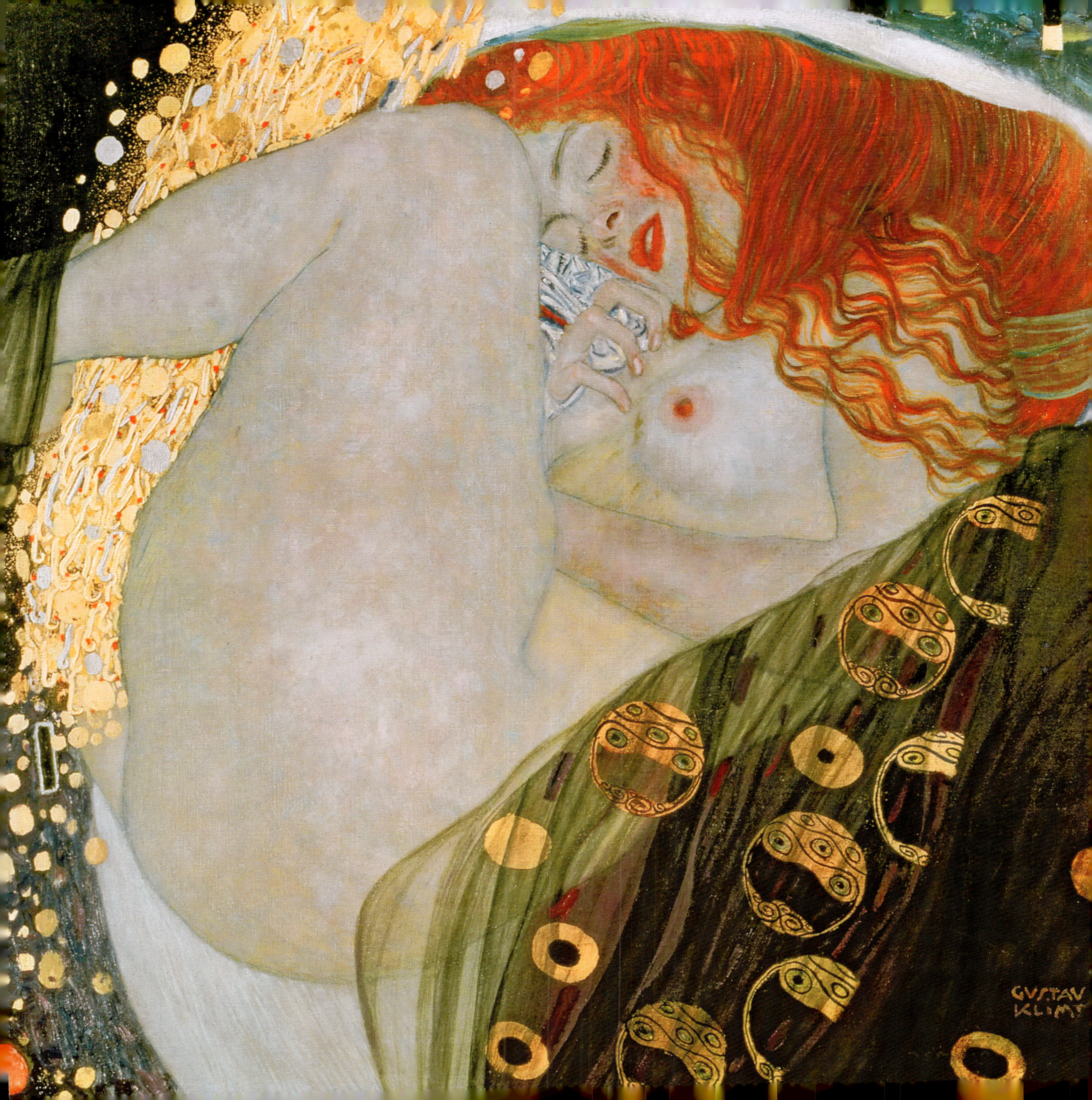
GUSTAV
KLIMT

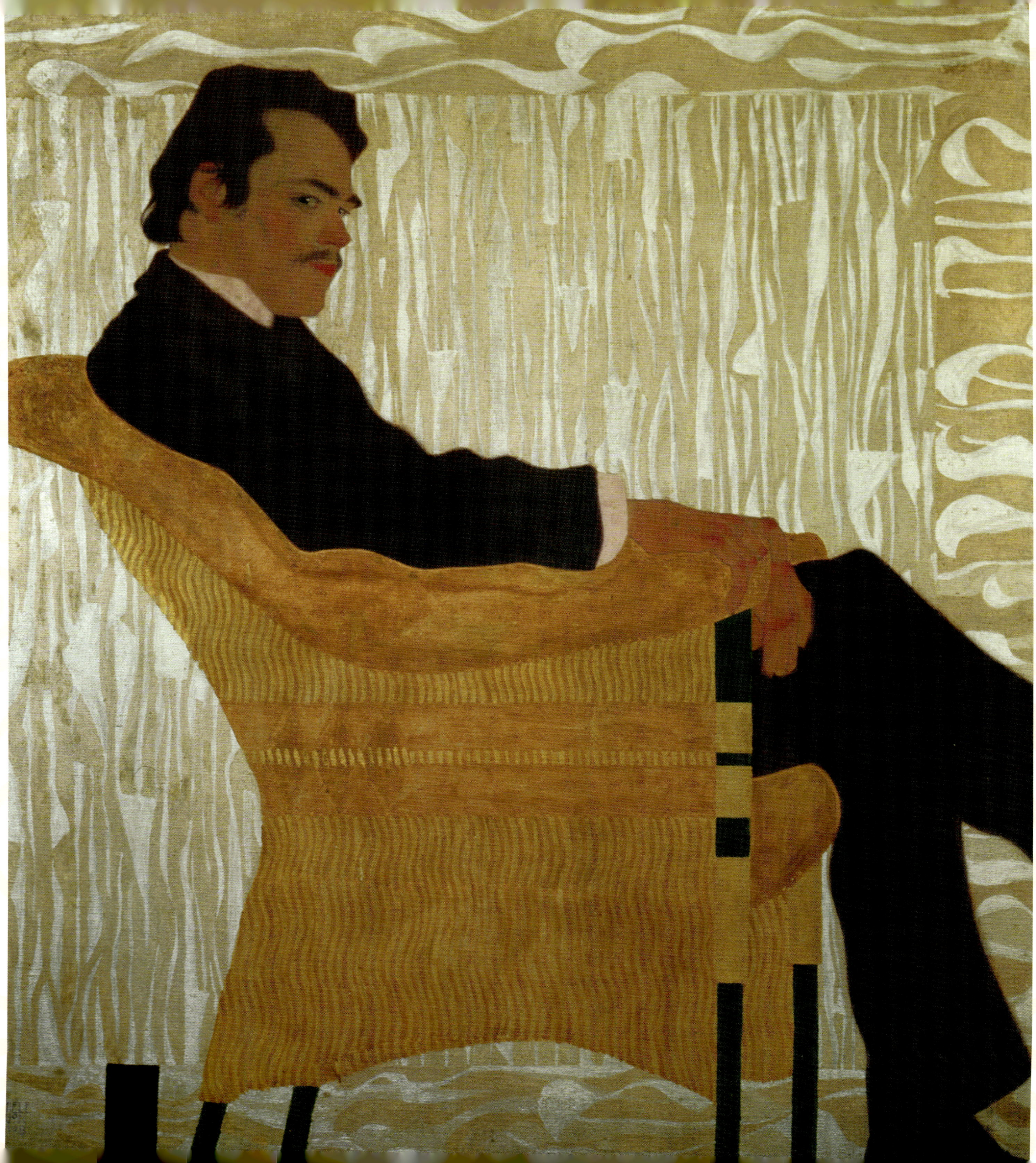

Glasgow School in Vienna

At the end of the year (November–December 1900) came the Eighth Exhibition, seen since as something of a milestone in Secession history. This exhibition brought Glasgow to Vienna in the work of Charles Rennie Mackintosh, the Macdonald sisters and Herbert McNair, along with that of a range of other applied artists from Austria and beyond. It's a testimony to the stir the stained-glass and panel-paintings of the Glasgow School caused that these artists were able to relegate to the status of exhibition also-rans such figures as Henri Toulouse-Lautrec (1864–1901), the late Vincent van Gogh and Paul Gauguin. In fairness, both Gauguin and his friend van Gogh attained artistic superstar status only after their deaths, while Toulouse-Lautrec was arguably old news as far as the *Jugendstil* and the Secession were concerned.

Even so, that the impact of the Glasgow artists should seem quite so extraordinary now is further evidence of the shift in attitudes the Vienna Secession represented. We'd be wrong to underestimate that impact, though. That Josef Hoffmann's friend, the textile magnate Fritz Waerndorfer, commissioned Charles and Margaret Rennie Mackintosh to envision and create a new music room (and subsequently other apartments) for his home may not mean too much – even if the resulting interior is now acknowledged as (at the very least) a minor masterpiece. Since Waerndorfer was already the proud owner of a couple of works by Klimt – *Pallas Athena, see* page 60) and a landscape, *Orchard in the Evening* (1898), as well as *Kneeling Youth* (1898, *see* page 160), a sculpture by the Belgian George Minne (1866–1941), a Secessionist idol – it did speak volumes for the Mackintoshes' prestige that this patron wanted to 'collect' them as well. But by drafting them in to consult with him on the goals and methods to be adopted by the *Wiener Werkstätte* he and Hoffmann were to found a couple of years later, Waerndorfer gave the Glasgow artists a vital place in the development of twentieth-century European design.

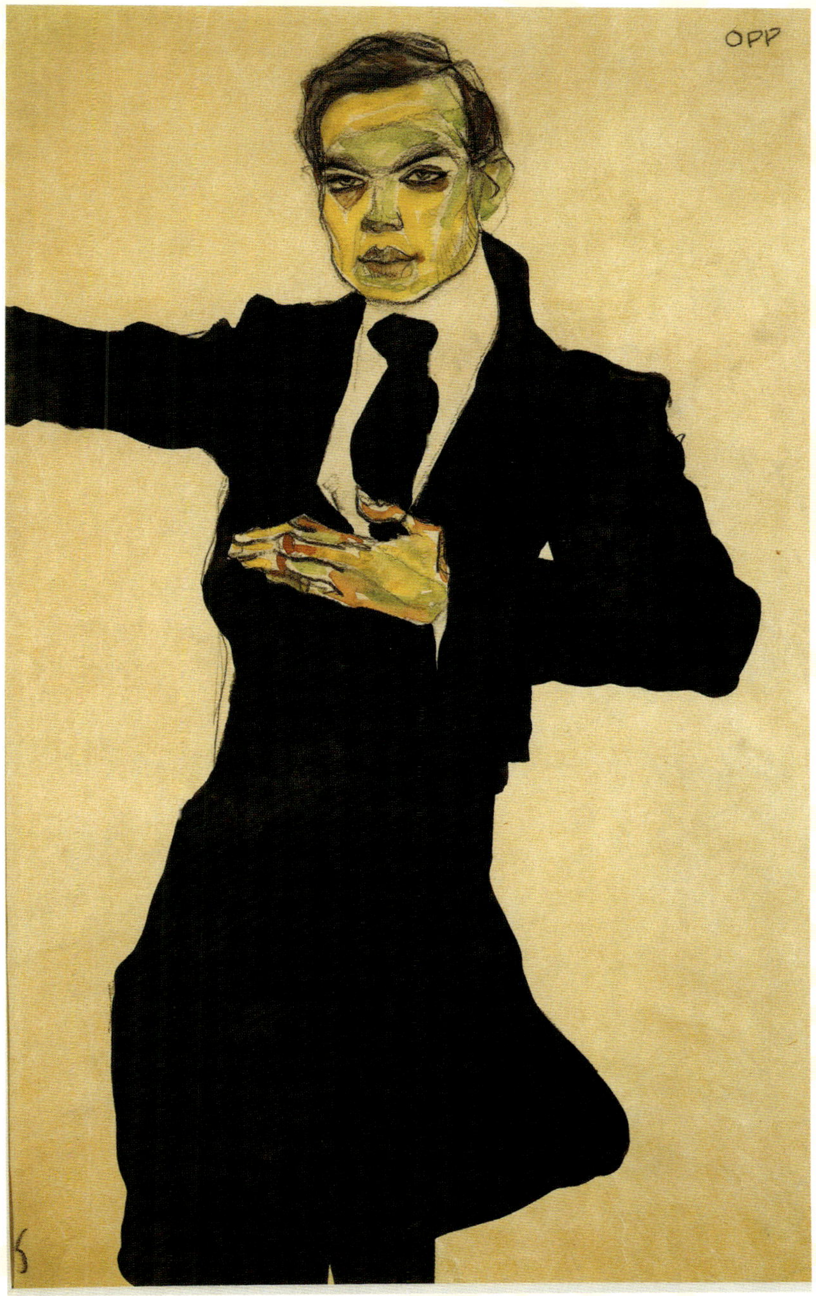

OPPOSITE ◆ PORTRAIT OF HANS MASSMANN, 1909, EGON SCHIELE (1890–1918)
RIGHT ◆ PORTRAIT OF MAX OPPENHEIMER, 1910, EGON SCHIELE (1890–1918)

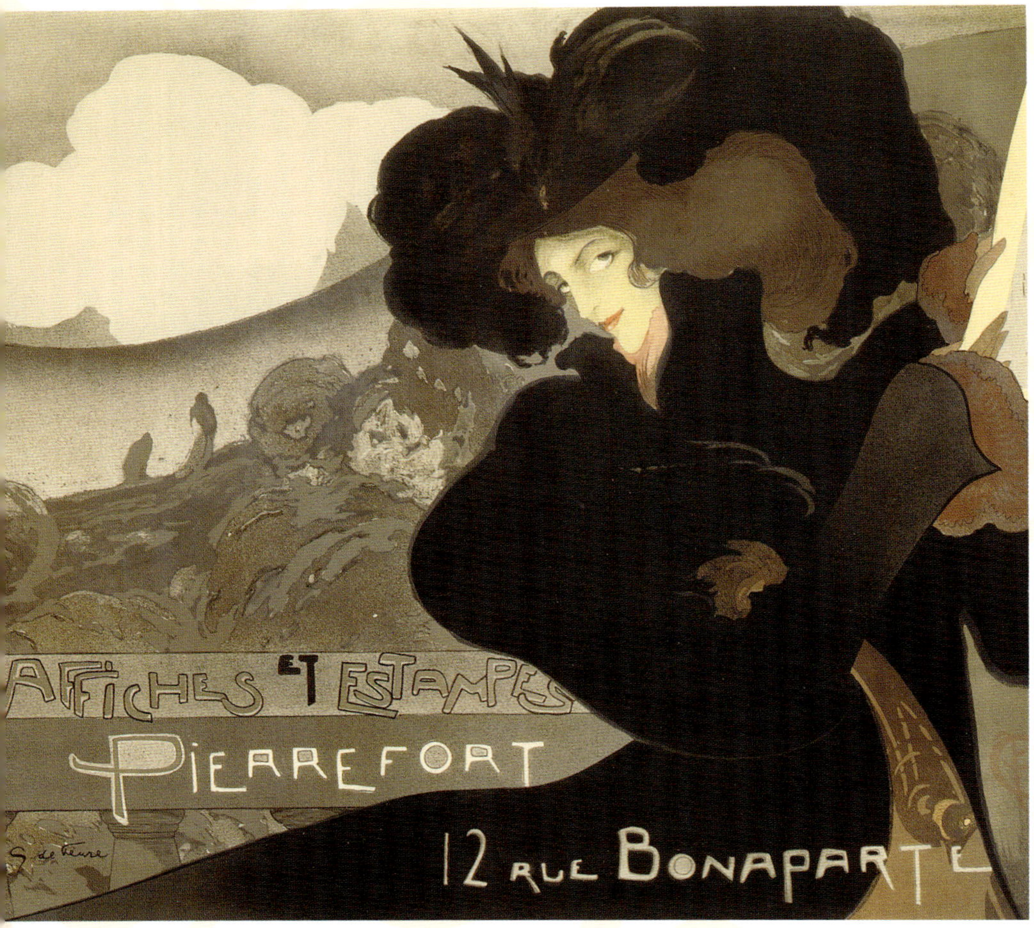

Glaswegian Geometry

The most immediate impact of the Glasgow Four was, however, the inspirational effect they had on Koloman Moser, who met them in Vienna and was much taken with their work. Moser's decorative designs for *Ver Sacrum* and elsewhere swing towards the geometric and the audacious use of empty space, which seems directly related to what he'd found in the art of the Glasgow Four. Josef Hoffmann too was directly influenced by the work of Charles in particular, as we can see from some of his posters for the *Werkstätte*'s exhibitions (and for that matter, from much of the jewellery and furniture he created around this time). The impact of the Glasgow artists on Klimt (although he seems to have loved their work) is a great deal harder to quantify. Works like Macdonald's *The Opera of the Sea* (*c.* 1902; *see* page 59) may have influenced him, some scholars have suggested.

Segantini Remembered

The Ninth Exhibition was staged between mid-January and the end of February 1901. It stood out largely for its memorial retrospective to Giovanni Segantini, who had died two years before – much mourned by his Secession comrades. Alfred Roller remodelled the main hall into an octagonal space around which Segantini paintings depicting *Becoming*, *Being* and *Death* respectively were deployed.

Quite how important a figure Segantini was to the Secessionists isn't quite clear to us until we appreciate, first, that though Italian, his Alpine homeland was in what they considered to be part of Austria-Hungary – so he was one of their own; and second, that although some of Segantini's more Impressionistic Alpine scenes looked (even then) as though they were created to cover chocolate boxes and biscuit tins, his more profoundly personal, Symbolist works seemed much more disturbing – as they do still. In paintings like *The Punishment of Lust* (1891, *see* pages 158–59) and *The Bad Mothers* (1894, *see* pages 164–65), Segantini's Alpine homeland becomes a dreadful background for scenes of the most appalling anguish and moral bleakness. If we then glance back at some of the more popular works, we'll often be taken by surprise, seeing that they aren't quite as charmingly innocent as they appear.

Also exhibited at this show were sculptures by Max Klinger and Auguste Rodin, including the plaster model Rodin had made for *The Burghers of Calais* (1889).

ABOVE LEFT: AFFICHES ET ESTAMPES PIERREFORT, 1898. GEORGES DE FEURE (1868–1943)
OPPOSITE: LADY WITH A HAT AND FEATHER BOA, 1909. GUSTAV KLIMT (1862–1918)

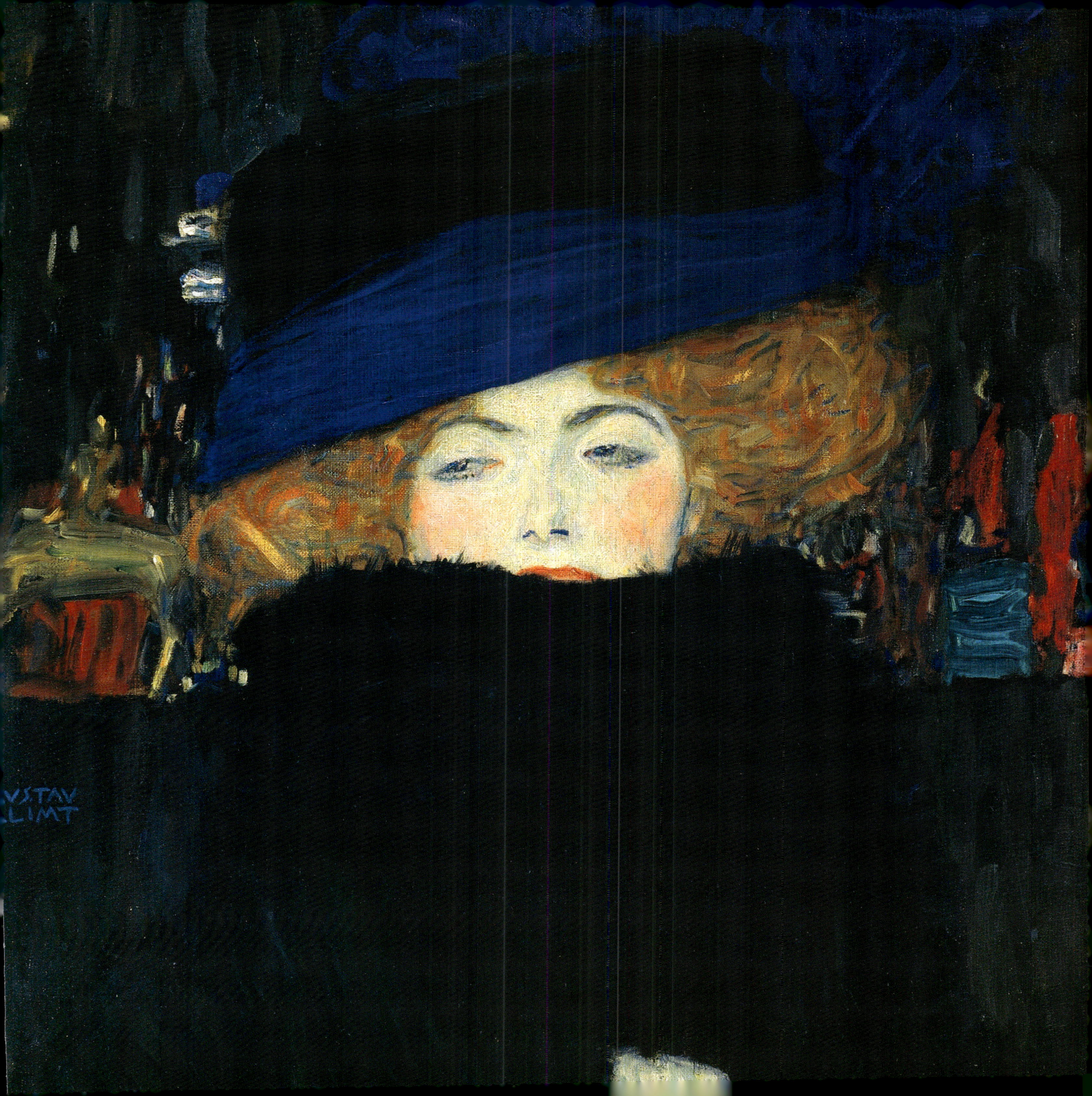

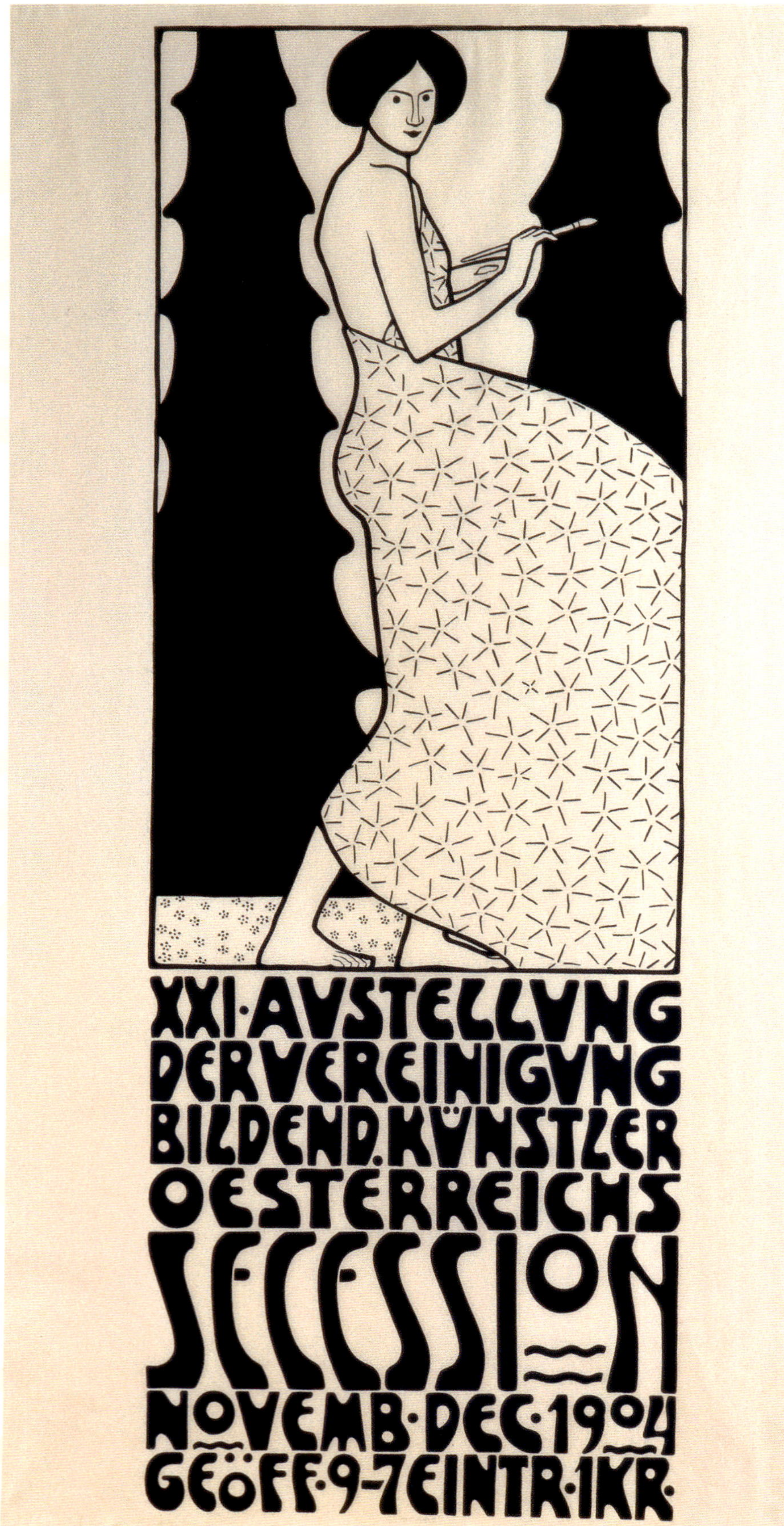

Medicine Man

For the Tenth Exhibition, which took place between March and May 1901, it was back to Klimt, and another round of scandal. Seemingly not the slightest bit disconcerted by the fuss that had greeted *Philosophy* the year before, Klimt now pitched in with his second University painting, *Medicine*. If the public had come in the hope of being scandalized, they were not disappointed. Indeed, some said this work surpassed its predecessor in outrageousness. If there were obvious similarities (most obviously the 'column of life and death', with its floating – and uncompromisingly naked – figures), the prevailing red colour immediately made it seem more startlingly lurid than the soft marine-green that had created the dreamy sense of doubt in *Philosophy*.

As for the central figure Hygeia (*see* page 161), Greek goddess of Good Health and Cleanliness and the daughter of the god of Medicine, Asclepius, she seemed shocking in just about every imaginable way. From the unborn baby floating above her head (and the matching man curled up in a foetal position to her right) to her expression, fixed in something not unlike a sneer; and from the golden snake twining round her outstretched arm, its coils picking up the aureate patterns of her glowing gown, to the spangled jewels of her headdress, she radiated an air of haughtiness and calm command. She could hardly be said to communicate the idea of health, however: just as *Philosophy* harnessed the iconography of human reason to suggest suspicions of anxious doubt, so this whole painting portrayed *Medicine* as a source of dread.

Cruel Beauty

Alarming as she was, however, *Hygeia* was arguably outdone by *Judith and the Head of Holofernes* (1901, *see* page 163), which also premiered at this

LEFT ◆ VIENNA SECESSION 21ST EXHIBITION POSTER, 1904. FRIEDRICH KÖNIG (1857–1941)
OPPOSITE ◆ PORTRAIT OF IDA ROESSLER, 1912. EGON SCHIELE (1890–1918)

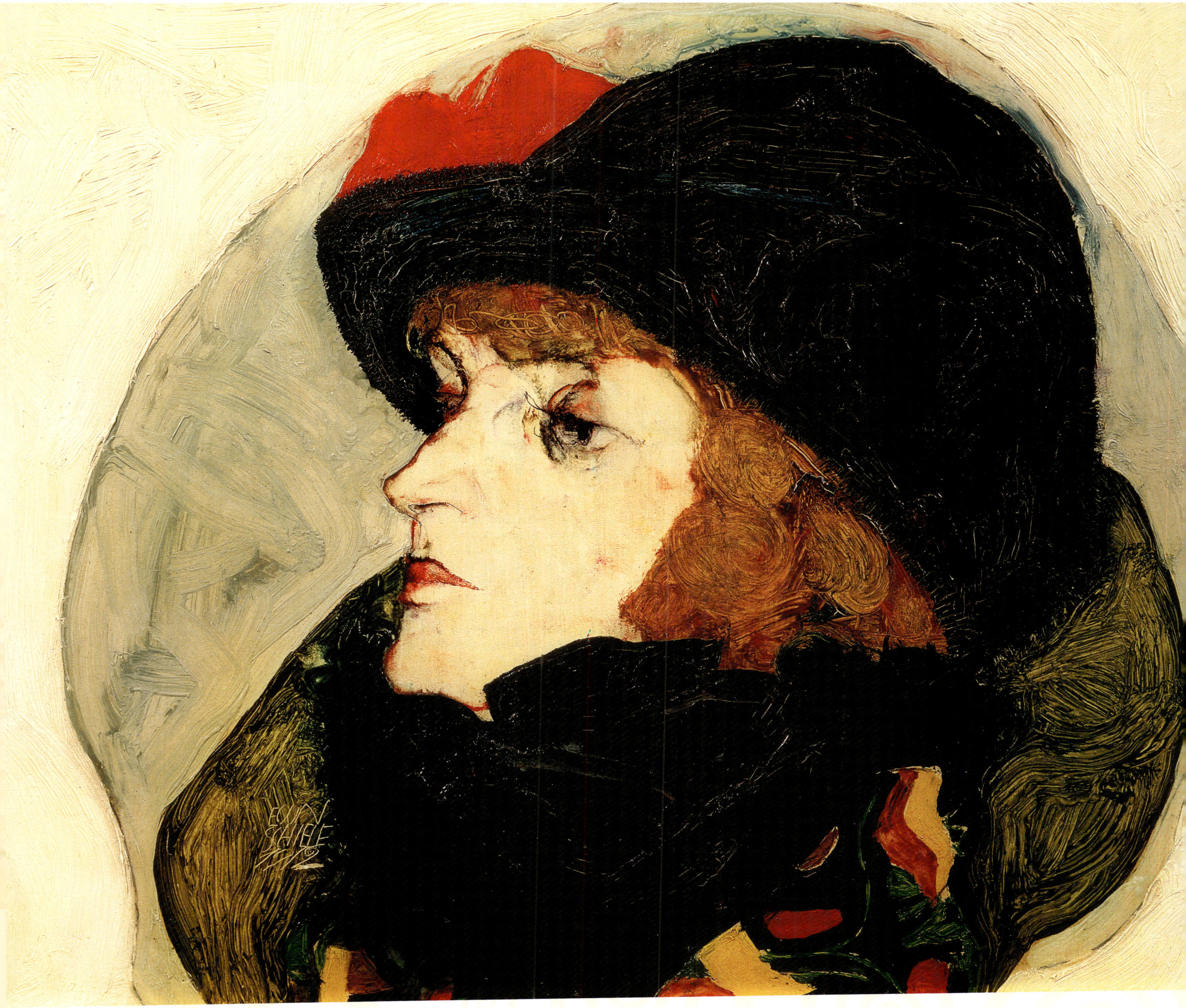

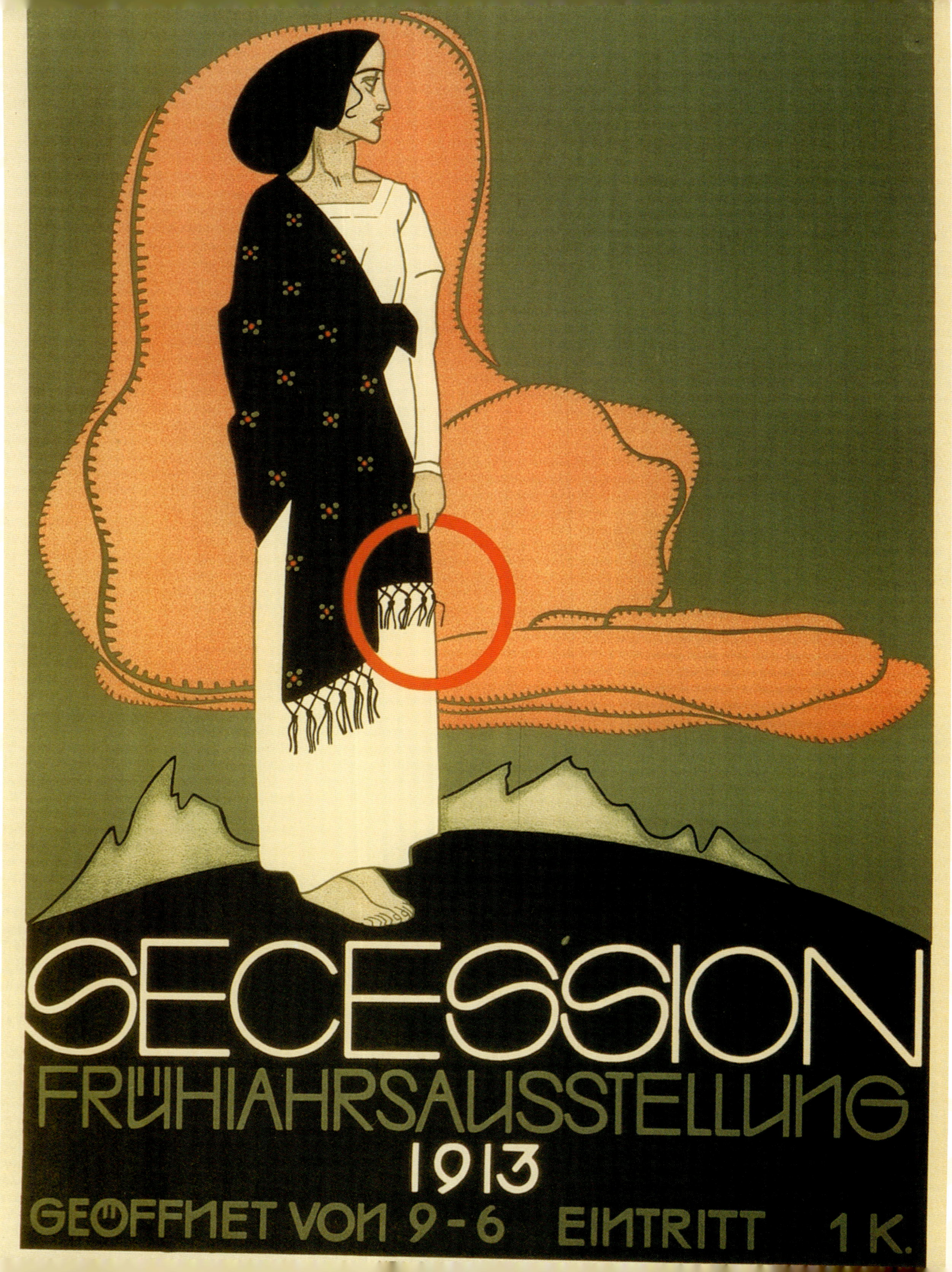
SECESSION
FRÜHIAHRSAUSSTELLUNG
1913
GEÖFFNET VON 9-6 EINTRITT 1 K.

exhibition. Those visiting the show would not, in many cases, have recognized as we do the face of Adele Bloch-Bauer (*see* page 189) in the sinisterly-smiling scriptural temptress here, but there was no mistaking the dangers this dark seductress represented – nor its fairly frank appeal to some seriously anti-Semitic stereotypes. For Judith was, as her name suggests, very definitely a Jewish heroine – if indeed a heroine she was.

One of the more peculiar texts that proliferated in Old Testament times, the Book of Judith has divided scriptural scholars in Christian times. Excluded from the King James and other Protestant Bibles (though it always made it into Catholic versions), it told the story of Israel's invasion by a foreign force, its menfolk's inability to defend it and a loyal wife's refusal to accept defeat. Making her way to the enemy camp with her maidservant, Judith seduced the enemy leader Holofernes, finally murdering him and carrying his head off in a bag. Inspired by her courage, the Jewish armies recovered theirs, and the alien invaders were quickly routed.

Unholy Seduction

Forget the historical detail (as does the Book of Judith, seemingly uncertain as to whether Israel's attackers originate in Assyria or Babylon). Mankind – or manhood – is arguably the 'real' victim in one of those ancient texts that seems positively to cry out for modern Freudian interpretation. Judith in her deadly eroticism sums up all that's most alluring – and most dangerous – in womankind. In that strange symbolic logic by which decapitation seems no more than a metaphor for the (somehow scarier) menace of castration, the story's climactic moment is not Holofernes' beheading, but something worse. So it certainly seems, here: the poor general's head is barely visible at bottom right, while to the 'male gaze', those lazy, post-coital-looking eyelids seem much more frightening.

OPPOSITE ◆ VIENNA SECESSION SPRING EXHIBITION POSTER, 1913. FRANZ WACIK (1838-1938)
RIGHT ◆ ART SHOW POSTER, 1908. RUDOLF KALVACH (1883-1932)

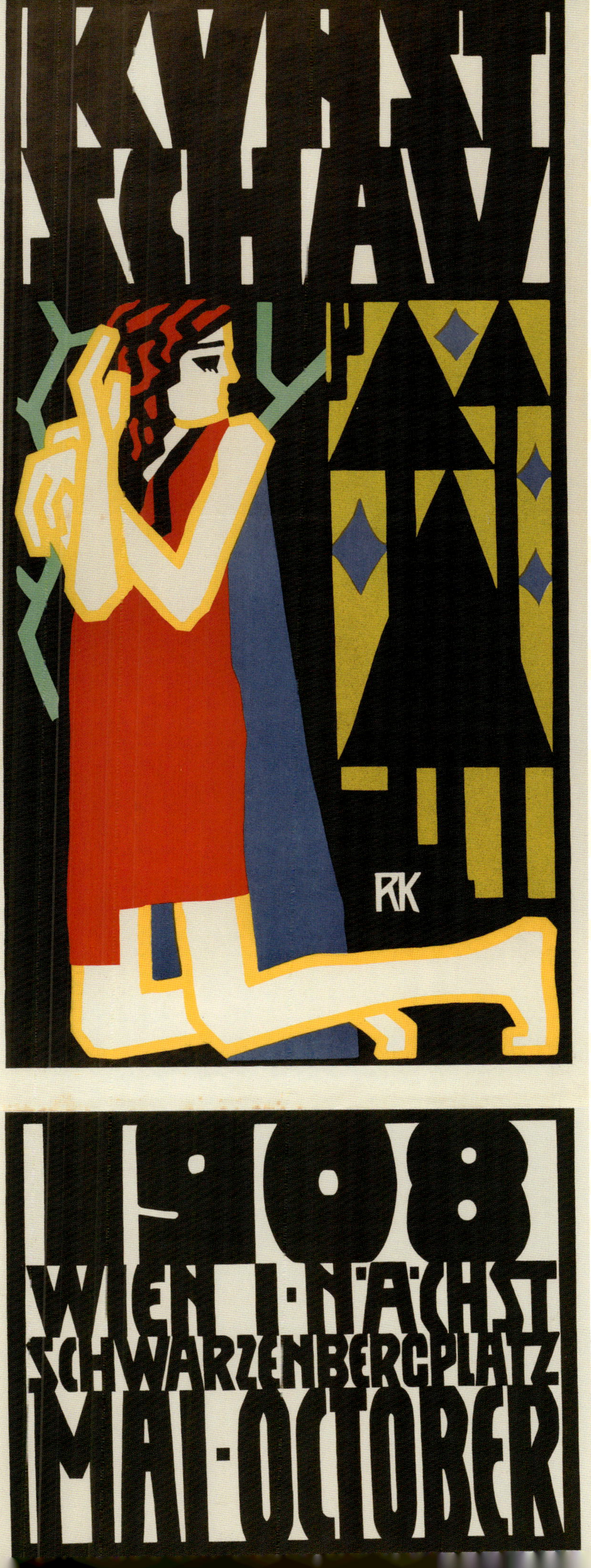

This painting is generally considered to have marked the start of Klimt's 'golden phase', but although it's certainly strikingly rich, the gold is used comparatively conservatively, here. Judith's seductive features – her face and breasts – are shown *au naturel* and the gold leaf is confined largely to her costume and to the background, as it might have been in a sacred icon – unholy as this subject is.

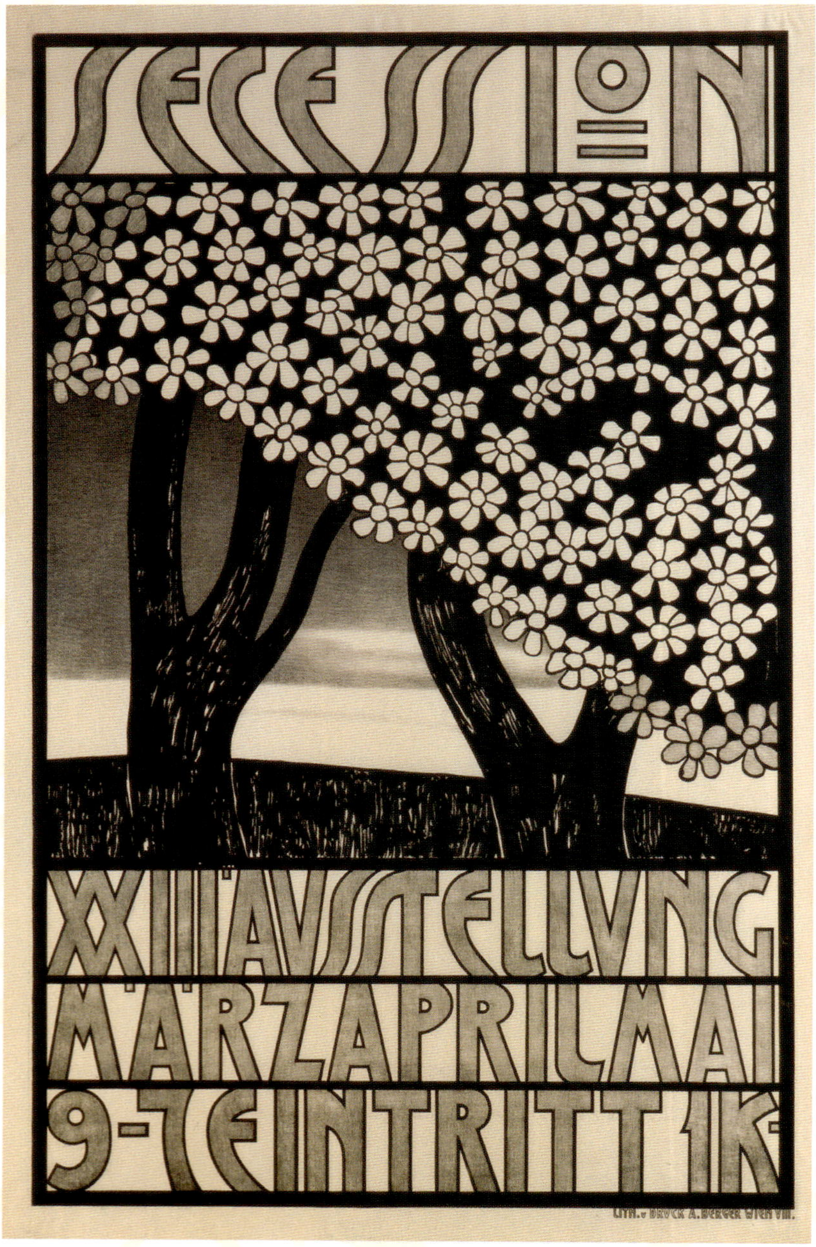

ABOVE ◆ VIENNA SECESSION 23RD EXHIBITION POSTER, 1905. LEOPOLD STOLBA (1863–1929)
OPPOSITE ◆ DETAIL OF THE SECESSION BUILDING, DES. BY JOSEPH MARIA OLBRICH (1867–1908)

The Dutchman and the Dancer

Johann Victor Krämer's work was spotlighted at the Eleventh Exhibition, held in May–June 1901, although readers of *Ver Sacrum* were already familiar with his work. In previous shows, the world of art had seemed to be beating a path to Vienna's door, but this intrepid traveller had taken Austrian art out into the world's wilderness, its deserts and its open fields. The Twelfth Exhibition gave Jan Toorop another outing. The Indonesian-born Dutchman had made his name in the 1880s as an Impressionist before taking a new Symbolist direction in the early 1890s. Of late, however, his work in graphics had shown an obvious kinship with that of the Secessionists, so it was no great surprise to see his work on show.

Boasting a striking – and borderline abstract – geometric poster by Moser, all repeated squares, rectangles and circles, the Thirteenth Exhibition (February–March 1902) featured paintings by the Austrians' 'elder brothers' from the Munich Secession, *Die Scholle*, as well as by the Swiss Symbolist Arnold Böcklin (1827–1901). The Norwegian painter Edvard Munch (1863–1944) was also represented. But the highlight of the exhibition was the appearance of the American dancer Isadora Duncan (1877–1927), giving one of her first public solo performances.

Symphonic Staging

And then of course it was Beethoven's turn. It's easy to see why, at the fourteenth time of asking, the Secessionists weren't fazed by the organizational challenges involved in staging such an exhibition. Although considerable efforts were obviously required to install Klinger's statue, and while Klimt had his work cut out to complete his frieze, on the whole, preparations were characterized by

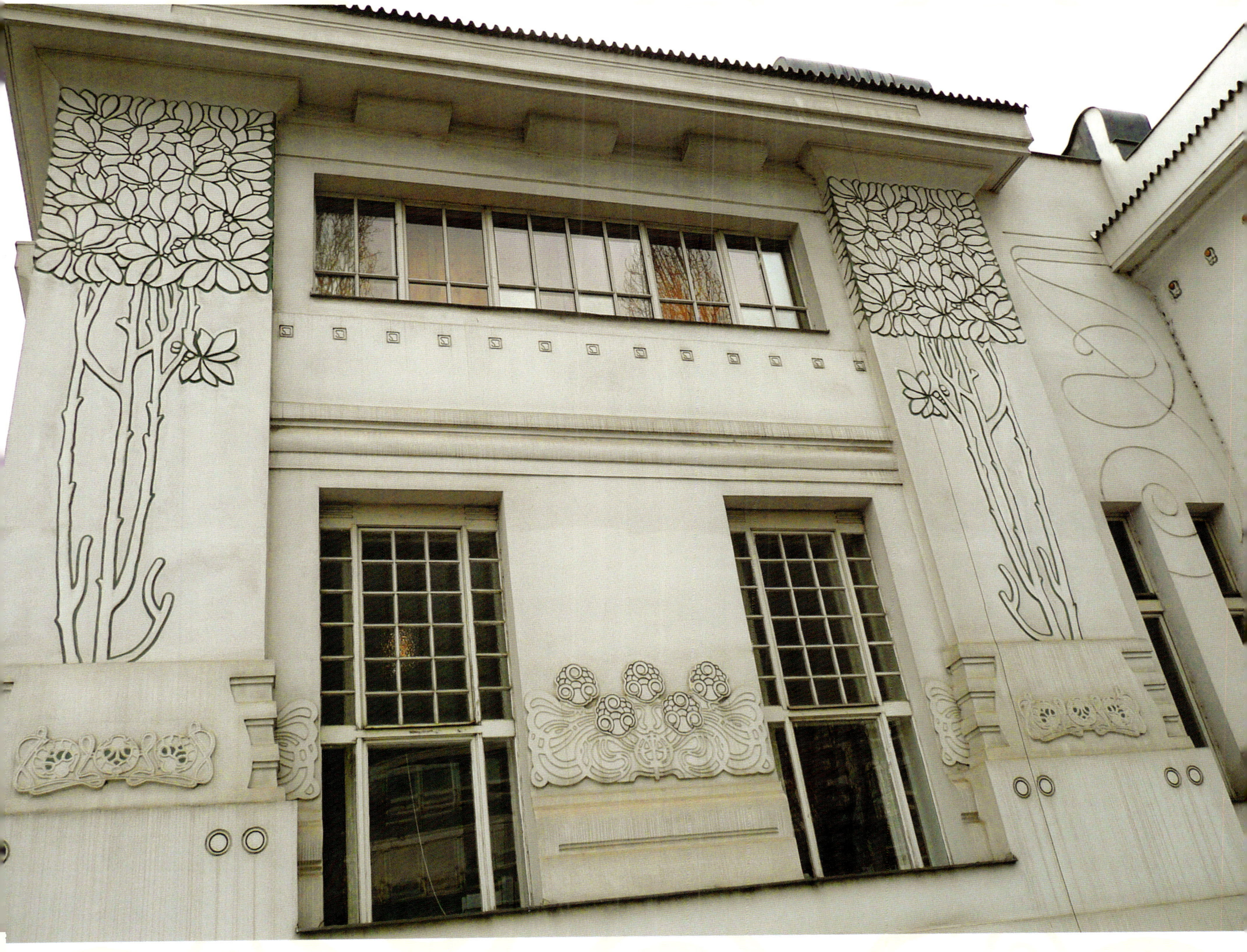

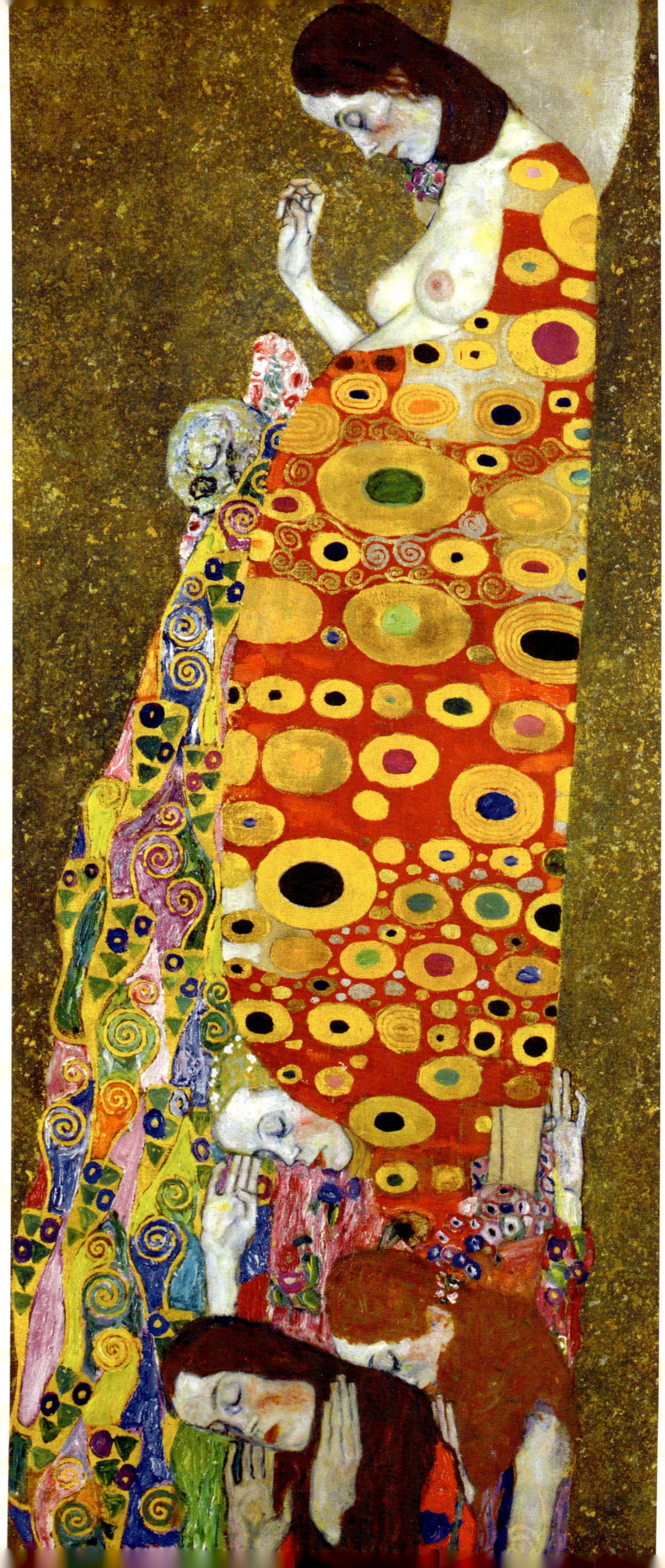

pragmatism. The cheery acceptance that, instead of having a whole symphony orchestra belting out Beethoven's Ninth, they would have to make do with Mahler's woodwinds, was a case in point. Given the enduring importance of the *Beethoven Frieze*, it's understandable that this Fourteenth Exhibition should seem to us to have stood out, and to some extent, it did – though not as much as we tend to assume.

Beginning of the End

At what point does an artistic 'secession' cease to be a breakaway and begin to be the mainstream movement of its time? George Minne's memorial to the late French-Belgian writer George Rodenbach (1855–98), named *Bruges la Morte* after one of its subject's novels, was the centrepiece of the Fifteenth Exhibition (November–December 1902), which was also a shop window for the Secession-style *Sztuka* school of Poland. This school included sculptors like Boleslaw Biegas (1877–1954) and Xawery Dunikowski (1875–1964), and painters such as Jan Stanislawski (1860–1907) and Julian Falat (1853–1929).

There was no sign of any loss of ambition in the Secession's aims, its next exhibition on Impressionism (January–March 1903) assembling a star-studded cast of modern French artists – including Édouard Manet (1832–83), Claude Monet, Paul Cézanne and Edgar Degas (1834–1917). By way of illustrating Impressionism's background, meanwhile, it tracked back as far as Jan Vermeer (1632–75) and Francisco Goya (1746–1828). A spectacular show then, and extremely well attended – but was there the merest suggestion of a 'dying fall' to be found in the faintly backward-looking aspect of the exhibition, in its historical sweep? And, come to that, in its emphasis on the 'fine' arts?

LEFT • HOPE II, 1907–08. GUSTAV KLIMT (1862–1918)

Secessionists Secede

In the Seventeenth Exhibition that same summer, the writing was arguably on the wall in a different way: this craft-centred show marked the inauguration of Josef Hoffmann's *Wiener Werkstätte*, which was ultimately to test the broad artistic principles of the Secession to breaking point. The triumphant success of the Eighteenth Exhibition in the autumn of 1903, an impressive Klimt retrospective designed by Moser and Hoffmann, was to be more literally retrospective than originally intended. It marked the first full showing of the University paintings: not just *Philosophy* and *Medicine*, but also the recently completed third and final picture. *Jurisprudence* proved every bit as controversial as its predecessors.

By now though, the bullish confidence of the craft 'wing', welcome as it was, had begun to create certain strains and stresses within the Secession as a whole. The exhibitions went on, but the mood was changing, with old rivalries resurfacing and old prejudices being restored. For some painters in particular, it was becoming clear that the Secession was simply the up-to-date version of the old Künstlerhaus, a union of painters (and, at a push, of sculptors) who felt no especial solidarity with their co-workers in crafts, nor any great commitment to the *Gesamtkunstwerk* ideal, and begrudged the need to make concessions to this cause. Accordingly, in 1905, the so-called 'Klimt Group' seceded from the Secession.

Back to the Start

This time, ironically, it was the 'old-guard' of the avant garde who broke away, for Klimt was accompanied by Carl Moll, Josef Maria Auchentaller and Adolf Böhm, as well as by more obviously 'applied'

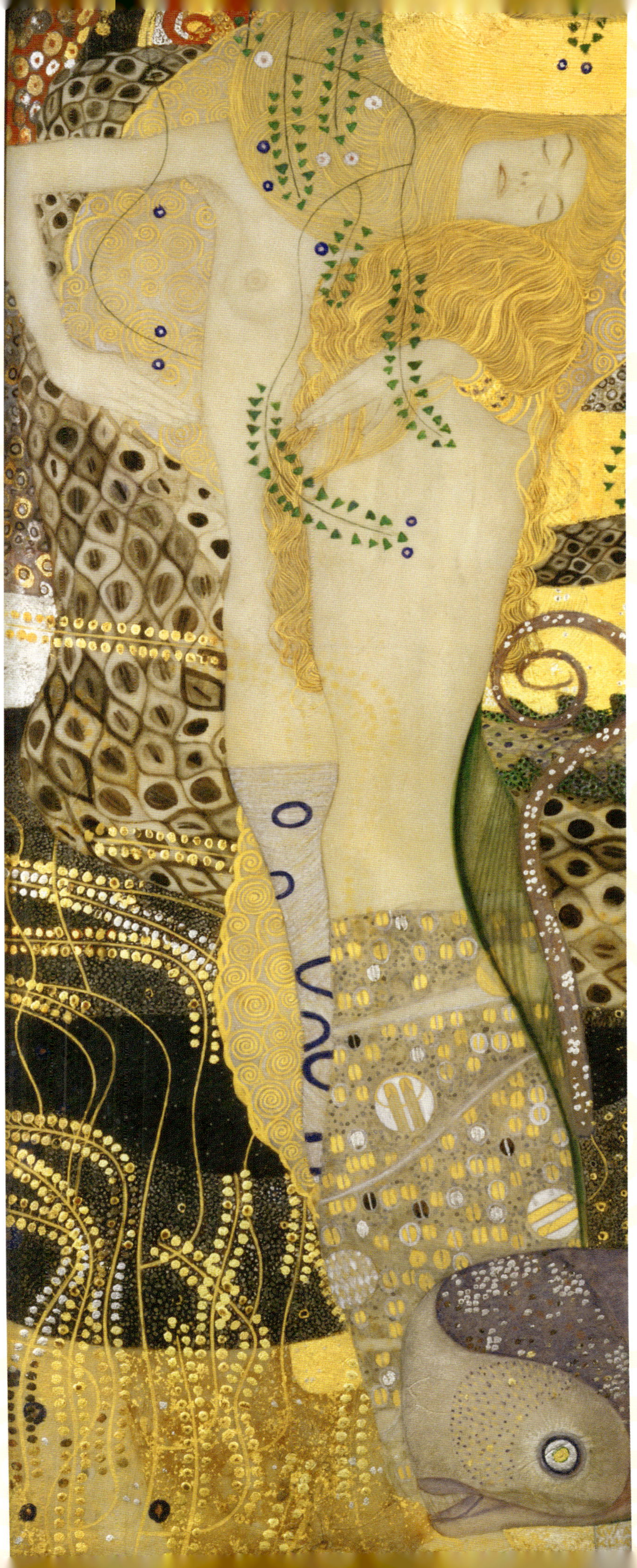

RIGHT ◆ WATER SERPENTS I, 1904. GUSTAV KLIMT (1862–1918)

artists like Koloman Moser, Josef Hoffmann and Alfred Roller. They held their first exhibition in 1908 in the Kunstschau, a temporary pavilion designed for the occasion by Josef Hoffmann, on the empty site awaiting the start of work on the building of Vienna's Konzerthaus, which opened just a few years later in 1911.

A temporary pavilion, perhaps, but the Kunstschau was conceived and constructed on an impressive scale, with no fewer than 54 exhibition rooms in all. To underline the epic implications, moreover, the Klimt Group took down the inscription from Olbrich's Secession Building – 'To every age its art, to every art its freedom' – and had it remounted above the main door of the Kunstschau.

Variety and Vision

The exhibition itself was arguably to put all its Secession predecessors in the shade: 176 different artists were represented. Klimt had pride of place, and many of what are now his most famous works were shown for the very first time here to his native Vienna and to a disbelieving world. *The Kiss* (*see* page 51) was here, for example: as were *Portrait of Adele Bloch-Bauer I* (*see* page 189) and *Portrait of Fritza Riedler* (1906, *see* page 169). Here too was *Danaë* (1907, *see* page 171), the mythical princess and mother of Perseus shown curled up in a cloak of imperial purple, seemingly in rapture as she's ravished by the god Zeus in the form of golden rain. *The Three Ages of Woman* (1905) shows a girl asleep in the arms of her mother, beautiful and tender. Off to their left stands a wizened old hag, bent and sagging with the effects of age.

There were other paintings too, by Max Kurzweil, Broncia Koller-Pinell and Elena Luksch-Makowsky, among many more, along with some stunning glass mosaics by Richard Teschner (1879–1948). Together with a wide selection of poster and other graphic art, there were jewellery, furniture and household items by the *Wiener Werkstätte*.

There was also theatrical art of several different sorts, including stage-paintings by Emil Orlik (1870–1932) for a production of Shakespeare's *The Winter's Tale*, as well as puppets and set designs by Alfred Roller. Newcomers to the Secessionist cause included the Czech 'Orphist' (or, as he preferred to call himself, 'Colour Symphonist') František Kupka (1871–1957) and Max Oppenheimer (1885–1954).

Expressionist Excursions

Oppenheimer is now best known to many from his memorable portrait by Egon Schiele (1910, *see* page 173) when the two men were sharing a studio. And there's a clear kinship of sorts between the types of figures to be seen in Oppenheimer's Expressionist works and the twisted, tormented subjects of his friend. Schiele, still a teenager, missed out on the 1908 Kunstschau Exhibition, though he was included in the repeat performance of the following year, at Klimt's invitation.

The paintings Schiele showed, such as the portrait of the painter *Hans Massmann* (1909, *see* page 172), were generally agreed to reveal the influence of his teacher in the posing of their subjects – and their use of metallic paint. However, it seems evident in hindsight that the master was meeting his student halfway in his move towards a less ostentatiously ornamental, more directly emotional, Expressionistic style.

Bloom and Fade

The fading of Klimt's palette for the depiction of the old hag in *The Three Ages of Woman* had been obviously symbolic in its intention, a

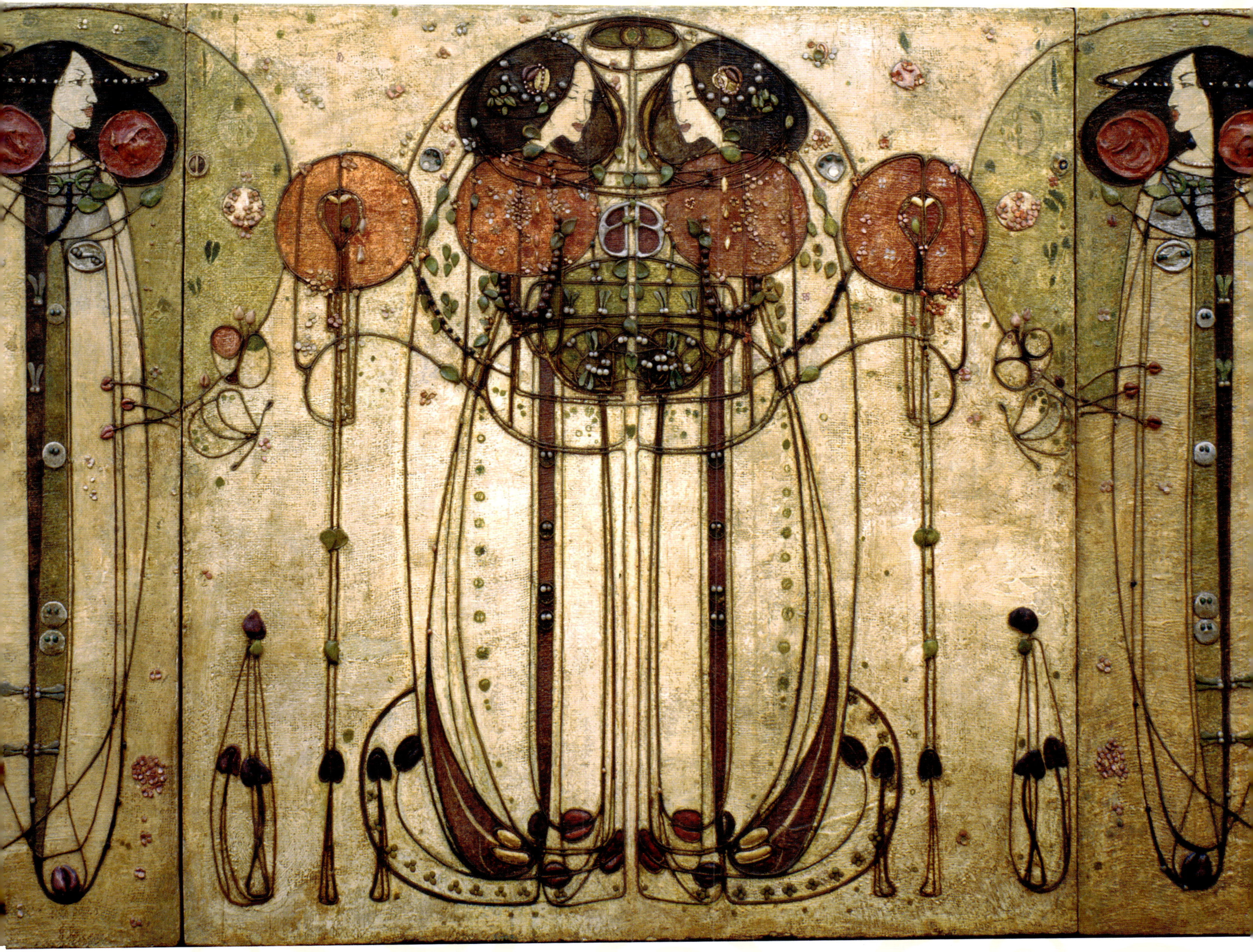

ABOVE • THE WASSAIL, 1900 CHARLES RENNIE MACKINTOSH (1868–1928)

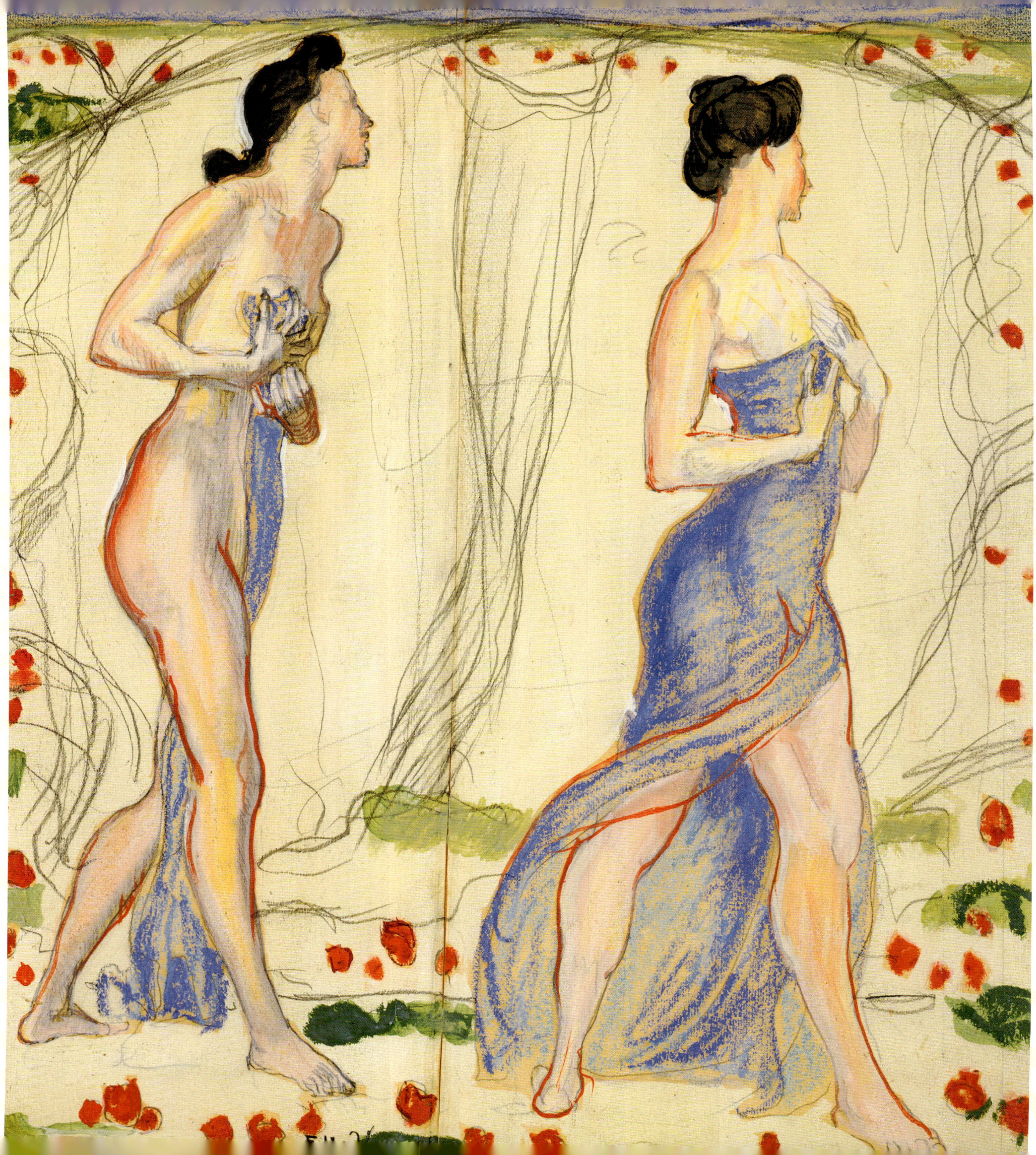

deliberate contrast with the blooming beauty of the young mother and her lovely child. In *Old Woman* (1909), the subject's characterization, though much less grotesque, still suggests a gradual ebbing away of life and colour. But gold and metallic ornamentation were generally coming to be conspicuous by their absence in the work of Klimt: although his *Lady with a Hat and Feather Boa* (1909, *see* page 175) has something of the look of an Impressionist image by Degas, the woman in his *Black Feather Hat* (1910), in her fleshy-pink halftones, might easily be the work of Schiele.

We wouldn't want to insist too much on this convergence, though: Schiele was ultimately never going to be anybody's follower but his own, while Klimt had too constantly questing an imagination to continue in any one course for very long. He was obviously excited both by Expressionism and by the French Fauvist influences brought to Vienna by Helene Funke – who herself went on to develop in an excitingly Expressionist direction. Later works of Klimt's like *The Girls* (1912–13) can be seen to explore both these artistic strands – while also recalling the experiments with ornamentation in his own earlier work. It's all-change again for *Girlfriends* (1916–17), though; with all the seeming restraint of these pastel shades, this work shows all the challenging audacity of the Fauves.

Secession Summation

When all's said and done, it may well be pointless to look to the Vienna Secession for the features of a school; for a consistent set of techniques – or even aims. What set these artists apart from each other in many ways mattered much more than what brought them together. They held few theories in common, and could hardly have been more diverse in their work. But the one great general principle

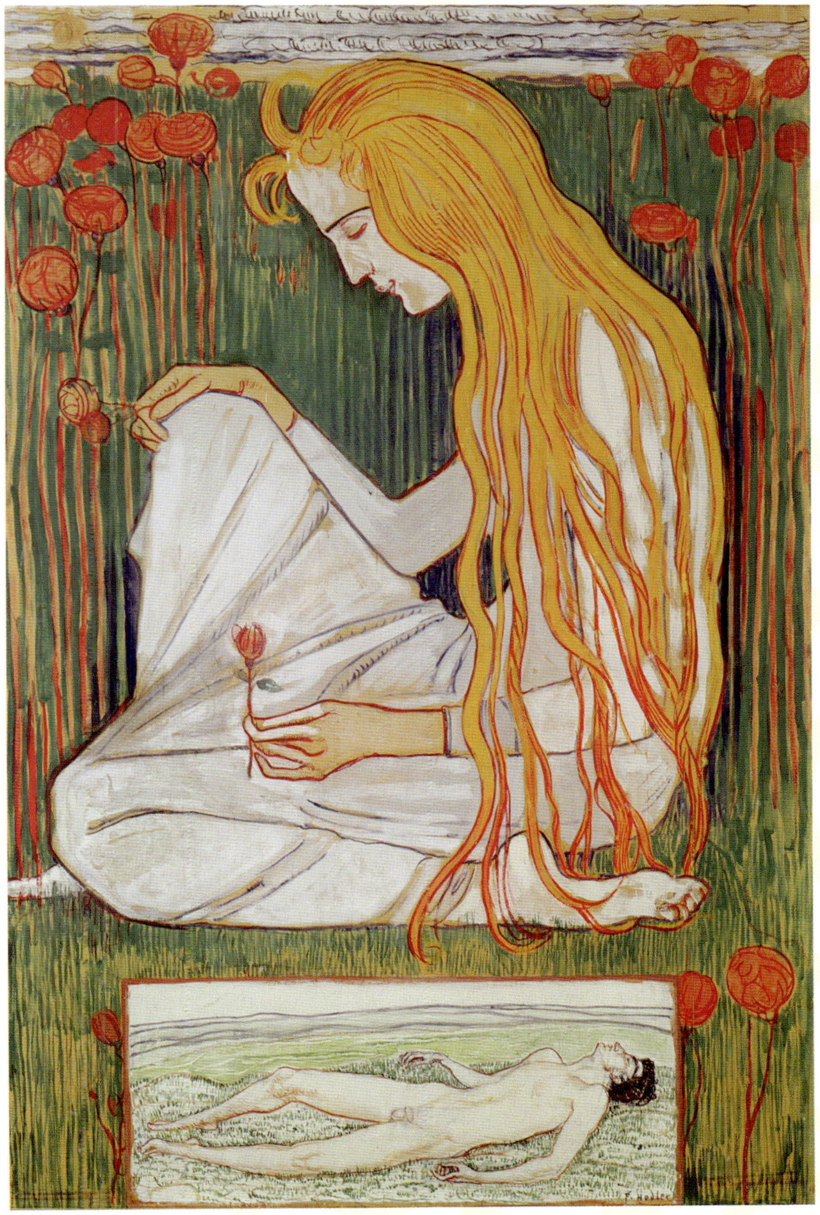

that they *did* share was all-important. Art, they felt, was, first, all-important and, second, indivisible: there were to be no boundaries between painting, sculpture, interior design, metalwork or jewellery-making, or between this more widely-defined world of art and that of life. This belief, although making the Secessionists' contribution maddeningly difficult to pin down at times, is also what makes their work so central to the development of modern art.

OPPOSITE • STUDY FOR DIE EMPFINDUNG I. c. 1901–02. FERDINAND HODLER (1853–1918)
ABOVE • THE DREAM. 1897. FERDINAND HODLER (1853–1918)

Further Reading

Bailey, C.B. (ed.), *Gustav Klimt: Modernism in the Making*, Harry N. Abrams, 2001

Brandstätter, C., *Wonderful Wiener Werkstätte: Design in Vienna 1903–1932*, Thames & Hudson, 2003

Cook, N., *Beethoven: Symphony no. 9*, Cambridge University Press, 1993

Howard, J., *Art Nouveau: International and National Styles in Europe*, Manchester University Press, 1996

Johnson, J., *The Memory Factory: The Forgotten Women Artists of Vienna 1900*, Purdue University Press, 2012

Karnes, K., *A Kingdom Not of this World: Wagner, the Arts, and Utopian Visions in Fin-de-Siècle Vienna*, Oxford University Press, 2013

Kallir, J. and Vartanian, I., *Egon Schiele: Drawings and Watercolours*, Thames & Hudson, 2003

Natter, T. and Grunenberg, C., *Gustav Klimt: Painting, Design and Modern Life*, Tate Publishing, 2008

Nebehay, C.M., *Gustav Klimt: From Drawing to Painting*, Thames & Hudson, 1992

Ormiston, R. and Robinson, M., *Art Nouveau: Posters, Illustration and Fine Art from the Most Glamorous Fin de Siècle*, Flame Tree, 2009

Staggs, J. (ed.), *Wiener Werkstätte Jewelry*, Neue Galerie, 2008

Teich, M. and Porter, R., *Fin de Siècle and its Legacy*, Cambridge University Press, 1991

Vergo, Peter, *Art in Vienna 1898–1918: Klimt, Kokoschka, Schiele and their Contemporaries*, Phaidon Press, 1994

Whalen, R.W., *Sacred Spring: God and the Birth of Modernism in Fin-de-Siècle Vienna*, Wm. B. Eerdmans, 2007

White, I.B., *Otto Wagner, Vienna 1841–1918: Designs for Architecture*, The Museum of Modern Art, Oxford, 1985

Whitford, F., *Klimt*, Thames & Hudson, 1990

Witt-Dörring, C. (ed.), *Koloman Moser: Designing Modern Vienna 1897–1907*, Prestel, 2013

Zweig, S., tr. Bell, A., *The World of Yesterday*, Pushkin Press, 2011

Acknowledgements

Michael Kerrigan is author of *Asian Art* and *Modern Art* from the 'World's Greatest Art' series, and co-author of *The Architecture Style Spotter's Guide* along with a great many other books and articles on art, culture and history. He lives in Edinburgh, where he writes regularly for the *Scotsman* newspaper and is a book reviewer for the *Times Literary Supplement* and *The Guardian.*

Images: © **akg-images** and the following: Imagno/Gustav Klimt 39br & 61; Sotheby's 92; © **Artothek**: 4 & 56, 108, 146, 163, 175, 183 and: IMAGNO 37, 62, 111; IMAGNO/Austrian Archives 43 131tr & 178, 154 & 155; IMAGNO 52, 98 & 99 & 157, 141, 161; Christie's Images Ltd 54; Städel Museum - U. Edelmann 57; Christie's Images Ltd 63, 118; Blauel/Gnamm 130 & 156; IMAGNO/Gerhard Trumler 143; Jochen Remmer 150 & 151 & 192; Hansmann 170; © **Bridgeman Images** and: De Agostini Picture Library/W. Buss 10 & 17; Private Collection/Piccadilly Gallery, London, UK 12; Mucha Trust 19 br & 33; Private Collection 20, 34, 42, 68, 1011 & 127 & 129, 102, 172; Private Collection/Photo Christie's Images 22, 174; De Agostini Picture Library 23, 85; Fogg Art Museum, Harvard Art Museums, USA/Bequest of Grenville L. Winthrop 24; Private Collection/Photo Christie's Images 27, 168, 186; Private Collection/The Stapleton Collection 29; Art Gallery and Museum, Kelvingrove, Glasgow, Scotland 36; De Agostini Picture Library/E. Lessing 39 l & 49, 104 & 105; Wien Museum Karlsplatz, Vienna, Austria 50, 88 & 89, 90 & 91; Lentos Kunstmuseum, Linz, Austria 53; Christie's Images 55, 134; Estate of Joseff Hoffman/Christie's Images 96 & 97; The Fine Art Society, London, UK 59, 128; Wien Museum Karlsplatz, Vienna, Austria 60; Museum der Bildenden Kunste, Leipzig, Germany 70 (foreground); Museum of Modern Art, New York, USA 73, 182; Zentralsparkasse-Bank, Vienna, Austria 94 & 95; De Agostini Picture Library/E. Lessing 100 & 120 & 122 & 123 & 125; Private Collection/Prismatic Pictures 110; Galerie Wurthle, Vienna, Austria 131 br & 171; The John R. Van Derlip Fund and gift of funds from Dr. Otto Kallir 140; Walker Art Gallery, National Museums Liverpool 158; Indianapolis Museum of Art, USA/Alicia Ballard Fine Arts Purchase Fund 160; De Agostini Picture Library/G. Nimatallah 164; Private Collection/Photo Peter Nahum at The Leicester Galleries, London 166; Osterreichische Galerie Belvedere, Vienna, Austria 169; Graphische Sammlung Albertina, Vienna, Austria/De Agostini Picture Library/G. Nimatallah 173; AISA 177; Culture and Sport Glasgow (Museums) 185; Kunsthaus, Zurich, Switzerland 187; © **Getty Images** and the following: Imagno/Hulton Archive 6, 7, 18 & 31, 40, 41, 81, 101br & 114, 107, 126, 134, 176; Imagno/Hulton Fine Art Collection 103; © **CSG CIC Glasgow Museums Collection**: 80; © **Mary Evans Picture Library** and: Imagno 65, 66; Estate of Josef Hoffmann/Imagno 64; © Photo Austrian Archives/**Scala** Florence: 39tr & 44, 58, 132, 162, 180; © **Shutterstock.com** and: A_Lein 16; hakne1 181; © **Superstock** and: DeAgostini 1 & 25, 48, 70 (background) & 71, 1311 & 138; Hemis.fr 45; Fine Art Images 72, 101tr & 106 & 112 & 116 & 117 & 119, 149, 152 & 153, 189; Fine Art Images 149; courtesy **Wikimedia Commons** and: Google Cultural Institute and © respective museums: 3 & 51, 21, 75, 115; public domain/User: Mefusbren69 9, 15, 19tr & 28, 191 & 32, 47, 66, 76, 77, 78, 79, 82, 83, 136 & 137, 139, 142, 144 & 145, 147; public domain/User: Waterborough 26; © Creative Commons 3.0/ Störfix 84; © Creative Commons 3.0/ Alberto Fernandez Fernandez 133; public domain/User: Lewenstein 179.

Page 112–13 full caption: The Beethoven Frieze: The Hostile Forces (Typhoeus accompanied by Lasciviousness, Wantonness and Intemperance) and Gnawing Sorrow, 1902. Gustav klimt (1862–1918)

RIGHT • PORTRAIT OF ADELE BLOCH-BAUER I, 1907, GUSTAV KLIMT (1862–1918)

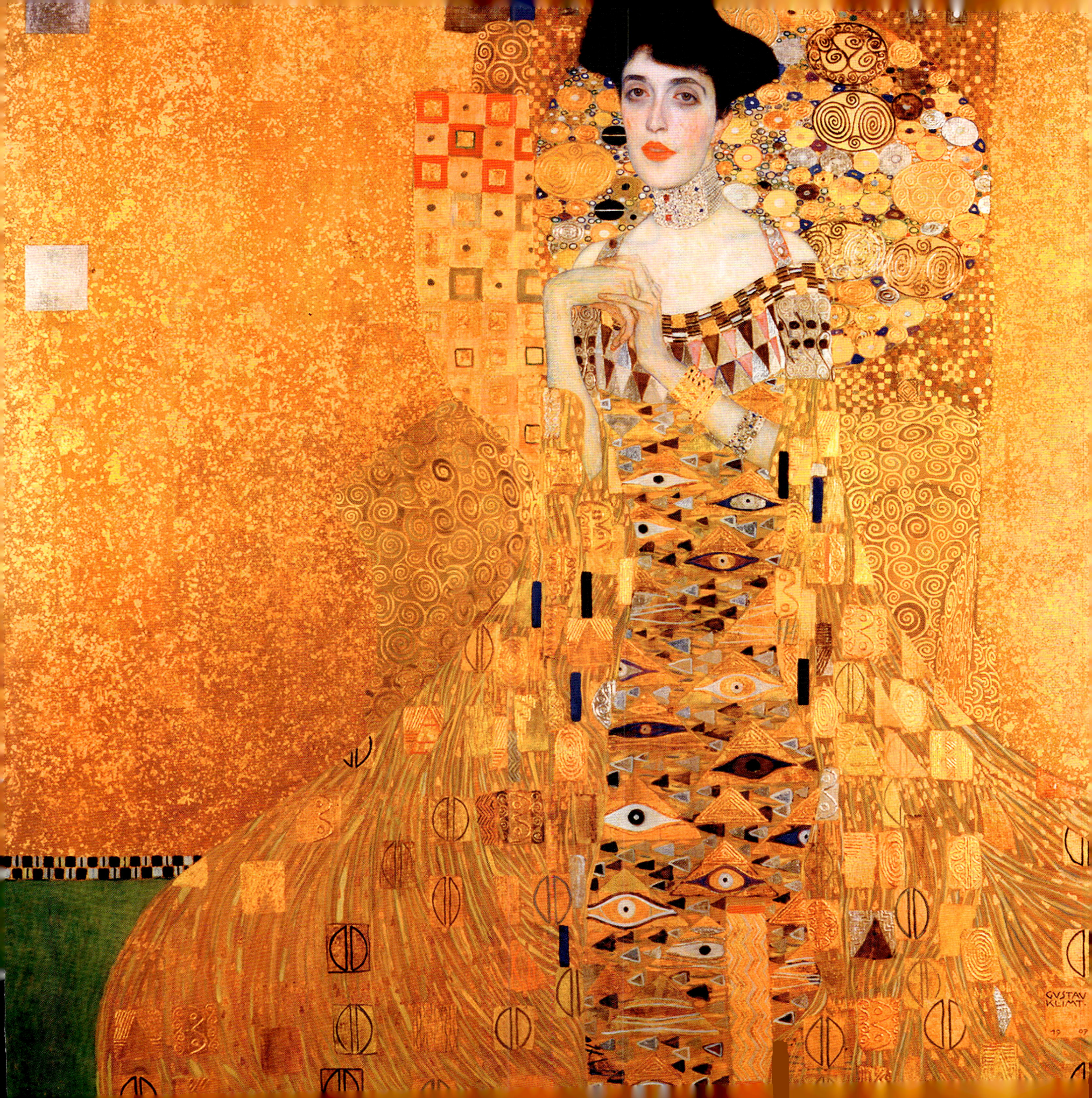
GUSTAV
KLIMT.
19 07

INDEX

Page numbers in *italics* refer to illustrations. Page ranges connected by hyphens take no account of intervening illustrations.

Works are listed by title under the name of each artist.

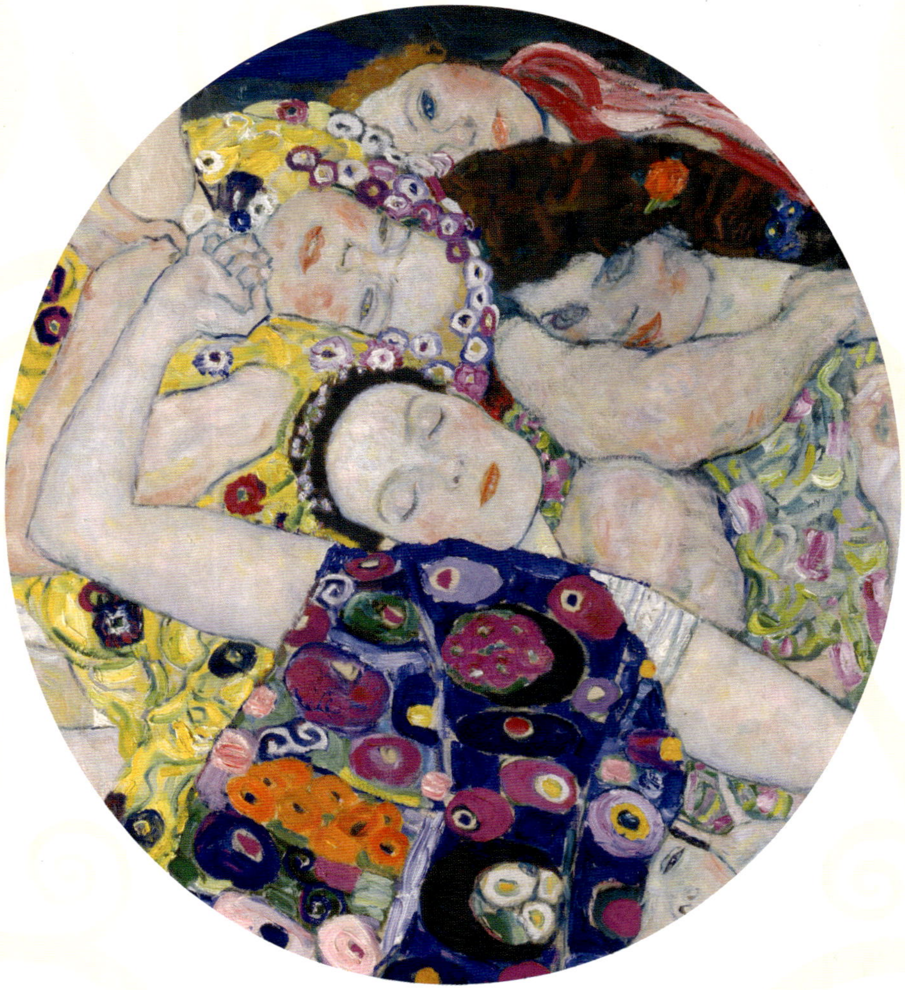

For further information about Klimt, Art Nouveau and associated art please visit us online:

blog.flametreepublishing.com